Confederate Odyssey

Confederate Odyssey

The George W. Wray Jr.

Civil War Collection at the

Atlanta History Center

GORDON L. JONES

Photography by

Jack W. Melton Jr.

Published in association with the
ATLANTA HISTORY CENTER

THE UNIVERSITY OF GEORGIA PRESS
Athens and London

© 2014 by the University of Georgia Press
Athens, Georgia 30602
www.ugapress.org
Designed by Rich Hendel
Set in Miller, Clarendon, and Egiziano by
    Graphic Composition, Inc., Bogart, Georgia

Manufactured by Everbest Printing Company
    for Four Colour Print Group

The paper in this book meets the guidelines for permanence and
durability of the Committee on Production Guidelines for
Book Longevity of the Council on Library Resources.

Most University of Georgia Press titles are available from
popular e-book vendors.

Printed in China
18 17 16 15 14   C   5 4 3 2 1

Library of Congress Cataloging-in-Publication Data
Atlanta History Center.
Confederate odyssey : the George W. Wray Jr. Civil War Collection
at the Atlanta History Center /
Gordon L. Jones ; photography by Jack W. Melton Jr.
        p. cm.
Includes bibliographical references and index.
ISBN 978-0-8203-4685-4 (hardcover : alk. paper)
ISBN 0-8203-4685-3 (hardcover : alk. paper)
1. United States—History—Civil War, 1861–1865—
Equipment and supplies—Catalogs.
2. Confederate States of America. Army—Equipment—Catalogs.
3. Atlanta History Center—Catalogs.
4. George W. Wray Jr. Civil War Collection (Atlanta History Center)
I. Jones, Gordon L., author.
II. Melton, Jack W., 1960– , photographer. III. Title.
E646.A75 2014
973.7′13—dc23   2013049816

British Library Cataloging-in-Publication Data available

Contents

Acknowledgments

The Atlanta History Center and the University of Georgia Press owe a special debt of gratitude to the Watson-Brown Foundation of Thomson, Georgia, which generously funded the publication of this book.

The Atlanta History Center also wishes to thank Anne C. Wray and the family of George W. Wray Jr., who worked to preserve his collection and his legacy.

The author wishes to express his grateful appreciation to his friends and colleagues at the Atlanta History Center, who aided in researching, cataloging, and processing the Wray Collection starting in 2005. He is especially grateful to Michael Rose, executive vice president, whose encouragement and active support made this work possible.

This book also owes much to the tireless efforts of photographer Jack W. Melton Jr. and his wife, Peggy. As proven by the beautiful photographs in this book, their dedication to their craft is simply extraordinary.

The author is profoundly grateful to his friends and colleagues in the private collecting community, from whom he has learned so much over the years. Many members of the American Society of Arms Collectors and the Company of Military Historians have selflessly shared their observations and expertise, especially Paul D. Johnson, who reviewed all the proof pages of this book, making many helpful comments and corrections.

Others who reviewed and commented on the manuscript include Frederick R. Adolphus, Craig D. Bell, Gregory G. Biggs, Michael C. Briggs, Robert J. Carlson, Paul J. Davies, Beverly M. DuBose III, the late Cleveland A. Huey, David Jarnagin, Frederick G. Novy, Tim Prince at the College Hill Arsenal, Russ Pritchard Jr., Robert S. Seigler, and Michael L. Vice.

Others who generously shared their knowledge and insight include Peter A. Albee, Thomas J. Bailey, Bryan Beard, William L. Beard, Richard L. Berglund, Trevor Bovee, Michael R. Carroll, Barton Cox, William "Kerry" Elliott, Ron Field, Charles L. Foster, Frederick C. Gaede, Robert M. Holter, Richard Hummel, Leslie D. Jensen, James R. Johnson, Ken Legendre, Walter Linberger, John W. McAden, Jack W. Melton Jr., Dr. Jack A. Meyer, Damon and Donna Mills, Josh Phillips, Robert A. Sadler, Brannen Sanders, John Sexton, Lewis F. Southard, H. Penn Templeman, Dennis Todd, Kent Wall, the late Gene K. Wilson, and Clifford M. Young.

All who work in this field are indebted to the work of previous generations of scholars and collectors, including William A. Albaugh, Claud Fuller, Howard M. Madaus, and many others. The author sincerely hopes that this book will encourage a new generation of collectors and historians to continue the important work begun by these pioneers. No work of this breadth is ever definitive; in time, new research will suggest new conclusions and overturn old ones. Meanwhile, any errors of fact or judgment are the author's.

Nomenclature

LONG ARMS

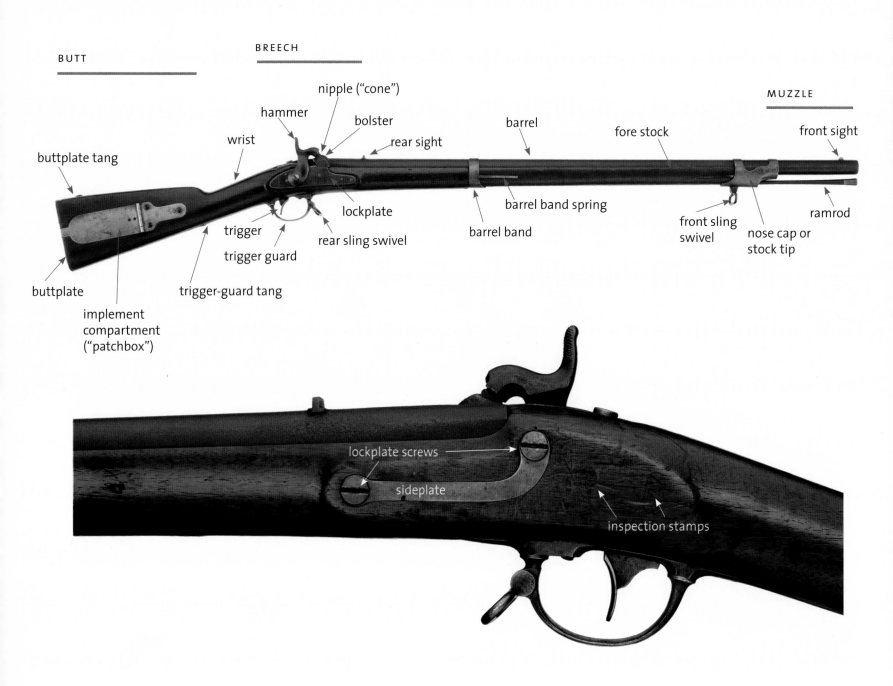

BUTT

BREECH

MUZZLE

nipple ("cone")

hammer

bolster

wrist

rear sight

barrel

fore stock

front sight

buttplate tang

lockplate

trigger

barrel band spring

front sling swivel

ramrod

rear sling swivel

trigger guard

barrel band

nose cap or stock tip

buttplate

trigger-guard tang

implement compartment ("patchbox")

lockplate screws

sideplate

inspection stamps

SWORDS AND SABERS

HILT   BLADE

pommel cap

grip

guard

ricasso

fuller

tip

pommel

knuckle bow or branches

throat

suspension rings

bands

edge

drag

SWORD BAYONET

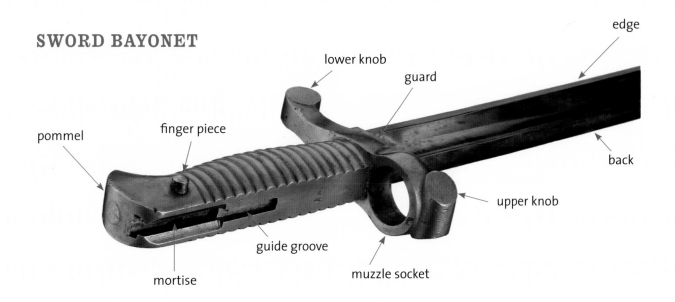

edge

lower knob

guard

pommel

finger piece

upper knob

back

mortise

guide groove

muzzle socket

Confederate Odyssey

Introduction Confederate Odyssey

The Confederate odyssey began in the early-morning darkness of April 12, 1861, in Charleston Harbor, South Carolina. Forty-three Confederate cannon and mortars — nearly all of them made in the North — opened fire on the federal garrison at Fort Sumter in the violent culmination of a cold war that had raged for more than forty years as Americans wrestled with the practical implications of their founding ideology. Though their republic was firmly rooted in the notion that "all men are created equal," white Americans on both sides of Mason and Dixon's line commonly made an exception that they saw as equally self-evident: white men were endowed by their creator not only with "certain inalienable rights," but also with intellectual and moral superiority over other races. It was the great paradox at the heart of the American Dream. In a republic founded on liberty, slavery would not go quietly, or without a cataclysmic fight to the death. Four years later, an estimated 750,000 Americans were dead, 4,000,000 enslaved people had gained at least nominal freedom, and a breakaway southern republic lay in ruins. This book is the story of that failed republic and its defenders as told through their artifacts, specifically those collected and preserved by one man: a devoted Atlanta-area collector named George W. Wray Jr.

Among the most compelling of these artifacts is the pillow-ticking frock coat worn by a Confederate private named Benjamin H. G. Schumpert. He was seventeen years old in September 1863 when a minié ball shattered his skull and killed him instantly. The war had already claimed his only brother as well as four cousins. Now young Ben, as his father called him, lay dead at the foot of Horseshoe Ridge on the battlefield of Chickamauga, where he was one of at least 2,300 Confederate soldiers killed — another 15,000 were wounded. Each had a family. Each had a story. Each had hopes and dreams that we will never know.

Today we know Ben Schumpert's story only because of two serendipitous events. First, his cousin Osborne, who probably witnessed the fatal shot, removed Ben's homemade, now blood-soaked frock coat from his body before it was buried. Granted a furlough three weeks later, Osborne traveled to Americus, Georgia, to present the bloody relic to Ben's bereaved forty-five-year-old father, Amos, who

This is not to be a static collection, but one I fervently hope will expand over time.

—Beverly M. DuBose Jr., upon donating his Civil War collection to the Atlanta History Center, 1985

"Ben" Schumpert's coat

George W. Wray Jr. (1936–2004)

treasured it for the rest of his life. Second, George W. Wray Jr. found out about the coat and purchased it in the mid-1970s. Captivated by his find, Wray immediately began researching the details of Schumpert's life. At first, all he had to go on were sketchy details from family stories. Within a year or two, he had several thick file folders and a ring binder full of photocopied service records and newspaper reports, hand-scrawled notes on yellow legal pads, and snapshots of family graves, all of which documented Ben Schumpert's life, as Wray liked to say, "from womb to tomb." George Wray's curiosity is the only reason anyone today knows about or even remembers Benjamin H. G. Schumpert, a soldier of Company E, 3rd South Carolina Volunteer Infantry, who gave his life for a white southern vision of America a century and a half ago.

Wray was more than an amateur collector. For more than fifty years, he was a detective, searching out long-lost clues, preserving physical evidence, and uncovering personal stories that would otherwise be lost forever. Wray's work with the International Silver Company took him all over the country, enabling him to build his collection in out-of-the-way places, anywhere from antique stores to old attics. Wherever he traveled, he usually visited a nearby historical society or cemetery, constantly on the hunt for the evidence that would give life and significance to otherwise meaningless objects. Even those objects without personal attributions became relevant when compared to other objects, for each told the story of the society that had created it. In small details, great truths are revealed. For Wray, recognizing in tangible form what had previously been known only in documents (and vice versa) was more than just the thrill of the hunt: it was a window into the Confederate experience of his North Carolina ancestors, a peek inside the bloodiest war in American history, a way to make that seminal event meaningful, relevant, even visceral.

In the mid-1970s, Wray purchased an unusually fine .40-caliber target rifle stocked in bird's-eye maple and built with a pivoting breech mechanism unlike that of any known Confederate arm. It was plainly marked "T MORSE / 1863." Wray noticed that a man named Thomas Morse had been granted Confederate States Patent 199 for a breech-loading rifle in September 1863. Yet the specifications and drawings for the rifle, like those of all other Confederate patents, burned in Richmond in 1865, never to be recovered. Could this .40-caliber rifle be the one mentioned in Patent 199? In reference books on American gun makers, there was only one Thomas Morse listed, and he worked from 1866 through the 1890s in Lancaster, New Hampshire. Yet the existence of a Morse rifle in the Museum of the Confederacy and a note referring to another in William A. Albaugh's classic

Confederate Arms (1957) suggested that this might indeed be the same man who had patented a breech-loading rifle in the Confederacy.

Wray spent the next thirty years penning inquiries to local historical societies, typing up research requests, and sending one- or two-dollar checks for copying fees, all in an effort to extract any scrap of evidence that would lead him to the elusive maker of his breech-loading rifle. Along the way, he discovered that there was indeed a Confederate connection. In 1858, Thomas Morse relocated from Lancaster, New Hampshire, to Macon, Georgia, and in 1863, at the time he submitted his patent claim, Morse was listed as a resident of Richmond. Immediately after the war, the Yankee-turned-Confederate gunsmith returned to Lancaster, where, according to a local storyteller, he freely admitted that he had not only sniped at Union soldiers from Confederate lines across the Rappahannock River at Fredericksburg, but also recognized his fellow townsmen along the bank and intentionally missed them. Clearly, Thomas Morse was not just an obscure New Hampshire gunsmith.

But was this breech-loading rifle really made by the same Thomas Morse? Wray thought so, but lacked positive proof. In the late 1990s, he discovered the existence of another Morse arm with a possible Confederate connection, this one a thirty-pound muzzle-loading target rifle marked "T MORSE / MACON, Ga." After many months of negotiating over the price, Wray finally purchased it in 2004. It was the last gun he ever bought; his death from cancer at age sixty-eight came just a few weeks later. Yet this target rifle turned out to be the Rosetta stone for which Wray had been searching all those years.

In a presentation to the American Society of Arms Collectors in the fall of 2008, I referred to the Morse breech-loading rifle as a Confederate arm. Afterward, Mike Carroll, a longtime collector of Morse's New Hampshire–made arms, expressed his disbelief. After our conversation, I too began to doubt the Confederate connection. So we reexamined the evidence. Mike noticed a number of physical similarities between all the extant Morse arms, regardless of where or when they were made, including the same set of dies having been used to stamp Morse's name. The bore of the Macon rifle also conformed precisely to the official .577 caliber specified by the Confederate chief of ordnance, Josiah Gorgas, in May 1862. Then, using tools that Wray never had—online newspapers, e-books, Fold3.com (an online collection of U.S. military records), Ancestry.com, and so on—we confirmed even more details of the story. Wray had been absolutely right. Furthermore, he had discovered not only what was probably the model or prototype arm for Confederate Patent 199, but also the first and perhaps only identified example of a Macon Armory sharpshooter rifle, the existence of which had been known up to that time only through historical

Thomas Morse's target rifle

documents. The long-lost story of Thomas Morse had finally come to life: here was one of the Yankee entrepreneurs on whom southern industry depended so heavily, even during the war. The arms collector and appraiser Damon Mills put it best: "If he had just lived a little longer, oh, what else George could have done!"

Wray did it because he loved it—and because his mind was precisely attuned to it. His was a near-photographic memory that was able to bank huge quantities of documentary knowledge and then retrieve it in an instant, recognizing small but crucial details that went unnoticed by everyone else. Wray found most of the items in his collection at Civil War relic shows, where he gained a reputation for never revealing what he knew until after he had made his purchase. One experienced bayonet collector sold Wray an unidentified sword bayonet with an unusual octagonal mounting ring. Only afterward did the tight-lipped Wray reveal that he not only knew the origin of the bayonet, but also owned the gun for which it was made: an almost one-of-a-kind Kemper, Shrivers, and Company altered rifle. Wray was a seasoned trader as well. He once told me that over the years he had owned four times as many arms as were now in the collection, but that he had traded up until he obtained just what he wanted, filling in the gaps and creating one of the finest and most comprehensive collections of Confederate artifacts in the world.

In December 2001, Wray invited me to lunch. I barely knew him. He got right to the point: he wanted to sell his collection to the Atlanta History Center, to be exhibited and studied alongside the collection of the DuBose family (Beverly M. DuBose Jr. and his son Beverly M. DuBose III, or "Bo"). Wray presented me with a small handwritten note card on which he had listed the contents of his collection by category: sixty-eight southern-made arms representing the full range of Confederate production from Virginia to Texas; fifty-one northern-made arms, many of which were altered or used by the Confederacy; thirty-three British arms imported through the blockade; twenty-one swords or sabers; fifteen uniforms; seven flags; and at least one hundred bayonets and dozens of accoutrements—some six hundred significant objects in all. (Later we counted thirteen hundred objects, including hundreds of bullets, tools, and gun parts.) Soon after our lunch together, I visited the cluttered attic-like collection room above the carport of Wray's house, tripping over a Tredegar Iron Works artillery tube and bumping past card tables filled to overflowing with research materials. He knew precisely and instantly where every object was and why it was important.

Wray had assembled a world-class collection; only after many years of studying it have we begun to fully appreciate the depth of his accomplishment. Today, assembling a collection of such a scope and significance would be almost impossible, even with unlimited funds. But for the Atlanta History Center in the early 2000s,

*George Wray's collection room
in his home, 2003*

acquiring this collection was a tall order: raising money for collections is always difficult, but raising millions for a Civil War collection—especially a Confederate one—seemed practically impossible. Most important, the center was already home to the famous DuBose Collection, probably the largest private collection of Civil War artifacts in the world at the time of its donation in the late 1980s. That was the collection that put the Atlanta History Center on the map among Civil War museums; it was also one of the primary motives for building the center's new museum in 1991–92 and the signature Civil War exhibition that went in it. For an institution already known for its Civil War collections but struggling to reach beyond its traditional white southern roots, the acquisition of another Civil War collection could be more than a little problematic.

Totaling at least 8,500 objects, from the largest cannon to the tiniest button, the DuBose Collection is known for its inclusiveness: it is essentially a sample of all military materiel produced during the war on both sides. Of course, given the Union's massive manufacturing output, the vast majority of that materiel is northern made. On the other hand, the 600 most significant objects in the Wray Collection are almost exclusively southern made or southern used, meaning that they were produced in small quantities, and are therefore the rarest and most telling evidence of Confederate materiel inferiority. In the Wray Collection lies the story of Confederate defeat, especially when seen alongside the DuBose Collection. The more that Bo DuBose and I examined Wray's collection, the more we realized the extent to which it complemented the DuBose collection without duplicating it. It complemented the artifact collections of fellow Atlantans Sydney C. Kerksis and Thomas S. Dickey too, as well as the center's extensive Civil War book, document, and manuscript collections, including the maps and artwork of Wilbur G. Kurtz, historian of the Atlanta Campaign. The addition of the Wray Collection would give Atlanta one of the most comprehensive Civil War collections in the world. It was an opportunity that would never come again. In 2005, soon after Wray's death, the Atlanta History Center made the largest collection purchase in its history.

The decision to purchase the Wray Collection rested not only in the knowledge of its content and quality but also in the expectation that it would enhance the center's educational mission without branding it as a one-dimensional institution bound up in traditional Confederate history or technical minutiae. This book is very much a part of that mission. It is not intended as a technical reference guide to Confederate artifacts, but rather as a visual catalogue of about three hundred of the most important artifacts in the Wray Collection, describing their stories, significance, and context to both general reader and Civil War buff alike. Traditionally, the study of Civil War history has been divorced from the study of its material remains — one the domain of professional scholars and the other the domain of amateur collectors. This book aims to bridge that gap.

Indeed, not so long ago the artifacts in the Wray Collection (and to a lesser extent, those in the DuBose Collection) would have been considered relics, near-sacred reminders of a great Confederate moral victory in a struggle that ended only, as General Robert E. Lee wrote movingly, when it was "compelled to yield to superior numbers and resources." In that version of history, Ben Schumpert's homespun coat was a sterling example of the devotion of white southern women whose loving handiwork was simply no match for the anonymous efficiency of northern mass production. But the era of Confederate relics is over.

Today the Wray Collection embodies a broader, multidimensional past, one inextricably tied up in slavery, industrialization, and a failed vision of the American Dream. Here, a delicate Kentucky-style hunting rifle altered for military use in the vain belief that the rifles that beat the British at New Orleans would stop the federals in Tennessee. There, one of George Woodward Morse's breech-loading carbines, one of the most advanced designs of the war, but produced in such minuscule quantities that it was irrelevant on the battlefield. There too a damaged rifle-musket made in 1862 from surplus U.S. parts at the Confederate States Armory in Richmond, assembled by mechanics who, a year earlier, were making the most mechanically perfect arms in the world at the U.S. Armory at Harpers Ferry. In 1864, those workers, using every ounce of creativity they possessed, refitted the damaged gun with a shorter barrel made from substandard iron and sent it back into the field as an ersatz cavalry arm. It was hardly mechanical perfection, but it worked. As these and many other artifacts demonstrate, there was more to the Confederate odyssey than the old myths of homespun coats, squirrel rifles, and raw courage against all odds.

To be sure, the cloth for Schumpert's coat was probably homespun, and the coat was certainly assembled by hand. But whose hands? Young Ben had no sisters, and his stepmother, Sarah, had married his father only in February 1863. Although she took a keen interest in the boy, it is unlikely that in a wealthy household with twenty-six slaves, at least one of whom was probably a skilled seamstress, Sarah Schumpert made the coat as well as a matching pair of trousers entirely on her own. More to the point, home production in the Confederacy was an anomaly. The vast majority of uniforms for Confederate enlisted men were mass-produced under the increasingly hard-handed authority of the Confederate central government. At Chickamauga, young Ben almost certainly stood out as a target among the men of his division who had just been issued jackets made from dark blue-gray English "army cloth" brought in through the blockade.

It is also unlikely that Thomas Morse fabricated his thirty-pound .577 target rifle entirely on his own. Hired out by their owners, African American slaves mined the iron ore, shoveled the coal, and cut the timber that kept the Macon Armory—and virtually all other Confederate factories—supplied with raw materials. They picked the cotton that purchased the British rifle-muskets that kept the Confederacy alive—one of which was probably in Ben Schumpert's hands when he was killed. Indeed, slave-grown southern cotton had fueled the Industrial Revolution in the North, which ultimately enabled the mass production of the modern firearms that accounted for more than 90 percent of all wounds during the Civil War—including the fatal one suffered by Ben Schumpert.

Like all those who made and used the objects in the Wray Collection, Schumpert was a product of his time and place, an American who held a vision of his country very different from that of the present day. Inspired by the American Revolution a scant eighty-five years before, it was a vision of an independent republic in which white supremacy was ordained by God and the perpetuation of a servile laboring class was the bedrock of personal liberty. This alternative vision of the American Dream gave birth to the Confederate States of America and was specifically protected in its Constitution. What if that vision had triumphed? What if General Lee had not been "compelled to yield to superior numbers and resources"? Herein lies perhaps the most crucial significance of Wray's collection: it is the tangible evidence of what was, what could have been, and most important, what was not. The Wray Collection is far more than a mere collection of relics, far more than the remnants of a failed republic or an esoteric lesson in firearms technology. It is the very stuff of American history. To explore its stories is to explore the single most important struggle in our nation's history, a struggle that determined the fate of slavery and republican government, and affirmed the ideals that today lie at the core of our nation.

1. Guns of the Industrial Revolution

In the 1790s, the U.S. Congress established two armories to produce firearms for the defense of the new nation against foreign invasion: one at Springfield, Massachusetts, powered by the Connecticut River, and the other at Harpers Ferry, Virginia (now West Virginia), harnessing the Shenandoah and Potomac Rivers. Both sites were personally selected by George Washington. The armories became engines of the Industrial Revolution in America, mass-producing the guns that would one day sustain the Confederacy and provide the models for nearly all its domestic arms production.

In the early 1800s, each gun was a unique precision instrument fashioned by a single, highly skilled craftsman who custom-made and fitted each part by hand. If a part broke, there were no ready replacements for it. The idea of using interchangeable parts to solve the problem dated back at least fifty years, but the technological challenges of implementing such a process seemed insurmountable. Functional interchangeability required never-before-imagined tolerances of ¹⁄₁₀₀th of an inch or less on metal parts. In the 1820s, the best that had been achieved was about ¹⁄₁₀th of an inch on parts for clocks. And unlike New England clock factories, where interchangeability had made products cheaper and therefore more profitable, private gunsmiths had no such incentive: the cost of the specialized machinery needed to produce interchangeable arms would make mass-produced guns far more expensive than those made by hand.

The U.S. government was the only entity in America for whom financial incentive was secondary to public need. As early as 1798, the U.S. Army Ordnance Department began issuing arms contracts encouraging interchangeability as a means of stimulating innovation among private gun makers. The results included the first practical milling machine for metals in 1818 (developed by the Connecticut gun maker Simeon North), a series of fourteen machines that automated the manufacture of wooden gunstocks by 1825 (perfected by the Massachusetts inventor Thomas Blanchard), and the turret lathe, which had a rotating tool head to speed up the manufacture of small precision parts (constantly improved by New England arms makers through the 1860s and beyond). Working under a special government

I have succeeded in establishing methods for fabricating arms exactly alike, & with economy, by the hands of common workmen, & in such a manner as to ensure a perfect observance of any established model, & to furnish in the arms themselves a complete test of their conformity to it.
—John H. Hall, director of the rifle works at Harpers Ferry Armory, December 30, 1822

Gambling of every description, and the drinking of Rum, Gin, Brandy, Whiskey or any kind of ardent spirits is prohibited in or about the public workshop.
—Rule number 15 for workers at the Springfield Armory, 1816

contract at Harpers Ferry, the Maine-born mechanic and gunsmith John H. Hall incorporated these and other inventions in dozens of different wood- and metal-working machines, each designed and built to perform one specific task in the manufacture of his specially designed Model 1819 breech-loading rifle. Special jigs and fixtures locked each part in place to ensure that holes could be drilled and edges cut to identical specifications over and over again. By 1827, John Hall's rifle works at Harpers Ferry had achieved experimentally something that no other nation — including the global powers France and Great Britain — had done: functional parts interchangeability in arms manufacture.

Building the specialized machinery was only part of the challenge: new machinery required a new organization of labor to operate it. What came to be called the "American System" relied on a few specialized workers who each repeated only one production step at a time until the final product was assembled from identical parts. By 1860, more than five hundred specialized operations were required to produce a single gun; each operation had its own machinery and its own wage. Because it rendered traditional trades obsolete, the American System was met with intense resistance from workers, even at the national armories. Gone were the days when craftsmen set their own hours and drank whiskey in the afternoon. Making guns — and nearly everything else — became a routine, not a craft, and workers went from being artisans to operators.

It took twenty years after John Hall's achievement for Springfield and Harpers Ferry to implement and perfect the new manufacturing techniques and organization. The first interchangeable arm to be mass-produced at both national armories was the U.S. Model 1842 musket. Although Springfield and Harpers Ferry turned out more than 272,000 nearly identical copies, each with tolerances of $\frac{1}{100}$th of an inch, some hand-fitting of parts continued through the late 1840s. By 1857, the next generation of rifles and rifle-muskets were fully interchangeable, and at one-fourth of the previous tolerances. Much of the intricate machinery required was built under government contract by a handful of private Connecticut River Valley arms makers whose expertise in interchangeability ignited the next phase of the Industrial Revolution. Such was the advanced state of American production technology in these few factories that when the British government set out to produce arms with interchangeable parts in 1856, it had to purchase the machinery in New England. By the end of the nineteenth century, the American System had spread to virtually all other areas of manufacturing as the United States became the world's industrial powerhouse.

Yet the revolution in interchangeability was by no means universal. Aside from the Harpers Ferry Armory, there were no such factories in the South, where incredibly profitable investments in land, slaves, and cotton left little incentive for industrial development. Nevertheless, on the eve of the Civil War, the products and ideals of the new technology had begun to trickle down into all corners of the United States. Under the Militia Act of 1808, federal arsenals used a quota system to distribute arms to each state for use by its militia in the event of an enemy invasion. In 1861, the states would use their stockpiles of weapons made by the U.S. armories not against a common invader but against each other. The guns of the Industrial Revolution would fundamentally shape the conduct and outcome of the war that followed.

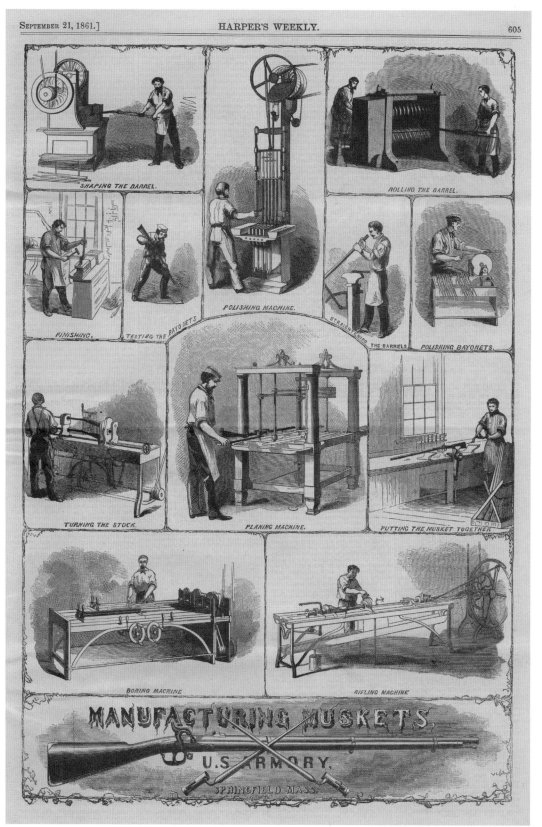

The interchangeable-parts machinery seized from Harpers Ferry and put to work in Richmond was virtually identical to that shown here at the Springfield Armory in Massachusetts. Note the barrel-rolling machine at upper right. (Harper's Weekly)

Marks of federal authority

To distinguish its arms from all others, the U.S. Army established a series of ownership marks that were both practical and symbolic. Beginning in 1795, the initials "us" were stamped on the lockplates and buttplate tangs of all firearms produced under federal authority. An eagle appeared on the lockplates of arms produced by the two national armories, and an eagle's head was used as an inspection mark on the barrel.

A traditional heraldic symbol of courage, strength, and immortality, the eagle was selected as the official symbol for the U.S. seal and coat of arms in June 1782. In its right talon, the eagle grasps an olive branch, a symbol of peace, while its left holds a bundle of thirteen arrows, a symbol for war. Usually the eagle faces its right, symbolically favoring the olive branch of peace. For reasons unknown, the eagles stamped onto Model 1855 arms were reversed.

U.S. Model 1816 musket lockplate

U.S. Model 1841 rifle lockplate

U.S. Model 1855 rifle-musket lockplate

U.S. Model 1855 rifle barrel with Harpers Ferry eagle's head inspection mark

U.S. Model 1855 rifle-musket buttplate tang with "us" and state arsenal inventory number

U.S. inspection stamps

To ensure absolute uniformity, U.S. Ordnance Department inspectors developed gauges that measured each and every part of a firearm to make sure that holes lined up, edges were aligned, and finishes were standard. The slightest deviation was cause for rejection. As proof of acceptance, inspectors stamped their initials on all major parts, while the foreman and master armorer marked the stock of the finished arm with their initials enclosed in a cartouche.

According to regulations, even the brass side plate of this U.S. Model 1841 contract rifle was gauged and stamped with an inspection initial. Aside from the usual "us," "V" (viewed), and "P" ("proved") marks, the barrel bears the initials "JH" (for the subinspector Joseph Hannis) and "JCB" (for the subinspector Joseph C. Bragg). The mark "STEEL" was applied to differentiate the stronger steel barrels fabricated by the gun makers Eli Whitney Jr. and Eliphalet Remington Jr. from the ordinary iron ones provided by other contractors. The "2CC" is a reinspection stamp applied after this rifle was upgraded by the Colt Firearms Company in 1861.

Marks of the router inletting machines at the U.S. Armory at Harpers Ferry

Three pilot holes in the base of the implement compartment (or patchbox) of the stock of this U.S. Model 1841 rifle are the distinguishing marks of the router inletting machines at the Harpers Ferry Armory, where workers could turn out a new stock every twenty-two minutes. There are no such marks on stocks made by private contractors without this machinery. Each rifle came with a spare nipple screwed into the lower-right corner of the compartment, as well as a wrench, wiper, and worm needed to maintain the rifle (not shown).

Flint and Steel: The Old Technology

In the early 1800s, the standard mechanism for igniting a firearm was the flintlock, which relied on the action of flint striking steel to create a spark. When the trigger was pulled, the flint on the cocking arm struck a steel frizzen just above an open metal pan filled with gunpowder. The resulting flame passed through a small vent hole in the barrel to ignite the powder charge inside the barrel. It was a simple system that had worked well for the past two hundred years.

Nevertheless, there were two drawbacks to the flintlock. First, the gunpowder in the pan could be made useless by rain. Second, there was a lag time between ignition of the gunpowder in the pan and ignition of the main charge in the barrel. Aiming a flintlock was tricky at best, especially for untrained troops.

Nearly all military firearms were made with smoothbore barrels of .69 caliber and were designed to fire a spherical lead ball of about .635 caliber. Being smaller than the bore, the balls could be loaded quickly and easily, even when the bore became fouled with gunpowder residue. Although smoothbore long arms, or muskets, were accurate against individual targets only to about fifty yards, when densely packed infantry formations fired at each other at seventy-five or even a hundred yards, muskets were devastating, especially when firing buckshot or a combination of round ball and buckshot known as "buck and ball." In that kind of fighting, there was really no need to aim at an individual target.

A smaller number of military arms were rifled, usually with seven grooves at about .54 caliber, which made them accurate against individual targets up to two hundred yards or more. To make the ball take the rifling, a soldier had to wrap it in a greased cloth patch and use a special starter and hammer to force it down into the bore. This time-consuming loading procedure—usually taking about forty-five seconds—meant that rifles could not generate as much firepower as muskets, which could be fired once every twenty seconds. In the early 1800s, rifles were specialized arms meant only for skirmishing at long ranges, thus screening and supporting the main line of infantry. Meanwhile, smoothbore muskets—faster to load and cheaper to make—remained the weapon of choice.

U.S. Model 1816 contract musket made by Lemuel Pomeroy, Pittsfield, Massachusetts, with socket bayonet (1825)

The Model 1816 musket was the mainstay of the U.S. Army and state militias through the Mexican War (1846–48). With its distinctive iron bands and double-strapped nose cap, the Model 1816 — like the Model 1795 before it — was copied from the French Model 1766 "Charleville" muskets sent to the fledgling United States during the Revolutionary War.

Between 1816 and 1844, the Springfield and Harpers Ferry Armories produced more than 550,000 Model 1816 muskets, and fifteen private contractors made another 190,000. All were made entirely by hand with no interchangeable parts.

This musket was produced in 1825 by the gunsmith Lemuel Pomeroy of Pittsfield, Massachusetts, and inspected by Justin Murphy at the Springfield Armory. As seen by the property stamp on top of the barrel, it was later issued to the State of North Carolina as part of its annual quota of arms under the Militia Act of 1808. Until the 1840s, contractor-produced arms were meant for issue to the states; arms produced at the national armories were reserved for the regular army and stored at national arsenals.

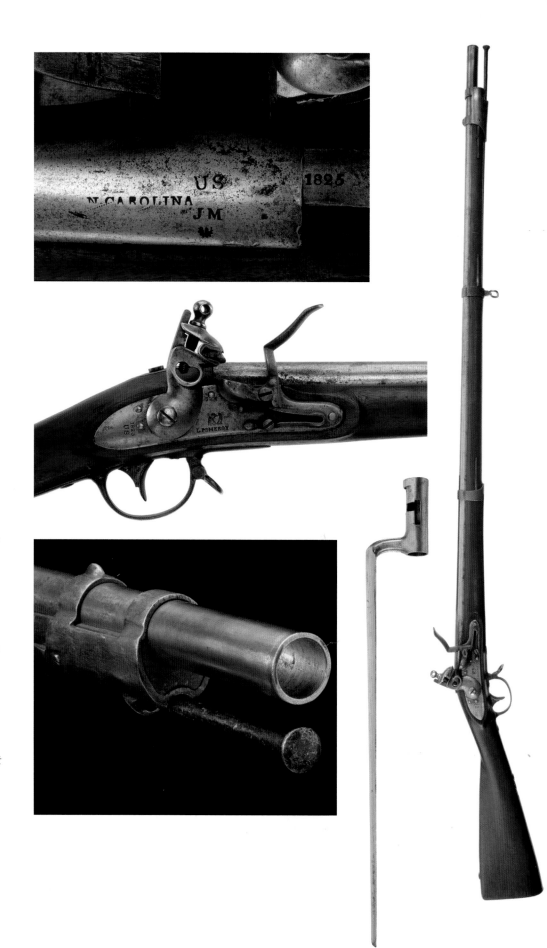

U.S. Model 1803 rifle made by the U.S. Armory at Harpers Ferry (1819)

The Model 1803 was one of at least six different models of rifles produced for the U.S. Army between 1792 and 1844, most of which were made by private contractors, and the remainder by the Harpers Ferry Armory. The early designs bore the graceful lines and seven-groove rifling of a classic civilian "Kentucky" sporting rifle. By 1814, military rifles began to bear a closer resemblance to their smoothbore cousins, with thicker, full-length stocks and iron bands.

This 1819-dated example is one of the last of the 15,700 Model 1803 rifles produced in response to the popular clamor for more and better arms after the disastrous War of 1812.

Rifle barrel made by a civilian gunsmith (ca. 1845)

The bore of this civilian sporting rifle, later altered to military use by a Tennessee gunsmith, clearly shows the deep, seven-groove rifling that made these arms more accurate but slower to load than muskets.

Fulminate of Mercury and the "Mississippi" Rifle

In the 1790s, the Scottish clergyman and amateur chemist Alexander John Forsyth discovered that the chemical compound fulminate of mercury produced a quick and strong explosion when struck by a hammer. By the 1820s, English, French, and American inventors (most notably Joshua Shaw) had developed and patented a new percussion ignition system based on Forsyth's discovery. It relied on a small charge of fulminate of mercury contained in a disposable copper percussion cap. With the new system, when the trigger was pulled, the cocking arm — now appropriately called a hammer — struck a percussion cap on a hollow anvil-like nipple, creating a spark that passed though an internal vent hole and into the barrel. The new, water-resistant percussion system solved the problem of wet powder in an open pan and reduced ignition lag time.

The U.S. Army first employed the new system for the .54-caliber Model 1841 rifle and the .69-caliber Model 1842 musket, both of which were in production from 1844 through 1855. In addition, the army altered about 400,000 now-obsolete flintlock muskets to the percussion system. Despite the more reliable priming system, the rates of fire and the tactical functions of each arm were unchanged: the slow-firing but accurate rifle was to be used only by a few specially trained marksmen in support of large infantry formations armed with faster-firing but relatively inaccurate muskets.

The near-legendary reputation of the Model 1841 rifle originated at the Battle of Buena Vista, Mexico, in February 1847, when it proved so deadly in the hands of Colonel Jefferson Davis's First Mississippi Rifles that it became known simply as the "Mississippi." It quickly became a favorite of the state militias, especially in the South. Harpers Ferry and five private contractors produced 92,800 Model 1841 rifles, but none of the contractor-made rifles were fully interchangeable until about 1853.

In the mid-1850s, the development of a new, quick-loading, long-range bullet, the minié ball, made obsolete about 50,000 new .54-caliber "Mississippi" rifles stored in government arsenals, none of which were sighted or bored to fire the new .58-caliber bullet. At the same time, as the U.S. Army experimented with the new French rifle-and-bayonet-based light infantry tactics, it needed a way to affix bayonets to these rifles, none of which were designed for use with a bayonet. In late 1854, Harpers Ferry began upgrading its Model 1841 rifles by fitting their ramrods with cupped iron tips that conformed to the conical head of the new minié ball, adding adjustable rear sights to take advantage of the additional range offered by the new bullet, and attaching sword bayonets for close combat. Harpers Ferry eventually altered more than 8,800 old Model 1841 rifles to this new "long range" configuration. These improvements extended the service life of the "Mississippi," and were also incorporated into the new generation of Model 1855 rifles and rifle-muskets.

In 1861 and 1862, dozens of private manufacturers in the North and South upgraded another 25,000 Model 1841 rifles, resulting in at least twenty variations. The "Mississippi" was the most widely modified arm of the Civil War and, not surprisingly, the one most often copied by private gun makers in the Confederacy.

U.S. Model 1841 contract rifle, original configuration, made by George and Edward Tryon, Philadelphia (1844)

Made in the Philadelphia shops of the gunsmith George W. Tryon and his son Edward, this is one of the first 600 rifles delivered to the U.S. Ordnance Department under the first contract for the Model 1841. This example is still in its original configuration: a simple, fixed rear sight and no provision for a bayonet. Because rifles were designed for long-range skirmishing, not hand-to-hand combat, bayonets were considered unnecessary.

Tryon completed 5,000 "Mississippi" rifles before 1849, none of which were interchangeable. Although the Tryon family had been making arms for government contracts since the War of 1812, this contract would be its last. Government prices were too low and the inspection process was too rigid for a small company—especially one without modern machinery—to make a profit.

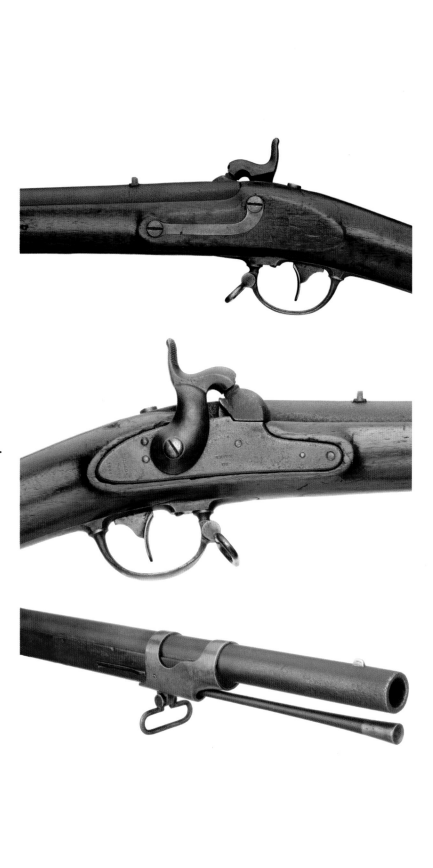

U.S. Model 1841 rifle, first long-range configuration,
made by the U.S. Armory at Harpers Ferry (1854–55)

This is one of the first 590 Model 1841 rifles upgraded to the new configuration at Harpers Ferry in late 1854 and early 1855. It features an experimental screw-type rear sight adjustable up to seven hundred yards, as well as two notches at the muzzle for attaching the newly designed Model 1854 sword bayonet (ring attachment type).

In May 1855, these 590 rifles were shipped to the St. Louis Arsenal. From there, some were issued to companies of the Sixth and Tenth U.S. Infantry Regiments, which used them in September 1855, against the Brulé Lakota at the Battle of Ash Hollow (or Blue Water Creek) in Nebraska Territory. The remainder probably went to the Third U.S. Infantry at Fort Leavenworth in "Bleeding Kansas," where they were used to enforce peace in the guerrilla war between pro- and antislavery settlers. In either place, this well-worn example would have seen hard service at a critical time in American history.

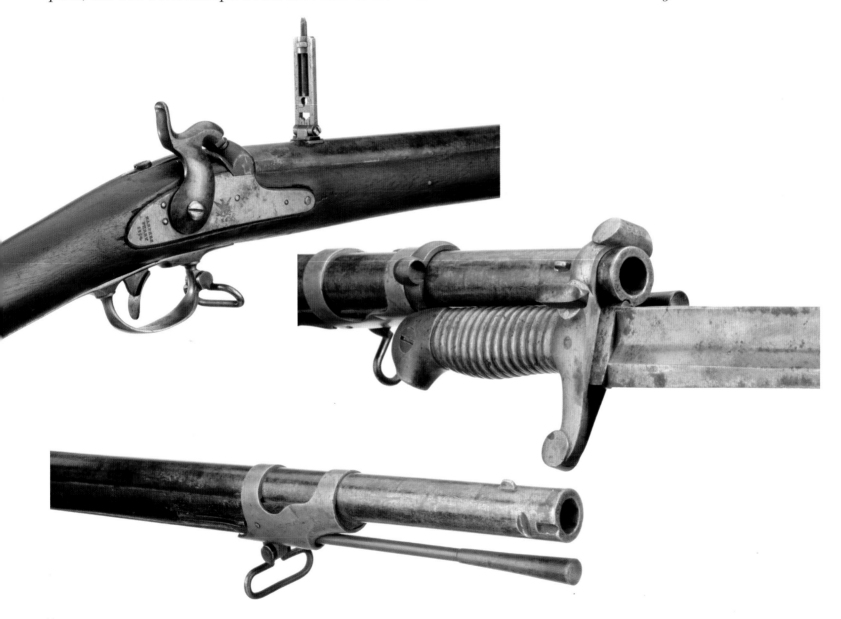

U.S. Model 1854 sword bayonet, ring attachment type, made by the U.S. Armory at Harpers Ferry (1854–55)

Because the Model 1841 rifle was never intended to be fitted with a bayonet, there was never any need to machine the exterior of the barrels to a standard dimension. This meant it was difficult to design a one-size-fits-all bayonet. In 1854 and 1855, Harpers Ferry tried to remedy the problem with 1,646 experimental sword bayonets, each with a ring and adjustable screw to compensate for slightly different barrel dimensions. Even so, the bayonets were not always interchangeable. Bayonet mating numbers, such as the "D37" seen here, were stamped into the top knob of the muzzle ring, thus ensuring that the bayonet would be fitted to the rifle with the corresponding number.

U.S. Model 1841 contract rifle, second long-range configuration, made by the Whitneyville Armory, New Haven, Connecticut (1855)

Delivered in November 1855, this rifle was among the last 600 Model 1841s produced under federal authority. Officially at least, it was the end of the line for the legendary "Mississippi." Like the last Model 1841s produced at Harpers Ferry, the last contract rifles made at the Whitneyville Armory in New Haven, Connecticut, were manufactured specifically for use with the new minié ball, albeit in .54 caliber. They used a rear sight copied from the British and a bayonet attachment copied from the French. To facilitate the interchangeability of bayonets, the exterior dimension of the barrel was specified at a standard 0.900 of an inch.

Reports from troops serving in the Kansas and Nebraska Territories revealed that the screw-type rear sight was too clumsy and delicate for field use. In mid-1855, the army adopted a new 1,000-yard "sliding pattern" sight like the ones on British Pattern 1853 arms. A smaller, third type of rear sight, sighted up to 500 yards with two folding leaves, was introduced in 1858 by the Springfield Armory and continued in production through the Civil War. These new sights would soon be used to alter thousands of older rifles, some of which were also rerifled to the new standard of .58 caliber.

U.S. Model 1854 sword bayonet, stud and guide type,
made by the U.S. Armory at Harpers Ferry (1855–56)

Like the screw-type rear sight, the ring-attachment bayonet proved too fragile for field service. In its place, the U.S. Ordnance Department adopted the "French pattern" of bayonet attachment, which consisted of a stud on the side of the barrel that fit into a grooved channel, or mortise, in the hilt of the bayonet. A flat iron spring in the hilt clamped the bayonet into place over the stud, while a small protruding guide key forward of the stud fit into a groove forward of the mortise, which helped guide the bayonet into place.

Though this alteration was an elegantly simple solution to the problem of different barrel dimensions, it required shortening the rifle's nosecap so that it could be removed for cleaning or repair without getting stuck on the bayonet stud.

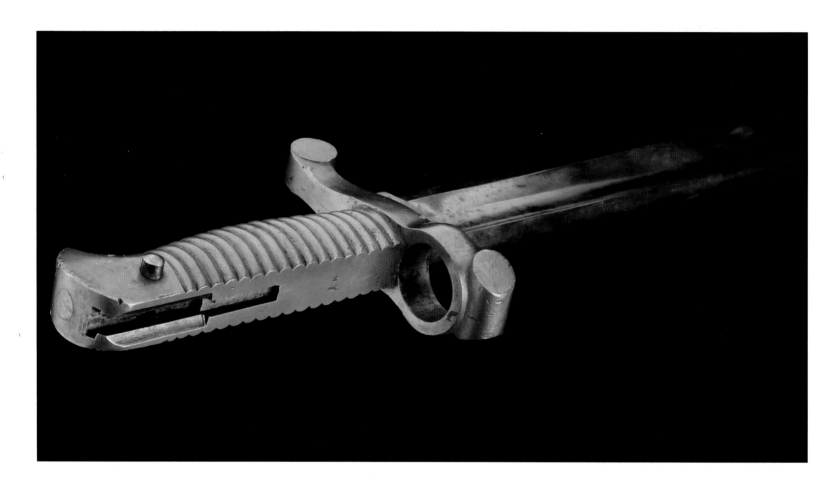

U.S. Model 1841 contract rifle made by the Whitneyville Armory, New Haven, Connecticut (1855), with alteration by the Colt Firearms Company, Hartford, Connecticut (1862)

In 1861, nearly all Model 1841 "Mississippi" rifles in northern and southern arsenals remained in their original configuration, that is, without long-range sights or bayonet studs. Among them was this Whitney contract rifle bearing an unusually sloppy double date stamping.

In late 1861, the Colt Firearms Company began upgrading more than 10,000 Model 1841 rifles for the U.S. Ordnance Department, including some 7,300 Whitneys from the New York Arsenal. Colt rebored the barrels to the new standard .58 caliber (although with seven-groove rifling), added a rear sight (surplus from Colt's Model 1855 revolving carbine), and fitted the barrels with a removable iron adaptor ring that held a bayonet stud.

This one, number 3511, was delivered to the U.S. Ordnance Department in May 1862. It was almost certainly among the 8,400 Colt-altered rifles shipped to the St. Louis Arsenal for issue to volunteer infantry regiments in Illinois, Iowa, Minnesota, and Kansas.

Lethality Perfected: The Model 1855 Rifle-Musket

Although the United States led the world in interchangeable production techniques, Great Britain and France led the world in ballistics technology. By 1853, the two global powers had developed the most lethal combination of loading speed and accuracy yet known: the hollow-base, expanding lead bullet, or minié ball, as well as a weapon designed specifically to fire it. Ironically, it was future Confederate president Jefferson Davis who encouraged the adoption and development of this new technology in the United States during his tenure as secretary of war (1853–57).

The minié ball was a conical lead bullet that could be loaded quickly like an undersized round ball, but featured a soft, hollow base that naturally expanded into the rifling upon firing, thus giving it the accuracy of a patched rifle ball. This meant that the rifling grooves could be fewer and shallower while still achieving the same purpose. The minié ball enabled the design of a new type of arm: the rifle-musket. Combining the loading speed of muskets and the accuracy of rifles, rifle-muskets turned the mass of ordinary infantrymen into riflemen capable of hitting enemy formations at four hundred yards or more.

Almost overnight, the rifle-musket made previous firearms and tactics obsolete — or so it seemed. At the beginning of the Civil War, no one fully understood how to maximize its lethality. Soldiers were seldom trained in sighting or estimating distances; many were not even allowed to practice firing their weapons before going into battle for the first time. Indeed, given the often wooded and hilly terrain of many Civil War battlefields, most of the real fighting was done at about a hundred yards (and often closer), where smoothbore muskets — by far the most numerous weapons on the battlefield through 1862 — were equally or more effective than rifle-muskets, especially with buck-and-ball ammunition.

The first U.S. rifle-musket was the .58-caliber Model 1855, produced between 1857 and 1861. It had a percussion lock, but with an added feature: an automatic tape primer system invented by Edward Maynard, a dentist in Washington, D.C. For all its promise of making firing even faster, the Maynard tape primer turned out to be too unreliable for field service and was eliminated in 1861. Aside from that change, all U.S. regulation rifle-muskets of the Civil War — the Model 1861, the "Special Model" 1861, the Model 1863, and the Model 1864, amounting to some 1,477,000 interchangeable arms — were essentially copies of the basic configuration established in 1855. Likewise, all arms produced at the Confederate national armories at Richmond, Virginia, and Fayetteville, North Carolina, not only used the Model 1855 design, but also were made on its U.S. machinery. Meanwhile com-

The United States musket, as now made, has no superior arm in the world. I say this with confidence, from my entire familiarity with the manufacture of these arms, and from the fact that the celebrated Enfield rifle of England is the result of a long visit and minute examination, and close study of the arms made at Springfield armory.
—U.S. Chief of Ordnance James W. Ripley to Secretary of War Simon Cameron, 1861

mercially made copies of the British Pattern 1853 rifle-musket — the arm that had helped inspire the design of the U.S. Model 1855 and its successors — became the standard-issue arm of Confederate forces.

By 1863, as northern mass production and southern blockade-running brought hundreds of thousands of quick-loading but accurate muzzle-loading rifle-muskets to the battlefield, their lethal impact became more apparent, but often in unexpected ways. The longer-range fire made possible by the rifle-musket gave rise to open-order skirmish tactics and sharpshooting; defensive earthworks came to dominate the battlefield; and frontal assaults across open ground became even more fatal for the attacker. It was this weapon that killed or wounded some 100,000 men in Virginia in May and June 1864 — fully half the strength of the armies engaged there. Ultimately, it was this weapon that robbed the Army of Northern Virginia of its mobility, sending it into ever more elaborate defensive earthworks around Richmond and Petersburg, where it slowly starved to death in 1865.

The deadly minié ball

In less than twenty years, the old technology of a round lead ball flying almost unguided through the air (left) gave way to a new technology of a conical lead ball spinning through the air (right). The latter's hollow base was designed to expand into the spiral grooves of a rifle-musket, sending it farther and faster than any other projectile.

While the new bullet bore the name of French captain Claude-Étienne Minié, who originated the idea in 1848, other engineers, including Americans James G. Benton at the Springfield Armory and James H. Burton at Harpers Ferry, perfected the shape of the new bullet in the early 1850s. Ballistics tests revealed that a .69-caliber minié ball was more accurate than the .54-caliber minié ball of the long-range Model 1841 rifles, but the recoil from the larger bullet was too severe. As a compromise, U.S. Ordnance officers settled on .58 as the new standard caliber.

Paper cartridge ammunition

During the Civil War, ammunition for muzzle-loading arms was prepackaged into paper cartridges. When loading, soldiers would bite the paper tail off the cartridge, pour the powder down the barrel, and then push the bullet down the barrel using a ramrod. A good soldier could load and fire about three times a minute. Pictured here are a .54-caliber minié ball cartridge for a "Mississippi" rifle (top), a .69-caliber buckshot cartridge for a musket (center), and a .58-caliber minié ball cartridge that has broken open, revealing the black powder still inside (bottom). The minié ball is at the other end.

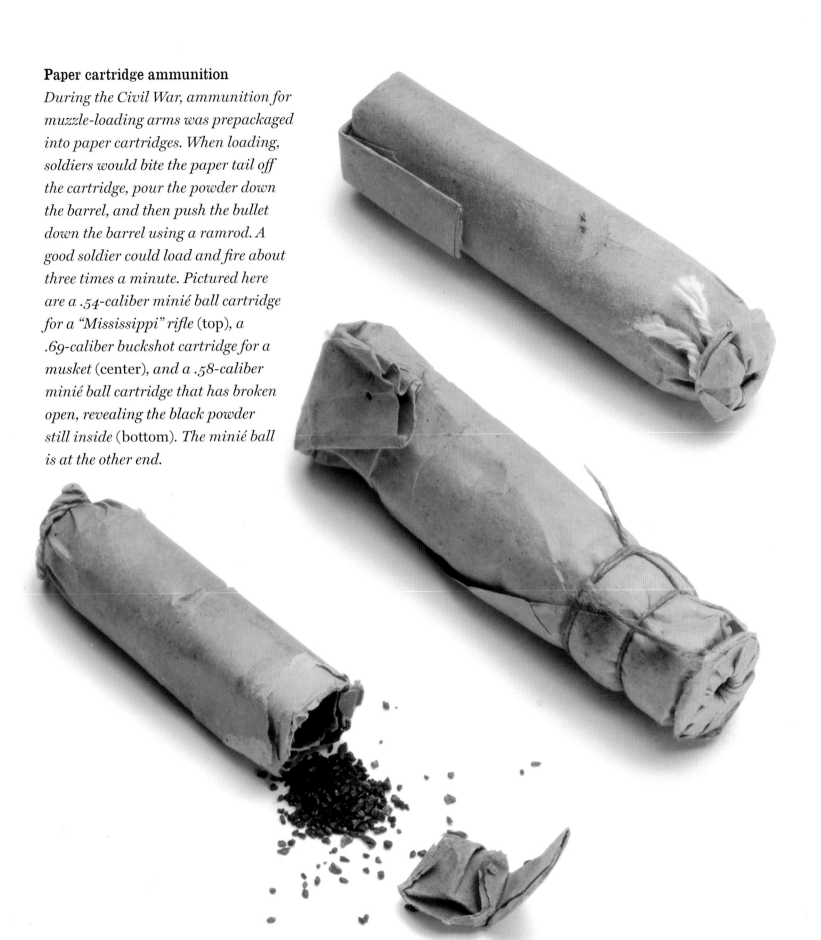

**British Pattern 1853
rifle-musket, second type,
made by the Royal Small Arms Factory,
Enfield, Britain (1856)**

*The new U.S. Model 1855 rifle-musket
copied the overall configuration of the
British Pattern 1853 rifle-musket, with its
brass stock tip and adjustable rear sight.
The Model 1855 was thus the first American
military arm since the Revolutionary
War to depart from the traditional French
configuration of a double-strapped nose
cap. Beginning about 1858, this was also
the first British government arm produced
with interchangeable-part machinery —
machinery it purchased from the Ames
Manufacturing Company in Massachusetts
and Robbins and Lawrence in Vermont.*

Copy of French Model 1859 "light minié" rifle made in Liège, Belgium (ca. 1860)

For its Model 1855 arms, the U.S. Army adopted several salient features of the French rifles developed in the 1850s around the new minié ball, including their shallow-groove rifling and stud-and-guide method of attaching a sword bayonet. This nearly mint-condition .56-caliber rifle is a close copy of the French Model 1859 made in Liège, Belgium, the arms-making capital of northwest Europe. Unlike its American counterparts, its parts are not interchangeable.

U.S. Model 1855 rifle-musket, first type, made by the U.S. Armory at Harpers Ferry (1857)

Fabricated in the last six months of 1857, this is one of the first 4,000 of the new Model 1855 rifle-muskets produced at Harpers Ferry. The bore is cut with the three-groove .58-caliber rifling that remained standard through the end of the Civil War.

For ordnance officers at the national armories, no detail or possible improvement was too small. As seen on this well-used example, the lip, or raised edge, around the striking surface of the hammer was prone to chipping as a result of repeatedly igniting percussion caps. In 1858, a small notch was machined into the top of the lip, which vented the force of the ignition and reduced chipping. Unissued stores of rifle-muskets were retrofitted with the modified hammers. Evidently, this example had already been issued.

Since the Revolutionary War, the U.S. Army had relied on private contractors to augment production at the national armories, especially for rifles. In 1855, the U.S. Army dispensed with contract arms altogether, believing its national armories could produce more than enough arms for any future emergency. Between 1857 and 1861, the Springfield and Harpers Ferry Armories turned out just over 70,000 Model 1855 rifle-muskets. No one envisioned the massive industrial effort that would be needed to fabricate millions more between 1861 and 1865.

Edward Maynard's patented tape primer system

In 1854, the U.S. government spent $50,000 to purchase the rights to Maynard's new priming system. It worked like a child's cap pistol: pulling back the hammer automatically advanced a waxed paper roll containing fifty fulminate of mercury charges onto the nipple, thus eliminating the need for individual percussion caps. The tip, or nose, of the hammer featured a small blade that cut the tape after each shot. Dr. Maynard's ingenious invention made him rich, but its delicate internal mechanism could not stand up to dirt, rain, and the hard use of military service.

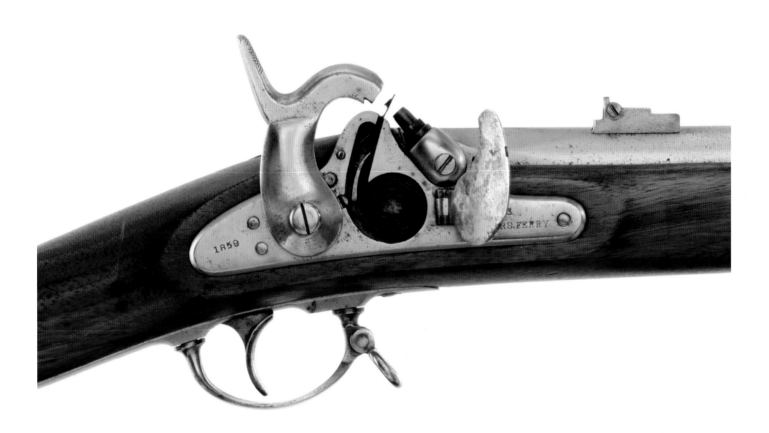

U.S. Model 1855 rifle-musket, second type, made by the U.S. Armory at Harpers Ferry (1859)

This second-type rifle-musket features an iron implement compartment and stock tip, as well as the Model 1858 leaf-type rear sight introduced into production at Harpers Ferry in March 1859.

On the night of October 16, 1859, this rifle-musket was either in production or already stored among 3,000 others at Harpers Ferry when the arsenal buildings were seized by a group of twenty-one armed men led by the militant abolitionist John Brown. But instead of distributing the arms as part of a slave insurrection, Brown and his men became besieged in the town, were attacked by an angry mob, and eventually surrendered to a company of U.S. Marines led by Colonel Robert E. Lee.

The inspection stamp "AMB" is that of forty-six-year-old master armorer Armistead M. Ball, who, along with the master machinist, the acting superintendent, and six other armory employees, was taken hostage by Brown and his raiders. "JAS" is the stamp of seventy-year-old John A. Schaeffer, foreman of the stock finishing shop. The script "NA" on the buttplate tang is unidentified; it may refer to a state armory or militia company.

U.S. Model 1855 rifle, first type, made by the U.S. Armory at Harpers Ferry (1858)

Although the new rifle-musket supposedly made shorter rifles obsolete, Colonel Henry Craig, the conservative U.S. chief of ordnance, as well as his boss, Secretary of War Jefferson Davis, insisted that the army retain its rifles, complete with the French-style sword bayonets.

The result was the Model 1855 rifle, 7,300 of which were fabricated at the Harpers Ferry Armory. This rifle was essentially the same as a rifle-musket, but about seven inches shorter and with the barrel bands, stock tip, and implement compartment made of brass instead of iron. Its British-style long-range rear sight and French-type bayonet stud had been successfully tested on the Model 1841 long-range rifles. Issued first to U.S. engineers, these early Model 1855 rifles were provided with a special rifleman's "figure 8" or "crosshair" front sight, which was fitted to the muzzle for more accurate shooting.

U.S. Model 1857 sword bayonet made by the U.S. Armory at Harpers Ferry (1857–61)

Bayonets designed for the new Model 1855 rifle featured a blade straighter than the Model 1854 stud-and-guide bayonet and eliminated the groove forward of the mortise, which fit over the guide key forward of the stud. In field tests, the groove and guide key were found to be unnecessary, so both were eliminated on the Model 1855 rifle.

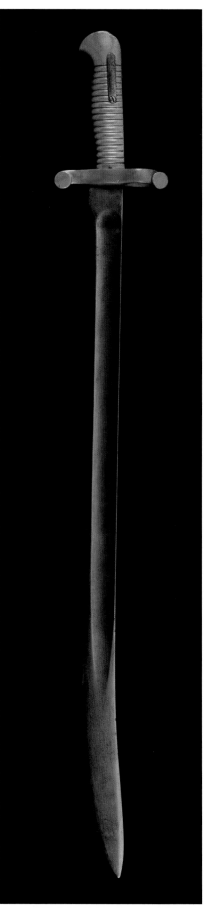

U.S. Model 1855 rifle, second type, made by the U.S. Armory at Harpers Ferry (1860)

Produced from late 1859 at Harpers Ferry, the second-type rifle was the same as the first except that it used the Model 1858 rear sight, and its bands, stock tip, and implement compartment were made of iron instead of brass. Since the army's eight regular infantry regiments had been rearmed with Model 1855 rifle-muskets, and the two light infantry regiments had been armed with altered long-range Model 1841 rifles, most of the Model 1855 rifles were issued to the states as part of their annual allotment of arms.

U.S. Model 1861 rifle-musket made by the U.S. Armory at Springfield (1861)

After abandoning the Maynard tape primer, the U.S. Ordnance Department redesigned its percussion locks around the more reliable system of disposable copper percussion caps. The result was the Model 1861 rifle-musket, the most widely produced firearm of the Civil War, so common that it became known simply as the "Springfield." It was the mainstay of Union armies throughout the war and, to a lesser extent, of Confederate armies as well, thanks to battlefield captures.

During the Civil War, the Springfield Armory alone fabricated nearly 800,000 interchangeable rifle-muskets of three models, about ten times the total Confederate production, public and private, of all types of firearms. By 1865, contract production of these and other arms had transformed the Connecticut River Valley into the arms-manufacturing center of the world, home to such well-known names as Colt, Remington, and Smith and Wesson. Here was the industrial ideal realized, but for a deadly purpose.

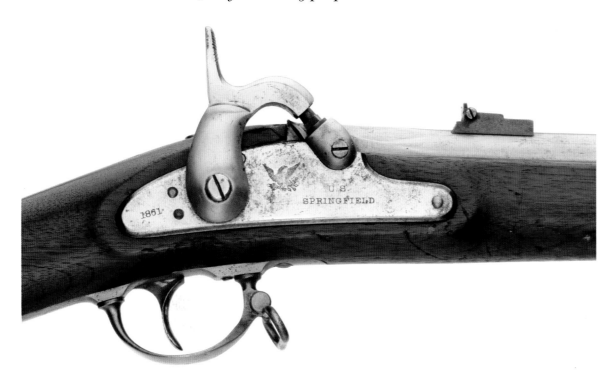

"Good and Serviceable": Eli Whitney and the Industrial Revolution

In 1792, the Connecticut native Eli Whitney Sr. (1765–1825) invented the cotton gin, a time-saving machine that made large-scale cotton cultivation enormously profitable—but only with the help of slave labor. In a dire example of unintended consequences, the rapid westward expansion of slavery that resulted from the development of Whitney's cotton gin became the central issue that tore the United States apart.

Because of legal issues with the patent, Whitney never realized a profit from his famous invention. Instead, he went into the arms business, establishing the Whitneyville Armory just north of New Haven, Connecticut. Here Whitney applied the methods of specialization and mass production that he had first attempted when manufacturing gins. According to legend, he also solved the problem of interchangeability. In a famous demonstration before Congress in 1801, Whitney assembled ten muskets from random piles of parts. But the show was rigged: he had had all the parts hand-fitted beforehand. His son, Eli Whitney Jr. (1820–95), assumed management of Whitneyville in 1842 and eventually transformed the armory to realize his father's dream of interchangeability. In one of American history's greatest ironies, the younger Whitney produced the guns for a war his father's invention had inadvertently spawned.

The Whitneyville Armory embodied the technological ideal of the Industrial Revolution. In the early 1850s, the armory employed about 300 workers and used specialized, state-of-the-art water-powered machinery capable of turning out at least 100 Model 1841 rifles each week. Between 1844 and 1855, the Whitneyville Armory produced 27,600 Model 1841 rifles for the U.S. government, more than any other contractor and nearly one-third of all Model 1841s produced.

At the same time, the Whitneyville Armory embodied the economic limitations of the Industrial Revolution. Having seen his father's dream of fully interchangeable parts become a practical reality at the national armories and for one or two of his fellow arms contractors, Eli Whitney Jr. did not need to achieve interchangeability at his factory until the Civil War. Before then, U.S. government contracts were a financial dead end: the cost of investment was too great, the inspection process too rigid, and the profit margin too low. In 1849, while the State of South Carolina was paying $14.50 each for noninterchangeable Whitney rifles, the U.S. Ordnance Department was paying $12.00 each for interchangeable ones—a price that dropped to $11.00 in 1853. Whitney later remarked that he had spent thirteen of his best years manufacturing the U.S. Model 1841 rifle, but never really made a profit.

I expect to be more particular in my government work than in my state work, as the state inspection is not with gauges. The inspector only examines the finished gun, which we agree to furnish good and serviceable.
—Eli Whitney Jr., testifying before the U.S. Commission on Ordnance and Ordnance Stores, 1862.

The impossibility of procuring the Mississippi Rifle, with sabre bayonet, has produced much dissatisfaction among the companies. . . . In consequence of the numerous applications for this rifle, the Adjutant-General . . . proceeded North in May last for the purpose of making contracts for this rifle. . . . The arms were received and examined, and proved to be old guns fixed up. Such an act being a violation of the letter and spirit of the contract, none of the arms were taken as part of the contract.
—Mississippi Adjutant-General W. L. Sykes, reporting to Governor John J. Pettus, January 1861

The real money was in selling arms to the states for their militias. Those arms did not have to be interchangeable, yet they commanded prices equal to (or higher than) those that did. Thus, when the U.S. government ended its procurement of arms from private contractors in 1855, Whitney focused on the lucrative state market. Some of the resulting arms, which Whitney advertised as "good and serviceable," are reasonably good copies of their U.S. models, while others can only generously be called derivative patterns. There were countless variations, and all were enormously profitable.

Although his political sympathies lay with the Republican Party, Eli Whitney Jr. always put business before politics. He sold guns to any state with the money to pay for them, regardless of whether that state was free or slave: Connecticut, New Hampshire, New York, Ohio, Maryland, South Carolina, Georgia, Mississippi, and probably other states as well. The nation's worst political crisis became Whitney's best business opportunity.

**"Good and serviceable" copy of U.S. Model 1841 rifle made
by the Whitneyville Armory (ca. 1856–57)**

*When Whitney's workmen assembled this rifle in 1856 or 1857, the stockpiles of surplus "us" marked
lockplates and buttplates were exhausted, although it still features one of the short front bands left over
from the last government-contract arms of 1855. The gun's most distinctive characteristic is its lack of
an implement compartment, an obvious time- and money-saving shortcut.*

*Lettering carved into both sides of the buttstock strongly suggests Confederate usage. "GWT" (with
a cursive T) and "ToTy" may refer to George W. Totty, a barely literate private of the Ninth Virginia
Infantry who was captured on July 3, 1863, at the Battle of Gettysburg. Although there are no
documented sales of Whitney "good and serviceable" arms to the State of Virginia, service records show
no other Union or Confederate soldier with these initials and last name.*

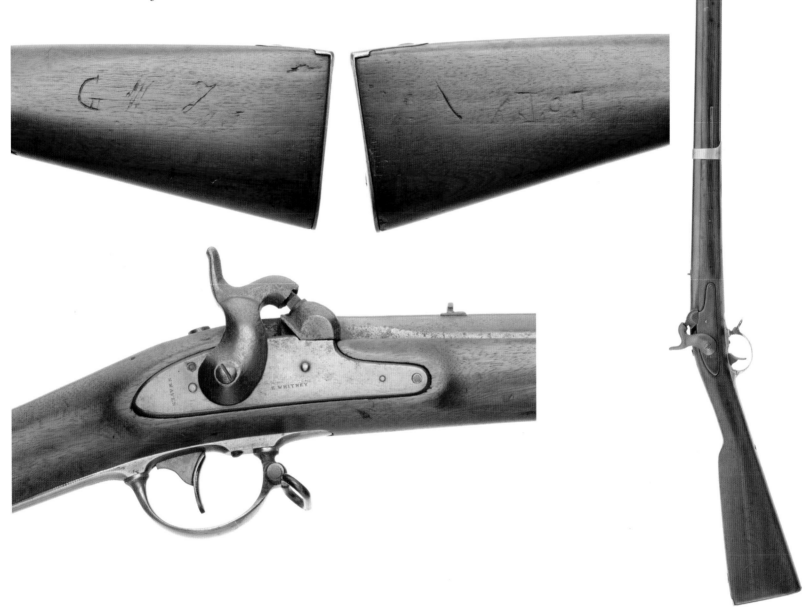

"Good and serviceable" copies of U.S. Model 1841 rifles made by the Whitneyville Armory (ca. 1858)

Assembled without implement compartments, bayonet studs, or any "US"-marked parts, and substituting iron instead of brass for the trigger guard bows, these inferior-quality Whitney rifles date to about 1858, making them some of the last ones made. The State of Georgia purchased 370 rifles of the Model 1841 configuration at the exorbitant price of $19.50 each from Whitney's New York agents between August 1860 and February 1861. Georgia inspectors were sorely disappointed, complaining, "The Mississippi Rifles recently furnished by you are not such as we desire to have."[1]

It was a similar story in Mississippi, where in 1860 the state found itself woefully short of the famous rifle that bore its name. Because Whitney had made the Model 1841 rifles used by Colonel Jefferson Davis's famous volunteers in Mexico, state officials again turned to the Connecticut gun maker in their hour of need. Having signed a contract with Whitney in June 1860 for 1,500 rifles, state inspectors found them to be "old guns fixed up" and therefore refused to pay for them. After heated negotiations between Whitney and U.S. senator Jefferson Davis, only 140 of the contracted rifles were delivered; none were ever paid for.

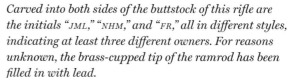

Carved into both sides of the buttstock of this rifle are the initials "JML," "NHM," and "FR," all in different styles, indicating at least three different owners. For reasons unknown, the brass-cupped tip of the ramrod has been filled in with lead.

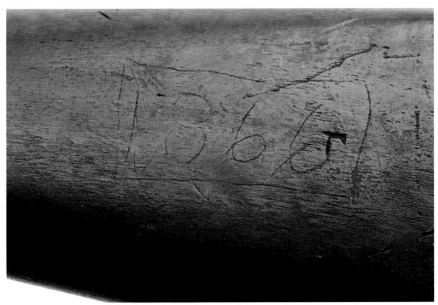

This heavily worn and crudely repaired rifle has the date "1866" scratched into the buttstock, suggesting use by self-armed militias in the South just after the war.

"Good and serviceable" copy of U.S. Model 1841 rifle made by the Whitneyville Armory (ca. 1856), with Confederate alteration (1861–62)

Similar in appearance to the rifles that Whitney sold to the State of Ohio in 1861, this example was assembled entirely of surplus parts made under U.S. government contract (including an 1848-dated lockplate and buttplate stamped "us"), but bears no government inspectors' marks.

As shown by its modifications, this rifle was probably sold to a southern state on the eve of the war. For reasons unknown, the Model 1855–type long-range rear sight has been replaced by a simple block sight, leaving two unfilled screw holes in the top of the barrel. For affixing a saber bayonet, a stud has been added at the muzzle. Most unusually, the upper strap of the front barrel band has been cut away to allow removal of the nose cap and bands over the stud during disassembly.

Three rifles (or remnants thereof) bearing the same bayonet stud and cut-down nose cap have been excavated from camp and battlefield sites near Richmond and Fredericksburg, strong evidence that this rifle was used by one of the Confederate states whose troops served in Virginia in 1861–62. The alterations were probably the work of a local gunsmith who also made noninterchangeable saber bayonets for the guns. Hence, the "16" on both the implement compartment and the buttplate may be a bayonet mating number.

"Minnie" or "Enfield" rifle derived from the British Pattern 1853 rifle-musket, made by the Whitneyville Armory (1860–61)

Perhaps the most bizarre and least attractive of Whitney's arms, this rifle bears little resemblance to its American-made British namesake except for the barrel bands. These bands were produced by Robbins and Lawrence, of Windsor, Vermont, as part of a British government contract for 25,000 Pattern 1853 rifle-muskets for use in the Crimean War (left). When the war ended unexpectedly in 1856, Britain canceled the order, sending Robbins and Lawrence into bankruptcy and, two years later, its assets to auction. Whitney snatched up 5,000 sets of barrel bands as well as stocks, screws, washers, and other parts, all at fire-sale prices. He incorporated these parts into an estimated 4,800 rifles and rifle-muskets that he advertised as "Minnie rifles" or "Minnie long-range muskets."

This rifle is believed to have been assembled in late 1860 or early 1861. It is distinguished by a unique Whitney-made rear sight, a pewter stock tip, and a brass trigger-guard bow mated to an iron trigger-guard plate. Whitney sold the rifles both to the U.S. Ordnance Department (which issued some to the Tenth Rhode Island Infantry) and to the states of Georgia and Mississippi. This one was fitted with a modified U.S. Model 1841 ramrod.

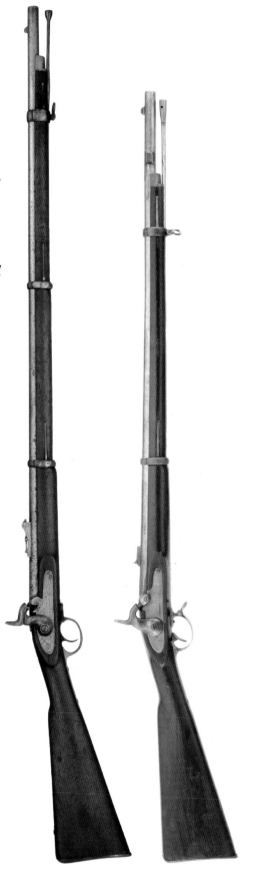

"Good and serviceable" rifle-musket derived from U.S. Model 1855 and 1861 rifle-muskets, made by the Whitneyville Armory (ca. 1861–62)

On April 19, 1861, the U.S. government declared an embargo on arms sales to the seceded states. With the lucrative southern market closed off, Whitney turned his attention to the northern states, which were clamoring for arms—any arms. In July 1861, Whitney turned down a federal contract for forty thousand interchangeable Model 1861 rifle-muskets in favor of a more profitable contract with his home state of Connecticut for fourteen thousand noninterchangeable copies of the same arm.

It is believed that this rare example was assembled in 1861 or early 1862 using the leftovers from that Connecticut contract as well as condemned and surplus parts previously auctioned off by the national armories. Its most distinctive feature is a "high hump" Model 1855–type lockplate (probably surplus from the Springfield Armory) that was never fitted for a Maynard tape primer. The three-groove barrel was made at Harpers Ferry (as indicated by the eagle inspection stamp), but bears the telltale c ("condemned") stamp under the breech. Only the barrel bands were made at Whitneyville, along with the brass (mostly copper) buttplate.

A State of Connecticut property mark stamped into the buttstock indicates that this arm was issued to the Eighth Connecticut Volunteers, Company D, soldier number 61. Though the identity of the soldier is unknown, his regiment received its baptism by fire at the Battle of Antietam, on September 17, 1862. The poor condition of the gun suggests that it was picked up from a battlefield, and there is a minié ball stuck about halfway down the barrel. Nearly half the soldiers of the Eighth Connecticut were killed or wounded that day. Was the owner of this gun one of them?

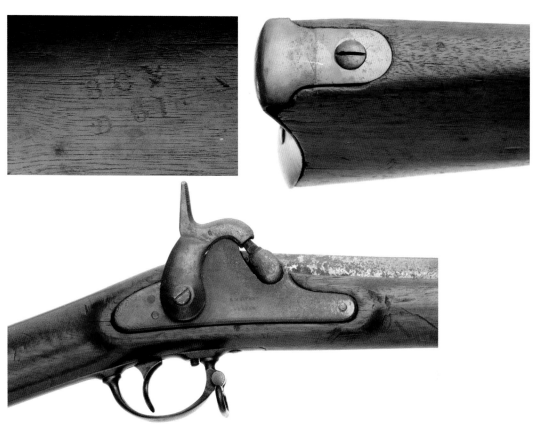

The Palmetto State's Yankee Armory

South Carolina began arming itself for war ten years before the first shots were fired at Fort Sumter. Built on cotton and slavery, the state threatened to secede from the United States first during the Nullification Crisis of 1832–33 and again following the Crisis of 1850 and the admission of California as a free state. In December 1850, the legislature of one of the richest states in the Union appropriated $350,000 "for the Defense of the State"—essentially to forgo years of private development and simply buy itself an arms industry. It was an unprecedented sum, greater than the entire state budget for the previous year and paid for by a 50 percent increase in all state taxes.

The core of the state's armament program was a contract signed on April 15, 1851, with William Glaze and Company of Columbia for six thousand copies of the U.S. Model 1842 musket, one thousand of the U.S. Model 1841 rifle, two thousand of the U.S. Model 1842 pistol, and two thousand of the U.S. Model 1840 artillery and cavalry saber. "These arms and their component parts, to be manufactured within the State of South Carolina," specified the contract, "and as far as practicable of material and by mechanics obtained in the state."[2]

With no previous experience in making weapons, Glaze partnered with an experienced mechanic named Benjamin Flagg and the manufacturer Asa Waters, both of Millbury, Massachusetts, to form the Palmetto Armory in Columbia. Flagg and Waters were in a familiar business but in a seemingly foreign land. They had delivered 760 noninterchangeable copies of the U.S. Model 1842 musket to the State of South Carolina in 1850. But because the state spent the funds allocated for the muskets on an elaborate funeral for native son and states-rights champion John C. Calhoun, it condemned 660 of the muskets so that it would not have to pay for them. It took three years to finally settle the account. Ironically, Waters was known for his antislavery sentiments; he joined the Free Soil Party in 1854 and later sold his muskets to free-state settlers in Kansas.

Politics aside, all three partners in the Palmetto Armory needed the business. Faced with a requirement that the arms be manufactured entirely in South Carolina yet understanding the prohibitive costs of setting up a fully functional arms factory for such a small order, they settled on the only logical course of action: assemble the arms from surplus and condemned parts made at the national armories or in New England factories. As a ruse, Flagg and Waters shipped some of their machinery south, along with workers who knew how to use it. Only a few small parts were made at the Palmetto Armory; the rest of the work there consisted of stocking, assembling, and final finishing. South Carolina military inspectors, who

If the State is sovereign, as we all hold she is, she is sovereign as well in war as in peace, and for warlike as well as peaceful purposes. To claim sovereignty without the readiness, or even the disposition to defend that sovereignty by force of arms, is simply absurd. It is the duty of the State, therefore, to retain the means of defence, and not to give up to any other power whatever all her military material, and in so doing, shift from her own shoulders the duty and labor of her defence.
—South Carolina chief of ordnance Edward Manigault, November 21, 1861

South Carolina is too small for a republic, but too large for an insane asylum.
—South Carolina Unionist James L. Petigru, soon after his state's secession, 1860

had even less experience in arms manufacturing than Glaze, either were unaware of the extent of the subterfuge or were induced to look the other way. By the end of 1853, the order had been filled and secession fever had abated, even if only temporarily.

Thus, the Palmetto State armed itself for war by using Yankee machinery, Yankee parts, and Yankee ingenuity. Given the lack of industrial infrastructure in South Carolina, it was the only way for the Palmetto Armory to meet the naive demands of the state legislature and still turn a profit. Thus, one of the South's first experiments in imposing industrialization from above succeeded in its immediate goal of procuring arms, yet its larger mission of promoting a private arms industry within the state failed miserably. It was a lesson that the Confederacy would be forced to learn on a much larger scale just ten years later.

Marks of state defiance

One of the most politically potent state symbols in pre–Civil War America, the palmetto tree recalled the June 1776 defense of Charleston, South Carolina, by a small patriot force that used palmetto logs to build a makeshift fort. The spongy logs proved impervious to British cannonballs, making the palmetto a symbol of South Carolina's defiance of royal tyranny. By the 1850s, the palmetto had come to represent the state's defiance of another supposed form of tyranny: a northern-led conspiracy to destroy the constitutional right to own slaves.

When the Palmetto Armory adopted the palmetto tree as its signature, it created one of the most distinctive, attractive, and often-faked makers' marks in firearm history. As if to wipe away any trace of U.S. authority, Palmetto Armory gun barrels used a palmetto tree in place of an eagle's head as an inspection mark, and the initials "SC" replaced the normal "US" stamp on the buttplate tang of Palmetto Armory muskets (left) and rifles (right). Ironically, the marks may have been applied by New England workers before the parts were shipped to South Carolina.

Copy of U.S. Model 1842 musket made for the Palmetto Armory (1852)

Outwardly at least, Palmetto Armory muskets differed from the U.S. pattern chiefly in the substitution of heavy brass bands in place of iron. But there were more subtle differences: crudely finished hammers, parts that do not line up precisely, and surplus or condemned barrels from the Springfield Armory, some of which bear palmetto trees struck over the eagle-head proof.

From the time of their delivery in 1853 through the first years of the Civil War, the 6,020 Palmetto Armory muskets saw extensive use in South Carolina militia companies. The lightly stamped palmetto tree mark on the lockplate of this example has been almost completely worn away.

Copy of U.S. Model 1841 rifle made for the Palmetto Armory (1852)

Aside from the markings and a barrel stud designed for socket bayonets, the Palmetto Armory rifles are almost indistinguishable from their U.S. counterparts, and for good reason. Many of the metal parts were probably purchased as surplus from Robbins and Lawrence of Windsor, Vermont, which had just finished delivery of twenty-five thousand Model 1841 rifles to the U.S. government. Other surplus parts probably came from Eli Whitney's armory in Connecticut.

In 1860 and 1861, virtually all one thousand Palmetto Armory rifles were in the hands of state militia companies; some eventually saw Confederate service in the Charleston area. By February 1865, some five hundred had been turned in for storage in Columbia, where General William T. Sherman's army destroyed them, along with ten thousand other firearms. As a result, rifles are the rarest of Palmetto Armory firearms.

**Copy of U.S. Model 1840
cavalry saber made for the
Palmetto Armory by
Schnitzler and Kirschbaum,
Solingen, Prussia (1852)**

*In April 1852, a year after receiving
its state contract, the Palmetto Armory
had made little progress toward
completing it. Perhaps in an effort to
simplify the task and hasten delivery,
the South Carolina Board of Ordnance
changed its original order from 1,000
cavalry sabers and 1,000 artillery
sabers to 2,000 cavalry sabers.*

*It mattered little to Glaze, Flagg,
and Waters. Their sabers were not
only not manufactured in South
Carolina, but were not even made
in the United States. Instead, the
partners purchased all two thousand
from the famous cutlery company
of Schnitzler and Kirschbaum, of
Solingen, Prussia, which had been
making sabers for the U.S. Ordnance
Department. It is not known whether
the "Columbia S.C." stamps were
applied in Columbia or in Solingen,
though the "AWZ" on the underside
of the brass guard is thought to be a
Prussian inspector's mark.*

U.S. Model 1816 musket made by the U.S. Armory at Springfield (1824), altered for the Palmetto Armory (1851–53)

On May 31, 1851, the Palmetto Armory received a second contract from the State of South Carolina, this time to alter the old U.S. Model 1816 flintlock muskets stored in the state's arsenals. By November 1853, the armory had been paid two dollars each for 5,960 muskets altered by adding a percussion hammer and a distinctive bolster brazed over the vent hole. Like most Palmetto Armory work, these alterations were done at the Flagg and Waters factory in Millbury, Massachusetts.

Originally issued to the state under the 1808 Militia Act, this 1824-dated musket bears the "S Carolina" state property stamp on top of the barrel. The barely discernible "N56" is a serial number that was applied when the arm was produced at the Springfield Armory.

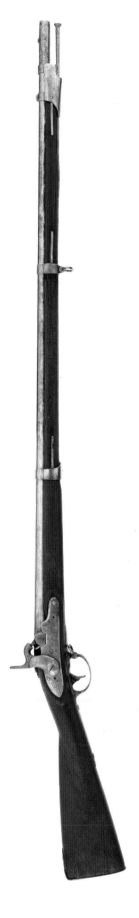

Copy of U.S. Model 1842 rifled musket made for the Palmetto Armory (1852), with rear sight added (1861)

Soon after declaring its independence on December 20, 1860, South Carolina hired William Glaze to upgrade muskets in the state's arsenals. By August 1861, Glaze's company, now known as the Palmetto Iron Works, had rifled and sighted 3,720 of the 6,020 Palmetto Armory muskets made in 1852–53. This example—fitted with a U.S. Model 1855 long-range ladder sight—is a restoration. Most of Glaze's rifled muskets had simple block sights. "I ame ready to doe any thing for the state or Confedret States you may see fit to order me," wrote Glaze to the state's ordnance department in 1861.[3] Although he possessed rifling machinery, Glaze clearly did not have the means to fabricate entirely new firearms, or else he surely would have been awarded a state contract to do so during the war.

2. Plowshares into Swords

On paper, at least, the northern states had all the resources necessary for winning a war, especially if it turned out to be a long one: 85 percent of all U.S. manufacturing, 80 percent of the military-age population, and 70 percent of the railroads. Northern iron and steel furnaces, firearms manufacturers, textile mills, and other industries were outproducing the rest of the world at an astonishing rate, while the South remained largely dependent on agriculture, with most of its capital tied up in land and slaves. Aside from the U.S. Armory and Arsenal at Harpers Ferry, Virginia — at the very tip of the Confederacy's exposed northern border — there were virtually no modern arms factories in the South.

But the war was not fought on paper. Instead, it was a contest among idealistic, emotional, and often irrational people, many of whom expected the war to be over in six months. Furthermore, the southern states were far from helpless. In 1861, the newly formed Confederate States of America was the fourth-wealthiest nation in the world, behind the United States, Great Britain, and France. Nor had the Industrial Revolution entirely left the South behind: newly established flour, paper, and textile mills as well as tanneries, iron foundries, rolling mills, and railroads had created a rapidly emerging industrial base. In 1861, southern cities and towns from New Orleans to Richmond were home to a small but vibrant class of entrepreneurs and artisans who swiftly took advantage of the Confederacy's pressing need to manufacture the modern tools of war.

When the war failed to end in six months, the champions of an independent agrarian South came to understand how much they needed these entrepreneurs and artisans — many of them northern- or foreign-born, and some of them Union sympathizers — to forge the sinews of war, to ensure national survival, and to literally beat plowshares into swords. And it all had to be done quickly. The Confederate States of America would never again control as much territory as it did at the time of its birth.

It is not men we lack, but muskets.
—Confederate secretary of state
Judah P. Benjamin to General Albert
Sidney Johnston, October 25, 1861

*The sooner our people free themselves
of the miserable delusion that "cotton is
King," the better off it will be for us. . . .
Bayonets and gunpowder is now "King."*
—Columbus (Ga.) Sun, March 25, 1863

Makeshifts and Alterations

In 1860 and 1861, the eleven seceding states took possession of approximately 165,000 military arms (including muskets, rifles, and pistols) from U.S. arsenals and forts located within their borders. More than two-thirds of these arms had been placed there thanks to the foresight (or perhaps paranoia) of John B. Floyd while he was U.S. secretary of war (1857–60). In December 1859, three months after John Brown's abortive raid on Harpers Ferry, Floyd, a former Virginia governor and future Confederate general, ordered some 115,000 muskets and rifles transferred to six federal arsenals in the South, citing self-defense in case the next Brown-style plot succeeded. In early 1860, Floyd authorized the sale from U.S. arsenals of an additional 34,000 percussion-altered and supposedly surplus muskets at bargain-basement prices. Southern states purchased 32,500 of them at $2.50 each. Considering Floyd's subsequently abysmal military career, this brazen bureaucratic stunt was by far his greatest contribution to the Confederate war effort, made well before the war even began.

Since 1816, at least another 150,000 small arms had been issued to these eleven states under the Militia Act of 1808, where they joined unknown thousands of older arms in state arsenals. In addition, Virginia had operated its own state armory in the early 1800s, which produced 60,000 muskets and rifles. South Carolina had purchased 9,000 guns through its Palmetto Armory venture in the early 1850s; Georgia, Mississippi, and other southern states bought perhaps another 8,000 arms from northern arms dealers on the eve of the war. Theoretically, the states of the new Confederacy owned close to 425,000 military firearms from all sources. Meanwhile, in Texas alone there were an estimated 40,000 civilian shotguns and sporting rifles, a figure that suggests at least ten times that number were on hand in the other states of the Confederacy.

These seemingly generous numbers conceal a hard truth: most of the military arms were obsolete, many were not even in working order, and some existed only on paper. A large number of the 165,000 arms from the former federal arsenals were pre-1855-era muskets as well as all manner of single-shot pistols, carbines, flintlock rifles, and at least 8,300 flintlock muskets. The state-owned arsenals were in even worse shape, housing a hodgepodge of broken and rusty weapons of different models and calibers, most of them flintlocks, some gathering dust since the Revolutionary War. Some states could not find all the arms they supposedly owned; once issued to the militias, state inspectors never saw the guns again. The Virginia Manufactory had not produced a single arm in the previous forty years; it had no modern machinery and its buildings were dilapidated. Of course, many of

It has been suggested that there are many thousand rifles and double barreled shotguns in the hands of citizens in the Southern States, which might be obtained for the use of the Army, which guns, if repaired, brought to a uniform size, rebored and rifled with a bayonet attached, might be found a very useful weapon, if not the best gun which could be placed in the hands of our soldiers.
—Appeal to Confederate secretary of war Leroy P. Walker from the citizens of Memphis, Tennessee, September 26, 1861

the young men who answered their states' calls for volunteers showed up with their own rifles or shotguns, fully expecting they would be sufficient for a ninety-day war. But professional military men knew better: fancy rifles and cheap shotguns could not long withstand the constant wear and tear of military life, any more than armies could long be supplied with ammunition in so many different calibers.

In reality, there were in the South probably no more than 225,000 serviceable military percussion muskets (most altered from flintlock), 25,000 Model 1841 rifles (most in their original configuration), and 10,000 Model 1855 rifles and rifle-muskets. That supply was considered more than adequate for the expected single-battle war, especially since most Union forces were armed with the same kinds of obsolete weapons. But in fact 260,000 serviceable arms of all types were hardly sufficient for the more than 360 Confederate regiments that were raised in 1861 alone, let alone the 900,000 soldiers who would serve the Confederacy at some point over the next four years.

Thus, the material challenge for the Confederacy was one of both quantity and quality. Buying arms abroad was the obvious solution, but that would take time — the war would not wait for blockade-runners. As a stopgap measure, Confederate and state ordnance agents set up arsenals and combed the countryside for old shot-guns, sporting rifles, and military muskets lost from the militia rolls. They searched for locks, barrels, machinery, raw materials, and any mechanics or gunsmiths who could make broken and obsolete arms into something reasonably deadly. Initially, the nascent Confederacy had to make do with what it had, putting its limited indus-trial capacity to work not on producing new arms, but simply on fixing up old ones.

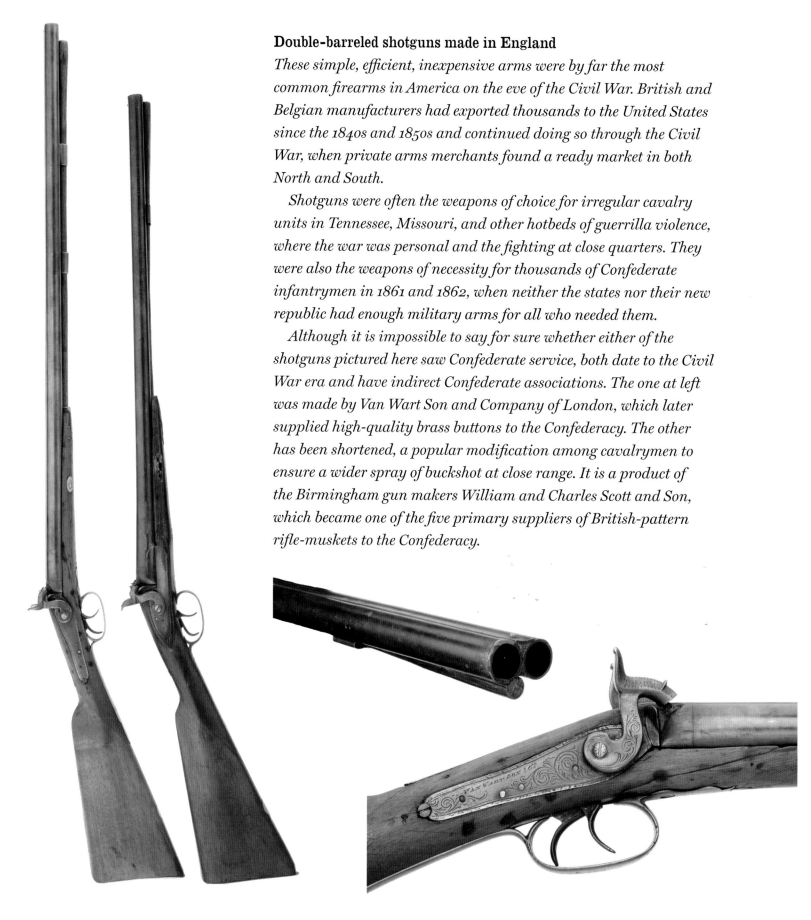

Double-barreled shotguns made in England

These simple, efficient, inexpensive arms were by far the most common firearms in America on the eve of the Civil War. British and Belgian manufacturers had exported thousands to the United States since the 1840s and 1850s and continued doing so through the Civil War, when private arms merchants found a ready market in both North and South.

Shotguns were often the weapons of choice for irregular cavalry units in Tennessee, Missouri, and other hotbeds of guerrilla violence, where the war was personal and the fighting at close quarters. They were also the weapons of necessity for thousands of Confederate infantrymen in 1861 and 1862, when neither the states nor their new republic had enough military arms for all who needed them.

Although it is impossible to say for sure whether either of the shotguns pictured here saw Confederate service, both date to the Civil War era and have indirect Confederate associations. The one at left was made by Van Wart Son and Company of London, which later supplied high-quality brass buttons to the Confederacy. The other has been shortened, a popular modification among cavalrymen to ensure a wider spray of buckshot at close range. It is a product of the Birmingham gun makers William and Charles Scott and Son, which became one of the five primary suppliers of British-pattern rifle-muskets to the Confederacy.

Half-stock sporting rifles made by John P. Murray, Columbus, Georgia (ca. 1860)

Many volunteers brought with them the only rifles they knew and the only ones they felt they needed for a ninety-day war. These elegant and nearly identical .45-caliber sporting rifles were crafted by John P. Murray, a thirty-five-year-old son of English immigrants who had started his gun-making business in Charleston before relocating to Columbus in 1859. Murray went on to work as the master armorer for Greenwood and Gray, a Columbus company that contracted for military rifles, before settling back into the firearms business after the war.

The pristine condition of the rifle with double-set triggers suggests that it was never carried into battle. The other rifle shows considerable wear, but its provenance is unknown. Many such rifles survive with stories of wartime use. True as these stories may be, the rifles probably survived only because they were sent home soon after being replaced with military arms.

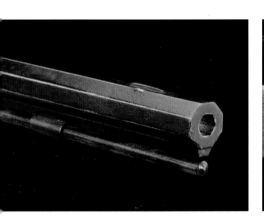

U.S. Model 1795 musket made by the U.S. Armory at Springfield (1811) with lock made by the Virginia Manufactory, Richmond (1812), and civilian percussion alteration (ca. 1861)

After John Brown's raid on Harpers Ferry in 1859, the State of Virginia appropriated $320,000 to refurbish the old Virginia Manufactory building in Richmond and to begin altering to percussion thousands of old flintlock muskets, including about 58,000 made there between 1803 and 1821. The work had barely begun when the war broke out. Desperate for arms of any sort, Virginia issued most of the old muskets in their original flint configuration in the spring and summer of 1861, gradually recalling them over the coming months for alteration.

This 1811-dated U.S. Model 1795 stock has been fitted with an 1812-dated Virginia Manufactory lock. Using a method typical of civilian gunsmiths, the flintlock was altered by replacing the cocking arm with a civilian-style hammer and inserting a drum-type bolster with a percussion nipple into the vent hole. It is not known where or when this marriage of parts took place, but the alteration resembles those done under contract by gunsmiths in western Virginia.

U.S. Model 1816 musket made by the U.S. Armory at Springfield (1837), presented to a member of the First North Carolina Militia Regiment (1844), with civilian percussion alteration (ca. 1855)

One reason that state arsenals often lost track of their property is illustrated by this U.S.-issued musket decorated and engraved as a personal gift. In 1844, the First North Carolina Militia Regiment presented this musket to Albert Gilbert Bogart, principal of the newly opened Washington Academy in Washington, North Carolina. Born in New Jersey and educated at Princeton, Bogart became a leading Whig in his adopted community, favoring government-funded "internal improvements" and public schools. Although Bogart was too old to serve in the Civil War, his youngest son, David, was a guard at the prisoner-of-war camp in Salisbury and eventually became lieutenant colonel of the same militia regiment in the 1880s. It is unlikely that either father or son ever fired a shot in anger using this musket.

It was altered to the percussion system using a common civilian-type hammer and drum-type bolster, most likely in the 1850s. Although North Carolina was home to dozens of gunsmiths skilled at brass inlay work for "Kentucky"-style long rifles, the craftsman responsible for this work remains unknown. George Wray considered this arm too special to be kept with the rest of his collection; instead he displayed it above the mantel in his den.

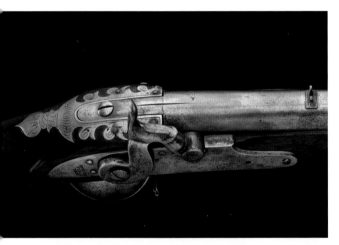

U.S. Model 1817 contract, or "common," rifle made by Simeon North, Middletown, Connecticut (1824), with alteration by Charles Kuester, Raleigh, North Carolina (1861)

Termed the "common rifle" to distinguish it from the U.S. Model 1819 Hall breech-loading rifle, the Model 1817 was fabricated in .54 caliber, requiring only percussion alteration and a bayonet attachment to make it suitable for Confederate use with the same ammunition as "Mississippi" rifles. This one was originally produced by Simeon North, who became famous in the 1830s as the first private manufacturer to fabricate interchangeable arms under John Hall's system.

Characterized by its distinctive hammer and bolster, this is one of the first fifty flintlock rifles altered to percussion by Charles Kuester, the sole gunsmith in Raleigh, under contract with the State of North Carolina in December 1861. Kuester went on to alter at least twelve hundred more arms for the state, including British and Hessian muskets captured during the Revolutionary War. The "24" struck above the bolster near the "N Carolina" property stamp is thought to indicate that this was the twenty-fourth arm that Kuester altered. He also shortened the stock to accommodate a North Carolina–style "footprint"-type bayonet stud, which fits a sword bayonet made by Louis Froelich's manufactory in Wilmington.

This rifle was likely issued to the Ashe County men of Company A, Thirty-Fourth North Carolina Infantry, who were bound for guard duty along the North Carolina coast before joining the Army of Northern Virginia for the battles of the Seven Days in June 1862.

U.S. Model 1836 contract pistol made by Asa Waters, Millbury, Massachusetts (1839), with alteration by the C.S. Armory at Fayetteville, North Carolina (1861–62)

Under the Militia Act of 1808, the State of North Carolina was issued some 5,650 single-shot flintlock pistols, including this U.S. Model 1836 pistol made by the famous arms maker, industrialist, and antislavery activist Asa Waters. By 1861, these old pistols had become practically useless for combat.

In late 1861 and early 1862, the C.S. Armory at Fayetteville altered about 1,100 Model 1836 flintlock pistols to the percussion system, adding a new S-shaped hammer, the signature design feature of the armory. Altering the pistols made them only marginally more useful, but still better than nothing. They were then issued to the First, Second, and Third North Carolina Cavalry Regiments on their way to service in Virginia. Even after the Confederate government assumed control of operations at Fayetteville, alterations totaling at least 3,600 arms continued on behalf of the State of North Carolina.

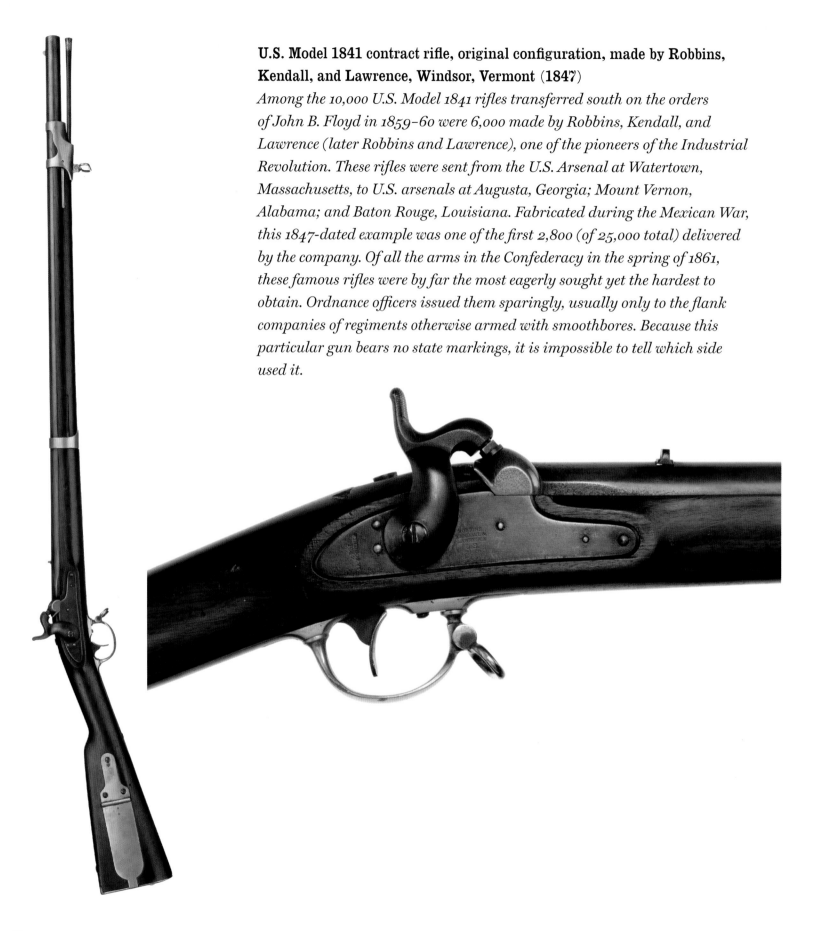

U.S. Model 1841 contract rifle, original configuration, made by Robbins, Kendall, and Lawrence, Windsor, Vermont (1847)

Among the 10,000 U.S. Model 1841 rifles transferred south on the orders of John B. Floyd in 1859–60 were 6,000 made by Robbins, Kendall, and Lawrence (later Robbins and Lawrence), one of the pioneers of the Industrial Revolution. These rifles were sent from the U.S. Arsenal at Watertown, Massachusetts, to U.S. arsenals at Augusta, Georgia; Mount Vernon, Alabama; and Baton Rouge, Louisiana. Fabricated during the Mexican War, this 1847-dated example was one of the first 2,800 (of 25,000 total) delivered by the company. Of all the arms in the Confederacy in the spring of 1861, these famous rifles were by far the most eagerly sought yet the hardest to obtain. Ordnance officers issued them sparingly, usually only to the flank companies of regiments otherwise armed with smoothbores. Because this particular gun bears no state markings, it is impossible to tell which side used it.

U.S. Model 1855 rifle-musket, first type, made by the U.S. Armory at Springfield (1858) and used by the Republican Blues, Savannah, Georgia

On the eve of war, only a lucky few had access to the latest rifle-muskets from the national armories. The underside of the stock of this one is marked with the property stamp of the elite Republican Blues, a volunteer militia company formed in 1808 by the well-born sons of Savannah, Georgia. In January 1859, political connections ensured that this 215-man company was the first in the state to receive the new U.S. Model 1855 rifle-muskets when they became available to Georgia as part of its annual allotment of arms under the Militia Act.

This gun accompanied the sharply uniformed Blues on their goodwill tour of New York City, which began on July 21, 1860, exactly one year before the First Battle of Manassas (Bull Run). While thousands fought and died in that battle, the Blues were posted to coastal defenses around Savannah. Redesignated Company C, First Georgia Infantry (Olmstead's), the company spent the next three years at Forts Jackson and McAllister. In June 1862, the Blues, then serving mainly as artillerymen, were required to turn in their cherished Model 1855s to the State of Georgia, which needed them for its infantry regiments.

This arm is believed to have been reissued two years later to an eighteen-year-old Butts County farm boy named William R. Parker of the Third Georgia Reserve Infantry Regiment, one of the regiments that Governor Brown insisted on keeping for state defense. Using a clothing stamp, Parker punched his name into the stock. He and his unit of men and boys were assigned to guard Union prisoners at Camp Sumter (or Andersonville) and Camp Lawton, Georgia, before fighting at the Battle of Coosawhatchie, South Carolina, in December 1864, and along the nearby Salkehatchie River in February 1865. Parker probably used this rifle-musket on the night of April 16, 1865, during the last-ditch defense of Columbus, Georgia, when Union cavalrymen routed the Third Reserves and he was taken prisoner. After the war, Parker drew a state pension until his death in 1913.

"Artillery muskets" believed made at the Alabama State Depot at Mobile (ca. 1861–62)

In the winter of 1861, the State of Alabama established an ordnance depot at Mobile where arms scavenged from across the state could be altered for military use. These two nearly identical muskets are believed to have been assembled there especially for artillerymen manning the forts around Mobile.

They are characterized by their diminutive size and mixture of parts. Nine inches shorter than a standard infantry musket and considerably lighter, these ersatz arms were suitable only for firing buckshot at close range against attacking infantry. Their thirty-four-inch-long .65-caliber smoothbore barrels were probably surplus taken from long-ago-condemned British flintlock carbines. The old barrels were then fitted with British-style bolsters and mated to percussion sporting locks made and sold in bulk by John P. Murray, a gunsmith in Columbus, Georgia.

Despite their antiquated origins, these guns present an outwardly modern appearance: "Mississippi" rifle–style hammers (obviously too large for the lockplate) and two-screw sideplates (even though the small lock requires only a single lockplate screw), as well as British military-style barrel bands and stocks (although with straight "Mississippi" butts). The oddest features of these muskets are the screws securing the bands to the stocks—perhaps applied to keep the bands from moving when the gun was fired.

There are three other known artillery muskets believed to have been made at Mobile, but they were built around cut-down U.S. Model 1842 musket barrels. Because none of the five bear the Alabama proof or inspection marks that were later applied to state contract rifles, it is impossible to say for sure where they were made.

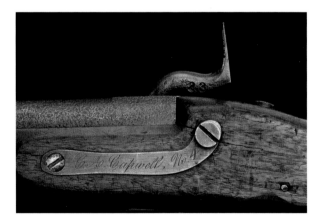

Previous page: *Both artillery muskets bear mating numbers stamped with the same set of dies under the barrels and in the stocks, indicating their assembly at approximately the same time and place. This one is number 10. The number "23" stamped on the inside of the hammer does not correspond to any other internal markings, probably indicating that the hammer was scavenged from another arm.*

Engraved on the sideplate of this musket is "C. A. Casswell, No.4" (what appears to be a cursive P is the typographic ligature for a double s). Unfortunately, the identity of this person remains unknown: perhaps a worker at the state depot or perhaps an artilleryman, "4" being the number of his battery or his station while manning the gun. Likewise, the name corresponding to the initials "GDA" punched into the right side of the stock is unknown.

This page: Stamped under the barrel with mating number 16, this musket bears what is probably a state inventory number on the buttplate tang. Similar numbers — although stamped with different dies — appear on Alabama contract rifles made later in the war.

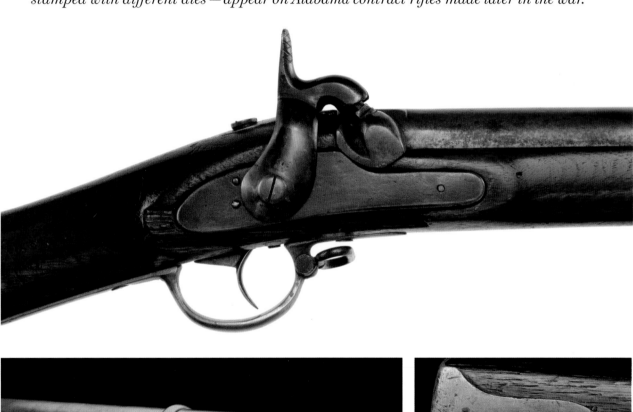

Tennessee's Ersatz Rifles

When the State of Tennessee officially joined the Confederate States of America on June 24, 1861, the fledgling nation gained not only a rich source of food and livestock, but also some of the South's few iron and gunpowder works as well as some of its best civilian gun makers. Yet with only a meager supply of serviceable flintlock muskets, no federal arsenals within its borders, and arms from federal arsenals elsewhere already in the hands of other states, Tennessee faced perhaps the most acute arms shortage of any state in the Confederacy—all this on the new nation's exposed northern border. Tennessee authorities moved quickly to establish military arsenals at Nashville, Memphis, Columbia, and Pulaski, from which agents fanned out across the state looking for anyone willing and able to make or repair weapons. Within a few weeks, they had contracted with seven new gun-making businesses in Middle Tennessee, mostly in the Nashville area. The state's model of choice was the famous Model 1841 "Mississippi" rifle.

Yet even this famous military rifle paled in comparison with the legendary civilian Kentucky (née "Pennsylvania," also known as "Tennessee") rifles. Though decidedly more attractive than their military counterparts, these handcrafted flintlock hunting rifles were not nearly as sturdy or reliable, nor were they suited for modern military use. Even the few that already had percussion locks still had to be cut down to a standard length, bored out to a standard caliber, and altered so that a bayonet could be affixed. None of that seemed to matter in 1861: Kentucky rifles and men skilled in their use were everywhere abundant in Tennessee and would surely be adequate for the coming fracas. Besides, it was reasoned, Kentucky rifles had won the great battles of the early republic: Saratoga, King's Mountain, and especially New Orleans, where Tennessee's own Andrew "Old Hickory" Jackson had beaten the best the Redcoats had to offer in 1815. Surely, such rifles could also beat the best the Yankees had to offer in 1861.

But the production and alteration of arms of any kind took time. Parts were hard to come by. The Confederate States Ordnance Bureau was slow to provide the nipples (cones) and hammers the state urgently requested for altering its flintlock muskets; indeed, the bureau was reluctant to share any of its scarce resources with states unless their troops were mustering into Confederate service. On September 16, 1861, the State of Tennessee quietly resolved the issue by transferring all its arms, supplies, and military contracts to the Confederate government, thus relieving itself of a considerable financial obligation while placing the burden of arming its defenders squarely on the national government. Among those defenders were three East Tennessee rifle regiments raised in the summer of 1861 by Brigadier

I have never yielded implicit credence to the prevailing idea that the musket is a superior weapon to the rifle. Such may be the case with the improved minie gun, but even the ordinary rifle, in the hands of the brave Tennesseans and Mississippians, saved and won the battle of Buena Vista during the Mexican War, as it did in the hands of the Carolinians at the battle of King's Mountain during the Revolution—in both instances with sad havoc to the enemy.
—Confederate secretary of war Leroy P. Walker to Tennessee governor Isham G. Harris, May 20, 1861

General William H. Carroll, whose father had commanded the center of Jackson's line at New Orleans. Each volunteer brought his own rifle, which Confederate authorities purchased and sent to the four Confederate arsenals for alteration into military arms. The race to defend Tennessee was on, but it would not last long.

In early 1862, Union naval and land forces punched through Confederate defenses on the Tennessee, Cumberland, and Mississippi Rivers, capturing Nashville in February and Memphis in June. Although the machinery in Nashville for altering arms and making ammunition was saved and sent to Atlanta, the fall of the state's two largest cities spelled the loss of most of Tennessee, a shocking disaster from which the Confederacy never fully recovered. Hence, the brief life span of these small arms companies and arsenals makes surviving examples of their work extraordinarily rare. The five rifles profiled here are by far the finest examples in the Wray Collection of ersatz Confederate arms production.

Confederate contract rifle made by the Pulaski Armory, Pulaski, Tennessee (1861)

Located about sixteen miles north of the Alabama state line in Middle Tennessee, the Pulaski Armory is believed to have been established by the brothers Napoleon B. and Joseph H. Zuccarello, who are listed in the U.S. census for 1860 as a wood molder and an engineer, along with James McLean, a wagon maker, and William N. Webb, a maker of cotton gins. The Zuccarellos later made corn-shelling machines.

Loosely patterned on the U.S. Model 1841, this .54-caliber rifle is made of parts scrounged from across Middle Tennessee, including an old flintlock made or imported by the Nashville hardware and cutlery company Fall and Cunningham. In altering the lock to percussion, armory workers fabricated an awkward-looking but serviceable hammer to reach the newly made bolster and nipple.

This is one of an estimated two hundred to three hundred rifles fabricated at the tiny armory in late 1861 before a Union raid destroyed it early the next year. Today, only seven are known to survive. One of them is firmly attributed to a soldier in the Thirty-Second Tennessee Infantry who had to surrender it when his regiment was captured at Fort Donelson on February 16, 1862.

After his failed venture in the arms business, Joe Zuccarello served as a lieutenant in Holman's Battalion, Tennessee Partisan Rangers (later the Eleventh Tennessee Cavalry) until he deserted in February 1864.

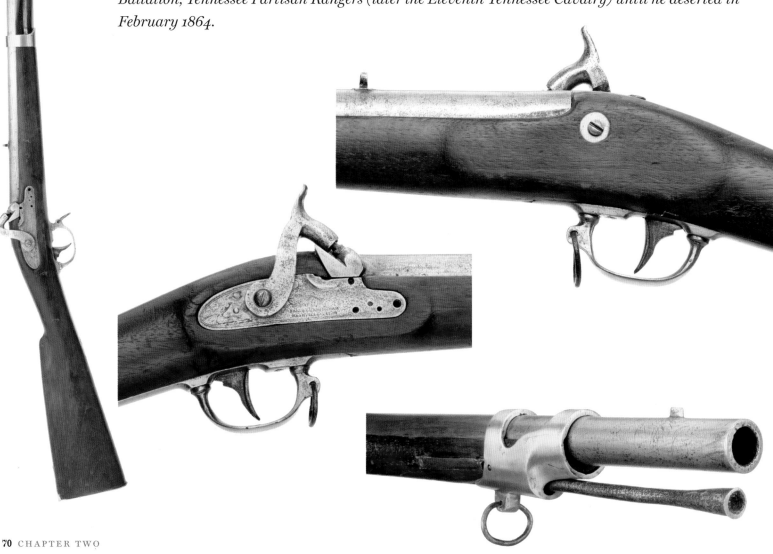

Confederate contract copy of a U.S. Model 1841 rifle made by Michael Cody and Son, Franklin, Tennessee (1861)

Believed to have been located in Franklin, Tennessee, the small gun shop of Michael Cody and Son delivered this extraordinarily well-made copy of a U.S. Model 1841 rifle to the C.S. Arsenal at Nashville in early December 1861. It bears serial number 7 on the barrel tang and interior parts, the lowest number observed among five known surviving examples (the highest is 80). The notable lack of wear on this arm suggests that it was never used in combat.

It was built around a .54-caliber seven-groove rifle barrel and a civilian-style percussion lock that the Nashville Arsenal provided Cody at the rate of fifteen dollars a dozen. Unusually, this rifle's neatly made furniture includes an implement compartment, a feature nearly all other private gun makers in the South later omitted for the sake of time and simplicity. The small stud under the barrel at the muzzle indicates that this rifle was meant to be fitted with a socket bayonet designed for U.S. Model 1842 muskets.

Kentucky rifle altered under Confederate contract by Kemper, Shrivers, and Company, Goodlettsville, Tennessee, with sword bayonet made by the Cook and Brother Armory, New Orleans, Louisiana (1861–62)

The Confederacy's pressing need for military arms was good news for a pair of enterprising men in the town of Goodlettsville, a few miles north of Nashville. Listed in census records as a farmer, fifty-four-year-old George C. Kemper probably financed the partnership with a twenty-seven-year-old gunsmith named N. Shrivers, who had previously been employed by a local gunsmith, Alexander T. F. M. Stalcup. In December 1861 and January 1862, the Confederate Ordnance Department paid Kemper, Shrivers, and Company $1,200 for 150 hunting rifles, "altered & prepared for Bayonets (Tenn. Rifles), rerifling, iron rods, single triggers & c."[1]

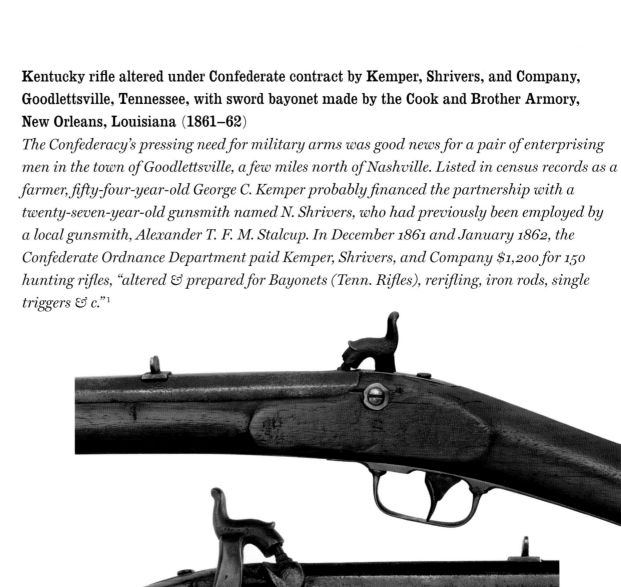

Built with a flintlock from the New York lock maker George Goulcher, this rather plain rifle was once at least forty-two inches long. Shrivers altered the lock to percussion and lengthened an off-the-shelf civilian-style hammer to fit it. He also cut down the heavy octagonal barrel to a thirty-inch military rifle length, rebored it to .54 caliber, and replaced the original wooden ramrod with an iron one. This arm may have been among those issued at Knoxville to the men of General Carroll's rifle regiments in early 1862, who complained bitterly about the rifles' quality.

With its distinctive octagonal muzzle socket and adjustable adaptor, the sword bayonet was fabricated especially for these arms by the Cook and Brother Armory in New Orleans, Louisiana. Thought to be the only surviving example, it was originally discovered for sale on eBay.

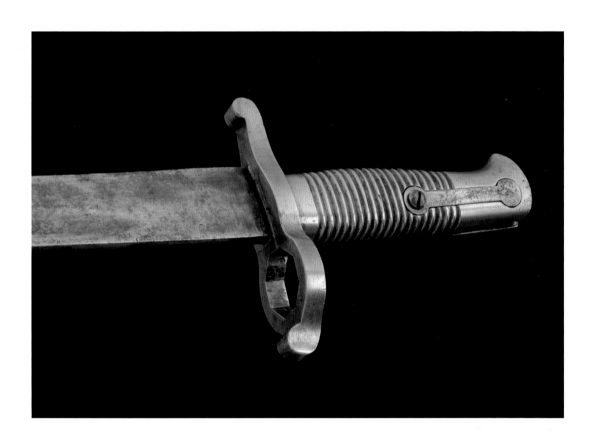

Kentucky rifle altered under Confederate contract by Alexander T. F. M. Stalcup, Goodlettsville, Tennessee, and the C.S. Armory at Holly Springs, Mississippi (1861–62)

On January 11, 1862, the C.S. Arsenal at Nashville paid thirty-three-year-old gunsmith Alexander T. F. M. Stalcup of Goodlettsville $510 for "Repairing 102 Rifles, Rebored, Stocked, & Locks."[2] This example is believed to be one of those 102 guns — one of only three known to survive. Although the Ordnance Bureau specified .44 as the standard caliber for adapted hunting rifles, most surviving examples from Tennessee — including this one — were rebored to .54 caliber so that they could use ammunition for U.S. Model 1841 rifles.

The assembly or serial number 7 is stamped inside the percussion lock, one of thousands sold by the New Jersey lock maker Henry Parker. Because this civilian-style lock required only one lockplate screw, there was no need to fabricate a Model 1841–style sideplate, yet Stalcup did so anyway, using a small screw to attach the forward end to the stock.

Soon after its delivery to the Nashville Arsenal and probably just before the Union army captured the city, this modified Kentucky rifle was shipped to the newly established C.S. Armory at Holly Springs, Mississippi, about forty miles southeast of Memphis. There, between March and June 1862, it received its final alteration: the last three inches of the octagonal barrel were milled down to a round military style and fitted with a small stud at the top of the barrel so it could be fitted with a standard U.S. Model 1816 socket bayonet. Established around a recently defunct private arms-making enterprise, the Holly Springs Armory operated until July 1862, when further Union advances forced the evacuation of its machinery to the C.S. Arsenal in Atlanta. It is possible that this rifle survived the war in storage there.

Kentucky rifle believed to have been repaired and altered by the C.S. Arsenal at Memphis, Tennessee, or Columbus, Mississippi, with sword bayonet made by the Cook and Brother Armory, New Orleans (1861–62)

Between October 1861 and February 1862, the C.S. Arsenal at Memphis altered more than 1,000 Kentucky rifles, including 520 at the personal insistence of General Carroll, who desperately needed them for his Second East Tennessee Rifles (later the Thirty-Eighth Tennessee Infantry) at Knoxville. Distinguished by its beveled-edge civilian-style drum bolster, which is believed to be a signature feature of the arsenal, this rebored .54-caliber rifle is probably one of the Memphis alterations. The original flintlock was made in Birmingham, England, by the gunsmith Henry Elwell; its new civilian-type hammer shows a break on either side of the screw hole, which has been repaired. The "c4s" stamped into the wood just forward of the buttplate tang combines an original assembly number, "c4," plus an "s" applied by a modern forger trying to give the rifle a more convincing (and valuable) Confederate States, or "cs," mark.

The other signature feature of the Memphis Arsenal was its use of sword bayonets instead of socket bayonets, as indicated by the delivery there of 1,079 Cook and Brother sword bayonets beginning in December 1861. Like the Stalcup rifle, this example has had the muzzle milled down, but with the addition of a stud and guide key that perfectly fits this unnumbered Cook and Brother bayonet with a large round muzzle socket. It is likely that the arsenal found it easier to mill down the octagonal muzzles to accept round muzzle sockets than to have Cook and Brother customize octagonal sockets and adaptor rings, as seen on the rifle altered by Kemper, Shrivers, and Company.

In February 1862, with the Union capture of much of middle and western Tennessee, the Memphis Arsenal was moved about 150 miles southeast to Columbus, Mississippi, near the Alabama border. Workers there altered a few more Kentucky rifles while concentrating on repairing existing arms. Operations continued through the end of 1862, when the machinery was moved to the safer confines of the C.S. Arsenal at Selma, Alabama.

U.S. Model 1817 contract, or common, rifle made by Henry Deringer, Philadelphia (ca. 1821), believed to have been altered by the C.S. Arsenal at Memphis, Tennessee, or Columbus, Mississippi (1862)

This is one of 13,000 U.S. Model 1817 rifles produced in the shops of the Philadelphia gun maker Henry Deringer, who became famous for his single-shot pistols—including the one used to assassinate Abraham Lincoln in 1865. At least several thousand of these antiquated yet still usable rifles lay idle in southern arsenals on the eve of the war. Because they were originally made in .54 caliber, they did not have to be rebored.

The size and beveled edge of the drum bolster applied to this rifle in place of the frizzen pan is nearly identical to the one applied to the Kentucky rifle pictured previously. It is impossible to say whether this alteration was accomplished before or after the C.S. Arsenal at Memphis relocated to Columbus, but operations at the latter location seem to have focused more on repair than alteration.

Emblems of Sovereignty

In 1861, the idea of large standing armies was an alien concept in the United States. Few people had ever seen a professional soldier (the regular U.S. Army numbered only about 16,000 men), and even fewer had any real military experience. For many Americans, whether in the North or the South, professional standing armies smacked of oppressive monarchies; they believed that the best way to safeguard their liberties in a time of crisis was by relying on themselves and their neighbors to serve as volunteer citizen-soldiers. After John Brown's raid on Harpers Ferry in 1859 and Abraham Lincoln's meteoric rise to national prominence in the following year, most white southerners felt that a national crisis was at hand. Moribund state militias were dusted off and reorganized, and volunteer militia companies, once known mainly for their fine uniforms and weekend barbecues, began drilling in earnest.

After the shooting started at Fort Sumter, white men volunteered by the thousands for their states and for the Confederacy. Entire families joined up together—fathers, sons, brothers, cousins, and uncles. They organized and named their own companies; they elected their own officers; they obtained their own uniforms and sometimes their own weapons. Their primary allegiance lay with their states, which they understood to be the sovereign guardians of their liberties and the sole basis of citizenship. Their regiments were formed under state authority, led by men with state commissions, and often armed and equipped from state arsenals.

Thus was the concept of state sovereignty literally embodied in southern volunteers as they marched off to war. State seals adorned their buttons and belt plates; state slogans graced their flags; state symbols embellished their hats. Even after state regiments formally entered national service, their soldiers often retained their own state emblems, cherishing them as symbols of local pride in an increasingly centralized and homogenous national army.

Everywhere you saw enthusiasm. The men of the West in their rude homespun, with their shot guns, rifles, antique muskets, and home-made bowie knives, were not one whit behind the sons of Louisiana, Mississippi, Alabama, or South Carolina, who have the advantage of superior drill and arms.
—Richmond Daily Dispatch, May 15, 1862

Mississippi headquarters or patriotic flag (1861)

State pride is emblazoned on this small faded flag. Almost certainly made by local women or a ladies' sewing society, it was made from a twenty-seven-by-seventeen-inch piece of polished cotton sheeting to which were stitched three red stripes and a canton of blue silk with eight six-pointed stars. Because it is so small and bears no resemblance to the "Bonnie Blue" flag (a single white star in a blue field, flown to celebrate the state's secession), or to the Mississippi state flag adopted in January 1861 (which bore the "Bonnie Blue" design and a green magnolia tree), this flag is unlikely to have been a secession banner or a volunteer company flag.

It appears that there were once three or four additional stripes of an unknown color stitched to the white field. If so, this flag may have resembled the Louisiana state flag, with its thirteen red, white, and blue stripes, as well as similar proposed (and rejected) designs for a Confederate national flag. Perhaps this flag was intended as some sort of prototype and was one of a series with the same design, each bearing the name of a seceded state. More likely, it was intended as a headquarters flag for a volunteer company or simply as a patriotic decoration in a home or business.

Hat worn by the Palmetto Guard of South Carolina (1861)

On the morning of April 12, 1861, two artillery batteries manned by the Palmetto Guard, a South Carolina volunteer militia company, were among the first to open fire on Fort Sumter. Formed in Charleston soon after the Crisis of 1850, the Palmetto Guard included some of the most committed secessionists in the South, including the Virginia fire-eater Edmund Ruffin, an honorary member who fired one of the first shots of the war from one of the Palmetto Guard batteries.

The State of South Carolina issued black slouch hats to its troops, although it is not known whether this was one of them. Whatever its origins, this hat was adorned with a wreath, the initials of the Palmetto Guard, and a homemade brass palmetto tree, the state symbol of South Carolina.

Louisiana officer's belt plate (1861)

This southern-made Louisiana belt plate is unusual in that it was not copied directly from a northern prewar design. The plate features the state symbol, a pelican, drawing blood from its own breast in order to feed its young, a traditional image of Christ's blood given in sacrifice for the salvation of all people. Such Christian symbolism was very much a part of Confederate ideology.

Confederate McDowell-style forage cap, believed to have been worn by a Georgia soldier (1861)

This distinctive variant of the French-style kepi was named for the Union general Irvin McDowell, best known as the losing commander at the First Battle of Manassas. Only a handful of these caps were made in the Confederacy, most in the first year of the war. Made of cadet-gray wool, with a leather visor and painted cloth sweatband, this cap was supposedly worn by a Georgia soldier named Hardin, but that attribution is unconfirmed. The only other clue to its origin are the two U.S. Ordnance Department buttons attaching the chinstrap, which were made between 1835 and 1851 and suggest use by a veteran of the Mexican War.

Georgia Militia canteen (ca. 1845) **and cartridge box plate** (ca. 1855, altered 1861)

The plain and unadorned tin canteens used by state militias practically cried out for colorful decoration and expressions of state or unit loyalty. This one, painted for an unidentified Georgia militia company, dates from the 1840s.

Produced by the Ames Manufacturing Company in Chicopee, Massachusetts, in the 1850s, the cartridge box plate depicts the state seal of Georgia: three classical pillars representing wisdom, justice, and moderation, supporting an arch bearing the word Constitution. *Beneath the arch is an armed militiaman prepared to defend the sacred edifice; Georgia volunteers imagined themselves to be taking his place. In 1861, state authorities ordered these cartridge box plates to be altered into belt plates by replacing the original iron loops with three copper-wire belt hooks.*

Virginia officer's belt plate (ca. 1855)

In the eyes of most white southerners, the state seal of Virginia perfectly symbolized the Confederacy's struggle in the face of northern despotism: a female figure representing liberty thrusting a spear through the body of a Roman tyrant, over the motto Sic Semper Tyrannis *("Thus always to tyrants"). These were the words John Wilkes Booth shouted to an astonished crowd at Ford's Theater to justify his assassination of Abraham Lincoln on April 14, 1865. Ironically, this officer's belt plate was manufactured in the North before the war.*

U.S. militia officer's belt plate (ca. 1855) **with a southern-made sword belt** (ca. 1862)

Not all Confederate volunteers marched to war wearing symbols of their states. Many still wore the trappings of the old union—after all, the American eagle was still a southern symbol. This 1850s-era militia officer's belt plate has been mounted on a southern-made sword belt; its iron hooks resemble those made by Louis Froelich's sword manufactory in Wilmington, North Carolina.

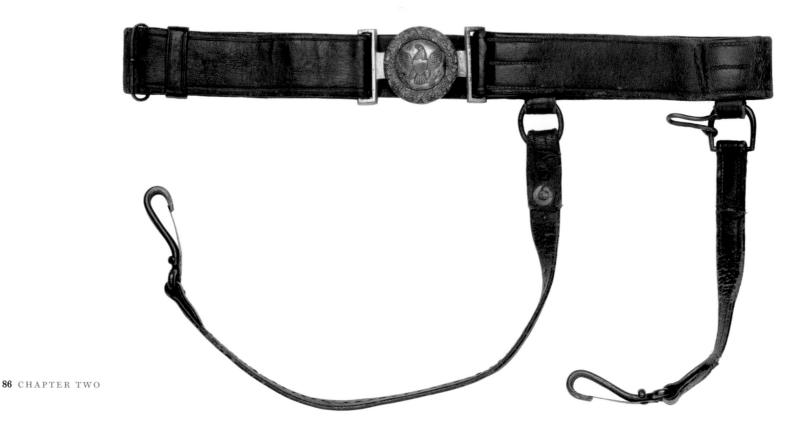

C.S. officers' belt plates and sword belts (ca. 1863)

Despite strong allegiance to their states, Confederate volunteers embraced the symbolic trappings of their new republic also as a sense of loyalty to "CS" came to replace that once implied by "US." The makers of these plates and sword belts are unknown, but the one with the laurel-leaf border (bottom) is believed to have been made in Virginia. Note the poor quality of the casting.

Cold Steel

No imagined vision of battle appealed to inexperienced southern volunteers quite like a massed bayonet charge. In the ultimate test of manly bearing, volunteers expected to kill or be killed while looking their enemies straight in the eye. Meanwhile, their comrades on horseback, bearing curved sabers designed especially for the purpose, would be slashing their way through the enemy's flanks, winning victory in a single gallant rush. Such was the mystique of cold steel.

The reality was far less glamorous: only a small fraction of wounds inflicted in the Civil War were the result of edged weapons; it was the musket or minié ball, not the bayonet or saber, that killed men in battle. Yet both of the latter retained their terrible reputations, and for good reason. Because a skillful bayonet thrust was usually fatal, bayonet charges, if wisely executed, could cause an enemy to take to its heels long before hand-to-hand combat became necessary. Likewise, saber charges, though suicidal against infantry, could break up opposing cavalry formations. Hence, both saber and socket bayonets remained standard issue for Confederate infantry; likewise, sabers were considered necessary weapons for cavalry and, sometimes, for artillerymen. Like firearms, cartridge boxes, and artillery pieces, they were mass-produced under the powerful authority of the C.S. Ordnance Bureau. For officers, edged weapons were less a matter of military necessity than of symbolic authority. Officers of all branches were expected to purchase their own swords (straight blades) or sabers (curved blades), the quality and design of which depended on the man's wealth and personal preference. In the prewar U.S. Army, sword designs differed according to rank and branch, but such fine distinctions were later seldom observed even in the U.S. Army, let alone in the Confederacy.

During the Civil War, the production of swords and sabers was exclusively the domain of private companies, most of which were formed in 1861 for the express purpose of making them. The same companies turned out the majority of the South's sword and socket bayonets too, except for those imported through the blockade. In all cases, it was a low-tech industry: brass founders, tinsmiths, and even ordinary country blacksmiths could make sabers for enlisted men, at least in limited quantities. But the most successful companies—usually ones with experience in making agricultural implements, tools, cutlery, and the like—were those that could produce in bulk. Among the largest were Boyle, Gamble, and MacFee in Virginia; Louis Froelich in North Carolina; and Haiman and Brother in Georgia, all of which became primary producers for the Confederate war effort. At least fifteen other significant manufacturers joined the fray, and dozens of smaller ones made what they could, even if it was just a few hundred sabers. Nearly all split their

God knows we have not desired war, but now that the North has thrust the alternative upon us, we are for war, and war to the knife.
—*Richmond Daily Dispatch*, May 10, 1861

Come on, boys, give them the cold steel! Who will follow me?
—Brigadier General Lewis A. Armistead at the Battle of Gettysburg, July 3, 1863

efforts between government contracts (for states or the CSA) and private sales to officers. Although the total number of edged weapons produced in the Confederacy remains unknown (and probably unknowable, based on surviving records), it likely exceeded 125,000 socket bayonets, 25,000 sword bayonets, and 50,000 enlisted sabers.

Like nearly all Confederate firearms, Confederate swords and sabers were copied from existing U.S.-regulation patterns, which had evolved over the previous thirty years into more than a dozen significant models based on rank and branch of service. Most U.S. patterns had been copied from French designs, often with blades produced in Solingen, Prussia, the great sword-manufacturing center of Europe. Many northern-made edged weapons saw Confederate service, just as some Solingen-made blades were incorporated into the products of some of the better southern sword factories. Even so, few Confederate-made edged weapons — especially cavalry sabers — were as well constructed or finished as even the most ordinary U.S. Model 1840 or 1860 sabers. The steel blades of Confederate sabers were often marred by forging flow lines or other faults. Some were beaten out by hand rather than rolled mechanically, resulting in blades of slightly different lengths and widths. Casting flaws in brass guards are common, as are grips wrapped in oilcloth rather than leather or sharkskin. But the most stunning examples of poor-quality finish are seen in the scabbards. In the North, saber scabbards for enlisted men were routinely made of sheet steel, with the long vertical seam on the reverse side neatly brazed and filed smooth. In the South, scabbards were often made of iron, with the long seam awkwardly joined with lead or tin solder, seldom filed smooth, and often filled with wax or putty. Such small and seemingly insignificant details hint at the limits of Confederate manufacturing capacity.

To be sure, the same shortages of raw materials that plagued the Confederate firearms industry also conspired against sword makers, forcing them to substitute softer metals and cheaper alloys. At least one company made wooden scabbards, probably as a way to save iron. Time, too, conspired against the Confederacy's sword makers: the struggle to turn out as many weapons as possible in the least amount of time required them to take all the shortcuts they could get away with and still pass inspection. From a historical perspective, the most egregious shortcut was the failure to mark their products. Today, identifying the weapons of a particular maker often hinges on only one or two extant examples bearing that maker's mark; there may still be unrecognized additional models or types made by the same company that bear different characteristics.

George Wray was only an occasional collector of Confederate edged weapons. Yet as with the firearms that were his primary focus, details of the construction and finish of the swords, sabers, and sword bayonets presented here reveal a great deal about Confederate manufacturing. Most important, the very existence of these weapons reveals an essential feature of the Confederate odyssey. If, as many volunteers had expected, victory had depended mainly on the bold application of cold steel, the Confederacy might have won its independence at Manassas or on the third day at Gettysburg. But the war was not a low-tech affair of sabers and bayonets. Instead it was a high-tech war of firepower and attrition, in which the Confederacy could not afford to waste its scarce resources on old-school weapons. In the end, the South needed a modern firearms industry, which it simply did not have and could not buy.

Sword bayonet made by Horstmann Brothers and Company, Philadelphia, Pennsylvania (ca. 1855)

Made in the 1850s by a famous Philadelphia militaria company, this odd combination of socket and sword bayonet was probably designed for commercially made militia rifles in the North. Two photographs taken near Mobile during the winter of 1861–62 clearly show these bayonets affixed to U.S. Model 1841 rifles in the hands of soldiers in Company I, Nineteenth Alabama Infantry. It is not certain how the rifles were made to fit these bayonets, or vice versa, but it was likely a makeshift solution by a northern contractor working for the State of Alabama, which had tried desperately to purchase arms in the fall of 1860.

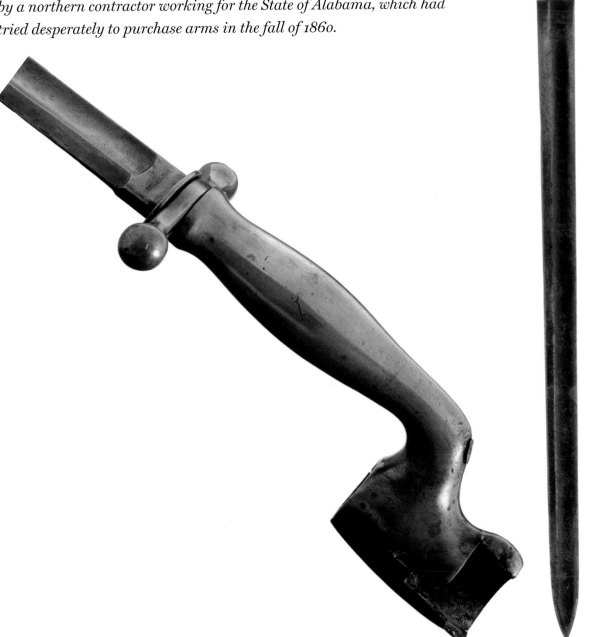

Shotgun bayonet made by the Cook and Brother Armory,
New Orleans, Louisiana, number 491 (1862)

Since so many volunteers were armed only with civilian shotguns and hunting rifles, Confederate and state ordnance officers tried to fit the guns with bayonets so that they might at least be of some use in hand-to-hand combat. This two-slot French-style sword bayonet attached to two studs braised on the side of a shotgun barrel. Because each bayonet had to be individually fitted, both bayonet and barrel bore a mating number, in this case 491.

This bayonet was made by the Cook and Brother Armory in New Orleans especially for a ninety-day unit of the Louisiana militia known as the Chalmette Regiment. In April 1862, its ill-trained men quickly surrendered to Admiral David Farragut's warships below New Orleans; the bayonet probably survived as a Union sailor's souvenir.[3]

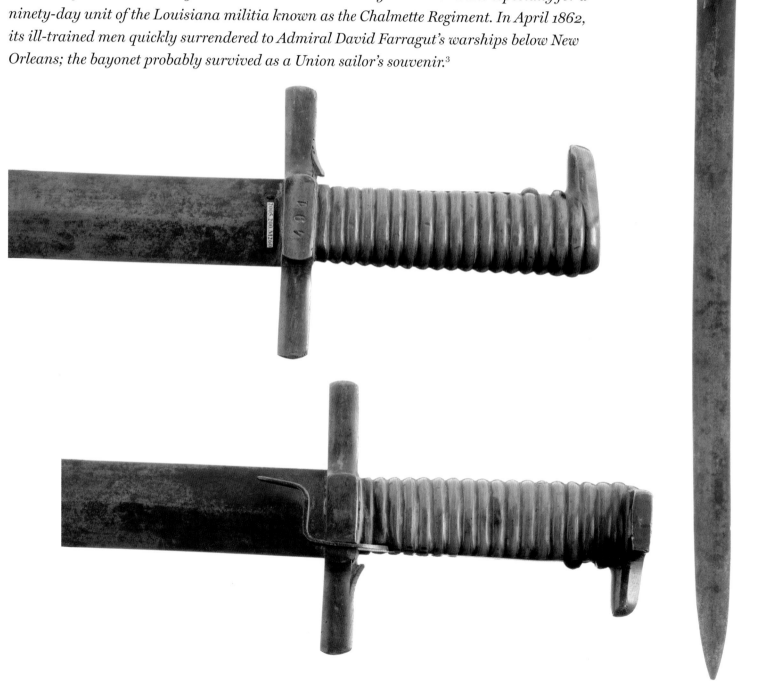

**Spear-point lanyard, or "lasso," knife made
by William J. McElroy and Company,
Macon, Georgia** (ca. 1862)

*Soon after the outbreak of war, the successful
tinsmith and merchant William J. McElroy
formed a partnership with Cornelius D. Wall
(machinist) and Alexander Reynolds
(brass founder) to make knives and swords.
This brass-handled fighting knife with
a fourteen-inch blade featured a small
loop in the base of the grip for a lanyard,
which was supposed to prevent loss of the
knife in close combat. At the same time,
a newspaper claimed these heavy knives
were designed to be thrown at the enemy.
Such wastage of copper, zinc, and steel on
practically worthless weapons was one reason
Confederate authorities exerted such strict
control over the private use of raw materials
later in the war.*

Enlisted artilleryman's short sword made by E. J. Johnston and Company, Macon, Georgia (1862)

In 1861, Edward J. Johnston and George S. Obear were running a successful business that sold watches, jewelry, cutlery, and musical instruments. Johnston volunteered for the army, but was discharged on medical disability after only three months' service. Thereafter, the partners turned some of their business toward the war effort, working closely with McElroy and Company to produce beautiful, finely crafted officers' swords for private sale, as well as a few cavalry sabers under Confederate contract.

These short swords are thought to have been made in 1862 for the Columbus Light Artillery (later known as Croft's Battery), which fought in the campaigns for Chattanooga, Atlanta, and Nashville. Based loosely on the U.S. Model 1832 foot artillery sword, these sturdy weapons were virtually useless against charging cavalry (their original purpose) but quite handy for cutting down brush to create a clear field of fire or cutting away traces from wounded battery horses.

Officer's cavalry saber made by Sharp and Hamilton (Nashville Plow Works), Nashville, Tennessee (1861–62)

Tennessee's call to arms meant financial opportunity for two Nashville businessmen, Thomas A. Sharp and James M. Hamilton. In a literal reversal of the famous biblical injunction, the two men put their agricultural implements company to work making implements of war. From September 1861 through January 1862, they delivered 964 cavalry sabers to the C.S. Arsenal in Nashville, in addition to leather accoutrements, gun slings, powder flasks, and large quantities of copper, zinc, and lead. The sabers alone were worth $10,398. All of that, plus private sales of handsome officers' sabers such as the one pictured here, made Sharp and Hamilton wealthy men.

Their fortunes came to an abrupt halt when Union troops captured Nashville on February 25, 1862, and arrested both men for treason. With the name of their country and the name of their business cast conspicuously into the guards, the evidence against them was hard to deny. Later released, they went back to making plows.

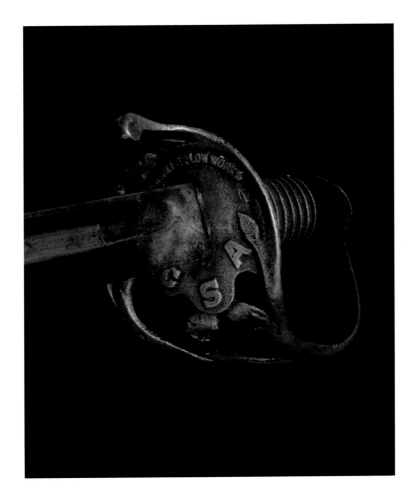

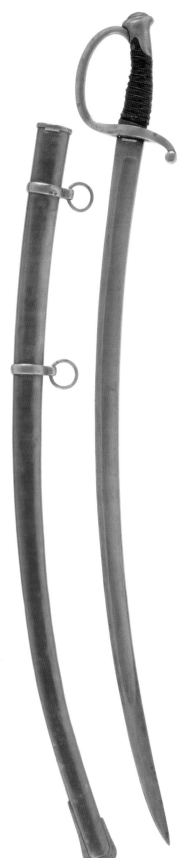

Enlisted artilleryman's saber and officer's cavalry saber made by Thomas, Griswold, and Company, New Orleans, Louisiana (1861–62)

With a population of nearly 170,000 in 1860, New Orleans was by far the largest city in the newly formed Confederacy. Among its many businesses was Thomas, Griswold, and Company, an import and manufacturing firm specializing in military goods, including "cavalry and artillery sabers, line and field officers swords and lances."[4] *The large number of militia companies in the city and surrounding parishes meant that the partnership among Henry Thomas Jr., A. B. Griswold, and William M. Goodrich was already doing a brisk business when the state seceded.*

With the outbreak of war, business boomed. The company made all types and grades of edged weapons for the Confederacy (including 760 naval cutlasses), at least 354 cavalry sabers for the State of North Carolina, and a variety of beautiful, finely crafted officers' swords for private sale. By January 1862, the company was claiming a production capacity of 300 sabers a week. Among them were these faithful copies of the U.S. Model 1840 artillery saber (left) and the U.S. Model 1840 cavalry officer's saber (right), both with the company's characteristic French-style brass scabbard and deeply stamped maker's mark. They were among the finest edged weapons produced in the Confederacy.

Thomas, Griswold, and Company met its untimely end on April 25, 1862, when Union naval forces captured New Orleans, immediately neutralizing the Deep South's most important port and manufacturing center. A year into hostilities, the Confederacy was already shrinking.

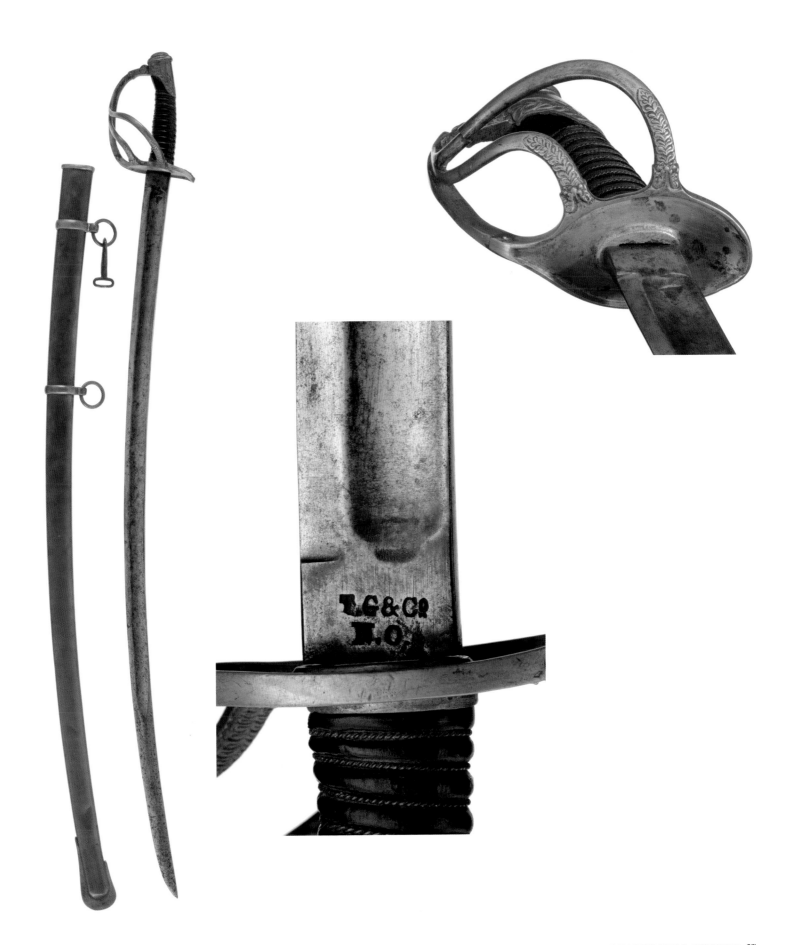

Staff and field officer's sword made by Louis Froelich, Wilmington and Kenansville, North Carolina (ca. 1862)

Louis Froelich's tireless persistence in the face of almost unimaginable hard luck was in many ways typical for entrepreneurs in the Confederacy. Described as "a thoroughly educated and scientific mechanic," the Bavarian immigrant in early 1861 settled in Wilmington, North Carolina, where he ran a small button factory.[5] After the outbreak of war, Froelich applied his considerable skills to making edged weapons, forming the Wilmington Sword Factory in partnership with a Hungarian émigré named Bela Estvan. As large-scale production of swords, knives, bayonets, and leather accoutrements got under way in March 1862, Froelich discovered that Estvan was a confidence man who had run off with the company's money. Later that year, a yellow fever epidemic shut down production for two months. In February 1863, Froelich suffered even worse misfortune: his renamed Confederate States Armory caught fire and burned to the ground. Undaunted, Froelich moved his operations about sixty miles north to Kenansville, North Carolina, but that July a Union raiding party burned the new factory. Still he did not give up. Salvaging what he could and taking on new financial backing, Froelich produced sabers, knapsacks, axes, and other supplies for the Confederacy until the very end of the war. Afterward, he took up farming.

During the first three years of the war, Froelich was reported to have manufactured 11,700 enlisted men's sabers, 2,700 officers' sabers, 6,500 sword bayonets, and 1,400 cutlasses, in addition to pikes, lance spears, knives, buttons, and leather accoutrements. Froelich's signature products were officers' swords with the letters "CSA" forming the guard, which were easily the most distinctive edged weapons manufactured in the Confederacy. This staff and field model, featuring a plain one-inch-wide blade, was probably made in 1862, the peak year of production. Assembly code slash marks "III" on the edge of the guard and at the throat of the scabbard ensured that the sword fit the correct scabbard.

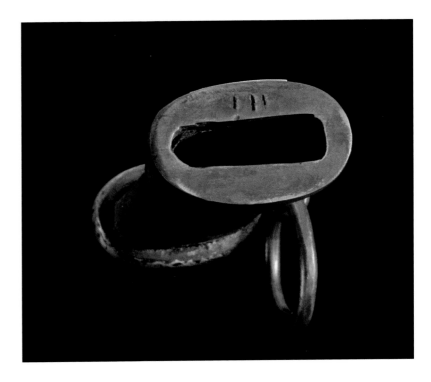

Sword bayonets made by Louis Froelich, Wilmington and Kenansville, North Carolina (ca. 1862)

Froelich produced sword bayonets under contract with the State of North Carolina as well as the C.S. Ordnance Bureau; most were copies of bayonets made privately by northern companies such as the Ames Manufacturing Company or Collins and Company. Of the eight examples in the Wray Collection, two bear "CSA" stamps in the guard or on the blade, and one bears the mating number 578 on the hilt. Forging flaws in the blades are common, as is the distinctively uneven milling of the muzzle sockets.

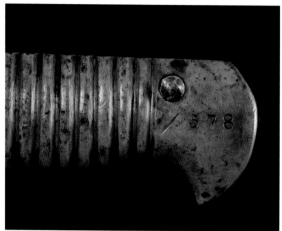

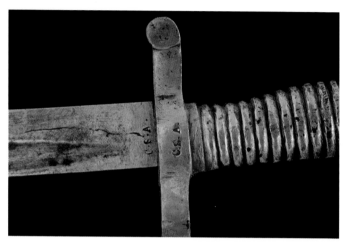

Staff and field officer's sword made by Boyle, Gamble, and MacFee, Richmond, Virginia (ca. 1863)

One of the most prolific makers of edged weapons in the Confederacy was the firm of Edward Boyle, Thomas Gamble, and Edward D. MacFee, located just a few blocks from the C.S. Armory in Richmond. Before the war, Boyle and Gamble had manufactured saw blades, axes, and other tools; in 1859, MacFee had won a prize from the Virginia Mechanics' Institute for a new model plow. In 1861, the partners expanded their product line to include swords, sabers, and sword bayonets, all available for private purchase or through government contract. In 1863, their annual profit was assessed at an impressive $18,000.

This staff and field officer's sword was at the top end of the company's catalogue, intended (theoretically) for officers above the rank of major. On its hilt, the corn represents southern agriculture, the laurel wreath around "CS" stands for victory, and the single star refers to the sovereign rights of a single state. The etched blade contains a shield with "CSA" beneath waving Confederate flags. Unlike enlisted men's models, this sword came with a leather scabbard.

Yet even this high-end southern sword was plainer than most of its northern counterparts: the floral patterns on the guard are fewer and more crudely rendered, and its simple leather grip is wrapped in a single strand of copper wire instead of a double strand of brass wire. There are casting flaws where the knuckle bow meets the pommel, and a fault line in the blade two inches below the guard, caused when the tang was forge-welded to the blade.

Sword bayonet adaptor made by Boyle, Gamble, and MacFee, Richmond, Virginia (1861)

Confederate ordnance officers faced the same problem as their northern counterparts when it came to fitting bayonets to the U.S. Model 1841 rifles in their arsenals. Boyle, Gamble, and MacFee invented its own version of the Colt adaptor ring and bayonet stud, for which it was granted Confederate States Patent 18 on September 2, 1861. The company sold these brass adaptors to the Confederacy as well as to private firms making copies of the famous rifles.

Bearing mating number 33, this adaptor was fitted to an Alabama contract rifle made by Greenwood and Gray of Columbus, Georgia. Because few southern-made rifles had standard-dimension barrels, adaptor rings were a popular solution.

Sword bayonet and bowie knife bayonet made by Boyle, Gamble, and MacFee, Richmond, Virginia (1861)

Left: *Realizing that it had more "Mississippi" rifles than it had bayonets to fit them, the Confederate Ordnance Bureau in July 1861 advertised for bids for three thousand sword bayonets. Designed to be used with Boyle, Gamble, and MacFee's patented adaptor, these bayonets were probably part of that contract. Some are known to have been issued in July 1861 to Company K, Third Alabama Infantry (encamped near Norfolk, Virginia), and to Company A, Eighth Alabama Infantry (near Yorktown, Virginia), both of which were armed with "Mississippi" rifles. These were probably some of the Robbins and Lawrence–made rifles seized from the U.S. Arsenal at Mt. Vernon, Alabama.*

Center and right: *Boyle, Gamble, and MacFee made these unique bowie knife bayonets with the company name boldly cast into the crossguard. This bayonet, which also relied on the patented adaptor ring, has the mating number 31 cast into its grip.*

Bottom: *Bowie knife bayonets were still in use in late 1862 and early 1863, as shown by this broken hilt recovered near Fredericksburg, Virginia. Its muzzle socket was bent inward and the blade snapped off, probably by Union troops disabling captured arms.*

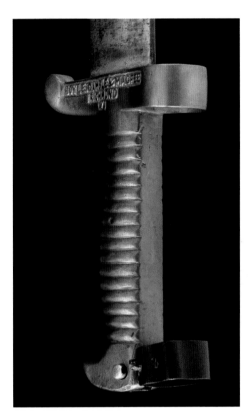

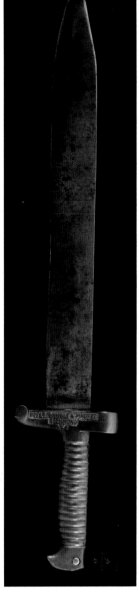

Enlisted man's cavalry saber made by Haiman and Brother, Columbus, Georgia (ca. 1863)

The Prussian-born brothers Louis and Elias Haiman were the proprietors of a successful tinsmithing business in Columbus, Georgia, before the war. In 1861, they turned the upper floor of the Columbus Iron Works into a sword factory, assembling and finishing a wide variety of edged weapons, accoutrements, and steel-tipped socket bayonets, using parts forged or cast in nearby buildings. By 1863, theirs was one of the largest manufactories in the South, covering most of a city block and employing more than four hundred workers. The end of the brothers' extensive operations (including a failed revolver factory) came on April 16, 1865, when Union cavalrymen under Major General James Wilson captured Columbus and put its factories to the torch.

Patterned after the U.S. Model 1840, this saber was probably among the eight thousand called for under Confederate contract, three thousand of which were delivered in 1862. As can be seen in their officers' swords made for private sale, the Haimans were capable of fine craftsmanship. Yet given material shortages and monetary inflation, they wisely chose quantity over quality when filling their government contracts.

The wooden grip of this saber is wrapped not in leather but in cheaper painted cloth, and the normal double-strand brass wire wrapping the grip is instead a single strand of iron wire. The thin iron scabbard was once disguised with black paint, perhaps to give it the appearance of leather, while the iron drag was painted gold to give the appearance of brass. Both were probably applied to protect the scabbard from rust — at least for a little while. While still an effective killing tool, this saber is hardly up to the standards of its northern-made counterparts, which had leather grips and polished steel scabbards.

Enlisted men's cavalry sabers, believed to have been made by Haiman and Brother, Columbus, Georgia (ca. 1863)

In size, weight, and configuration, these U.S. Model 1840–type cavalry sabers bear a strong resemblance to the Haiman and Brother saber pictured on page 104, but with a slightly finer finish. The oil-cloth-covered grips are wrapped with double-strand brass wire, the steel scabbard bears no evidence of paint, and the drag is brass instead of iron. Both sabers are characterized by small inventory or assembly numbers stamped into the guards, pommels, and drags.

Although the Haimans were aided in no small measure by Elias's trips to Europe to procure steel and Solingen-made blades, they were never secure from wartime shortages. The reddish shade of the brass hilts reflects an unusually high copper content, evidence of the periodic shortages of zinc that beset the Confederacy—and a further indication that these sabers were made either by a different maker or, more likely, at a different time. Because material shortages fluctuated during the war, it is impossible to say whether these sabers were made earlier or later than the one with a painted scabbard on page 104.

Enlisted man's cavalry saber made by B. Douglas and Company, Columbia, South Carolina (ca. 1863)

This is one of the rarest and most enigmatic of Confederate edged weapons, identified only in the mid-1990s when a marked example was discovered. Even today, the maker's first name is unknown. Located at the "Old Foundry" on Washington Street in Columbia, South Carolina, the company advertised itself as a supplier of bits, spurs, and swords, though it also made sword bayonets under Confederate contract beginning in February 1862.

This sturdy cavalry saber was patterned after the U.S. Model 1840, with a prominent scabbard drag similar to that of the U.S. Model 1833 dragoon saber. Several features suggest the maker's attempt to dress up the quality of the weapon's fit and finish: the hilt has a cloth-and-leather throat washer, designed to help keep the hilt tight around the blade, and the scabbard, made of rust-prone sheet iron, was once coated with copper or bronze, with the drag and throat dipped in tin. But defects remained: the distinctively shaped pommel does not fit the grip properly, and there are small flaws throughout the steel blade.

Wooden scabbard believed to have been made by Lewis L. and T. R. Moore, Atlanta, Georgia, with enlisted man's cavalry saber, maker unknown (ca. 1863)

Famous as evidence of material shortages in the Confederacy, these wooden scabbards may have owed as much to practicality as to desperation. Their construction is painfully simple: two wooden slats carved with a groove for the sword blade and then bound up with tin bands. The only brass parts are the rings, drag, and throat. Their simple widemouthed construction easily accommodated small differences in the sizes and shapes of blades, making the scabbards as close to interchangeable as possible. These are believed to have been the products of Lewis L. and T. R. Moore, who delivered 556 "wooden saber scabbards" to the C.S. Arsenal at Charleston in 1863. This may be the same company that made fighting knives for the State of Georgia in 1862.

Such scabbards are often found with swords made by two firms in Columbia, South Carolina: B. Douglas, and Kraft, Goldschmidt, and Kraft. In 1863, Douglas is known to have delivered at least 379 sabers without scabbards to the Charleston Arsenal, suggesting that the wooden scabbards were meant as cheap substitutes for the iron ones that Douglas normally made. These scabbards (and by extension, the sabers in them) are associated also with Hammond Marshall and Company of Atlanta, Georgia. Marshall was a dentist known for engraving presentation swords, but was accused of shoddy workmanship in the manufacture of sabers in 1862. The maker of this saber is unknown, although it is similar to those produced by Kraft, Goldschmidt, and Kraft. It may or may not be original to the scabbard.

Enlisted man's cavalry saber, maker unknown (ca. 1863)

This crudely made cavalry saber is one of thousands made by small-town blacksmiths across the South whose names are now lost to history. Like this one, many are distinguished by their unusually thin guard branches and protruding quillons, though variations are as numerous as their now-nameless makers. Typical of most, the roughly joined seam of the sheet-iron scabbard appears to have once been filled with wax or putty.

In the 1960s, William A. Albaugh, the legendary historian of Confederate weapons, speculated that 90 percent of all Confederate edged weapons had been produced by the larger manufacturers whose products had already been identified. Today, although many more manufacturers have been identified, even more unidentified weapons have been discovered, suggesting that our knowledge of the subject is far from complete.

3. The Confederate National Armories

In his postwar recollections, Josiah Gorgas, the Pennsylvania-born chief of ordnance for the Confederate States of America, exaggerated his adopted country's predicament in 1861—but only slightly. Although it had perhaps 260,000 serviceable arms within its borders, the Confederacy had practically none of the modern facilities or machinery needed to mass-produce new arms once the supply of old ones was exhausted.

Unlike most of the South's volunteer soldiers and many of its political leaders, Gorgas and the other professionals at the core of the newly formed Confederate army (especially its commander in chief, Jefferson Davis) recognized the nearly overwhelming logistical challenges that would face their new nation in the likely event that it failed to win independence in a single battle. Using massive governmental appropriations, Gorgas ordered the overhaul of existing arsenals and the creation of new ones, supervised construction of a gunpowder factory, and sent agents throughout the South to scrounge up weapons, raw materials, skilled labor, and everything else the Confederacy needed to survive. But all these efforts paled in importance beside the secession of Virginia on April 17, 1861.

The Old Dominion had more men, more railroads, and more manufacturing capacity than any other Confederate state. Home to the largest ironworks in the South, Richmond alone produced more manufactured goods than Alabama, Arkansas, Florida, Mississippi, South Carolina, or Texas. Most important, the secession of Virginia gave the Confederacy Harpers Ferry. The seizure of one of the two U.S. armories in 1861 was the Confederacy's greatest windfall: one of the largest and best sets of arms-making machinery in the world, as well as gauges, tools, belting and shafting, and thousands of parts for fully interchangeable U.S. Model 1855 rifles and rifle-muskets. Control of Harpers Ferry gave the agrarian nation a realistic chance of fighting an industrial war—but not until a bureaucratic fight over states' rights and strategic imperatives was settled.

After capturing the armory with its own militia and then relocating the machinery to Richmond, Virginia insisted that the machinery rightfully belonged to the state; the Confederate government would have to fend for itself. Meanwhile, North

Within the limits of the Confederate States there were no arsenals at which any of the material of war was constructed. No arsenal, except that at Fayetteville, N.C., had a single machine above a foot-lathe. . . . All the work of preparation of material had been carried on at the North; not an arm, not a gun, not a gun-carriage, and, except during the Mexican War, scarcely a round of ammunition had for fifty years been prepared in the Confederate States.
—Former Confederate chief of ordnance Josiah Gorgas, ca. 1880

109

Carolina governor John W. Ellis requested that some of the Harpers Ferry machinery be set up in his state at the former U.S. Arsenal at Fayetteville. Ellis's request highlighted a vital strategic question: was it wiser to place all the Harpers Ferry machinery in one location, which would allow it to maximize output, or to divide up the machinery among two locations so that the loss of one would not mean the loss of all? In the end, the decentralization argument prevailed: Virginia lent the machinery for making rifles to North Carolina, but kept the machinery for making rifle-muskets in Richmond. In a face-saving compromise, Virginia also agreed in late June 1861 to lend its machinery to the Confederate government as long as the state retained title and the rifle-musket machinery was operated in Richmond. For all practical purposes, however, the central government took complete charge of the newly formed C.S. armories at Richmond and Fayetteville.

In May 1862, Union troops were advancing rapidly on Richmond in the first of many threats to the Confederate capital. The Confederate secretary of war ordered the armory to prepare to evacuate, first by moving the stock-making machinery to central Georgia, as far away as possible from potential Union advances. By mid-July, the danger to Richmond had passed, but thirty boxcar loads of machinery were sitting idle at the railroad depot in Macon. Rather than haul the precious cargo all the way back to Richmond, the Confederate superintendent of armories, James H. Burton, set up the stock-making machinery in Macon, where, he believed, it would soon be joined by the rest of the Harpers Ferry machinery.

Believing centralization to be the key to efficiency, Burton intended to construct a new national manufacturing complex in Macon, a hub facility situated close to raw materials and linked by rail to the rest of the South. Under one roof, the new C.S. armory would house all the Harpers Ferry machinery and all the machinery scrounged from private armories and gun shops, plus new machinery purchased from Great Britain. Nearby, the C.S. Central Laboratory would supply all the nation's artillery and small-arms ammunition by using the high-quality gunpowder already being produced at the new, state-of-the-art C.S. Powder Works in Augusta. Burton planned to make Macon the Springfield of the South; all other Confederate ordnance installations were temporary expedients for keeping up production until the new factories at Macon were finished.

Meanwhile, the problems inherent in decentralized production were becoming painfully clear. Division of the Harpers Ferry machinery among three national armories meant that none of them were self-sufficient: Richmond depended on Macon for gunstocks; Fayetteville depended on Richmond for barrels; and all three depended on raw materials from other regions. Ultimately, all their efforts relied on the railroads. With numerous gaps in its network, which had track of at least six different gauges, the southern railroad system had never been terribly efficient, even in peacetime. In wartime, its overused and undermaintained rails literally sagged under carloads of food, forage, coal, iron, and military supplies of all kinds. Meanwhile, draconian Confederate conscription policies—as well as real military crises—frequently diverted what few skilled mechanics the South had into the army. To ease labor shortages, the C.S. Ordnance Bureau impressed slave laborers for support tasks and building projects, but in the end, the lack of skilled white labor meant that none of the national armories ever really operated at full capacity. Even the best arms-making machinery in the world was worthless without the men to run it. Transportation and labor problems exacerbated shortages of raw materials, especially coal, iron, and copper. A lack of iron for gun barrels shut down the C.S. Armory at Fayetteville for three months in 1863 just as its production was peaking.

Incredibly, the Confederacy ran out of the seasoned black walnut needed (or at least insisted upon) for gunstocks in March 1864. Although the new C.S. Armory at Macon was located in the heart of Georgia's timberlands, Burton had for many months tried unsuccessfully to purchase and dry the vital wood—a much scarcer commodity than he had imagined. In September 1864, with William T. Sherman occupying Atlanta, uncomfortably close to Macon, Burton ordered the stocking machinery moved to the safer confines of Savannah, Georgia. Josiah Gorgas instead recommended the machinery be shipped to the C.S. Armory in Columbia, South Carolina, where black walnut was reportedly available. There, rifle and stocking machinery laboriously moved from the defunct armory in Asheville, North Carolina, was finally ready, awaiting only the precious walnut for production to begin. But beginning in November, Sherman's mercilessly efficient march first to Savannah and then north toward Columbia ensured that stock production never resumed. In February 1865, workers at the Columbia Armory barely managed to save the stocking machinery from Sherman's army. As the city burned, the vital machinery sat on a railroad siding in Lincolnton, North Carolina, safe from the Yankees, but never to be set up again. So it was that in April 1865 the Richmond Armory had on hand all the metal parts for ten thousand new arms, but not a single wooden gunstock.

Thus the relentless Union war effort uncovered the essential weakness in the Confederacy's nascent military-industrial complex: no location in the South was truly safe. At Richmond, well before the city finally fell to Ulysses S. Grant in April 1865, Union raids interrupted production at least three times when armory workers were called out to man the trenches. At Macon, the nearly finished armory buildings sat empty and cut off from the rest of the South after Sherman's troops obliterated four hundred miles of railroads in Georgia. Even Fayetteville, perhaps the safest location of all, fell victim to Sherman's "hard hand of war" in 1865. The Confederacy's inability to protect what little industrial infrastructure it possessed spelled doom for all its arms factories, whether centralized or not.

Between October 1861 and February 1865, the C.S. Armories at Richmond, Fayetteville, and Asheville together produced an estimated forty-nine thousand muzzle-loading rifles, rifle-muskets, and carbines, or nearly 60 percent of all firearms produced in the Confederacy during the war. By mid-1863, the Springfield Armory in Massachusetts was producing the same number of rifle-muskets every two months.

The Fall of Harpers Ferry

On the night of April 18, 1861, First Lieutenant Roger Jones had only forty-nine soldiers to defend the U.S. Armory at Harpers Ferry, one of the most important military installations in the nation. Marching on Harpers Ferry were two thousand Virginia militiamen intent on capturing the armory and seizing as many as fifteen thousand arms in the arsenal. Assisted by a former armory superintendent, Alfred M. Barbour, the militia had been planning the seizure since the night of April 16, when it became obvious that the state's secession convention would vote Virginia out of the Union the next day.

With little hope of reinforcement, Jones made preparations to destroy the armory workshops and machinery as well as the arsenal — in all, at least $1.25 million worth of governmental property. The soldiers placed gunpowder charges in the buildings and sent out a guard of about thirty armory workers and local unionists to warn of approaching danger. Alerted that Virginia troops were about twenty minutes away, Jones's men set off the charges at 10:00 p.m., and fled north into Maryland. The resulting flames consumed the two arsenal buildings but not the workshops, where local residents, fearing that the entire town would burn, quickly organized to put out the fires. Jones and other eyewitnesses reported that all fifteen thousand arms in the arsenal were destroyed.

Recognizing that its exposed position on the Maryland border made Harpers Ferry practically indefensible, troops under the command of Thomas J. (soon to be "Stonewall") Jackson and Joseph E. Johnston began moving the vital machinery to the safer confines of the old state armory building in Richmond. Over the next two months, 430 arms-making machines, 57,000 tools, and ready-made components for at least 3,000 U.S. Model 1855 arms were inventoried, crated, and loaded onto railroad cars. The lack of a direct railroad connection meant that all the crates had to be offloaded in Winchester onto wagons for the twenty-mile trip to the next railhead, at Strasburg, and then reloaded onto trains bound for Richmond. It was an extraordinary logistical feat.

Pressed by advancing Union forces, the Confederates pulled out of Harpers Ferry on June 14, 1861, and put the remaining buildings to the torch. After sixty years of production, the U.S. Armory at Harpers Ferry — engine of the Industrial Revolution, birthplace of interchangeable parts, mother of the Confederate arms industry — ceased to exist.

At length one man, more daring than his neighbors, made his appearance, rushed into one of the burning arsenals, and hauled therefrom into the street a box of arms, which he at once opened. On finding that it did not contain the rifle muskets, he rushed again towards the building for the probable purpose of trying his luck upon another. . . . In the meantime large crowds had gathered near the workshops, and were industriously engaged in subduing the flames, in which they succeeded before any very serious injury had been done to the machinery.
—Captain Charles P. Kingsbury, superintendent of the U.S. Armory at Harpers Ferry, before a congressional committee, November 15, 1861

U.S. Model 1855 rifle, second type, made by the U.S. Armory at Harpers Ferry just before its capture (1861)

This U.S. Model 1855 rifle was one of the last arms made at the Harpers Ferry Armory. Bearing a lockplate and barrel dated 1861, it was one of perhaps two hundred rifles completed in the fourteen weeks before the armory's capture. Well aware of the vulnerability of its armory on Virginia soil, the U.S. Ordnance Department tried to distribute arms manufactured there as quickly as possible to more secure locations. This example probably went to the Washington, D.C., or New York Arsenal.

Every Model 1855 rifle completed at Harpers Ferry under U.S. authority carried proof, inspection, and date marks on the barrel as well as two inspector stamps, or cartouches, in the stock opposite the lock. This one bears the stamp "AMB" for master armorer Armistead M. Ball as well as "TR" for Thomas Russell Jr., an English-born armorer and stock inspector.

**U.S. Model 1855 rifle, second type, believed to have been assembled
at Harpers Ferry just after its capture (1861)**

*Although Virginia troops began removing machinery from the Harpers Ferry musket works
almost immediately, the undamaged rifle works continued in operation through May. Under the
supervision of the Harpers Ferry armorer Phillip Burkhart, prosecessionist workers had time to
finish about 1,500 rifles then in production, for which parts had already been made.*

*This is believed to be one of those rifles. It is identical in all respects to the 1861-dated U.S.
Model 1855 rifle pictured on the opposite page except that it lacks the usual U.S. proof, inspection,
and date marks on the barrel as well as inspector stamps in the stock. The lack of these marks
indicates that it was not assembled under U.S. authority.*

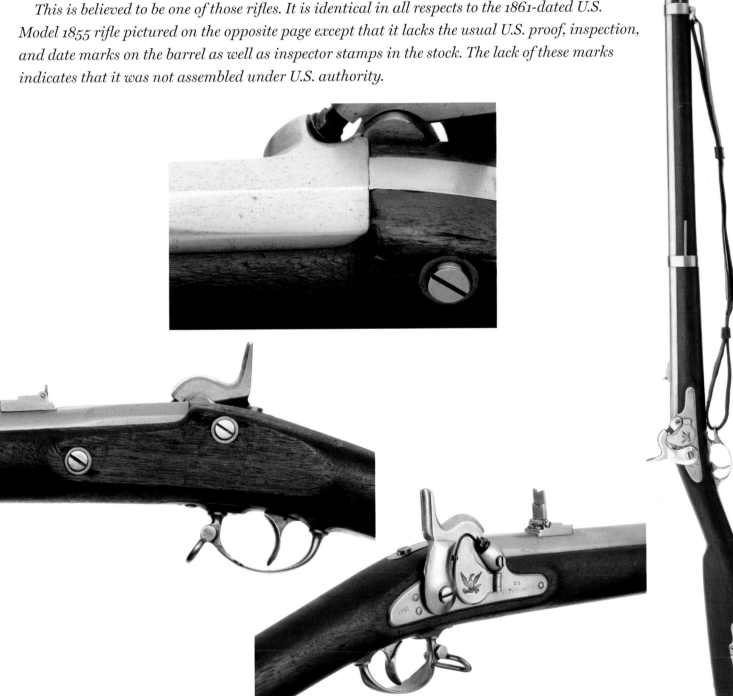

THE BURNING OF THE UNITED STATES ARSENAL AT HARPER'S FERRY, 10 P.M. APRIL 18, 1861.—[SKETCHED BY D. H. STROTHER.]

As flames consumed the arsenal buildings at Harpers Ferry, local residents rushed in to take what they could, especially the valuable rifles. (Harper's Weekly)

U.S. Model 1855 rifle, first type, made by the U.S. Armory at Harpers Ferry (1858), saved from the arsenal fire (1861)

Distinguished by its lack of a rear sight, this rifle was one of a few dozen rescued from the flames that engulfed the arsenal at Harpers Ferry on the night of April 18, 1861. Moved to action by both patriotism and potential profit, local citizens dashed into the burning arsenal and grabbed as many guns as they could (a new rifle could fetch $100 or more). Many of their stolen treasures remained hidden in their homes until ferreted out later by Virginia troops.

It was only due to a bureaucratic glitch that this rifle was still stored in the arsenal that night. In 1858, 615 rifles were assembled after the Model 1855 British-style rear sight had been eliminated from production but before the Model 1858 leaf-type sight was officially approved. Those rifles were supposed to be retrofitted with the new sight, but armory workers never got around to this one.

The heavy pitting around the bolster suggests that this rifle saw considerable use either by the local resident who saved it or by Virginia troops who subsequently discovered it. Without a rear sight, it would have been difficult to fire accurately.

U.S. Model 1855 rifle, transitional type, made by the U.S. Armory at Harpers Ferry (1859) and believed to have been used by Senator James H. Lane's Frontier Guard

When Virginia left the Union on April 17, 1861, the U.S. Army barely had enough troops to guard its own capital, let alone Harpers Ferry or anywhere else along the newly declared front line. In the panic that followed, army officers combed the streets of Washington, rounding up volunteers and assembling them into makeshift militias to guard the White House, the Capitol, and other vital points.

Forty-six-year-old James H. Lane, a militant Kansas Free-Soiler, had just arrived in town to take his seat in the U.S. Senate. Senator Lane quickly recruited about fifty fellow Jayhawkers and formed his own militia company, which he dubbed the Frontier Guard. On the night that Harpers Ferry burned, the Frontier Guard marched to the White House and "encamped" in the East Room, where they were assigned to protect their president and political champion, Abraham Lincoln.

At the White House, Lane's men were issued U.S. Model 1855 rifles. This is believed to be one of them, as evidenced by a photograph taken at the time in which Lane grasps a Model 1855 rifle curiously lacking the normal implement compartment, or "patchbox." It is one of about two hundred rifles assembled in the midst of an 1859 specification change that resulted in the temporary omission of this otherwise standard feature. These rifles had been sent to Washington just weeks before the secession of Virginia.

The Frontier Guard remained on duty in and around the White House for the next two weeks. As northern volunteer regiments flooded into the capital at the end of the month, the crisis passed and the Frontier Guard was disbanded after receiving the personal thanks of the commander in chief.

That night [April 18], Kansas had Supreme possession of the White House, and fifty of her "Old Guard" slept sweetly on the President's rich Brussels, with their arms stacked in martial line down the center of the hall, while two long rows of Kansas ex-Governors, Senators, Judges, Editors, Generals and Jayhawkers were dozing upon each side, and the sentinels made regular beats around them.
—Kansas State Journal, May 9, 1861

Richmond: The Confederacy's Best Effort

Although the Virginia Manufactory of Arms had produced its last musket in 1821, its sixty-year-old building became the home of the C.S. Armory at Richmond, by far the most productive of the Confederate national armories. In January 1860, with John Brown's raid fresh on everyone's mind, the Virginia General Assembly allocated $500,000 to renovate the old Virginia Manufactory building on the James River so that it could produce modern interchangeable firearms for the state militia. To oversee the operation, the commonwealth hired the thirty-seven-year-old Virginia native James H. Burton, who had applied his mechanical genius for ten years at Harpers Ferry and for another five at the Royal Small Arms Factory at Enfield, the national armory of the United Kingdom. Burton began by designing a new "Virginia pattern" rifle-musket, which was based on the British Pattern 1853.

To manufacture the new arms, Burton needed new arms machinery, which at first was to be purchased from the Ames Manufacturing Company in Massachusetts. Chided for its reliance on Yankee manufactures (on August 9, 1860, the *New York Times* had called Virginia "poorly prepared for the dangerous experiment of independence"), the Old Dominion ended up contracting for most of the arms machinery with Joseph R. Anderson's Tredegar Iron Works, whose rolling mill abutted the old armory building. But in April 1861, just as the first of the new machines was being installed (drive shafting from Tredegar and two drop-hammers from Ames), Virginia unexpectedly inherited the Yankee machines from Harpers Ferry. Although tooled to fabricate U.S. Model 1855 arms, the machinery needed only slight modification—most notably, the elimination of the Maynard tape primer—to approximate the design of Burton's Virginia pattern arms, the production of which was now unnecessary. But the plans, preparations, and building renovations that Burton had completed for Virginia saved the Confederacy many months' effort in getting a new national armory into operation—and just when it needed it most.

In July 1861, with the touchy matter of ownership of the Harpers Ferry machinery settled, Burton became superintendent of what was (officially at least) the C.S. Armory at Richmond. Most of the industrial infrastructure he needed was literally right next door. The Tredegar Iron Works rolled iron for gun barrels; just down the river, James Hunter's Richmond Steel and Iron Works rolled iron for the other components. Bayonets, gun tools, brass stock tips, and other parts would also come from Richmond contractors. Aside from the raw materials that had to be supplied from outside the city by railroad, the armory was almost self-contained. But it lacked one important time-saving device: the barrel-rolling machine, installed at Harpers Ferry just two years before but abandoned the previous summer before it

Nearly every mechanic in the Confederacy competent to manufacture small-arms is believed to be engaged in the work. The manufacture of small-arms is a slow and tedious process, and the accumulation of supplies necessary for such an army as we now require is the result of the labor and expenditure of long series of years.
—Confederate secretary of war Judah P. Benjamin to President Jefferson Davis, March 12, 1862

No adequate arrangements have been entered into for the certain supply of gunstocks. . . . One great difficulty appears to be that the walnut timber abounds only in regions of the country occupied by disaffected persons to a considerable extent. Owners of mills are therefore loathe to undertake the work for fear of their mills &c. being burned by incendiaries.
—Confederate superintendent of armories James H. Burton to chief of ordnance Josiah Gorgas, August 12, 1864

ROLLING THE BARREL.

*The barrel-rolling machine at Harpers Ferry was virtually identical to the one shown here at the Sprinfield Armory. (*Harper's Weekly*)*

could be moved. In January 1862, Burton, who well knew the value of the heavy and unwieldy apparatus from having patented an improvement of it in 1860, insisted that Confederate forces undertake the dangerous mission of hauling it out from under the noses of Union artillery on the surrounding hills. The risk was worth it: the armory gained ownership of a state-of-the-art machine that eliminated the need to weld barrel seams, making them much stronger and at half the cost and time. Ultimately, the Richmond Armory became the main supplier of barrels to the government armories at Fayetteville and Asheville, North Carolina, and at Tallassee, Alabama.

Despite its interchangeable-parts machinery, the C.S. Armory at Richmond was seldom able to produce truly interchangeable arms. Specific features of Richmond arms were constantly in flux, depending on available parts and materials as well as the resourcefulness of armory workers. Throughout the war, Burton and subsequent armory superintendents understood that their focus had to be on production, not perfection; strict adherence to pattern was a luxury the Confederacy could not afford. At first, with thousands of ready-made U.S. Model 1855 parts on hand, the armory was more an assembly than a manufacturing operation. As the Harpers Ferry parts were used up, the Richmond mechanics made new ones and cannibalized old ones from guns collected off the battlefields. The armory was loath to waste parts that could be used for any other type of arm: flawed barrels and stocks could be cut down to make rifles, carbines, or even shortened muskets. Of the fifteen arms in the Wray Collection that were assembled or fabricated by the C.S. Armory at Richmond, only two are constructed entirely of Richmond-made parts.

In March 1865, Richmond was clearly running out of time. Burton was ordered back to the Confederate capital to see that the Harpers Ferry machinery was properly crated and loaded onto railroad cars for possible evacuation. On the night of April 2, 1865, as the Confederate government fled and the armory buildings burned, all machinery except the heavy barrel-rolling machine was headed west for

The C.S. Armory at Richmond in ruins, April 1865 (Library of Congress)

the relative safety of Danville, Virginia. From there, Burton planned to move everything to Macon, but Macon was captured and the Confederacy collapsed before even that desperate measure could be enacted. With no place to go, the trains were seized in Danville by Union troops on April 27; the ultimate fate of the Harpers Ferry machinery on board is still unknown.

According to the best estimate, between October 1861 and March 1865, the C.S. Armory at Richmond produced about 39,600 new arms of four types, in addition to repairing at least 48,000 others. Compared to the nearly 1.5 million rifle-muskets turned out during the same period by the Springfield Armory and its private contractors, Richmond's production was minuscule. On the other hand, considering all its handicaps — a lack of raw materials, inadequate railroad transportation, and a dearth of skilled labor — the Richmond Armory represents a remarkable achievement for a nation otherwise unprepared to fight a modern industrial war on its own soil.

Marks of Confederate authority

In general, the Confederacy was not as concerned with marking its property as with simply producing it. The only mark of Confederate government ownership stamped on arms at the Richmond Armory was a simple "CS" over "RICHMOND, VA" on lockplates. The Fayetteville Armory went further, often stamping "CSA" on brass buttplates and the guards of sword bayonets.

  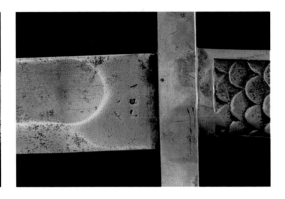

Reclaiming the traditional American eagle symbol as its own, the Fayetteville Armory used the same stamping dies on its lockplates that had once been used on U.S. muskets and rifles, but added "CSA" in place of "US." At the Asheville Armory, workers using old lockplates from U.S. Model 1841 rifles simply struck over the U in "US" and replaced it with a C. The Richmond and Fayetteville Armories continued to use the old Harpers Ferry eagle-head stamp as an inspection mark for barrels as well as the V ("viewed") and P ("proved") marks.

U.S. Model 1841 rifle lockplate   Fayetteville Armory lockplate   Asheville Armory lockplate

Rifle-muskets made by the C.S. Armory at Richmond, using Harpers Ferry parts (1861–62)

Top: *Bearing an unmarked lockplate, this rifle-musket was probably among the first completed at the Richmond Armory in October or November 1861, before lockplate stamping dies were created. Aside from its Richmond-made cloth sling (a later addition), a crudely fashioned Richmond hammer, and the lower barrel band, it is made entirely of Harpers Ferry parts. The brass stock tip was left over from the early production of U.S. Model 1855 rifle-muskets, while the brass buttplate is believed to have been cast for a U.S. Model 1855 rifle, but was never cut with a slot for the implement compartment cover.*

Bottom: *By contrast, this rifle-musket, finished in December 1861 or January 1862, is made almost entirely of Richmond-manufactured parts, including its stock and welded barrel. Other than the lock, which probably contains parts originally forged at Harpers Ferry but finished at Richmond, only the rear sight, ramrod, and middle and lower barrel bands are Harpers Ferry products. Even though it had not yet exhausted its entire Harpers Ferry inventory, the Richmond Armory was already producing most of its own parts by this time.*

Lockplates made or finished by the C.S. Armory at Richmond (1861–62)

Superintendent James H. Burton had decided to eliminate the pesky Maynard tape primer even before the Harpers Ferry machinery was installed in Richmond. Although armory workers could easily omit the primer door and its internal mechanisms, their Harpers Ferry lock-profiling machine was still set up to fabricate U.S. Model 1855 lockplates. Workers also had on hand 1,600 unfinished Harpers Ferry lockplates of the same design.

Top: *The Model 1855 lockplate's distinctive "high hump" shape made placing and removing a percussion cap difficult. The Richmond Armory assembled an estimated 3,900 rifle-muskets with this type of lockplate between October 1861 and February 1862.*

Bottom: *In March 1862, a former Harpers Ferry mechanic named William H. Wentzel spent two days modifying the lock-profiling machine so that it would produce this easier-to-use "low hump" configuration, which the armory produced through the end of the war. The "C.S." stamp was added in early 1862.*

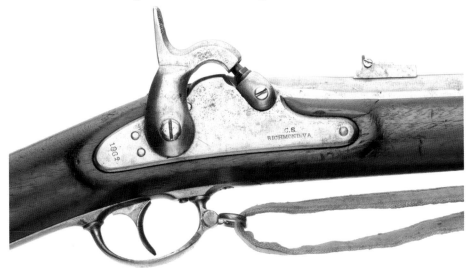

Locks and stocks made or used by the **C.S. Armory**
at Richmond (1861–63)

Top: *The internal mechanism of the Maynard tape primer on U.S. Model 1855 arms
included a "feeding finger," which reached into the lockplate cavity to advance a roll
of percussion caps every time the hammer was cocked. This feeding finger required a
special cut just behind the bolster in the stock's lockplate cavity. The presence of this
cut is the distinguishing feature of the two thousand completed stocks captured at
Harpers Ferry and used in the first months of production at Richmond.*

Bottom: *By eliminating the Maynard tape primer, the C.S. Armory at Richmond
did away with the need for at least seven parts and a dozen manufacturing steps.
The absence of a cut for the Maynard feeding finger is the distinguishing feature of
Confederate-made stocks. Completed in 1863, this stock is one of more than twenty-
six thousand shaped and cut on the Harpers Ferry machinery at Macon between
October 1862 and March 1864, when the supply of black walnut was exhausted.*

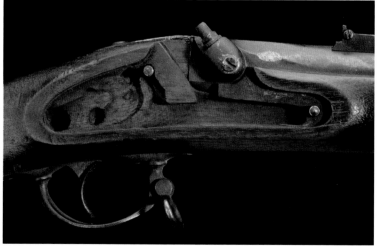

Buttplates made or used by the C.S. Armory at Richmond (1861–62)

During his years at Enfield, James H. Burton came to favor the British practice of using rustproof brass in place of iron for the buttplates, trigger guards, and stock tips of rifle-muskets. Burton was quick to incorporate brass into Confederate-made rifle-muskets whenever possible.

Top: *Among the parts seized from Harpers Ferry were about seven hundred U.S. Model 1855 iron buttplates. This one, which had already been stamped "us," was fitted to a Richmond rifle-musket made in early 1862.*

Middle: *By May 1862, the armory had switched over to brass buttplates. Many of them were provided on contract by the Bargamin family, which ran a large plumbing-fixture business in Richmond. This rifle-musket dates to 1863.*

Bottom: *The armory still used any parts it could scrounge up, regardless of material or pattern. This well-worn 1862-dated rifle-musket bears an iron buttplate originally made for a Model 1855 rifle, as indicated by the slot milled for the cover tab of an implement compartment.*

Stock tips made or used by the C.S. Armory at Richmond (1861–62)

The C.S. Armory at Richmond was lucky that so many of the Harpers Ferry mechanics agreed to work for the Confederacy. They understood the newest methods of fabricating arms and, more importantly, still remembered the old ones. When material or parts shortages threatened production, these mechanics were able to revert to older methods in order to accomplish the same goal.

Top: *Stock tips prevented the wooden stock from being split or damaged when a soldier returned the ramrod to its channel after loading. The first U.S. Model 1855 rifles used brass stock tips and brass rivets, but later ones, such as this 1860-dated example, used more durable iron tips with iron screws.*

Second from top: *Among the many parts captured at Harpers Ferry were about sixteen hundred brass tips and rivets. Unwilling to waste parts, the Richmond workers reverted to riveting. Dated 1862, this rifle-musket was probably assembled in January or February of that year.*

Second from bottom: *In February 1862, the supply of Harpers Ferry tips and rivets being exhausted, the armory began using newly cast brass tips along with more durable—but rust-prone—iron screws. This rifle-musket was made in late 1863.*

Bottom: *Ultimately, workers used whatever parts were available. It is unknown whether the iron stock tip and screw on this 1863-dated rifle-musket were made at Harpers Ferry or Richmond. Perhaps it was cannibalized from a U.S. Model 1861 rifle-musket.*

Percussion hammers and barrel bands made or used by the C.S. Armory at Richmond (1861–62)

Despite their great resourcefulness and creativity when it came to reusing parts, Richmond Armory mechanics were never able to match the quality they had known at Harpers Ferry. The iron was poorer, the urgency of production far greater. Even in the smallest details, the differences were telling.

Top: *The twenty-four crossed lines of checkering on the hammer of this 1860-dated U.S. Model 1855 rifle are deep and well defined.*

Bottom: *By comparison, the eighteen crossed lines on the hammer of this 1861-dated Richmond rifle-musket are shallow and imprecisely applied.*

Bottom left: *The iron barrel bands of U.S. Model 1855 arms (as well as subsequent models) were marked on the right side with a capital letter U (for "up") to indicate their correct positioning during disassembly and reassembly. The Harpers Ferry-made barrel band at the top of this photograph is evenly formed, and the U is evenly stamped. By contrast, the Richmond-made band below is thicker, more unevenly formed, and because it was stamped by hand rather than by a machine press, the U is lopsided.*

Bottom right: *Even when the U mark was evenly stamped, the mark itself did not always line up with the barrel band spring, as had been the practice at Harpers Ferry.*

Rifle-musket made by the C.S. Armory at Richmond, using Confederate-made parts (1863)

In the first half of 1863, rifle-musket production at the Richmond Armory averaged just over twelve hundred a month. Nearly all these arms were assembled entirely from iron and brass parts made in Richmond and black walnut stocks made in Macon. Their rolled (not welded) barrels were all rifled at a standard .577 caliber, the same as thousands of British arms imported through the Union blockade. During these months, the Confederacy came as close to interchangeability and mass production as it ever would.

It is likely that this 1863-dated rifle-musket was fabricated during this peak period. Except for its brass buttplate and the shape of its lockplate, it is a reasonably close copy of the U.S. Model 1861 rifle-musket, the standard arm issued to Union infantrymen, but lacks the same quality finish. It is one of only two Richmond-made arms in the Wray Collection made entirely of Confederate parts; the other is an 1863-dated carbine.

Having peaked at 1,700 in April 1863, rifle-musket production at the Richmond Armory plunged to 580 in July, mainly because its entire workforce was summoned to the defense of the city during a Union cavalry raid. In March 1864, another such raid captured sixty prisoners from the defense battalion made up of armory workers. Neither production nor quality ever again reached the levels seen in early 1863.

Major, it is my duty to inform you [of] loosing John Jones, one of our barrel straighteners, who was killed in the late fight around Richd. . . . It will take several months to educate a new man to this peculiar and difficult branch of work. . . . The late fight has produced disastrous results on this armory and it will be a long time before we shall recover if we ever do.
—Salmon Adams, master armorer of the C.S. Armory, Richmond, to Superintendent Frank F. Jones, March 8, 1864

Carbine made by the C.S. Armory at Richmond, using Confederate-made parts (1863)

Faced with increasingly well-armed opponents, Major General J. E. B. Stuart desperately needed accurate long-range carbines for his shotgun-toting cavalrymen in the Army of Northern Virginia. The Richmond Armory responded in late 1862 by producing muzzle-loading carbines. At first, some were improvised from captured U.S. Model 1861 rifle-muskets or damaged Richmond-made barrels cut down to the required twenty-five-inch length.

Over the next two years, the Richmond Armory turned out nearly forty-eight hundred .58-caliber carbines fabricated entirely from Confederate-made parts, including barrels rolled for the purpose and Macon rifle-musket stocks whose tips or forearms had broken during manufacturing but could be shortened and used for carbines. Produced in late 1863, this carbine has all the features associated with Richmond-Macon production, including a brass buttplate and stock tip, iron bands, a leaf-type rear sight, and a distinctive "pinched" front sight designed especially for cavalry carbines.

Although an improvement over shotguns, these muzzle-loading carbines were still hopelessly obsolete. By 1863, nearly all Yankee troopers were armed with breech-loading and repeating carbines, which were by then being mass-produced by the tens of thousands in northern factories.

Rifle-muskets reassembled as shortened muskets by the C.S. Armory at Richmond, using spare parts (1864)

In the summer of 1864, with stock production at Macon halted, Richmond Armory workers collected old rifle-musket stocks whose forearms had failed in the later stages of manufacture, after the slot for the middle-band retaining spring had already been cut. The stocks could not be used for carbines, but they could be made into two-banded rifles with thirty-three-inch barrels or even shortened muskets with thirty-inch smoothbore barrels, both of which may have been intended for issue to cavalry units. Production levels at the Richmond Armory dropped off in 1864, and as demonstrated by these examples, so did quality and standardization.

Top: *This smoothbore .61-caliber shortened musket was assembled entirely from Richmond-made parts except for the top barrel band, which was taken from a U.S. Model 1861 rifle-musket. Though its lockplate dates from early or mid-1863, this arm was likely assembled a year later. The original .577-caliber rifling in the barrel was probably already worn down when it was bored smooth, almost certainly for use with buckshot.*

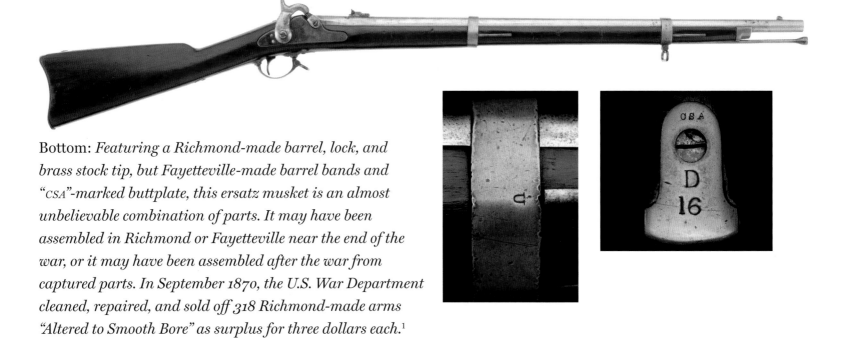

Bottom: *Featuring a Richmond-made barrel, lock, and brass stock tip, but Fayetteville-made barrel bands and "CSA"-marked buttplate, this ersatz musket is an almost unbelievable combination of parts. It may have been assembled in Richmond or Fayetteville near the end of the war, or it may have been assembled after the war from captured parts. In September 1870, the U.S. War Department cleaned, repaired, and sold off 318 Richmond-made arms "Altered to Smooth Bore" as surplus for three dollars each.[1]*

Rifle-musket repaired and reassembled as a rifle by the C.S. Armory at Richmond (1864)

This forty-six-inch-long rifle was originally a fifty-six-inch-long rifle-musket assembled in Richmond from Harpers Ferry parts, including a complete 1860-dated U.S. Model 1855 lock. Probably as a result of damage, it was turned in to the Richmond Armory, where its stock and ramrod were cut down and it was refitted with an 1864-dated barrel. The pinched front sight indicates that the refitted rifle was intended as a cavalry weapon.

The poor quality of iron available to the armory is obvious from the tiny flaws along the barrel's surface, which appear as irregular black streaks. Much of this iron came from Samuel W. Hairston's Union Furnace Company in southwestern Virginia, and from the Cranberry Iron Works in western North Carolina. Hairston iron was considered so vital that the Confederacy bought the ironworks in 1863.

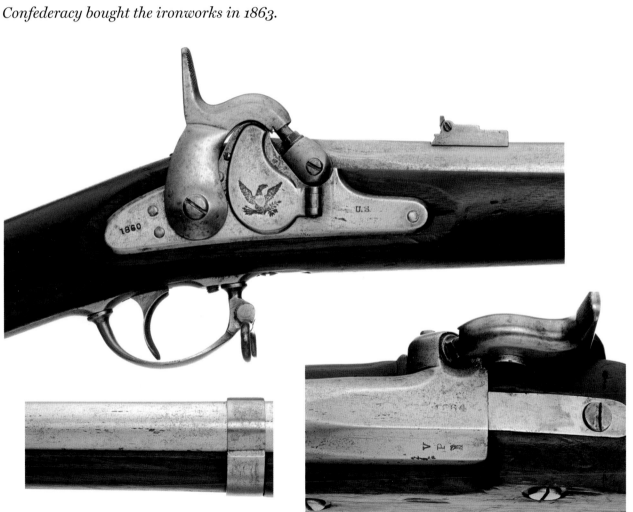

Rifle-musket assembled from captured parts by the C.S. Armory at Richmond (date unknown)

This rifle-musket demonstrates the Richmond Armory's creative but almost random use of parts. It is based on U.S. Model 1855 Harpers Ferry–made parts, including the stock, stock tip, bands, and ramrod. To these parts have been added an 1858-dated Springfield-made barrel, complete with the early Model 1855 "sliding pattern" rear sight.

The only part of this arm made in Richmond is the 1862-dated lock, and even this has been modified with a hammer from a U.S. Model 1861 contract rifle-musket. The shield-shaped checkering on the thumb of the hammer, which was not introduced until late 1863, suggests that this rifle-musket was assembled after that date. It is also possible that the hammer was replaced while the gun was in field service or that this arm was assembled well after the war. Herein lies the problem for modern researchers and collectors: it is as easy to assemble spare parts into a Confederate arm today as it was during the Civil War.

Socket bayonet made by or for the C.S. Armory at Richmond, with scabbard made by unknown contractor (ca. 1863)

Socket bayonets for Richmond Armory rifle-muskets were copies of the U.S. Model 1855 rifle-musket bayonet, but were sometimes made without the weight-reducing fluting or grooves on the blade (hence these are popularly known as "three-square" bayonets). Despite steel shortages, the C.S. Ordnance Bureau always tried to incorporate steel, even if the socket or the lower part of the blade had to be made of softer, less durable iron. On this example, the weld seam where the lower part of the iron blade joins the iron socket is clearly visible; less visible is the seam where the steel tip is welded to the upper part of the blade. Such bayonets were produced at the Richmond Armory and also by private contractors, including Haiman and Brother in Columbus, Georgia, and Heck, Brodie, and Company in Raleigh, North Carolina.

Unlike their U.S. counterparts, Confederate bayonet scabbards were often tipped with lead instead of more expensive brass. This remnant is lacking the frog that attached the scabbard to a waist belt.

Rifled 1.75-inch "infantry gun" made at the Tredegar Iron Works, Richmond (1862)

Chief among the private enterprises supporting the Richmond Armory was the Tredegar Iron Works, which did business almost exclusively with the Confederate government during the war, fabricating some 1,160 artillery gun tubes. Among them was this one-of-a-kind experimental "infantry gun" fabricated in the summer of 1862. Made as a swivel gun, its precise function and mounting arrangement is unknown, but its five-groove ratchet-type rifling and exterior casting flaws are distinctively Confederate. The Thomas S. Dickey Collection at the Atlanta History Center includes a 1.75-inch rifled iron bolt recovered from a test range near Richmond, but unfortunately the rifling pattern imprinted on the lead base does not match the rifling pattern of this gun.

On the eve of the Civil War, Tredegar's owner, Joseph Reid Anderson, employed 1,000 men, including many northern- or foreign-born whites as well as 130 enslaved and ten free blacks. By 1864, the size of the workforce had doubled to 2,000, of which 1,500 were enslaved African Americans, some of whom performed the most highly skilled tasks. The Tredegar Iron Works proved that slave labor could be used profitably in heavy industry; if the Confederacy had survived, Tredegar's example may have provided a model for the future.

Wartime view of the Tredegar Iron Works (Library of Congress)

Fayetteville: The Safest Place in the Confederacy

The C.S. Armory at Fayetteville, North Carolina, had its origins in the U.S. Arsenal begun there in 1838 as a storage facility for both federal- and state-owned arms. From the beginning, the arsenal suffered from its remote location, connected to the rest of the country chiefly through the Cape Fear River, "the use of which for carrying heavy articles," wrote the U.S. chief of ordnance in 1859, "is impracticable for the greater part of the years for the want of sufficient depth of water, and difficult at all times from the light construction of the boats engaged in that transportation."[2] A planned railroad through Fayetteville never materialized except for a short spur line connecting it to the small town of Egypt, from which the armory received coal during the war. Otherwise, all raw materials going in and completed arms going out depended upon 120 tenuous miles of the Cape Fear River flowing southeast to Wilmington, North Carolina, the closest port and railhead.

On April 15, 1861, North Carolina governor John W. Ellis joined the governors of four Upper South states in refusing to answer President Lincoln's calls for volunteers to put down an insurrection. Instead — and even before his own state formally seceded — Ellis ordered the state militia to seize the U.S. Arsenal at Fayetteville and the forty-one thousand arms stored there. Ellis ordered the arms distributed to volunteers in his own and other states. On July 9, his military secretary reported, "We are nearly out of arms. I am scouring the state for them."[3] Fortunately for North Carolina, in 1857 and 1858 the U.S. Army Ordnance Department had installed about $50,000 worth of northern-made arms machinery in the arsenal, including trip-hammers, a rifling machine, giant wood lathes for making artillery carriages, and a thirty-horsepower steam engine to drive the shafts and belts. None of it had ever been used. State authorities soon put the machinery to work repairing, altering, and upgrading at least five thousand unserviceable arms already in the arsenal, plus thousands of others being turned in from all over the state.

This machinery made Fayetteville a logical place to install the Harpers Ferry rifle-making machinery — or so it seemed to Governor Ellis. Richmond Armory superintendent James Burton disagreed. For one thing, splitting up the machinery meant splitting up the four hundred skilled mechanics from Harpers Ferry, about one hundred of whom moved to Fayetteville along with the machinery. For another, the arsenal buildings at Fayetteville had to be expanded to accommodate the new machinery and two seventy-five-horsepower steam engines to drive it, all of which required bricks, lumber, iron shafting, and additional laborers to be ferried up the Cape Fear River. As a result, the machinery did not go into operation until January 1862. Finally, because the U.S. Model 1855 rifle-musket and rifle both used the same

It should be on navigable waters to permit easy communications with the forts, seaports, and counties along the coast. . . . It should, if possible, be along the great road leading north to south. . . . As it would necessarily be placed in the midst of the black population, it should be at or near some town where, in any emergency, it might be aided by the citizens; and from whence mechanics might be obtained.

—Stipulations for location of a new U.S. Arsenal in the South Atlantic region, 1836

We claim for the arms turned out here superiority in workmanship over those made elsewhere in the Confederacy and desire to keep up the quality of the arms. . . . Every effort will be made to meet your espoused expectation, but we require an immediate supply of barrels and four good figures [skilled workers] to do it.

—Frederick L. Childs, superintendent of the C.S. Armory at Fayetteville, to Josiah Gorgas, chief of ordnance, June 6, 1863

lock, Harpers Ferry had maintained just one set of lock-making machinery, not two, and that set belonged to Richmond. Therefore, locks had to be manufactured in Richmond and shipped to Fayetteville until that armory completed its own set of lock-making machinery in October 1862.

Despite these obstacles, the C.S. Armory at Fayetteville turned out a respectable three hundred rifles a month from October 1862 through June 1863. But when the supply of Richmond-made barrels ran low because of a shortage of iron (Unionist guerrillas had interrupted the supply from the Cranberry Iron Works in western North Carolina), production dropped steadily until October 1863, when it ceased altogether until the next year. When the supply of barrels was renewed in early 1864, Fayetteville was able to turn out an estimated four hundred rifles a month until the end of the year, but still never reached the modest target of five hundred a month set by Josiah Gorgas. All told, the armory turned out an estimated 8,600–8,900 rifles between late 1861 and early 1865 — an amazingly high number, considering all the handicaps it faced, but still only a fraction of its machinery's capacity. Using the same machinery and an uninterrupted supply of raw materials, the Harpers Ferry Armory had produced 7,300 U.S. Model 1855 rifles between late 1857 and early 1861, albeit without the urgency of wartime.

The only advantage of the Fayetteville Armory's location was its insulation from Union military movements. As long as the Confederacy held the massive earthen ramparts of Fort Fisher, it held Wilmington, and as long as it held Wilmington, it held the mouth of the only highway leading to the armory. The fall of Fort Fisher on January 15, 1865, effectively sealed the fate of Fayetteville, but it was Sherman's army moving up from South Carolina that got there first. On March 11, 1865, Sherman occupied Fayetteville; four days later the armory had been thoroughly demolished — except for the Harpers Ferry rifle machinery. Hidden in a mine shaft near the town of Egypt, it was not discovered until May, when it was confiscated and shipped downriver to Wilmington. From there, its fate is unknown.

Rifles made by the C.S. Armory at Fayetteville, first type, using Harpers Ferry parts (1861–62)

In addition to the Harpers Ferry rifle-making machinery, the C.S. Ordnance Bureau shipped thousands of parts for U.S. Model 1855 rifles to the Fayetteville Armory in the summer of 1861. These included about fifteen hundred stocks and eighteen hundred barrels in various stages of completion, but not the critical lock parts, most of which were retained in Richmond. The three rifles featured here were among the first several hundred assembled at Fayetteville with Harpers Ferry parts beginning in the fall of 1861.

Left: *Some of the U.S. Model 1855 rifle parts captured at Harpers Ferry were surplus brass fixtures that had been phased out in 1859 in favor of iron parts. Except for the Model 1858 leaf-type rear sight, this well-worn rifle was assembled almost entirely from these older parts, including a stock cut for the early "figure eight," or "crosshair," sharpshooter's sight inside the implement compartment. The Richmond-made high-hump lock has been fitted with a hammer that appears to have been forged at Harpers Ferry but finished—rather crudely—at Richmond. Only the brass buttplate and barrel bands were made at Fayetteville.*

Right: *Bearing an 1860-dated Harpers Ferry barrel, this rifle was assembled mainly from the newer iron parts introduced in 1859 for the second-type U.S. Model 1855 rifle. The exceptions are the first-type Harpers Ferry–made trigger guard, the Fayetteville-cast barrel bands, and an unmarked Richmond-made lock distinguished by the "c2" assembly code stamped on its interior surface. Evidently, the experienced Harpers Ferry mechanics at Fayetteville tried to avoid intermixing the brass and iron parts from first- and second-type Model 1855 rifles as much as possible. They probably used the newer parts first.*

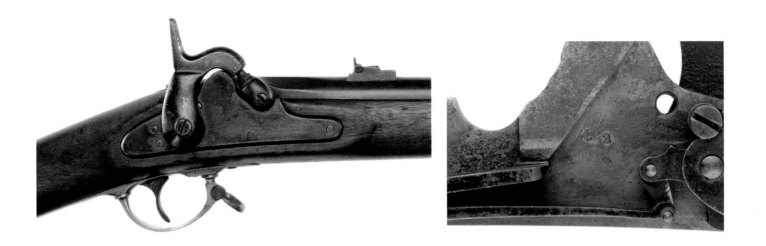

Below: *Except for the Fayetteville-made buttplate and barrel bands, this rifle was assembled entirely from Harpers Ferry parts, including a hammer that had already been milled with a cutting edge for the tape primer. The lockplate was stamped "CSA" over "FAYETTEVILLE, NC," in the same format as the "CS" over "RICHMOND, VA" mark, which was introduced at about the same time. It is likely that this lock was finished and stamped in Richmond, but it is also possible that it was one of the thirty-nine unfinished plates shipped directly from Harpers Ferry and finished at Fayetteville. Later Fayetteville locks dropped the "NC" and added an eagle and a date stamp.*

Rifle made by the C.S. Armory at Fayetteville, transitional type (1862)

As they worked to reduce their dependency on Richmond by building their own lock-making machinery, mechanics at the Fayetteville Armory designed a distinctive S-shaped hammer, similar to those used on Sharps carbines. This one has been fitted to a Richmond-made low-hump lockplate.

Produced in mid-1862, this .58-caliber rifle features brass bands, buttplate, and trigger guard, no implement compartment, and a copy of the U.S. Model 1858 rear sight. These features—as well as a generally high quality of workmanship—remained remarkably consistent through the end of the war.

This rifle bears the name "A Boyd" scratched into the wood opposite the lock. This may refer to Private Abner Boyd of Craven County, who enlisted in August 1863 in the First North Carolina Sharpshooters before being transferred the following January to the Sixty-Seventh North Carolina Infantry. Boyd survived the war and died in 1917.

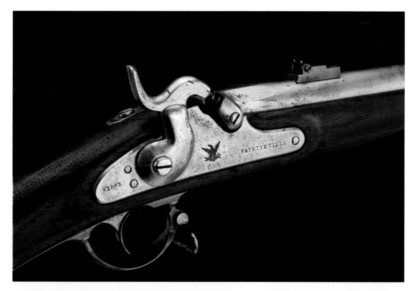

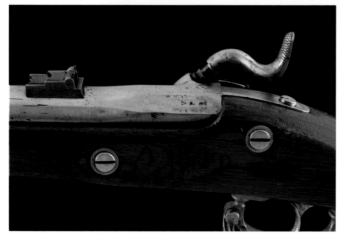

**Rifle made by the C.S. Armory at Fayetteville,
third type, with sword bayonet (1863)**

*This 1863-dated rifle is equipped with a lock made entirely at Fayetteville. Except
for the hammer, it is a close copy of locks made for U.S. Model 1861 rifle-muskets.
This arm also bears the "PB" inspection stamp of Phillip Burkhart, the former
Harpers Ferry mechanic and John Hall protégé who served as master armorer for
the Fayetteville Armory.*

*Like the U.S. Model 1855 rifle upon which it was based, the Fayetteville rifle was
designed initially with a stud on the right side of the muzzle for affixing a sword
bayonet. Thousands of these distinctive "fish scale"-grip bayonets (right) were
fabricated at the armory in 1862 and 1863.*

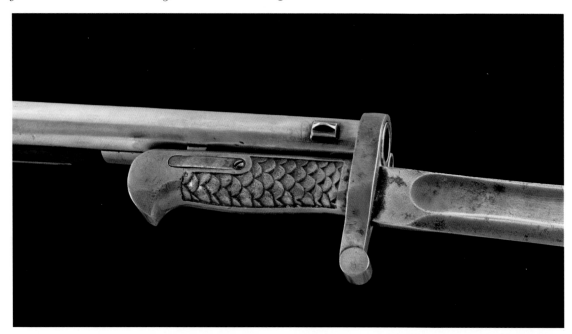

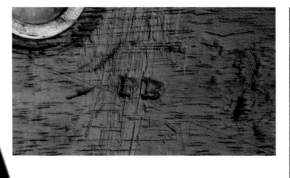

Rifle made by the C.S. Armory at Fayetteville, third type (1862)

Confederate soldiers were well known for carving their initials into the stocks of their guns. Though punishable by fines, such defacing of governmental property served a practical purpose: initials or other marks allowed a soldier to readily distinguish his rifle from those of his comrades. At rest, soldiers usually placed their guns in a triangular stack with the buttplates resting on the ground and the muzzles leaning against one another and interlocked. In this position, a gun's top surfaces face downward, which is why most initials seem to have been carved upside down.

This unusual 1862-dated Fayetteville rifle with iron Harpers Ferry bands and stock tip bears the initials "TWM" and a large X (later filled in with putty) on one side of the buttstock, a large W on the other, and "EHM" in the wood opposite the lock. If a soldier was sick, wounded, or killed, Confederate ordnance officers usually issued his gun to another soldier. It is common to see two or more sets of initials on a single arm, a chilling reminder of the high mortality rate among Confederate soldiers. Unfortunately, it is rarely possible to trace the initials to a specific individual among the estimated 900,000 who served in the Confederate army at some point during the war.

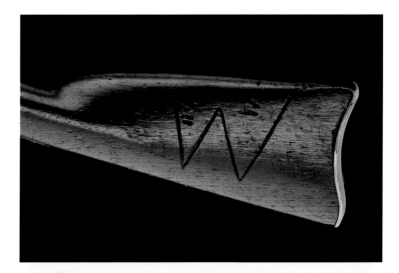

Rifle made by the C.S. Armory at Fayetteville, fourth type, with socket bayonet (1864)

Understanding only too well the impact of metal shortages on production, Major Frederick Childs, superintendent of the Fayetteville Armory, recommended the elimination of saber bayonets in the summer of 1863. He and his mechanics considered them a waste of time and materials, especially since they did not fit any other government-made arms. Socket bayonets, common in the Union army and mass-produced by the C.S. Armory at Richmond, simply attached to the front sight, eliminating the need for a stud on the side of the barrel. Childs's recommendation was officially accepted in January 1864.

At about the same time, a shipment of barrels from Richmond allowed rifle production at Fayetteville to resume and the fabrication of socket bayonets to begin. Although unmarked, these bayonets are usually distinguishable by their undulating blades and, as seen here, a grossly off-center slot in the base for fitting over the front sight. Such work would never have passed U.S. inspection, but was functional enough for the Confederate war effort.

In view of the expectation of the department to turn out at this armory 500 arms for the month of July, Inst., I deem it essential to state that the wishes of the department cannot be met in consequence of the want of Material for the Manufacture of Barrels. . . . I must respectfully decline the assumption of any responsibility in a quarter where it is not in our Power to Control.
—Phillip Burkhart, master armorer of the C.S. Armory at Fayetteville, to Josiah Gorgas, chief of ordnance, July 3, 1863

Asheville: The Confederacy's Most Costly Failure

Nestled deep in the Blue Ridge Mountains of western North Carolina, the tiny hamlet of Asheville was known mainly as a stopover for cattle and hog drovers along the main road connecting Asheville to the closest railheads, Greeneville, Tennessee, and Greenville, South Carolina, each about sixty miles away. Although far from potential Union incursions and close to a dozen or more iron furnaces, Asheville had virtually no industrial infrastructure or specialized mechanics among its 1,100 inhabitants. It was hardly a location that Josiah Gorgas or James Burton would have chosen for a national armory.

As it turned out, that decision was made for them. In the summer of 1861, Robert W. Pulliam, a supplier of uniforms and camp gear for Asheville-area volunteer companies, was designated an official agent of the C.S. Ordnance Bureau. On August 5, 1861, an enthusiastic Pulliam went well beyond his original charge—collecting and repairing old arms—and entered the Confederacy into a contract with Ephraim Clayton and George W. Whitson, the owners of a steam-powered wood-planing and lumber mill, for fabricating arms from scratch. All production expenses—including wages, use of the mill building and its machinery, the purchase of additional machinery, and, above all, the cost of transporting raw materials in and completed guns out—were to be borne by the Confederacy.

Gorgas and Burton first learned of their government's commitment to the Asheville enterprise in March 1862 when Pulliam submitted a copy of the contract along with a bill requesting reimbursement for expenses already incurred. Keenly aware of his country's desperate need for arms, Gorgas decided to make a go of the venture, surprise or not. Two months later, he dispatched a twenty-nine-year-old mechanic named Amasa W. King from the Richmond Armory to act as master armorer at Asheville. King was appalled at what he found. "I condemned all the locks," he reported, "examined the barrels and found them very bad indeed, having to condemn a large majority of them. . . . I have changed the patterns for mountings and changed some tools, making them work to a better advantage."[4]

King insisted on appointing his own foremen on the basis of merit and on organizing the workforce by specialty areas, a move that quickly angered everyone in the armory. Like most businessmen in a preindustrial economy, Clayton, Whitson, and Pulliam (who was still nominally in charge of the armory) maintained an informal management structure. Pulliam ran the armory out of his dry goods store and often paid his hundred or so white workers in store scrip instead of Confederate currency. Most of the men operating the machinery were jacks-of-all-trades, used to setting their own hours and doing piecework. Despite the best intentions, neither Pulliam

As far as I can learn, the tools and machines, before Mr. King arrived at Asheville, were makeshifts and the work carried on almost at the discretion of the men employed. Consequently the guns were made worthless and the labor performed (at the expense of the Department) worse than thrown away.
—Report of Major William S. Downer, superintendent of the C.S. Armory at Richmond, after inspecting the C.S. Armory at Asheville, November 22, 1862

nor his workers had any idea of the massive scale and industrial-style discipline necessary to make the armory a viable operation. Thus, what seemed like commonsense changes to King seemed like abusive treatment to the armory's workers and thus made them all the more determined to resist his efforts. On the heels of a damning inspection report from Major William S. Downer of the Richmond Armory, the Ordnance Department replaced Pulliam with Captain Benjamin Sloan in December 1862. King was kept on. Sloan attempted to make peace, firing the most incompetent workers but retaining Clayton as his manager in order to maintain the loyalty of the rest. Yet Sloan's peace was never perfect. Part of the problem was the strong Unionist sentiment in the area, which was shared by some of the white workers who, Sloan feared, would "embrace the first opportunity of joining the enemy."[5]

Racial tensions also permeated the workforce of the Asheville Armory. The traditionally nonslaveholding region had become home to an increasing number of enslaved people sent by nervous owners from threatened coastal areas to the relative safety of the mountains. Some slaves were hired out to the armory for hauling wood or making charcoal; others, including eight men belonging to Ephraim Clayton (who were probably already working at the planing mill), performed mechanical jobs traditionally reserved for whites. Among them were three armorers, one steam engineer, and a master carpenter who earned three dollars a day for his owner at a time when unskilled white workers made as little as one dollar a day. Resentment boiled over in January 1863: a white mob whipped an enslaved worker originally from York, South Carolina, after he was discovered outside the armory without a pass.

In December 1862, King accompanied the first lot of two hundred completed arms to the Richmond Armory. By then, the Asheville Armory was suffering from the same shortages that eventually halted production at the Richmond and Fayetteville Armories. Despite the iron ore and furnaces all around him, Sloan discovered that some of the iron was so poorly smelted as to be almost worthless. He found a source of high-quality iron for gun barrels in Cranberry, North Carolina, about eighty miles northeast of Asheville, but washed-out mountain roads and bridges as well as Unionist guerrillas severely limited deliveries. In January 1863, guerrillas sacked the nearby town of Marshall, forcing Sloan to temporarily halt production as he and his workforce joined a punitive expedition against the raiders.

Nevertheless, the tiny Asheville Armory persevered. By March 1863, Sloan and King had coaxed out another two hundred rifles, most with barrels provided by

Richmond and some, perhaps, with stocks from Macon. But the supply of parts from the other armories was so erratic that Sloan became determined to make the Asheville Armory self-sufficient and so began work on his own barrel-making and stocking machinery. In late April, he dispatched King to the Macon Armory to make notes on the Harpers Ferry stocking machinery there and to confer with James Burton. It is likely that King discussed with Burton the particulars of a "model arm," probably intended as a new pattern rifle, that King had submitted to the Ordnance Bureau in Richmond the previous December. Finally, in June 1863, Sloan and King achieved their goal: the furnaces and trip-hammers for welding barrels and the machinery for turning stocks were complete; virtually all major parts for a rifle could be made in Asheville, at the rate of two hundred a month. Against all odds, the C.S. Armory at Asheville was teetering on the brink of success.

But it was not to be. In July and August, production ground to a halt as guerrillas cut off the supply of Cranberry iron. Even with the iron, the armory could not have made barrels. "Our Foreman of the Blacksmith Shop has kicked up and says he won't weld any more barrels," King reported. "[He] has raised a mutiny in the shop & none will work . . . there being no Provost Marshall here we are completely powerless."[6] Major Downer at the Richmond Armory denied Sloan's request for a skilled barrel welder and barrel borer; he simply did not have the men to spare. In September 1863, U.S. troops occupied Knoxville, Tennessee; the next month, a raiding force came within forty miles of Asheville before being turned back. In early November, well aware of the strong Unionist presence in the area, a worried and thoroughly frustrated Josiah Gorgas pulled the plug. Over the previous twenty-six months, the Confederacy had pumped at least $375,000 into the Asheville Armory. In return, it had received 875 rifles, each costing the Confederacy an astounding $429. It was a price in time, labor, and materials the young nation could ill afford to pay.

Gorgas ordered the armory's machinery packed up and moved to the presumably safer environs of Columbia, South Carolina, a move that ended up taking five months to complete. Meanwhile, skilled and competent workers were lent to the other armories; all others were released for army service. By the end of 1864, with buildings, motive power, and overhead shafting finally completed and all machinery in place (including stocking machinery from Macon), the new C.S. Armory at Columbia was ready to start production where Asheville had left off. But the entire effort went for naught when the supply of black walnut for making stocks failed to materialize. Finally, in February 1865, only the stocking machinery was saved from destruction as the Columbia Armory was put to the torch by Sherman's army; the rest of the dearly bought machinery removed from the Asheville Armory went up in flames.

To date, collectors and historians have located fewer than twelve confirmed examples of Asheville Armory rifles. No two are exactly alike; only one bears a date stamp. Although the armory used inspection marks and serial numbers, they were not consistently or consecutively applied. Nevertheless, surviving examples generally fall into two basic types. The first comprises the rather makeshift rifles assembled through May 1863, using parts from other government armories and including features of the U.S. Model 1855–type arms produced at Fayetteville. The second type comprises the surprisingly well-made and standardized rifles fabricated after June 1863, when the armory was making its own stocks and barrels. Unlike other Confederate government arms, these rifles closely resemble the U.S. Model 1841–style rifles made by private manufacturers. Two of the three Asheville rifles in the Atlanta History Center's collection are of this latter type (including one from the DuBose Collection presented here for comparison). Both exhibit a level of quality at least as high as arms produced at Richmond or Fayetteville, proving that the Asheville Armory achieved its greatest success at the moment of its demise.

Rifle made by the C.S. Armory at Asheville, first type, number 116 (1863)

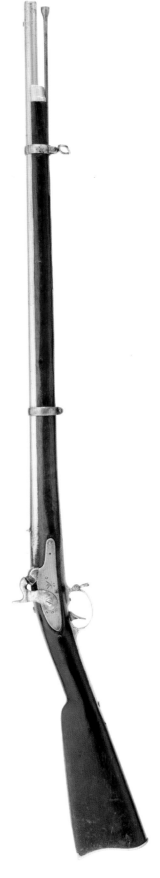

This rifle was probably among the second lot of two hundred arms delivered to the Atlanta Arsenal in March 1863. Its most distinctive feature attests to the makeshift nature of the armory's early production: a reused lockplate from a Harpers Ferry–made U.S. Model 1841 rifle. The tail section was ground down to obscure the original markings, and the "US" under the American eagle symbol was struck over to form "CS." The left side of the stock bears the faintly visible remains of Amasa W. King's inspection stamp, "AWK," inside a rectangular cartouche. King had requested these stamps from the Ordnance Bureau in October 1862 so that he could mark inspected arms according to regulations.

Another distinguishing feature of this rifle is the shape of its U.S. Model 1855– or Fayetteville-style stock, distinguished by a curved butt and buttplate as well as separate lockplate screw washers. Although the Macon Armory may have furnished such stocks to Asheville in 1863, this one appears to be handmade, probably from locally grown walnut. Asheville rifles are characterized also by rounded British-pattern barrel-clamping bands on the stock, which were normally made of brass. Here they are made of iron, perhaps the result of a temporary shortage of tin or copper. Significantly, there is no ramrod-retaining spring in the stock, as would be expected with these bands.

The thin-walled, six-land-and-groove barrel was probably rifled at Asheville using one of the "short rough musket barrels" that Benjamin Sloan received from the Richmond Armory after he took command in December 1862. The S inspection stamp at the breech may be his initial. The X punched on the underside of the barrel is probably an assembly-code marking, while the stamped "116" may be an inventory number applied to the barrels sent from Richmond. It is also possible that the number signifies the 116th rifle completed in the second lot of arms.

This rifle evidently saw a great deal of use. The wood behind the bolster is deeply burned out, the .577-caliber barrel is worn to about .60 caliber; the bayonet stud on the right side of the muzzle has been filled in. The left side of the stock bears a large carved B beside an x over the faint initials "GDM," indicating use by at least two soldiers.

Rifle made by the C.S. Armory at Asheville, transitional type, number 423 (1863)

This is probably one of the first new-pattern Asheville rifles that went into production about June 1863. This example from the DuBose Collection was assembled almost entirely from new and machine-made parts; it represents a significant qualitative improvement over earlier production. Its solid and well-formed lockplate is completely unmarked. Some of the early arms bear an "ASHEVILLE, N.C." stamp, but apparently that die quickly wore out from being stamped on old but case-hardened U.S. Model 1841 lockplates. The left side of the stock bears the deep and clear inspection stamps "AWK" and "ASHEVILLE, N.C."

The most distinctive feature of this rifle is its Model 1841–style stock with a squared-off butt and buttplate, undoubtedly turned by the Asheville Armory's new stocking machinery. Most significantly, the stock channel of this rifle includes a ramrod-retaining spring of the type introduced by James H. Burton at the Royal Small Arms Factory at Enfield, and the barrel-clamping bands are made of brass. Both features may have been recommended (and probably specified) by Burton in April 1863 when King visited the Macon Armory to examine the stocking machinery. In these small features, the later-production Asheville rifles anticipated the design of the British Pattern 1853 rifle-muskets that Burton planned to put into production at Macon as the Confederacy's standard long arm.

At the same time, this rifle was not assembled entirely with Asheville-made parts. It still bears the U.S. Model 1855–style lockplate screw washers, perhaps left over from previous production or provided by another armory. The thick-walled, six-land-and-groove .577-caliber barrel bears no proof or inspection marks, but both the underside and the breech plug bear the number "423," strong evidence that it was among the 459 barrels rolled in Richmond especially for the Asheville Armory in May 1863. The bayonet stud, with its guide key extending toward the muzzle, is a replacement. So far, no saber bayonets have been located that fit any of the three Asheville rifles in the Atlanta History Center collection.

This well-worn rifle may have been part of the third lot of two hundred rifles received at the Atlanta Arsenal on August 27, 1863; 135 of these rifles were issued to the Third Battalion of the Georgia State Cavalry, also known as the "Atlanta Fire Battalion."

Rifle made by the C.S. Armory at Asheville, second type, number 85 (1863)

This rifle is believed to have been among the last ones produced at Asheville, perhaps as late as September or October 1863. In configuration and detail, it is nearly identical to the previous rifle (with barrel number 423), including the unmarked lockplate, Model 1841–style stock with a squared-off butt, brass British-pattern clamping bands, and a ramrod-retaining spring. There are no proof or inspection marks anywhere on the gun.

Significantly, the underside of the barrel is stamped with the number "85." Because the same number stamped with the same die appears in the barrel channel, the interior of the lockplate, and the inside surface of the hammer, it is almost certainly a serial number and not just an assembly code, indicating that all these parts were stamped at the same time and by the same maker. It therefore seems likely that this rifle was assembled almost entirely from Asheville-made parts. The only exception is the hammer, which appears to have been taken from a northern-made contract copy of a Model 1841 rifle. Also of significance is the Model 1841–style sideplate used to secure the lockplate screws. Reversing the evolution seen in rifles produced by most private arms contractors in the Confederacy, the Asheville Armory replaced features of the U.S. Model 1855 and reverted to those of the Model 1841. The fate of the last arms produced at Asheville is unknown, but it is possible that some were held back for local defense. Interestingly, the barrel of this rifle has been bored smooth to about .61 caliber, indicating civilian use after the war as a shotgun.

4. A War between the States

In 1861, despite the windfall inheritance from the U.S. Armory at Harpers Ferry, the most far-thinking of Confederate leaders—including Secretary of War Judah P. Benjamin and President Jefferson Davis—understood that this machinery alone might not be able to produce enough arms to sustain the young Confederacy in a prolonged war. They also realized that in the absence of a sufficiently capitalized private banking system in the South, only their new national government could provide the financing required to create a private military arms industry from scratch. In 1861 and 1862, the C.S. Congress authorized advances to arms makers of up to 50 percent of estimated start-up costs, the money to be repaid without interest in the form of guns and bayonets. What followed was an unprecedented entrepreneurial frenzy.

Combining patriotism with the quest for profit, at least thirty private companies were formed across the South to fabricate new arms—usually hybrid copies of the U.S. Model 1841 and Model 1855 rifles, but occasionally the British Pattern 1856 "Enfield" rifle. Most of the new arms businesses were formed as partnerships between planters, attorneys, or merchants, many of whom already had substantial investments in other businesses, such as textile and lumber mills or iron furnaces. Some partnerships included men experienced in producing wagons, farm tools, or the few machines essential to an agrarian economy, such as cotton gins or syrup presses. But only a handful of the new ventures included experienced mechanics or gun makers, and even those few specialists failed to grasp the size of their task. Building modern gun factories would require machinery, labor, and materials on a scale theretofore unknown south of Harpers Ferry.

Two-thirds of the new enterprises worked under state contracts. North Carolina, Georgia, Alabama, Tennessee, and Texas followed the example of the Confederate government and provided incentives designed to arm their militias against both Union invasion and possible central-government coercion. Previously, private manufacturing had suffered from competition with the immensely profitable cotton industry. Now state governments were attempting to bypass years of private-sector development and simply create an arms industry by fiat. It was the same approach

The constant tendencies of the war seem to have been the subordination of civil authorities and laws to the military, and the concentration of supreme power in the hands of the Commander-in-Chief of the armies. The longer the war lasts . . . the less probability at its termination of a return to the Constitutional forms and republican simplicity which existed at its commencement.
—Georgia governor Joseph E. Brown, November 3, 1863

The difficulty is not in the want of legislation. Laws cannot suddenly convert farmers into gunsmiths.
—Confederate secretary of war Judah P. Benjamin to President Jefferson Davis, March 12, 1862

tried by the State of South Carolina in the early 1850s, but when isolated from northern manufacturers, it yielded dismal results. With the notable exception of the Cook and Brother Armory, virtually none of the private enterprises succeeded, at least not for long. Start-up costs, even when machinery, buildings, and workers could be procured, were prohibitive. New factories in the Mississippi, Cumberland, and Tennessee River valleys—the most productive regions of the new nation—quickly became targets of advancing Union armies. Some businesses and their factories were forced to pack up and move multiple times, with each move interrupting production. Sometimes the disruptions sank the enterprise altogether. Confederate currency began losing its value as soon as it was printed; contractors could not make a profit, and profits could not keep up with rising production costs. And as always there were shady characters such as Thomas E. McNeill, a man who knew how to talk his way into governmental funding without producing anything to show for it.

Ultimately, all industries in the South competed for the same constantly shrinking pool of manpower and raw materials. The conservative champions of state sovereignty—most famously, Governors Joseph E. Brown of Georgia and Zebulon B. Vance of North Carolina—fought hard for their states' share of those resources, and their contractors naturally expected a free hand to make a fair profit. But neither the Confederacy nor its private economy could provide sufficient resources for all who needed them. In a war between states' rights and national necessity, there could be only one winner: the Confederate central government, which by early 1864 had established a virtual monopoly on arms and munitions production. In violation of much of its founding philosophy, the Confederate States undertook the greatest expansion of central-government power Americans would see until the New Deal and World War II. Popular acquiescence to such control, though hardly universal, was in large measure aided by long-standing distrust of stereotypical businessmen and greedy industrialists. Simply put, many white Southerners trusted their own government before they trusted the private sector, at least when it came to manufacturing.

One key to central-government control was the railroads. The absolute necessity of moving soldiers and supplies to battlefronts trumped all other needs and rendered irrelevant the usual flow of freight, passengers, and profit. Unlike its northern enemy, the Confederacy never officially nationalized its railroads; instead, in 1861 they were placed under the jurisdiction of the C.S. Quartermaster Department, whose inefficient administration became legendary. Regardless, the Confederate government controlled and directed the limited supplies of coal, iron, copper, lead, wood, and other raw materials needed for arms manufacturing. The national armories took first priority; all others — including private armories working under state contracts — had to wait in line or try to procure supplies locally. Sometimes, that meant obtaining no supplies at all.

The other key to government control was labor. In April 1862, the Confederate States enacted the first conscription law in American history; by 1864, the laws had made all men age seventeen to fifty liable for Confederate service. Workers in vital industries could be exempted by order of the War Department; likewise, skilled men already in the army could be detailed to work in arms factories. But with such great authority came great coercive power: companies that failed to deliver the right products at the right time and for the right price might find their workers' exemptions suddenly revoked or their detailed men returned to the front lines. It was much the same story in North Carolina, Georgia, and Alabama, where state authorities used their powers of exemption from militia duty to obtain the most favorable terms for state contracts, often paying less than market price in exchange for exempting workers. Yet the states were at a decided disadvantage when it came to labor: as with raw materials, the central government was the first (and usually only) priority. The C.S. Ordnance Bureau never had enough skilled workers for its own national armories, let alone for anyone else.

In the end, the lack of skilled labor proved fatal for the Confederacy's private arms industries. By April 1865, only two survived, both tucked away in southwestern Georgia. Virtually all others — even the successful Cook and Brother Armory — had gone out of business or sold out to the Confederate government. The same was true for iron foundries, copper mines, and related ordnance businesses. Since it already controlled the means of production, the C.S. Ordnance Bureau found it most efficient to cut out the enterprising middleman and operate arms businesses directly — a savings in time, money, and paperwork. Meanwhile, most state governments gave up on their private arms contractors. Never-ending (and usually losing) battles with the Confederate government over labor and raw materials combined with the often-sketchy quality of the contracted arms to convince state officials that the product was simply not worth the effort. Selling out to the Confederacy was the only logical alternative.

Most private arms enterprises in the Confederacy managed to produce only a few hundred arms, making surviving examples extremely rare. Yet these few examples generally followed the same evolution in their overall form and configuration. Initially, most of the South's gun makers fell back on their own experience in making civilian or Kentucky-style hunting rifles, altering them with the addition of a bayonet, percussion lock, and standard-size rifled bore into an ersatz military arm. As the war progressed and these lightweight rifles failed the test of field use, gun makers began building sturdier, military-style rifles from the ground up, usually based on the ever-popular U.S. Model 1841 "Mississippi." Early on, especially in North Carolina and Alabama, military-style arms were characterized by civilian-style features such as slightly built stocks or reused octagonal barrels with multigrooved rifling. Only gradually did gun makers add muscle to their products: thicker stocks, military-style three-land-and-groove rifling, heavier bands, and tighter mainsprings. Yet just as their country's fragile infrastructure and labor supply were deteriorating in 1864 and 1865, a few private southern arms makers—most notably, Dickson, Nelson, and Company—were improving the quality and standardization of their work. Hence, the story of private arms manufacture in the South also is a tale of remarkable adaptation and resourcefulness in the midst of an extremely harsh business environment.

The Guns of Guilford County

In the summer of 1861, the State of North Carolina found itself short of arms, having issued to its own troops or given to other seceded states all thirty-seven thousand guns it had seized at the U.S. Arsenal at Fayetteville. To help make up for the shortfall and to ensure that its own state troops would be sufficiently armed, state ordnance officers turned to Guilford County, home of the largest concentration of private gun makers in the South. More than eighty craftsmen were engaged in the trade centered on Jamestown, about ten miles southeast of the county seat at Greensboro. The Jamestown school of gunsmithing was famous for its highly decorated, finely crafted Kentucky-style rifles.

In July 1861, North Carolina established a small armory in Florence, just north of Jamestown, where it hired Guilford County craftsmen to rework Kentucky rifles into military arms by altering them to percussion and providing them with bayonets. But the delicate "country" rifles broke easily; they simply were not suitable for the constant stress of military service. In response, the state issued five contracts in early 1862 for entirely new "North Carolina rifles" to be patterned on the U.S. Model 1841 "Mississippi" rifle. All five contractors were located in Guilford County within twenty miles of Greensboro and close to the Florence Armory: Henry C. Lamb and Company, of Jamestown; Mendenhall, Jones, and Company (soon to be Mendenhall, Jones, and Gardner), which eventually settled in Jamestown; Gillam and Miller of High Point (just south of Jamestown); Clapp, Huffman, and Company (soon Clapp, Gates, and Company) on Alamance Creek eleven miles east of Greensboro; and Searcy and Moore on Hogan's Creek twenty miles northwest of Greensboro.

Among the partners in these companies only two — Henry C. Lamb and Grafton Gardner — were true gun makers; the rest were merchants, attorneys, and businessmen anxious to combine patriotism with profit by organizing local gun makers and gunsmiths into a factory labor force that could turn out arms more efficiently and in greater quantity than ever before. In details both large and small, the guns of Guilford County reflect the ersatz nature of this proto-industrialization: among at least eleven rifle subtypes, none are exact copies of the U.S. Model 1841 and no two are exactly alike. In 1862, at least one-fourth of all rifles delivered were rejected by state inspectors. Yet the guns also demonstrate a remarkable resourcefulness on the part of their makers. The contractors made maximum use of their limited resources, sharing raw materials, laborers, and parts. Clapp, Gates, and Company made hammers, lockplates, buttplates, and other parts for Lamb and Company and Mendenhall, Jones, and Gardner; Lamb and Company and Gillam and Miller

I wish to call your attention to an objection in your rifle. It is not well balanced, there being too much weight at the muzzle, which I think you can remedy by keeping the present thickness at the breech & grinding down the muzzle until you reduce the weight of the barrel to five pounds. In issuing guns yesterday to troops, I found that yours were universally rejected on account of the object mentioned above.
—North Carolina ordnance officer Thomas G. Hogg to Henry C. Lamb and Company and Mendenhall, Jones, and Gardner, September 10, 1862

sold locks and stocks to the Florence Armory. All five contractors reused old civilian rifle barrels with traditional seven-groove rifling. Remarkably, these rifles show a gradual improvement in quality and standardization. By 1863, stocks had become heavier, construction sturdier, and markings more consistent; calibers had been increased from the state standard of .50 to the Confederate government standard of .577.

Yet no improvement in quality could save the gun makers of Guilford County. In January 1863, recognizing that its previous practice of offering fixed-price contracts could never keep up with inflation, North Carolina agreed to guarantee its contractors a net profit of $10 a rifle. While such generous terms eventually yielded some five thousand arms for the state, prices skyrocketed from $20 a rifle in early 1862 to more than $50 by mid-1863. Meanwhile, British arms imported through the Union blockade were better made and far easier to obtain. In July and August, the state's parsimonious governor, Zebulon Vance, terminated the contracts with four of the five enterprises, leaving only Mendenhall, Jones, and Gardner (the most prolific of the contractors) in operation through 1864. The state bought out the tiny firm of Searcy and Moore, transferring its remaining parts and materials to the Florence Armory. Finally, on October 31, 1864, even the Mendenhall, Jones, and Gardner contract was canceled after inflation pushed production costs to an unbearable $164 a rifle.

As was the case throughout the South, financial incentive alone could not transform a local craft into a modern industry without massive additional investments in machinery, infrastructure, and skilled labor. As Governor Vance recognized, industrialization in Guilford County simply did not make economic sense as long as domestically made arms cost more than foreign imports. More ominously still, by 1864, where there had once been a shortage of arms and a surplus of men, now the situation was reversed. In the end, guns were cheap; soldiers were irreplaceable.

North Carolina contract rifle made by Henry C. Lamb and Company, Jamestown, second type (1862)

Since the 1820s, the Lamb family had been among the most successful and prolific of the Guilford County gun makers. By 1862, the family business, headed by Henry Clarkson Lamb, was busy altering civilian rifles for the State of North Carolina and delivering its first Model 1841–type rifles.

This example was probably among the 554 rifles delivered between February and August 1862. Its seven-groove barrel is in .54 caliber, which is neither the North Carolina nor the Confederate standard. The muzzle is equipped with a double-peaked "footprint"-type sword bayonet stud, a feature unique to North Carolina–made rifles. But as shown by two uncompleted stud slots, a mechanic working on this barrel either did not understand the proper placement of the stud or else had trouble milling the slot. The assembly number 3 stamped on the hammer matches only one part inside the lock; all others are marked 5.

As indicated by the "Nc" stamped into the wood opposite the lock, these minor anomalies did not prevent the gun from passing state inspection. In September 1862, state ordnance officers complained about weak mainsprings and poorly balanced barrels. Subsequent deliveries showed marked improvement.

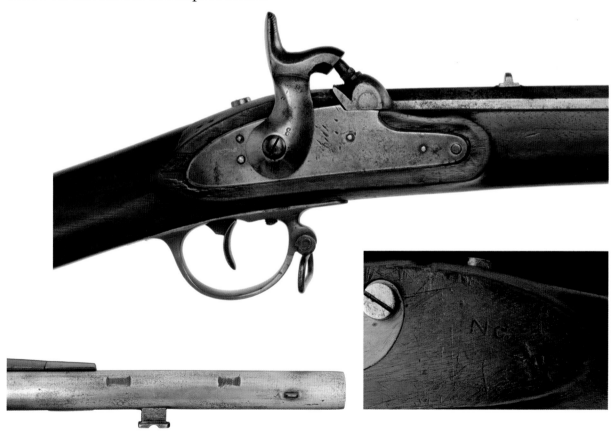

North Carolina contract rifle made by Henry C. Lamb and Company, Jamestown, third type (1862–63)

This North Carolina rifle was probably made in late 1862 or early 1863. It is heavier and about an inch longer than the previous example, and its bayonet stud is now the standard single-peak "flat" type. Though it bears assembly numbers 6 and XV on the underside of the barrel and in the stock channel, it has no inspection marks or serial numbers.

This gun was most likely made in .577 caliber, though its rifled barrel was later bored smooth and now measures .63 inches, or about 20 gauge. After the war, military arms were often altered in this way for use as civilian shotguns.

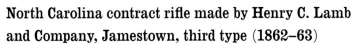

North Carolina contract rifle made by Henry C. Lamb and Company, Jamestown, third type, serial number 234, with bayonet made by Louis Froelich, Wilmington or Kenansville (1863)

Probably made in the spring of 1863, this .577-caliber rifle is the best made of the three Lamb and Company rifles in the Wray Collection. By then, Lamb had standardized the length of its arms at forty-nine inches and the caliber of its barrels at .577; under a contract signed in January 1863 for 1,000 rifles, it also applied consecutive serial numbers to major parts. This one is stamped "234" on the barrel, the inside of the hammer, and in the stock opposite the lock. It is also marked P ("proved") and "N.C." on the barrel, as well as "N.C." and "H.C. LAMB & Co." on the stock opposite the lock.

In August 1863, Governor Vance terminated the state's contract with Lamb through an escape clause allowing North Carolina to pay $5,600, or $10 for each of the 560 rifles yet to be completed under the January 1863 contract. Vance used the same method to close out contracts with Gillam and Miller, and Clapp, Gates, and Company, saving the state at least $35,500 but ending production just as it was achieving some measure of quality. In total, the state accepted just over 1,000 Lamb rifles.

This bayonet was among at least 2,500 and perhaps as many as 7,000 manufactured under contract for the State of North Carolina by Louis Froelich's factory in Wilmington and later in Kenansville.

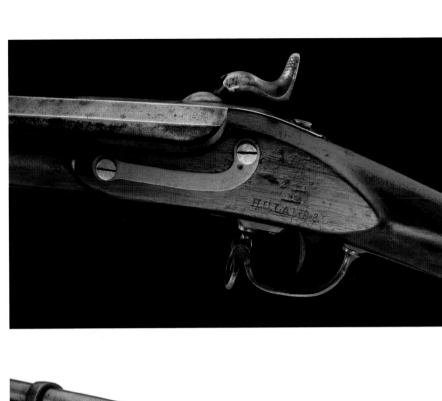

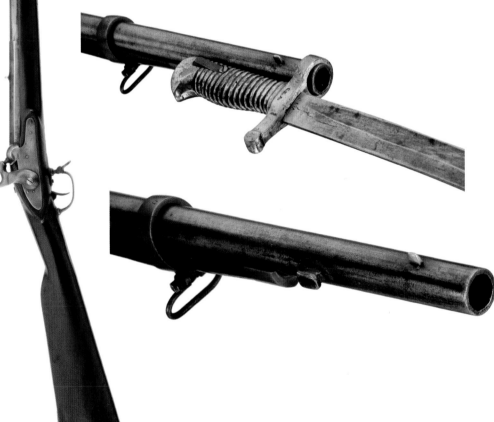

North Carolina contract rifle made by Mendenhall, Jones, and Gardner, Jamestown, first type, serial number 66, with matching-number bayonet made by unknown maker (1862)

Soon after North Carolina's secession, the planter and attorney Cyrus P. Mendenhall and the tobacco merchant Ezekiel P. Jones formed a partnership to make arms, initially renting space and machinery from Clapp, Huffman, and Company at the Cedar Hill Foundry and Machine Shop on Alamance Creek. Mendenhall and Jones later admitted into the partnership Grafton Gardner, an experienced mechanic who became the superintendent of the factory, which was relocated to Jamestown in February 1862.

This early-production Mendenhall, Jones, and Gardner rifle is one of only two of its type known. Bearing serial number 66 on the interior of the lockplate, under the barrel tang, and in the stock opposite the lock, this .50-caliber rifle may have been among the first one hundred rifles delivered in July 1862, three months before North Carolina adopted .577 caliber as the standard. Like the early Lamb rifles, it features a double-peak footprint-type sword bayonet stud, and its stock is of lighter construction than that of the guns later made by the company.

Because bayonets for these arms were not interchangeable, each was marked with the serial number of its parent rifle. Incredibly, bayonet number 66 has survived with this gun. It is one of the only known instances in which a numbered southern-made rifle matches a numbered southern-made bayonet.

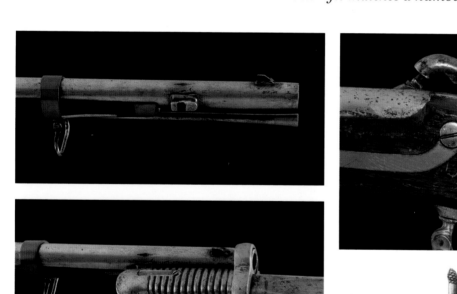

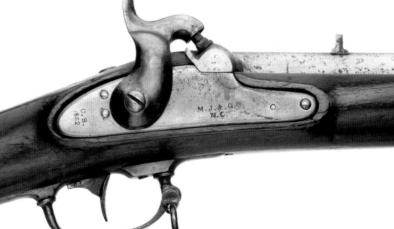

North Carolina contract rifle made by Mendenhall, Jones, and Gardner, Jamestown, third type, serial number 258 (1864)

In quantity and quality, Mendenhall, Jones, and Gardner was the most successful of the Guilford County gun makers. Between July 1862 and October 1864, the State of North Carolina accepted 2,239 Mendenhall, Jones, and Gardner rifles, almost as many as it accepted from the four other contractors combined.

This 1864-dated .577-caliber rifle is significantly sturdier and better finished than the 1862-dated rifle pictured previously. It also bears the influence of blockade-run British Pattern 1853 rifles and rifle-muskets, including an engraved British-style hammer as well as brass washers for its lockplate screws instead of the U.S. Model 1841–type sideplate. The rifle bears a cursive "MJ&G" company cartouche stamped into the stock under the rear lockplate screw, but for reasons unknown it has been scratched out.

The tops of the barrel bands are stamped U (for "up") to indicate their correct positions during disassembly and reassembly. These bands — which are often found facing the wrong way — are identical to the ones on Lamb and Company rifles.

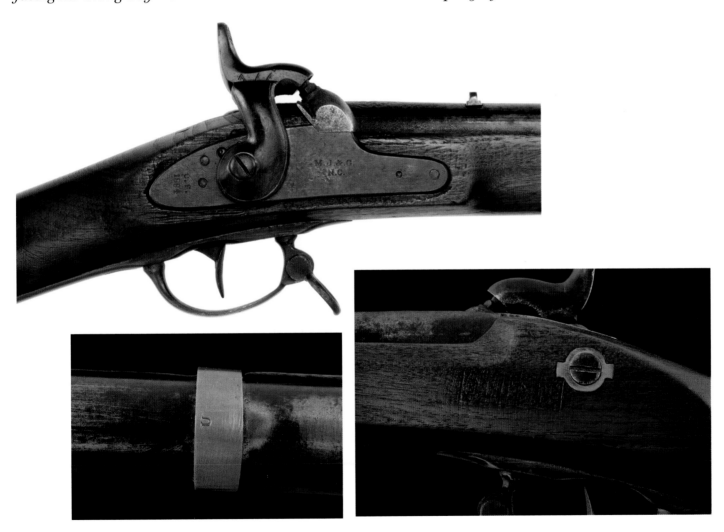

North Carolina contract rifle made by Gillam and Miller, High Point (1863)

By mid-1862, Dr. L. M. Gillam and James Miller had established a small factory with the evident intention of producing rifles under a Confederate government contract. But with the Confederacy offering only $30 a rifle, Gillam and Miller sought a more lucrative deal with the State of North Carolina. Between January and July 1863, the company delivered some 889 rifles in .577 caliber (of which 677 passed state inspection) before their contract was canceled.

Among the Guilford County guns, Gillam and Miller rifles are distinguished by a protruding toe on the buttstock and a barrel that is round, not octagonal, at the breech. Many rifles, including this one, lack a sword bayonet stud, suggesting that they were intended to be fitted with sword bayonet attachment rings such as those made by Boyle, Gamble, and MacFee of Richmond.

Aside from the P ("proved") stamp on the barrel, the exterior of this example is unmarked. The interior of the lock bears assembly number 5 (which also appears under the barrel) and the slash marks "IIV," which aided the makers in fitting the custom-made lock parts. The letter W may be an inspector mark; a similar W appears on the buttplate of the second-type Lamb rifle. The cloth sling is almost certainly original to this rifle and was probably made in one of the many textile mills in the area.

North Carolina contract rifle made by Clapp, Gates, and Company, Alamance Creek, third type (1862–63)

In the 1850s, the brothers Joshua and Jacob Clapp operated the Cedar Hill Foundry and Machine Shop on Alamance Creek, along with Joshua's three sons and a business partner named C. C. Huffman. By the fall of 1862, Huffman had left the company, but Joshua Clapp had enlisted Charles C. Gates, a Vermont native and former Amherst College friend, as a partner and marketing agent.

This seven-groove .50-caliber rifle was produced before March 1863, when Clapp, Gates, and Company finally began making its arms in .577 caliber. Its thirty-six-inch barrel and lightweight stock are typical of the earlier 1862 production, but its flat-faced bayonet stud and British-style lockplate-screw escutcheons are more typical of 1863 production. The lock and bands are probably recent additions, the result of a skillful restoration using parts excavated from the ruins of the factory.

In August 1863, the termination of the state arms contract came as a personal blow to Charles Gates, for it also ended his exemption from Confederate military service. In February 1864, as the Clapp family turned to producing supply wagons for the Confederacy, Gates embezzled $5,000 from his partners and fled north. After the war, in a letter to his former friend Jacob Clapp, Gates explained that he "always held the resolution to run rather than go into the Rebel army."[1] Gates later became a successful lawyer in Chicago, albeit one with a secret past.

North Carolina contract rifle made by Clapp, Gates, and Company, Alamance Creek, fourth type (1863)

With its heavier stock and shorter 33½-inch barrel in .577 caliber, this rifle was probably manufactured in the summer of 1863. Its most distinctive feature is the awkwardly replaced bolster; it was meant to repair the original one, which had burst—a common problem for North Carolina rifles. Although the new bolster resembles the U.S. Model 1855–type used by the C.S. Armories at Richmond and Fayetteville, it is larger than normal, suggesting that it was replaced elsewhere. The hammer and the sword bayonet stud also appear to be replacements. On the buttplate just above the lower screw is a small "NC" stamp. Is this a reinspection or repair mark?

The most significant clue to the history of this gun is carved on the left buttstock: "WEW / Co. B 28TH / NORTH CAROLINA." The only soldier with these initials in this company was seventeen-year-old Private William E. Whitesides (or Whiteside), who enlisted on July 30, 1861, along with two older brothers. He fought at the Seven Days, Second Manassas, and Antietam before contracting typhoid fever in December 1862. Whitesides was transferred to a hospital in Charlotte, North Carolina, close to his home in Gaston County, in April 1863. His confinement there may have saved his life: 40 percent of his regiment was killed or wounded in July at Gettysburg. By April 1864, Whitesides had returned to active duty; he remained with his hard-fighting regiment through its surrender at Appomattox a year later. Two of his five brothers died in Confederate service.

It is believed that many North Carolina state contract rifles were used only for training purposes. Whitesides was probably issued this rifle in late 1863 or early 1864 in a North Carolina convalescent camp, where recovering soldiers would drill before being sent back to their regiments. It is unlikely that Whitesides carried his state rifle back to a regiment in Confederate service that was already well supplied with blockade-run British rifle-muskets. If such was indeed the case, this rifle may have never left the state, and was therefore most likely repaired at the Florence Armory.

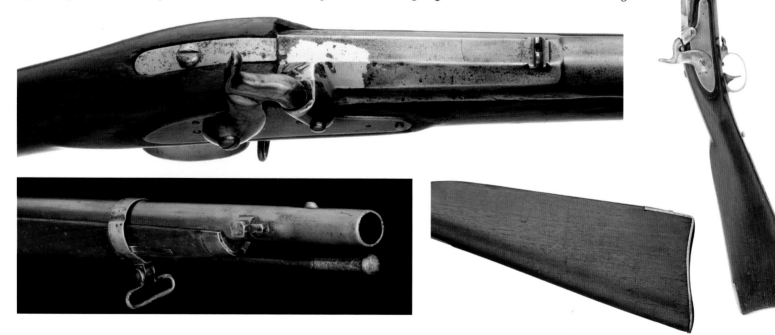

Governor Brown's State

Situated at the base of the Appalachian Mountains, Georgia was the strategic hinge point of the Deep South, linking the eastern and western halves of the Confederacy with an extensive railroad network and boasting the most advanced industrial infrastructure south of Richmond. Georgia thus became the ideal location for the Confederacy's most essential war industries, many of which relocated there from the western borderlands of the Confederacy in the wake of dramatic Union advances in early 1862. In February, the C.S. Ordnance Bureau moved the entire Nashville Arsenal to Atlanta, resuming the manufacture of ammunition and accoutrements, as well as the alteration and repair of small arms, in about two months' time. Arsenals in Louisiana and Mississippi followed soon after. In June, the Ordnance Bureau moved its infant revolver factory as well as the vital Harpers Ferry stocking machinery from Richmond to Atlanta and Macon. Ultimately, dozens of private arms manufacturers—including Cook and Brother, Leech and Rigdon, Greenwood and Gray, and Dickson, Nelson, and Company—all sought refuge in Georgia.

By the end of 1862, Georgia was home to four of the C.S. Ordnance Bureau's largest arsenals (Atlanta, Augusta, Macon, and Columbus), its sole source of gunpowder (the C.S. Powder Works at Augusta), its national revolver manufactory (Spiller and Burr in Atlanta), and its only permanent (but never completed) national armory at Macon. Georgia was also home to at least one hundred major private contractors, including the South's most prolific manufacturers of long arms (Cook and Brother in Athens) and revolvers (Griswold and Gunnison, near Macon), plus innumerable minor manufacturing operations spread out in small towns such as Dalton, Rome, Milledgeville, Dawson, and Adairsville. In Atlanta alone, 5,400 men and women—fully a quarter of the city's population in early 1864—were employed in war industries, both public and private. The combined output of governmental and private manufacturing establishments in Georgia exceeded even that of Richmond, transforming the state into the military-industrial heartland of the South.

Georgia was also home to Governor Joseph E. Brown, the Confederacy's most vocal proponent of states' rights. Brown envisioned Georgia as a semiautonomous self-sustaining state responsible for defending itself with its own troops. To that end, he balked at Confederate impressments of food, raw materials, and labor; he fought the Confederate army's attempts to seize control of his state-operated railroads. Brown was particularly irked by Confederate conscription laws, which drained more and more manpower from his state militia. The governor responded by raising new regiments of his own with men too old or too young for national

The entire force of Armorers & Machinists will be employed in the repair of arms as soon as the arms are received. . . . Those who neglect to do so after being notified will be sent to the front. You will make arrangements to fill the places of such watchmen as may be ordered to the front today with men unfit for Garrison Duty. You will substitute negroes for the white "helpers" also sent to the front. There is a great demand for infantry arms and the repair of arms must be pushed on vigorously.
—Confederate superintendent of armories James H. Burton to acting master armorer Jeremiah Fuss, Macon Armory, July 23, 1864

The houses, lands, and effects of the people of Georgia are daily seized and appropriated to the use of the Government or its agents without the shadow of law, without just compensation. . . . In this state of things the militia are necessary to uphold the civil tribunals of the State. . . . Measured by your standard this is doubtless disloyalty. Tested by mine it is high duty to my country.
—Georgia governor Joseph E. Brown to Confederate secretary of war James A. Seddon, November 14, 1864

service, believing that they would act as a deterrent against Confederate violations of state sovereignty and personal liberty. To a greater degree than any other state in the Confederacy, Georgia attempted to arm, equip, and clothe its own regiments, even those that later entered Confederate service.

As early as 1858, there was a movement to establish a national armory in Georgia as a means of economic development; following John Brown's raid in October 1859, the idea of building a Harpers Ferry for the Deep South gained traction as a means of self-defense. Yet as secession loomed in the fall of 1860, both time and economy dictated a simpler solution: state agents fanned out across the North to buy all the arms they could find — including Sharps and Maynard carbines, Colt revolvers, and Whitney "good and serviceable" rifles — but none were available in sufficient quantities. In January 1861, Georgia troops seized more than twenty-two thousand arms at the former U.S. Arsenal at Augusta, but all quickly went to regiments entering Confederate service. State agents spent another $100,000 buying arms in Britain, only to have many of them confiscated by Confederate authorities upon arrival at southern ports. Finally, at the end of 1861, the state legislature appropriated $350,000 for manufacturing its own rifles. In the buildings of the state penitentiary in the capital of Milledgeville, a former Harpers Ferry armorer named Peter Jones oversaw machinery built at the Tredegar Iron Works in Richmond or purchased from William Glaze of Columbia, South Carolina.

One of only two state-run armories in the Confederacy after 1861 (the other was in South Carolina), the Georgia Armory had a painfully brief lifespan as a rifle factory. Ultimately, the same shortages of raw materials and skilled labor that plagued the national armories and doomed the private ones also conspired against the Georgia Armory. From the late summer of 1862 through the spring of 1863, the armory was able to produce only about 350 rifles. Ironically, production ended in large measure because the Confederacy was finally able to provide arms (usually British or Austrian rifle-muskets) to all Georgia regiments entering national service. At the same time, the shrinking number of state troops required fewer state arms. Brown reached the same conclusion as North Carolina's governor Vance: a state-level arms industry simply did not make economic sense, especially when foreign imports were cheaper and of better quality than rifles made in Georgia. And so Governor Brown finally got his rifles, but then found he no longer needed them.

Determined to recoup the state's investment for the benefit its citizens, the ever-adaptable Brown refocused the armory on mass-producing cotton cards, which were needed to prepare ginned cotton for spinning. Although Georgia was the largest textile-producing state in the South, cloth produced in most of its thirty-eight mills was contractually obligated to the C.S. Quartermaster Bureau before it was ever woven. Brown reasoned that with an ample supply of cotton cards, at least civilians would have the means of making their own cloth. It was an odd end to the dream of a Harpers Ferry of the Deep South—or at least one under the control of a semiautonomous Georgia. Ironically, such an armory was founded at Macon—but under the strict control of the Confederate States of America.

In the end, the states' rights tug-of-war between Brown and the Confederacy was a moot point: Sherman's men made no distinction between national, state, or private war industries as they wrecked and burned their way through Georgia in 1864. The same factors that had transformed the state into the most critical military-industrial complex in the Confederacy also made it the most critical strategic target of the Union war effort. Its destruction was nothing less than fatal.

Rifle made by the Georgia Armory, Milledgeville, Georgia, serial number 30 (1862)

In December 1861, master armorer Peter Jones visited the C.S. Armories at Richmond and Fayetteville in his quest for machinery, patterns, and model arms for the State of Georgia. Not surprisingly, his new "Georgia Rifle" was patterned on the U.S. Model 1855–style rifles then being made in Fayetteville, though with rounded "winged" lockplate screw washers of the British style, perhaps copied from the Whitney "Enfield" rifles acquired by the state on the eve of war. The first few rifles were made in .58 caliber; in July 1862, the state switched to .577 to conform to the new Confederate (and British) government standard.

Bearing serial number 30 on the buttplate tang and under the barrel, this .58-caliber example is one of six known survivors. Its barrel bands, stock tip, and forearm forward of the rear band are replacements, made to restore the rifle to its original appearance after it had been cut down into a sporting configuration after the war. The number "48" on a brass plate on the buttstock is an inventory number attached by a modern collector.

It is believed that most Georgia Armory rifles, including this one, were issued to the Sixty-Third Georgia Infantry, which was formed in December 1862 from several smaller infantry and artillery units in the Savannah area. The Sixty-Third garrisoned Fort McAllister, Fort Thunderbolt, and Rosedew Island until May 1864, when it joined the Army of Tennessee in the Atlanta Campaign. The meaning of the letters "JB" carved into the stock remains a mystery; there were at least fifty soldiers in the regiment with those initials.

We have the satisfaction to announce that Georgia is now manufacturing in her State Prison a variety of arms, a specimen of which we examined a few days ago. . . . The "Georgia Rifle" with sword bayonet attached is a beautiful piece of workmanship, not surpassed by any arm manufactured in the United States or in Europe.
—"Georgia Armory," *Milledgeville Southern Recorder*, August 12, 1862

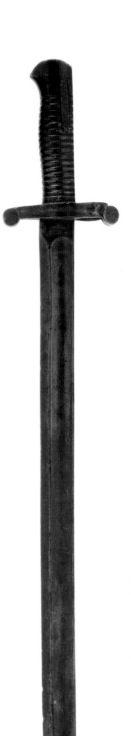

Sword bayonets made by the Georgia Armory, Milledgeville, Georgia, serial numbers 32 (1862) and 289 (1863)

Like the rifles for which they were made, Georgia Armory sword bayonets followed the U.S. Model 1855 pattern, with a grooved mortise designed to fit a stud on the barrel. The earliest 1862-dated bayonets featured a brass Model 1855–style hilt, while later 1863-dated bayonets featured a British-style wood and iron hilt. The stamped numbers were probably meant for matching each bayonet to its serial-numbered rifle; thus, bayonet number 32 does not fit rifle number 30. It is also possible that they were state inventory numbers, since the dies used for stamping the bayonet were different from those used to stamp the buttplate tang of the rifle.

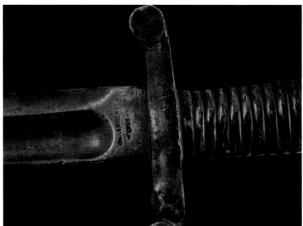

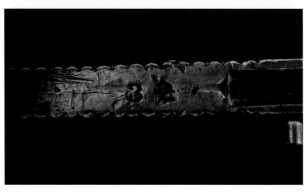

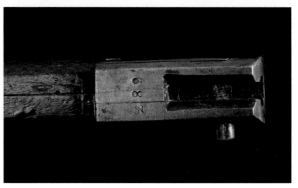

Georgia contract "D-Guard" side knife, maker unknown (1862)

After the disastrous Confederate defeats in Tennessee in February 1862, an unnerved Governor Brown, worried that his armory was not yet ready to fabricate rifles, exhorted Georgia's blacksmiths to instead make pikes and side knives. "Let every army have a large reserve, armed with a good pike, and a long heavy side knife," urged the governor in a public proclamation, "let them move in double quick time and rush with terrible impetuosity into the lines of the enemy."[2] Soon after, pattern knives were sent to prospective makers all over northern and central Georgia.

The state's offer of $4.60 for each knife, scabbard, and belt delivered to Milledgeville stimulated a veritable cottage industry in knife making. By June, the Georgia Armory was home to at least six thousand virtually useless pikes and about forty-nine hundred slightly more functional knives, all inspected by master armorer Peter Jones. Most were still collecting dust at the Armory in November 1864, when Sherman's men put it to the torch during the March to the Sea.

This neatly crafted example with an eighteen-inch blade is today one of the most commonly encountered of at least seven variants. It may have been fabricated by R. J. Hughes, a wagon maker in Monroe, or by J. W. and L. L. Moore of Atlanta, the two firms that together produced half of all knives delivered.

Confederate contract "Spiller and Burr" revolver assembled by the C.S. Armory at Macon, serial number 1086 (1864)

Among the many war industries that settled in Georgia was a public-private partnership formed in November 1861 between James H. Burton, then superintendent of the Richmond Armory, and Edward N. Spiller and David J. Burr, two entrepreneurs from Virginia. Backed by a massive $60,000 advance from the Confederate government, the Richmond Small Arms Factory planned to produce copies of Eli Whitney Jr.'s second-model .36-caliber "navy" revolver, then in production in New Haven, Connecticut. The Confederacy stood to gain at least fifteen thousand revolvers for its cavalry troopers, and each of the three partners stood to make a spectacular $116,000 in what seemed to be a relatively simple, low-risk venture. It turned out to be anything but.

In the wake of the Union offensive toward Richmond in June 1862, the factory was moved to the safer confines of Atlanta, where production got under way in September. The renamed Atlanta Pistol Factory suffered from a lack of skilled workers, a problem exacerbated by the army's refusal to release mechanics from service for a nominally private enterprise. In late 1863, after their best efforts had yielded only 854 revolvers, the partners finally gave up and sold the factory to the C.S. Ordnance Bureau, which then packed up the machinery and moved it to the Macon Armory in early 1864. Each partner walked away with a tidy $32,300, a far cry from their original expectations, but a far better return than most other private arms contractors realized.

Although the Confederate buyout eased the labor shortage, it could not end the shortage of raw materials. Burton had successfully substituted a brass frame for an iron one, but discovered that he could not safely substitute twisted iron rod for steel in the cylinders. Unfortunately, Edward Spiller, in what seemed to him a smart business move, had sold off the factory's excess steel the year before. To make up the shortfall, Burton purchased three tons of steel in England in August 1863, but the shipment was misplaced upon arrival in the South and did not appear in Macon until almost a year later. By April 1865, as the Pistol Department of the C.S. Armory at Macon closed its doors, total production stood at just 1,532 revolvers, one-tenth of the number originally envisioned. Meanwhile, the Whitneyville Armory in Connecticut had turned out about 33,000 all-steel revolvers of the same design.

This example was assembled in Macon about March 1864, probably from parts originally made in Atlanta; it almost certainly saw service in the Atlanta Campaign by cavalrymen of General Joseph Wheeler's command. The faint diagonal striations in the cylinder bear witness to the twisted iron rod used in its construction, and the nipples are all broken from hard use. Evidently, the trigger guard and wooden grips were also broken or damaged; they have been replaced with parts from a Whitney-made revolver.

Confederate contract revolver made by Griswold and Gunnison, Griswoldville, Georgia, second type, serial number 3024 (1864)

The most successful manufacturer of revolvers in the Confederacy was also one of its most unusual. Connecticut-born Samuel Griswold moved to Jones County, Georgia, in 1822, where he began a lucrative business making cotton gins. By 1860, he had established a prosperous New England–style manufacturing town along the railroad nine miles south of Macon, which included saw and grist mills, an iron foundry, a blacksmith shop, and a soap and candle factory in addition to houses, a store, a post office, and a church for his workers.

The outbreak of war afforded the seventy-one-year-old entrepreneur with new business opportunities. Griswold began in early 1862 by producing at least eight hundred pikes in answer to Governor Brown. Later that year, he was joined by a former employee and New Hampshire native named Arvin N. Gunnison, who had been displaced from his own cotton gin business in New Orleans when the city was captured. Together, the two men contracted with the C.S. Ordnance Bureau to fabricate brass-framed copies of the Colt third-model "dragoon" revolver.

But Griswoldville was no New England town: most of Griswold's workers were enslaved African Americans. "I found 22 machines worked by 24 hands," reported a Confederate agent in July 1862, "22 of whom are Negro slaves."[3] Griswold and Gunnison thus had an unbeatable business advantage: the only skilled labor force in the South beyond the reach of Confederate conscription. Although they suffered the usual material shortages, a captive labor force (forty workers by 1864), combined with the town's modest industrial infrastructure, allowed the partners to maintain their arms business long after most others had ceased to exist.

Griswold thus maintained a steady production of about 140 revolvers a month from October 1862 through November 1864, when his factories were put to the torch by Sherman's cavalry. Griswold and Gunnison had fabricated nearly 3,700 revolvers, more than any other manufacturer in the South, and almost as many as all others combined. While remarkable in the Confederacy, Griswold's production pales in comparison with the 649,000 Colt revolvers of four models manufactured in Connecticut between 1850 and 1865. The example pictured here was probably fabricated in June or July 1864 and likely saw service in the Atlanta Campaign.

Ammunition box made at the C.S. Arsenal at Columbus, Georgia, with bundle of .69-caliber buckshot ammunition (1862)

Perhaps Georgia's greatest material contribution to the Confederate war effort lay in its massive ammunition factories at Augusta, Atlanta, Macon, and Columbus, which together produced about thirty-nine million small arms cartridges during the war, or almost 20 percent of the Confederacy's total production. Given the ephemeral nature of paper cartridges and black powder, little evidence of this production has survived.

This October 1862–dated ammunition box is a rare exception. It was discovered in rural Georgia in the early 1990s, still partly filled with .69-caliber buckshot cartridges wrapped ten to a bundle. What makes these artifacts so significant is what they reveal about the nature of warfare in 1862. At a time when battlefields were still dominated by old .69-caliber muskets, most ammunition came in the form of round ball, buckshot, or "buck and ball," a deadly combination of the two. Buckshot was favored for close-quarters fighting, since flying lead pellets inflicted more wounds than any other type of round. Despite the dominance of smaller-bore rifle-muskets later in the war, Georgia arsenals continued to produce .69-caliber buckshot rounds for smoothbore-armed reserve or militia regiments through 1864.

The Odyssey of Francis and Ferdinand Cook

With a population approaching 170,000 in 1860, the booming port and commercial hub of New Orleans, Louisiana, was the sixth-largest city in the United States, and by far the largest city in the South. It was the ideal location for the British-born mechanics and entrepreneurs Ferdinand and Francis Cook to try their hand at making rifles of "Southern material, for Government purposes and without Government aid," thus proving that "rifles could be made here as well as in Yankee land or Europe."[4] In the summer of 1861, they collected $25,000 in private capital to set up a small armory, where about thirty employees began making copies of the British Pattern 1856 rifle at the rate of about ten guns a week.

Business was brisk. Over the next six months, the armory fabricated rifles, carbines, bayonets, scabbards, and waist belts for volunteer companies; naval cutlasses for the Confederate government; and at least eighteen hundred pikes for the State of Louisiana. In March 1862, the Cook brothers signed a contract for one thousand rifles for the State of Alabama. But it was the C.S. Ordnance Bureau that ensured the long-term success of the Cooks' enterprise with a contract for fifty thousand arms in early April 1862. By then, the Cook and Brother Armory was the largest private arms manufactory in the Confederacy, with four hundred employees making at least two hundred guns a month, or about thirteen hundred arms since its inception. But on the morning of April 24, 1862, Admiral David Farragut threatened to wipe out the booming business in a single stroke when his Union warships smashed through Confederate river defenses below New Orleans, guaranteeing the capture of the city within a day or two. The brothers moved quickly, commandeering two steamboats and loading on board as much of their machinery as possible for the journey upriver to Vicksburg. Left behind were steam engines, 130 tons of iron, and the entire machine shop. From Vicksburg, the heavy machinery was hauled overland to temporary facilities in Selma, Alabama, where workers assembled New Orleans–made parts to fulfill their order for the State of Alabama. By the end of the year, they had completed another eight hundred arms.

In August 1862, Ferdinand and Francis Cook purchased a vacant mill building in the small town of Athens, Georgia, about sixty-five miles east of Atlanta and connected to it by rail, seemingly far from the possible reach of Yankee armies. Borrowing heavily from the Confederate government, the brothers purchased additional machinery and enough raw materials (in particular, iron from Alabama) to resume production in March 1863. But their armory was still plagued by a shortage of skilled labor, and by the end of the year it had produced only twelve hundred additional arms. Confederate chief of ordnance Josiah Gorgas intervened, detail-

These rifles have been delicately tested against the English and Belgian arms of the same pattern, and have proved to be truer. Where some of the European barrels have been shown to be thicker on one side than the other, those of Mr. Cook's are true to a hair. . . . Mr. Cook, determined to establish from the very beginning a reputation for his rifles, spares no pains to make them perfect weapons in every respect, and weapons that will stand the rough use of battle.
—"The New Orleans Rifle Factory," *New Orleans Bee*, August 5, 1861

We are pained to learn that Maj. F. W. C. Cook, the gallant commander of the Athens Battalion, so greatly distinguished at the battles of Griswoldville and Honey Hill, was killed by a sharp-shooter at or near Hardeesville, S.C., one day last week. He was shot through the head. It is said he had shot five of the enemy's sharp-shooters before he received the fatal wound. Maj. Cook was a gallant soldier, and his loss will be deplored by all who knew him.
—*Athens Southern Watchman*, December 21, 1864

ing skilled workers from the army to assist the private enterprise in fulfilling its government contract. As a result, during the first seven months of 1864 the Cook and Brother Armory turned out approximately 4,500 rifles and carbines, or about 640 arms a month, a rate of production second only to that of the government-run Richmond Armory. Confederate superintendent of armories James H. Burton praised the firm, claiming that Ferdinand Cook "exhibited a much better appreciation of the requirements of an armory than any other person who has attempted a like enterprise in the Confederacy."[5]

Like virtually all private arms manufacturers in the South, Cook and Brother's increase in production came about only with an increased dependence on the Confederate government. By August 1864, the armory was in debt to the Confederacy for $250,000 and yet had not received a payment for arms since March. As inflation made Confederate currency practically worthless, the brothers struggled to feed their employees, using scarce raw materials as well as sugar boilers, syrup mills, and even spittoons made at the armory to barter for food. Trying to salvage a profit while they still could, the Cook brothers sought a deal with the C.S. Ordnance Bureau to sell their facilities, which they claimed were worth much more than their debt. The Ordnance Bureau, for its part, coveted the potential cost savings of cutting out the middleman.

Events on the battlefield almost scotched the deal. In September 1864, unable to pay their workers and faced with the previously unimaginable reality of a Yankee army on their doorstep, Ferdinand and Francis Cook were forced to halt production. With Major Ferdinand Cook in command and armed with the products of their own labor, the armory workers were organized as the Twenty-Third Battalion, Georgia Infantry, Local Defense. In November 1864, they joined with the Georgia militia in trying to slow Sherman's March to the Sea, fighting at Griswoldville, Georgia, and Honey Hill, South Carolina. On December 11, 1864, near Hardeeville, South Carolina, Major Cook was shot dead by a federal sharpshooter. It was the last straw for the Cook and Brother Armory. In spite of it all, they had managed to fabricate seventy-eight hundred rifles and carbines, the largest production of any private arms maker in the Confederacy.

Though General Sherman bypassed Athens and left the armory intact, its workforce had been decimated. Francis Cook reached an agreement with the C.S. Ordnance Bureau to sell his arms machinery to the government while still retaining title to the armory buildings. Incredibly, operation resumed in mid-March 1865, though it was limited to arms repair, not new production. Determined to the last,

James Burton sought to further consolidate governmental ordnance production by relocating the embryonic but now-threatened carbine factory in Tallassee, Alabama, to the newly established C.S. Armory at Athens. The war ended before his plans could be realized.

After the war, a heavily indebted Francis Cook sold the armory property to the Athens Manufacturing Company, which for many years operated a cotton mill in the buildings. Through the 1960s, local enthusiasts continued to unearth parts of arms and machinery on the grounds. After 150 years of adaptive reuse, the armory buildings are still in use today as offices on the University of Georgia campus.

Marks of Confederate loyalty

Cook and Brother arms are distinguished by the small C.S. first national-pattern flag stamped on the lockplate behind the hammer. The rather static flag on New Orleans–made arms (left) differed slightly from the "waving" Athens flag (right), which was often double-stamped, giving it a blurry appearance.

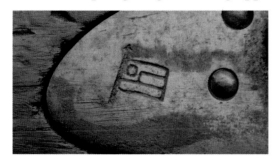 

Sword bayonet made by the Cook and Brother Armory, New Orleans, for the Sunflower Guards of Mississippi, number 10 (1861)

In July 1861, representatives of the Sunflower Guards, a volunteer company from Sunflower County in northwestern Mississippi, visited the newly established Cook and Brother Armory in search of arms. Impressed by what they saw, they placed one of the company's first orders: $5,000 for one hundred new rifles and accoutrements, complete with sword bayonets specially stamped on the hilt "SUNFLOWER GUARDS." The bayonets were designed for the fixed studs applied to the first few hundred Cook and Brother rifles. This one bears serial number 10 on the blade and guard.

In mid-September 1861, the first fifty of these arms were shipped to Virginia, where the Sunflower Guards were organized as Company I, Twenty-First Mississippi Regiment. The guards received their baptism of fire during the Seven Days battles near Richmond in the summer of 1862 and fought again at Sharpsburg (Antietam), Maryland, in September. During bitter street fighting in Fredericksburg, Virginia, on December 11, 1862, the Twenty-First Mississippi suffered eight killed, twenty-five wounded, and thirteen captured.

This bayonet may have belonged to one of those men. Along with the brass upper mount from its scabbard (the leather deteriorated long ago), it was excavated in the Fredericksburg area. It is one of only two examples known; the other was recovered near Sharpsburg.

Confederate or Alabama contract rifle, made by the Cook and Brother Armory, New Orleans, serial number 772 (1862)

Except for the very first arms produced, Cook and Brother rifles and carbines were stamped with consecutive serial numbers from the beginning of production in New Orleans to the end of production in Athens. For these noninterchangeable arms, serial numbers served the practical purpose of identifying parts, allowing each to be customized for a specific gun. These are the only arms made in the Confederacy to be so extensively marked; numbers are commonly found on lockplates, barrels, screws, stock tips, and other parts.

For present-day historians, consecutive serial numbers allow a reasonably accurate estimate of production dates based on documented numbers of deliveries. This rifle was probably fabricated about February 1862; it may have been among the first of the one thousand arms made for the State of Alabama, at least one hundred of which were issued to the Twenty-Eighth Alabama regiment.

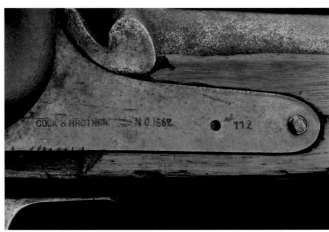

**Sword bayonet made by the Cook and Brother Armory,
New Orleans, number 770 (1862)**

*Like the British rifles from which they were copied, Cook and Brother rifles
were designed to be fitted with sword bayonets. But unlike British arms makers,
Ferdinand and Francis Cook believed (probably correctly) that brazing a sword
bayonet stud to the side of the barrel could weaken it at the muzzle. So the brothers
designed an adjustable—and therefore interchangeable—brass adaptor ring for
sword bayonets, similar to those being made in Massachusetts by the Colt Firearms
Company and in Virginia by Boyle, Gamble, and MacFee for U.S. Model 1841 rifles.*

*These adjustable adaptors, which are often found still attached to bayonet hilts,
should have made matching serial numbers on sword bayonets unnecessary.
Nevertheless, of nine Cook and Brother bayonets in the Wray Collection, four carry
serial numbers reaching into the 1100s, suggesting that interchangeability was
imperfect, at least through the end of production in New Orleans. It is extremely
unusual to find a bayonet and rifle numbered within two digits of each other. As
seen here, casting flaws in the brass hilt were common.*

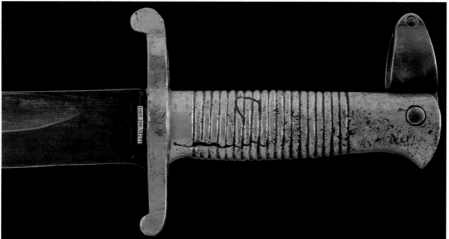

Confederate contract rifle made by the Cook and Brother Armory, Athens, serial number 6271 (1864)

Except for the omission of a long-range rear sight and a bayonet stud, Cook and Brother rifles were remarkably faithful and well-made copies of the .577-caliber British Pattern 1856 rifle. They were also among the most consistently configured arms in the Confederacy, varying in only a few minor details whether produced in New Orleans, Selma, or Athens. This one was probably fabricated in May 1864; the only significant difference between it and one made two years before is the simpler, one-piece trigger guard.

In accordance with Ordnance Bureau specifications ending the production of sword bayonets in January 1864, the front sight of this rifle has been placed 1.2 inches behind the muzzle so that a socket bayonet could be attached to it. Nevertheless, it still carries an adaptor ring, indicating that sword bayonets may have continued in use well into 1864. The ring remains on this rifle probably because it is so difficult to remove over the front sight.

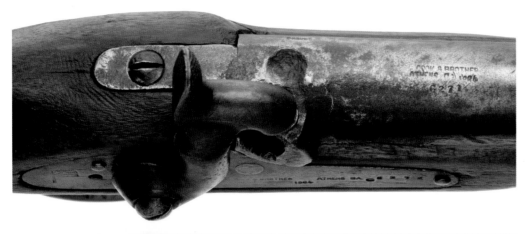

Confederate contract cavalry carbine made by the Cook and Brother Armory, Athens, serial number 7670 (1864)

With its distinctive ramrod swivel and a sling ring opposite the lock, this .58-caliber carbine is a direct copy of the British Pattern 1856 cavalry carbine. During the last year of the war, most Cook and Brother arms—whether designed for cavalry use or not—were issued to Confederate cavalry units in Tennessee, Georgia, and Alabama. This example was probably fabricated in July 1864, just before the armory was forced to cease production for lack of funds. Its serial number is among the highest known.

Confederate contract artillery carbine made by the Cook and Brother Armory, Athens, serial number 3625 (1863–64)

Except for the omission of a ramrod swivel and sling ring, the so-called artillery carbine was virtually identical to the cavalry carbine. Cook and Brother carbines of both types were issued almost exclusively to cavalry units in the western theater; at least sixty-three Cook and Brother artillery carbines were issued to Nathan Bedford Forrest's command in May 1864.

On the right side of the buttstock of this example are carved the words "NaNcy. / AL," which may refer to Albert Nanny ("Nancy" or "Nanney" in military and census records), a semiliterate thirty-five-year-old farmer from Marshall County, Kentucky, whose wife was named Nancy. Albert Nanny enlisted on October 6, 1861, in Company D, Seventh Kentucky Mounted Infantry, in which he served as a teamster in the regimental wagon train. In December 1862, Nancy was caught by Union troops on his way home to Marshall County, having earlier deserted his unit. While a prisoner of war in St. Louis, Nanny did his best to avoid being exchanged and sent back. In a dictated statement, Nanny asserted that his reason for enlisting was "opposition to the Federal Gov't whose policy I then understood was Emancipation of the Slave and Confiscation of Confederate property." He went on to claim, "I am willing to Enlist in Federal service and use my best Endeavors to crush the rebellion . . . [but] . . . on account of my health I would prefer taking the oath of allegiance." A week later, one of his interrogators wrote: "I would respectfully recommend exchange in this instance. This man is not to be trusted."[6] In the end, Nanny got his way: after taking a loyalty oath to the United States and promising not to leave Marshall County, he went home to his wife Nancy in June 1863. His promise was secured by a $1,000 bond signed by his older brother and a neighbor.

The serial number on this 1863-dated carbine indicates that it was probably produced in late 1863 or early 1864, at least six months after Albert Nanny had returned home. In that same month (June 1863), Albert's younger brother John A. Nanny traveled south from Marshall County to Paris, Tennessee, where he enlisted in the Twelfth Kentucky Cavalry on December 11; he deserted on May 23, 1864. On April 15, 1864, an eighteen-year-old Marshall County man named G. A. Nanny (probably a younger relation) enlisted in Albert Nanny's old outfit — Company D of the Seventh Kentucky Mounted Infantry; he deserted on June 8, 1864. Both regiments were in the same brigade under Forrest's command; both men bore the same middle initial (was the A for "Al" or "Albert"?) and deserted just before Forrest's spectacular victory at Brice's Crossroads, Mississippi; either man could have taken this carbine home with him. Perhaps John A. or G. A. Nanny then gave

it to Albert and Nancy. Or perhaps Albert Nanny violated his oath and joined Forrest, but there are no records to prove it. In any event, this carbine was likely connected with this family, which, like so many in Kentucky, felt a profound ambivalence about slavery, secession, and the Union.

Confederate contract naval cutlass made by the Cook and Brother Armory, New Orleans or Athens (1862–63)

In March and April 1862, the Cook and Brother Armory produced 563 cutlasses for the crews of the River Defense Fleet on the Mississippi River. Commanded by the Confederate army (additional vessels were under the command of the Confederate navy or the State of Louisiana), this ragtag fleet comprised fourteen merchant steamboats converted to military use, better known as "cottonclads." All six cottonclads defending New Orleans in April 1862 were lost; the other eight continued to operate through the summer.

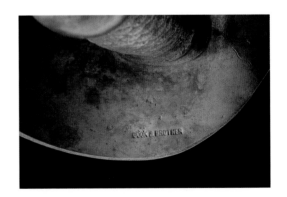

In February 1863, Cook and Brother delivered another five hundred cutlasses, this time for the Confederate navy. This close copy of the U.S. Model 1841 naval cutlass is probably one of these later deliveries; twenty-two Cook and Brother cutlasses of this type were captured with the css Tennessee *at the Battle of Mobile Bay, Alabama, on August 5, 1864. Given the rarity of hand-to-hand combat and ship-to-ship boarding actions in the Civil War, this cutlass is unlikely to have been used in combat.*

Alabama Iron

Alabama's greatest material contribution to the Confederate cause—and the genesis of its postwar industrialization—lay in the rich layers of limestone, coal, and iron ore of its north-central counties. In 1860, there were only six or seven blast furnaces for producing iron in the state. Between 1862 and 1865, the Confederate government financed the construction of thirteen more, which together produced more iron than all other Confederate states combined. In June 1863, as currency inflation made fixed-price contracts all but impossible, the C.S. Nitre and Mining Bureau was authorized to impress the output of all of Alabama's iron-making facilities. One of the largest and most significant of these was the Shelby Iron Works, located about twenty miles southeast of Birmingham. Shelby produced iron for virtually all the Alabama and Georgia arms makers, including the two most prolific, Cook and Brother, and Dickson, Nelson, and Company. Most of the rest of its output went into artillery, ammunition, and armor plate at the massive C.S. Arsenal at Selma.

Given its natural resources and seemingly safe location in the Deep South, Alabama appeared to be ripe for the development of an arms industry. On December 7, 1861, the state legislature passed "An Act to encourage the Manufacture of Fire Arms and Munitions in this State" that included a $250,000 appropriation for capitalizing new arms enterprises.[7] Governor John Gill Shorter, a longtime advocate of manufacturing as a means of achieving economic independence, supported the measure. The most ambitious proposal to acquire some of those funds came from Alabama quartermaster general Duff C. Green and the entrepreneurs Thomas E. McNeill and William B. Gilmer. In 1862, the state advanced some $500,000 to their newly formed Alabama Arms Manufacturing Company, while the Confederate government advanced another $200,000 to support its subsidiary, the Red Mountain Iron and Coal Company. In addition to breech-loading carbines, the partners proposed making copies of the British Pattern 1856 "Enfield" rifle. The success of their venture depended on James H. Burton, the Confederate superintendent of armories and former chief engineer at Britain's Royal Small Arms Factory—and the only man in the South who possessed a complete set of plans for the machinery needed to produce the rifles. Despite Burton's nominal assistance, by March 1864 the company had run through all the advance funds without fabricating a single arm.

Blaming failure on the not-unreasonable claim of "the difficulty in procuring suitable labour without coming into competition with the Confederate Government," the company offered to sell its Montgomery factory to the C.S. Ordnance Bureau, provided it would produce arms for the State of Alabama.[8] After inspecting

I cannot get ¼ enough men[,] what I have is some got out from New Orleans run the Blocade[,] yet in hopes to get in operation in about six weeks, this is the slowest country that I ever saw[,] nobody wants to do any thing but waite for Somebody Else to do a thing for them, Very discouraging for a Person in a hurry.
—Sylvester Bennett, superintendent, Alabama Arms Manufacturing Company, to James Burton, Confederate superintendent of armories, September 29, 1862

All detailed men and conscripts leaving their work or refusing to work, will at once be turned over to the nearest Enrolling Officer to be tried and punished as deserters.
—Regulations issued by the office of the C.S. Nitre and Mining Bureau, Selma, Alabama, June 1863

the facility, Burton diagnosed the real problem: the machines, purchased from a defunct New Orleans firm two years before, "present to the unexperienced eye the appearance of well-constructed machines," but in reality were "of cheap construction and not well adapted for the intended purpose."[9] The building was too small and the power plant unfinished; there was neither a model arm, nor tools or gauges, nor the mechanical expertise to make them; and the cost of accomplishing any of those things would have been prohibitive. Burton wisely declined the offer. Alabama authorities had learned a hard lesson: there was more to creating an arms industry than local iron, some cheap machinery, and enthusiastic but naive (or possibly crooked) businessmen.

Although its half-million-dollar investment in the Alabama Arms Manufacturing Company went to waste, the state's advances to smaller companies yielded tangible results, though often in negligible quantities. Over the course of the war, the State of Alabama arranged contracts for copies of the U.S. Model 1841 rifle with seven gun-making companies: Wallis and Rice in Talladega; Casper Suter and Company in Selma; Christian Kreutner in Montgomery; Lewis G. Sturdivant and Company in Talladega; Davis and Bozeman in Coosa County; Dickson, Nelson, and Company in Colbert County (eventually relocated to Dawson, Georgia); and Greenwood and Gray in Columbus, Georgia (just east of the Alabama state line). Of these, only the last four delivered rifles in any quantity; Wallis and Rice delivered no arms, Kreutner only about 36, and Suter and Company just 50. The most successful contractor was Dickson, Nelson, and Company, which, despite four moves in three years, may have produced upward of 3,600 arms of all types (including, perhaps, repaired older arms), though only 645 new rifles are actually documented. Otherwise, the grand total produced by all seven contractors was about 2,500 rifles and carbines.

In 1863, as its investment in the Alabama Arms Manufacturing Company evaporated and with much of northern Alabama occupied by Union forces, the state redoubled its efforts to secure arms from its contractors. In the end, southwestern Georgia turned out to be one of the safest regions of the Confederacy, a place where Dickson, Nelson, and Company, and Greenwood and Gray could, unlike virtually all other southern arms makers, work unmolested through the closing months of the war. Only the arrival of James H. Wilson's Union cavalrymen in April 1865 ended their operations.

Alabama contract rifle believed to have been made by Lewis G. Sturdivant and Company, Talladega (ca. 1863)

This badly weathered rifle is believed to be one of the only surviving arms made by the jeweler turned gunsmith Lewis G. Sturdivant. In March 1862, Sturdivant secured a state contract for two thousand rifles and rented a workshop on West Battle Street in Talladega. Despite advances from the state totaling some $21,000, Sturdivant immediately ran into trouble in obtaining skilled workmen and keeping them out of the army. "Mr. Sturdivant says you told him that all who were to work on these guns would be exempt from enrollment or conscripts," wrote one of his employees to Governor John Gill Shorter. "I want to know as soon as possible so I will know what to do."[10]

This .54-caliber rifle is distinguished by its short, 46½-inch length, a lightweight stock, and diminutive furniture, of which only the hammer appears to be full sized. The only markings are "22" inside the lock and hammer (probably a serial number) and "76" on the buttplate tang (probably an inventory number). If the serial number of this rifle is indeed 22, it could have been made by Christian Kreutner or Suter and Company. If the serial number is 76, it must have been made by Sturdivant, since all other Alabama contractors who made more than fifty guns are identified by lockplate markings.

There are no visible remains of any proof or acceptance marks on the barrel. Sturdivant delivered 280 rifles in 1863 and 1864 under order of the governor without going through the usual state inspection process. These guns were issued directly to the First Regiment of Alabama Reserves in the defenses of Mobile. Other Sturdivant arms are believed to have been rejected for their unusually small size and fragile construction. The bottom of the trigger guard of this example is dented, giving it an unusually rectangular appearance.

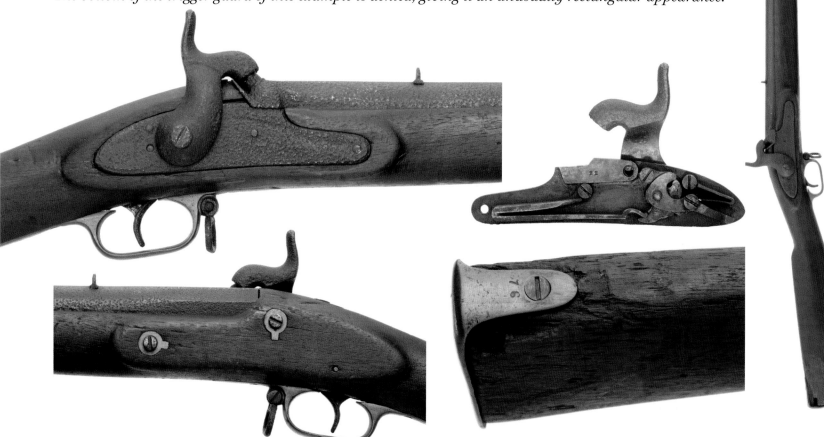

Alabama contract rifle believed to have been made by Davis and Bozeman, Coosa County, serial number 57 (ca. 1863)

In early 1862, the cotton-gin manufacturers Henry J. Davis and David W. Bozeman applied their mechanical skills to the fabrication of 1,000 .58-caliber copies of the U.S. Model 1841 rifle. Deliveries of the first 280 rifles began in October 1863, but state inspectors rejected almost half of them because of poor barrels and weak mainsprings. Davis and Bozeman cut down some of the rejected rifles into carbines and struggled to improve the quality of their arms. It took almost a year before they again submitted rifles for inspection.

This unmarked rifle is believed to be one of the company's early failures. It was fashioned using an octagonal Kentucky-style flintlock rifle barrel that was turned over (note the old sight slot on the underside), fitted with a new bolster, and rounded off from the rear band forward. The matching slash-marked roman numerals underneath the barrel and breech-plug tang are consistent with later Davis and Bozeman manufacture, as are the unusually narrow grooves in the .54-caliber rifling. However, unlike most 1864-dated examples, this one has a U.S. Model 1841–style sideplate and rounded British-style clamping barrel bands instead of flat, spring-retained ones.

The serial number 57 under the barrel suggests that this arm was among the first lot of eighty rifles submitted for inspection on October 1, 1863, of which thirty were rejected. At some point, perhaps after failing initial inspection, the barrel was cut down from the normal rifle length of thirty-three inches to only thirty inches, giving the rifle an oddly stunted appearance. As indicated by the beveled grooves on the face of the muzzle, the barrel was rifled (or rerifled) at this length. Yet it would also appear that rifling made the barrel too thin at the muzzle, essentially ruining the gun. Not surprisingly, this arm bears no state acceptance mark.

Alabama contract rifle made by Davis and Bozeman, Coosa County, serial number 220 (1864)

In September 1864, Davis and Bozeman submitted 680 rifles for inspection, but this time, only 52 failed. The lockplate of this rifle bears a faint "D&B" over "Ala" forward of the hammer, and the date "1864" behind it. The state acceptance mark "ALA. 1864" is stamped into the barrel opposite the lock. Though rifled in the same distinctive pattern as the previous example, the barrel is in .58 caliber.

Despite representing an obvious improvement in quality, this rifle still bears all the hallmarks of painfully slow hand assembly. Because the wood of each lock cavity had to be hand-finished to accommodate each lock, the serial number 220 is stamped inside both parts as well as on the hammer. Likewise, since each breech plug had to be customized for each barrel, the roman numeral XIV appears on both parts. Additionally, the arabic numeral 16 stamped on the bottom of the barrel matches the same number penciled into the stock channel. The mark "VIX" has been stamped into the channel, perhaps an intentional reversal of the "XIV" on the barrel and breech plug or else an incorrect rendering of "16." These often-inconsistent roman numerals were really just personal assembly codes invented by individual workers who could apply them quickly with a single punch mark instead of a set of arabic-numeral stamps.

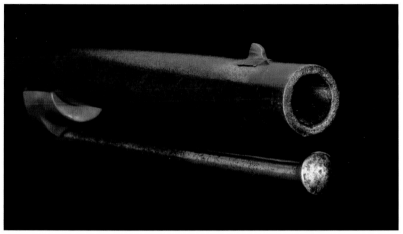

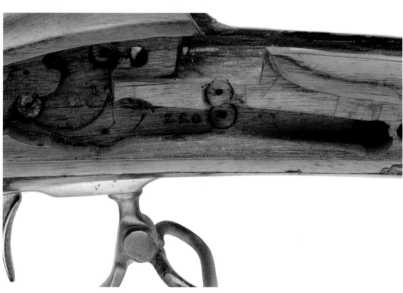

Alabama contract carbine believed to have been made by Davis and Bozeman, Coosa County (1864)

This carbine was built around a cut-down rifle barrel (perhaps one of the ones rejected by state inspectors in 1863), but its stock and bands were cut and spaced for a carbine. Nevertheless, the stock was incorrectly milled by about an eighth of an inch, as seen by the small slot that had to be cut out of the rear band to accommodate the band spring. The stock forward of the rear band is a modern replacement; the U.S. Model 1841 nose cap—which makes this carbine resemble those built by Greenwood and Gray—was not originally part of the arm.

Although its lockplate is unmarked, this carbine bears common Davis and Bozeman characteristics, including the rifling and internal markings. The assembly number 1 is stamped inside the lock and lock cavity, as well as on the heads of the lockplate screws, while the buttplate is marked with a single dot. This barrel, as well as all others accepted by the State of Alabama, was marked with "PRO" ("proved"), "FCH" (Frederick C. Humphries, commander of the C.S. Arsenal at Columbus, Georgia), "ALA." (Alabama), and the year of inspection. When not inspecting barrels for the Confederacy, Humphries did so on behalf of the State of Alabama.

Like the gun makers of Guilford County, North Carolina, Davis and Bozeman's qualitative improvement could only go so far before being outweighed by the state's financial burdens. In November 1864, Alabama canceled its contract with Davis and Bozeman and turned its workers over to Confederate enrollment officers. By then the state had purchased a total of 922 rifles and 109 carbines at an inflated cost of nearly $60,000, or about $58 an arm.

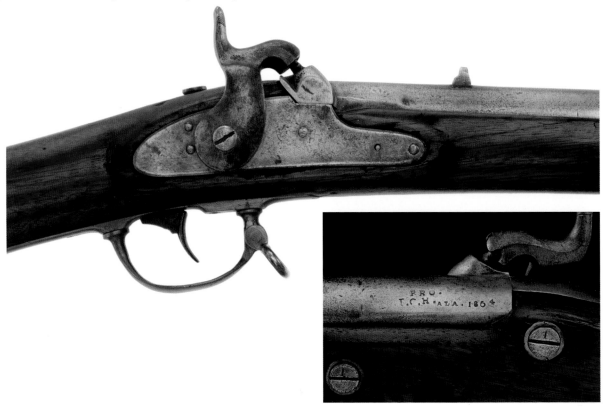

Alabama contract rifle made by Greenwood and Gray, Columbus, Georgia, third type (1864)

In January 1862, Eldridge S. Greenwood and the brothers William C. and John D. Gray set up a small private armory near the C.S. Arsenal at Columbus. Greenwood and William Gray had been the proprietors of a cotton warehouse; John Gray ran a toolmaking company. To supervise operations at the armory, the partners hired a thirty-seven-year-old New York–born gunsmith named John P. Murray, who had been in the sporting-arms business about six blocks away. The lockplates of most Greenwood and Gray arms bear the same name stamp that Murray had used in his own business.

Greenwood and Gray managed to secure contracts for rifles and carbines with both the State of Alabama and the C.S. Ordnance Bureau. The first rifles produced for Alabama bore nose caps, bands, and sideplates copied from the U.S. Model 1841 rifle; subsequent production for the Confederacy featured U.S. Model 1855–style stock tips, bands, and lockplate washers. This is one of the later-style arms, but as indicated by the "ALA" stamp beside the proof and inspection marks, it was fabricated for the State of Alabama, which accepted at least 262 Greenwood and Gray rifles between October 1863 and November 1864.

Unusually, there is a slot in the barrel for a sword bayonet stud, but it has been placed incorrectly and is too far back from the muzzle to fit a bayonet. Instead, the barrel features an adjustable bayonet adaptor patented and produced by Boyle, Gamble, and MacFee of Richmond.

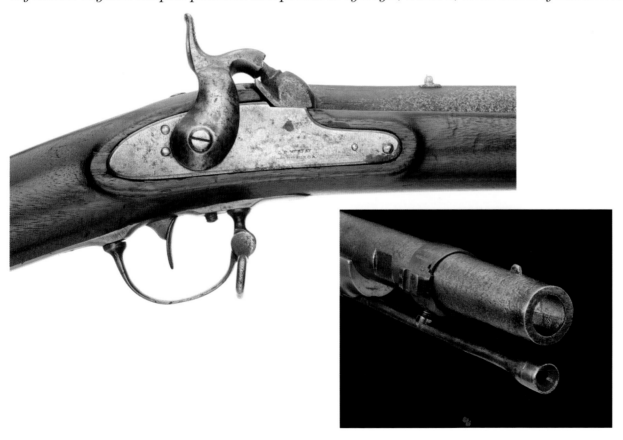

Alabama contract rifle made by Dickson, Nelson, and Company, Dawson, Georgia, second type (1865)

In late 1861, William Dickson (a planter from northern Alabama), Owen Nelson (an attorney from Tuscumbia), and Lewis H. Sadler (a physician from Leighton) formed the Shakanoosa Arms Company in Colbert County, Alabama, to take advantage of the state's incentives for new arms businesses. With a state contract and $7,000 in advance funding, the future of the company looked bright.

But in the summer of 1862, before the Shakanoosa factory could be completed, Union forces advancing toward Corinth, Mississippi, forced its relocation to the safety of Rome, Georgia. Operations there had barely begun when fire gutted the armory on September 4, 1862, destroying all the machinery. Under the name Dickson, Nelson, and Company, the enterprise started over again in nearby Adairsville, Georgia, but in August 1863, Union incursions from Chattanooga forced operations to move south to Macon. In February 1864, Dickson, Nelson, and Company settled in Dawson, Georgia (its fourth and final move), about sixty miles southeast of Columbus. There the hard-luck company made most of its rifles; at least 645 (and probably many more) were accepted by the State of Alabama.

Aside from the omission of an unnecessary implement compartment, this sturdy 1865-dated rifle is a faithful copy of the U.S. Model 1841 and one of the best-quality southern arms manufactured during the Civil War. Like many other Alabama contract rifles, it lacks a sword bayonet stud, suggesting that it was intended to be fitted with a bayonet adaptor ring. This arm bears the "ALA. 1865" acceptance marks on the barrel opposite the lock, as well as the "windmill" stamp of state inspector Nathaniel D. Cross under the barrel.

Carbine stock blank made for or by Dickson, Nelson, and Company, Dawson, Georgia (1865)

This is one of dozens of carbine-length walnut stock blanks found after the war in one of the Dickson, Nelson, and Company factory buildings in Dawson. The company was evidently preparing to make a large number of carbines when the end of the war interrupted its plans. Unlike the C.S. Armory at Macon, Dickson, Nelson, and Company found a reliable source of walnut.

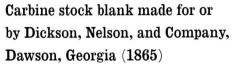

Texas Rifles

Like many of its neighbors east of the Mississippi River, the Lone Star State found itself woefully short of military arms by mid-1862. The fifty-four hundred muskets, rifles, and carbines seized at the U.S. Arsenal at San Antonio the year before had long ago been issued, and although there were still as many as forty thousand shotguns and sporting rifles in the state, few were suitable for military use. Many regiments drilled and even took to the field with no arms at all. Operating on a shoestring line of communications stretching fifteen hundred miles east to Richmond—a line effectively cut by Union control of the Mississippi River in the summer of 1863—Governor Francis R. Lubbock had no choice but to fall back on the sparse resources of his own state. Armed with the proceeds of a $500,000 issue of state bonds, the newly formed Texas Military Board signed contracts with five new arms-making firms in the summer and fall of 1862: D. E. Bartley of Hempstead (Waller County); Short, Biscoe, and Company of Tyler (Smith County); Whitescarver, Campbell, and Company of Rusk (Cherokee County); Billups and Hassel (or Billups and Son) of Mound Prairie (Anderson County); and N. B. Tanner and Company of Bastrop (Bastrop County). The first two enterprises produced virtually nothing under their state contracts; the last three managed to turn out a mere seventeen hundred rifles.

State contracts called for these rifles to be approximate copies of the U.S. Model 1841, but with the back-action locks and single lockplate screws characteristic of locally made Kentucky-style rifles. The resulting "Texas" rifles bore a much closer resemblance to French pattern arms of the 1850s, making them unlike any others manufactured in the Confederacy. Yet given the similarities in contract specifications and the extreme rarity of surviving examples—the Wray Collection's two Texas state contract rifles may be the only ones extant—it is difficult to distinguish the products of one manufacturer from another. What is clear from both documentary and material evidence is that these rifles were of notoriously poor quality. "I would not use them if I had shotguns or the ordinary hunting rifle," reported one commander in north Texas. "I was compelled to take this poor apology for a weapon or leave these troops behind."[11] Even so, soldiers issued with Texas contract rifles were considered well armed compared with most others.

The most ambitious state arms-manufacturing partnership was that of the Tyler gunsmiths James C. Short and William S. N. Biscoe, formed with the pecuniary backing of a successful merchant named George Yarbrough in May 1862. Armed with a state contract for five thousand rifles, Short, Biscoe, and Company purchased 125 acres just south of town and there constructed its own private armory. From the beginning, the enterprise was plagued by problems, especially a shortage

I would call your attention especially to this arm. A regiment armed completely with these guns are armed but badly. These guns are nothing more than a cheat, badly put together, and very unreliable, being liable, a great number, to burst.
—Captain Julius J. DuBose to Brigadier General Samuel B. Maxey, commanding the District of the Indian Territory, 1864

We have had much troubles about stock timber and a large number of our hands have been sick. We have been delayed on account of unexperienced hands, having to take such as we could get, as we have been invariably refused gunsmiths from the regular army, and we are much annoyed by hands wanting advanced wages, as everything has so much advanced above the usual prices of the Guns.
—Report of Short, Biscoe, and Company to the Texas Military Board, September 17, 1863

of skilled labor. In September 1862, Short complained to the governor that Confederate authorities had refused his requests to release skilled men from the army because "it is a private enterprise for the State, and that they are not to be benefited by it, and that you, as Governor of the State, had refused to let them have arms belonging to the State to arm their regiments, etc."[12] Despite repeated pleas from the governor and other state authorities, the impasse between the State of Texas and the Confederate government continued unabated for the next year.

As a direct result, by September 1863, Short, Biscoe, and Company had managed to deliver only a single model arm. Although one hundred rifles were nearing completion, that number was nowhere near the five hundred that the company was supposed to have delivered in August. The following month, the Texas Military Board reached the same conclusion as the State of Tennessee had two years earlier: the only solution was to sell out to the Confederacy, which was already confiscating most of the state's production anyway. "Under the direct control of the Government," the board commented, "much more dispatch in the manufacture of these arms could be obtained."[13] In the process, the Confederate States of America paid Short, Biscoe, and Company $100,000 for its land, buildings, and machinery in Tyler, enabling the partners to repay $25,000 advanced by the state of Texas and still break even on their failed venture. It was a far more successful outcome than that of most other private arms makers in the South.

Beginning in December 1863, the private armory built for Texas functioned as a national armory for the Confederacy, though it operated virtually independently of central-government control. In Tyler was concentrated all available arms-making machinery in the Trans-Mississippi Department, including machinery evacuated from Arkadelphia and Little Rock, Arkansas, as well as whatever could be purchased from state contractors at the end of their production. Over the next sixteen months, the former Short, Biscoe, and Company employees turned Confederate government workers (including the long-sought workers detailed from the army) completed 2,223 arms of at least five types, depending upon which kinds of used or captured barrels were available. All other features, such as forward-action locks and iron French-style nose caps, were remarkably standardized. Production included .577-caliber "Texas" rifles (nearly identical to state contract arms but with forward-action locks), .54-caliber "Hill" rifles (named for armory commander Gabriel H. Hill), .577-caliber "patent breech" rifles (made with barrels taken from old Hall breech-loading rifles), and .577-caliber "Enfield" and .54-caliber "Austrian" rifles (made with barrels taken from British Pattern 1853 and Austrian Pattern 1854 rifle-muskets). Hundreds of other arms, including civilian sporting arms, were repaired, restocked, or altered to percussion.

Unlike virtually all its counterparts, the C.S. Armory at Tyler operated without interruption from Union military incursions through May 1865. With news of the collapse of the Confederacy east of the Mississippi River, most of the armory workforce simply walked away, leaving only a few men to guard the twelve hundred arms stored there. A few days before the formal surrender of the Trans-Mississippi Department, Confederate brigadier general Joseph O. "Jo" Shelby sent a regiment to take charge of the guns, some of which are believed to have been traded the following month for passage into Mexico by Shelby and six hundred of his diehard Missourians. At the armory, remaining stockpiles of gunpowder and ammunition were blown up, leaving a massive crater. Union troops occupied the site and turned it over to the U.S. War Department, which sold off the property in 1866.

Today, the fate of almost all Tyler Armory rifles is a mystery; only eight are known to survive intact. There are even fewer extant state contract rifles. Because some of the units armed with Texas-made rifles did not surrender formally at the end of the war, many rifles probably went home with the troops, where they were used until discarded. In the lean and turbulent years after the war, few people in the region had the luxury of saving guns as keepsakes. It is also likely that many rifles stored at the Tyler Armory were intentionally destroyed at the end of the war. In 1931, a group of twenty-nine Tyler locks, all showing evidence of use, were found stashed away in a post of the Grand Army of the Republic (GAR), the Union veterans association. The precise origin of the locks has never been firmly established, but it is possible that soldiers of either side detached them as a means of disabling the arms. Today these locks constitute the largest single source of physical evidence relating to the Tyler Armory.

Texas contract rifle believed to have been made by Billups and Hassell (Billups and Son), Mound Prairie (or Plenitude), Texas (1863)

Because the contract specifications for Texas state rifles varied only slightly, details within the specifications provide vital clues for identifying otherwise-unmarked arms. In this case, the presence of an ordinary, notched-block rear sight — not the "raised sights, style of the Sharps" specified in the contract for Whitescarver, Campbell, and Company — suggests that this rifle was a product of either Billups and Hassel or N. B. Tanner and Company.

Fortunately, there are other clues: carved into the butt is "William Malloy" (right side) and "TEX" (not shown), which links the rifle to a twenty-three-year-old private in the Twenty-Ninth Texas Cavalry. In May and June 1863, Whitescarver, Campbell, and Company and Billups and Hassel are known to have delivered five hundred Texas rifles to William H. Steele's command in the Indian Territories, where the Twenty-Ninth was serving. Since it lacks the Whitescarver "raised sights," and since there were no known deliveries of Tanner rifles to Steele's command, this rifle was probably made by Billups and Halsell, a partnership between the cotton gin manufacturer John D. Billups and a wealthy farmer and slaveholder named Daniel D. Hassell. The business produced 650 rifles in the small, later-abandoned town of Mound Prairie (also known as Plenitude) southeast of Dallas. By early 1864, Billups had brought his son Joseph into the business and renamed it Billups and Son.

Unfortunately, little is known about Private Malloy. He enlisted in the Twenty-Ninth Texas Cavalry in April 1862, and in June 1863 was listed as "under arrest at Brigade Headquarters."[14] No cause was given and no further record exists, though it is likely he was among the many deserters from this regiment. It is unknown whether he was present when the Twenty-Ninth fought its most famous engagement, at Honey Springs, Indian Territories, facing the First Kansas ("colored") Infantry on July 17, 1863.

Malloy's rifle is undoubtedly the crudest arm in the Wray Collection, with an ungainly, thick-walled barrel and undersized, poorly made iron bands. It is also one of the most heavily used: the wood behind the bolster has been chipped away (despite a nail inserted for repair), the .577-caliber rifling has been worn smooth, and the ramrod is a replacement from a British Pattern 1853 rifle-musket. Such wear suggests that this rifle may have been issued to another soldier or perhaps that Malloy took it home with him when he left the army.

Texas contract rifle believed to have been made by N. B. Tanner and Company, Bastrop, Texas (ca. 1863)

Given its missing back-action lock and near-relic condition, positive identification of this .577-caliber state-contract rifle is almost impossible. Nevertheless, its French-style nose cap and triangular lockplate-screw washer distinguish it from the previously identified Billups and Hassel rifle; likewise, it does not feature the raised sights thought to be characteristic of Whitescarver, Campbell, and Company rifles. By process of elimination, this rifle, once thought to have been made in Arkansas, is believed to be the work of the Bastrop gun maker Napoleon B. Tanner. With the blacksmiths James R. Nichols and Adolf A. Erhard, Tanner completed 294 arms for the State of Texas from mid-1862 through early 1864.

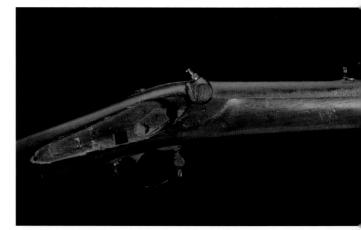

With better luck and a little cooperation from the Confederacy, Tanner and Company could have made more rifles. In July 1862, three weeks after Tanner made his first deliveries, a fire destroyed his workshop. It took until May 1863 for Erhard, who had enlisted in the Confederate army sixteen months earlier, to be detailed back to Tanner and Company to make barrels. By December 1863, the skyrocketing cost of iron had nearly driven Nichols and Erhard out of business. "To make gun barrels & bayonets longer at $9 I beg to decline," wrote Nichols. "I have a family to support which is my only care."[15]

Unlike Billups and Hassel, N. B. Tanner and Company rifles were to be fitted for sword bayonets. With a notch on the left of the muzzle and a small peg underneath the front sight, the barrel of this rifle was clearly designed for such a bayonet (probably one with a screw attachment device), though an example has never been found. As with all Texas contract rifles, the first of Tanner's guns were made in .54 caliber, but by 1863 all were being made to the Confederate standard of .577 caliber. This one still retains its crisp six-land-and-groove rifling.

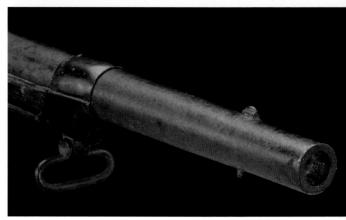

Sword bayonets believed to have been made for Texas contract rifles (ca. 1863)

Featuring unusually severe "yataghan" curves in their blades, these sword bayonets are thought to have been made for the Texas Military Board. Their muzzle sockets fit the oversized barrels of the two contract rifles pictured previously, but were clearly not intended for either: Billups and Hassel's contract called for socket bayonets, and Tanner and Company appears to have used a different mounting system. It is possible that these bayonets were made for the 750 rifles produced by Whitescarver, Campbell, and Company, none of which are known to survive. It is also possible that these bayonets were intended to be fitted to sporting rifles or to Tyler Armory rifles, perhaps with the use of an adaptor ring. The one at left bears mating number 36 on the grip; the other is unmarked.

Lock made by the C.S. Armory at Tyler, Texas, "Enfield" configuration, serial number 64 (1864)

The Tyler Armory produced the most elaborately marked and thoroughly numbered arms in the Confederacy. Each lockplate was stamped with the type and caliber of the arm (perhaps to ensure the use of correctly sized ammunition), and barrels, lock interiors, and other parts were stamped with corresponding serial numbers. Different serial-number ranges were used for different types of arms.

Between September 1864 and March 1865, the armory built 508 "Enfield" rifles based on .577-caliber British Pattern 1853 rifle-musket barrels scrounged from battlefields in Louisiana and Arkansas. Featuring a reworked British-made hammer, this lock was fabricated for one of the 181 rifles assembled in September 1864, most of which were issued to the Thirty-Third Texas Cavalry (battle flag featured in chapter 8). The lock was among those recovered from the GAR cache in 1931, suggesting that the rifle-musket to which it once belonged was destroyed at the armory in May 1865.

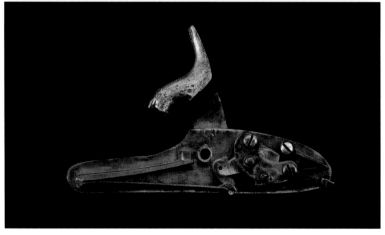

Lock made by the C.S. Armory at Tyler, Texas, "Austrian" configuration, serial number 42 (1865), with reconstructed rifle-musket (ca. 1975)

In January and February 1865, the Tyler Armory assembled fifty-four "Austrian" rifles using .54-caliber Austrian Pattern 1854 rifle-musket barrels that had been scavenged from battlefields along with the five hundred British rifle-muskets. This lock, also from the GAR cache, is one of only four of its type known to survive and the only one to make use of a hammer taken from an Austrian rifle-musket.

The lock is the only part of this arm made in Tyler during the war. All other parts, including the Austrian Pattern 1854 rifle barrel, were built around the lock in the 1970s as a reconstruction. The only known complete and original Tyler "Austrian" rifle is part of the Claud Fuller Collection at the Chickamauga and Chattanooga National Military Park.

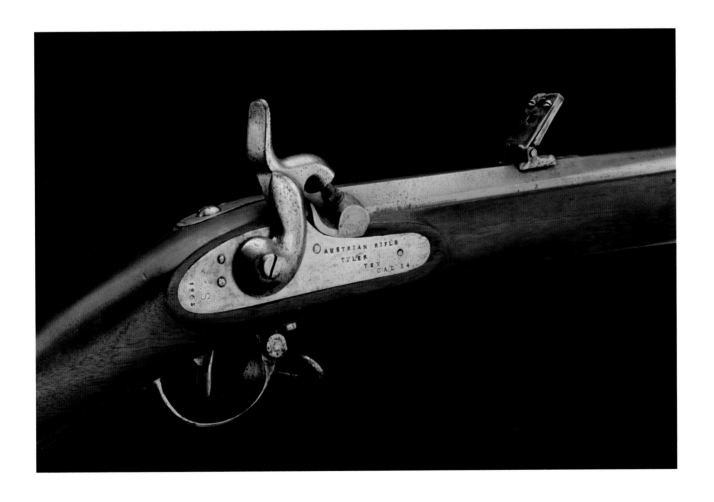

Sword bayonet and scabbard made by the C.S. Armory at Tyler, Texas (1863–64)

Made with a solid iron hilt, this sword bayonet is thought to be unique to the Tyler Armory. The 1862 contract between Short, Biscoe, and Company and the State of Texas mentioned "the improved bayonet invented by Mr. Short," which was to "have a point of five inches of steel, and the remainder to be of good iron, well tempered."[16] It is believed that the 331 bayonets produced by the Tyler Armory in late 1863 and early 1864 were of Short's crude but effective design and were meant to be attached to the barrels of "Texas" rifles using brass adaptor rings. It is probable that production ended because of the shortage of iron.

5. Guns for Cotton

On April 19, 1861, President Abraham Lincoln declared a military blockade of all southern ports as a means of starving the Confederacy into economic ruin. Like the bombastic Senator Wigfall, many Confederate leaders expected Britain to use military force to break the U.S. Navy blockade and keep its vital textile industry supplied with southern cotton. With precisely this goal in mind, southern planters intentionally withheld their cotton shipments from Britain in 1861. Intervention did indeed follow, but not in the way they anticipated. As it turned out, King Cotton diplomacy failed: the world's superpower remained neutral throughout the war. No British soldiers, warships, or in-service government arms ever fired a shot in defense of the Confederacy. Yet in the hands of the Confederate army and navy, English ships, weapons, and supplies—all privately made and mostly legal under British neutrality laws—kept the southern nation alive for four long years in the face of otherwise overwhelming northern material superiority. After 1862, at least a third of the Confederacy's raw materials and military equipment and two-thirds of its firearms were imported from Britain. Instead of political leverage, cotton became the Confederacy's currency of necessity as it tried to barter its way to independence through a largely porous blockade.

Confederate chief of ordnance Josiah Gorgas had no illusions about the South's capacity for producing modern firearms: at the start of the war, he dispatched to Britain a thirty-year-old Massachusetts-born artillerist and military instructor named Caleb Huse to buy as many arms as he possibly could. From the dozens of specialized designs developed by the British army, Huse tried to select the best and most modern arms whenever he could. His weapon of choice was the .577-caliber British Pattern 1853 "Enfield" rifle-musket, one of the most technologically advanced weapons of its time and the arm that most closely resembled (and had helped inspire) the U.S. Models 1855 and 1861. The British government was making first-class interchangeable versions of the Pattern 1853 at the Royal Small Arms Factory at Enfield (just north of London), but they were reserved for the British army. Confederate agents thus entered the shadowy world of the

We are a peculiar people, sir! We are an agriculture people; we are a primitive but a civilised people. . . . We want no manufactures; we desire no trading, no mechanical or manufacturing classes. As long as we have our cotton, our rice, our sugar, our tobacco, we can command wealth to purchase all we want from those nations with which we are in amity.
—Texas senator Louis T. Wigfall to the British war correspondent William Howard Russell, May 1861

You will purchase at the earliest possible moment all the arms suitable for our purposes which can be obtained, from whatever places and at whatever price. . . . Spare no expense or risk which may be necessary to secure the largest quantity of arms, of the best quality, at the earliest possible moment, sufficient to arm, if need be, not less than 500 regiments. To this end increased sums of money, to whatever amount may be necessary, will be placed at your disposal.
—Confederate secretary of war Leroy P. Walker to Confederate purchasing agents in London, July 22, 1861

commercial firearms trade in which noninterchangeable second-class copies of the Pattern 1853 were available to the highest bidder.

They played the game extraordinarily well. In all, Huse purchased and shipped an estimated five hundred thousand commercial copies of the Pattern 1853 rifle-musket, making it, for all practical purposes, the standard-issue infantry arm of the Confederacy. So numerous were these English-made weapons that in June 1862, Gorgas established .577 as the standard caliber for all domestically made rifles and rifle-muskets, thus allowing ammunition to be interchanged. Indeed, superintendent of armories James H. Burton, who had worked as the chief engineer at the Royal Small Arms Factory as the Pattern 1853 was going into production, intended the arm to be the chief product of the Confederacy's new central armory at Macon, Georgia. In 1863, he traveled to Leeds, England, to place a $300,000 order with the newly established firm of Greenwood and Batley for the machinery needed to mass-produce interchangeable Pattern 1853s at Macon. Most of it never made it into the Confederacy before the war ended.

By February 1863, Huse had incurred a debt of nearly £1.2 million (about $3 million in U.S. gold), of which only about half had been paid, and there was little prospect of paying the rest. Gold specie shipped to Britain had long ago been expended, and currency inflation at home made the C.S. Treasury Department's bills of exchange (essentially bank drafts or checks) unworkable. The Confederacy's credit was running out. Meanwhile, cotton that sold for eight cents a pound in the South was fetching at least three or four times that amount on the docks of Liverpool. In March 1863, the Treasury Department, which had purchased 400,000 bales of cotton through an 1861 bond issue, used its stockpile of white gold to back a massive $15 million international loan with Erlanger and Company, a Frankfurt-based bank with offices in Paris and Amsterdam. The former Confederate congressman and cotton trader Colin J. McRae was dispatched to London as the Confederacy's chief financial agent in charge of supervising the implementation of the new loan.

With a new source of credit, Confederate purchasing increased dramatically. In addition to Pattern 1853 rifle-muskets, over the course of the war the Confederacy bought at least a hundred thousand Austrian rifle-muskets as well as English-made cannons, ammunition, swords, accoutrements, uniforms, shoes, medicines, food, and vital raw materials, including 3 million pounds of lead for bullets and 2.25 million pounds of saltpeter for gunpowder. Not all of it came from Europe: shoes, raw materials, and, especially, salted and tinned meats made in the North were surreptitiously routed through Canada and Britain on their way to southern ports. The C.S. Navy purchased small arms, heavy guns, armor plate, marine engines, and several entire ships outfitted as commerce raiders. Cotton went out, armaments came in; business was booming. Cotton was still king.

At first, slipping such massive quantities of supplies past the Union blockade was relatively easy. In 1861, the U.S. Navy only had about forty ships to patrol thirty-five hundred miles of southern coastline from Chesapeake Bay to Texas. Slow-moving cargo ships sailing directly from British shores could easily reach any one of the dozen major ports in the South. In early 1862, as the navy added more warships to the blockade, cargo ships began to be intercepted. Shipping companies soon established transshipment points in Nassau, Bermuda, and Cuba (and, for a short time in 1864, Nova Scotia), where cargoes were transferred from large, slow-sailing ships into small, fast steamships for the run into port. Though too small and unstable for transatlantic crossings, these light-draft vessels were perfect for blockade-running: their low profiles made them hard to spot at night, and their powerful engines and sleek designs made them fast enough to elude pursuers. By 1865, British shipyards had turned out more than one hundred steamships designed specifically for blockade-running. Between 1861 and 1865, about three hundred steamers tested the blockade; of thirteen hundred attempts to run it, a thousand were successful. At the same time, thousands of small sailing ships, most of which were engaged in coastal trade, also attempted to outwit federal blockaders. It was a constant game of cat and mouse.

Nearly all runners were owned by newly formed private enterprises. Their primary market was not in armaments, but luxury items: cigars, wine, porcelain, carpets, antique furniture, and the like, scarce goods in the wartime South that often rendered the runners' cargoes more valuable than the ships themselves. Rather than continue to compete for expensive cargo space on private vessels, the Confederate government in late 1862 began purchasing its own blockade-runners, in addition to many others it chartered. During most of 1863, four government-owned ships operated by the C.S. Ordnance Bureau made regular runs between its sprawling warehouse complex in St. George, Bermuda, and the South's most important and best-defended port, Wilmington, North Carolina. Meanwhile, the C.S. Quartermaster Bureau operated five runners in partnership with Crenshaw and Collie and Company, a private shipping line, while the C.S. Navy and the States of North Carolina and Georgia had their own blockade-runners as well. Most of the Quartermaster Bureau and state-owned ships brought in cloth, thread, and shoes, not only to clothe their soldiers, but also to serve as barter for food and other necessities.

Yet by early 1864, the Confederate government had lost all of its Ordnance Bureau and Quartermaster Bureau ships and many of its charters to an increasingly well-armed and vigilant U.S. Navy. Worse for the Confederacy, only four major southern ports remained open to blockade-runners: Galveston, Mobile, Charleston, and Wilmington. Under these increasingly dire circumstances, the Confederacy could no longer afford to compete with private enterprises — it had to control them. Colin McRae was put in charge of all Confederate purchasing abroad, consolidating the efforts of the various Confederate departments, agents, and states into a single centralized authority. In February and March 1864, the C.S. Congress passed legislation giving President Jefferson Davis sweeping powers to regulate all foreign commerce, controlling the export of cotton and prohibiting the import of a long list of luxury items. Private shipping lines and state-operated runners were required to offer half their cargo space for Confederate government use. Such draconian measures brought positive results: from October 1864 through January 1865, the C.S. Ordnance Bureau imported more than fifty thousand arms and four hundred thousand pounds of lead; from April to November 1864, the Quartermaster Bureau imported more than 311,000 pairs of shoes, 170,000 blankets, and 803,000 yards of uniform cloth. The hard-fighting Army of Northern Virginia lived on salt pork imported through Wilmington.

Even so, the Confederacy's fortunes on both the home front and the battlefield were rapidly diminishing. Despite the relative ease of blockade-running, the federal blockade had reduced the South's seaborne trade to less than one-third of prewar levels by simply discouraging — even if not entirely preventing — normal commerce. Deprived of hard currency, the badly inflated southern economy was in a state of collapse: all basic necessities had long since been diverted to the war effort, leaving nothing for the civilian population. Although cargoes continued to arrive in southern ports, the Confederacy's weak transportation system meant that they did not always make it to frontline troops when and where needed. The last straw came on January 15, 1865, as Union naval and land forces captured Fort Fisher, the massive earthen bastion that had for so long protected Wilmington. Charleston was evacuated the following month. With its last ports closed and life-line cut, the Confederacy's slow starvation became acute. In April 1865, when the Army of Northern Virginia surrendered at Appomattox, most of its soldiers were equipped with the best English-made arms, accoutrements, uniforms, shoes, and blankets that money could buy. And yet the men were starving, as were many of their families, who pleaded for their return home. In the end, cotton could equip an army, but it could not win a war.

No one will ever know exactly how many arms the Confederacy procured abroad, nor how many reached its shores. Given the confusing and often-secretive nature of the business as well as the intentional destruction of Confederate-related sales records by English gun makers after the war, documentation of Confederate purchasing is sketchy at best. As a result, the myriad markings on English-made arms, especially markings that might indicate Confederate purchase, remained largely inexplicable well into the 1980s. Extensive research by collectors and historians—including the discovery of Colin McRae's business papers in 2003—has yielded substantial documentary evidence explaining some (but by no means all) of these markings, many of which were in use only during the first year of the war. At the same time, it appears that arms produced after 1863 either did not survive in large numbers or, being unmarked, have yet to be identified positively as Confederate purchases.

George Wray assembled his collection of thirty-three English-made long arms (not including Whitworth rifles) in concert with these research efforts. He was among the first to study markings associated with Confederate use, even if their precise meanings were still unknown. The result is a substantial pool of material evidence attesting to the importance of the guns-for-cotton trade, the lifeline of the Confederacy.

The Birmingham System

Of an estimated half million English-made arms imported into the Confederacy, at least 90 percent were hand-made under a two-hundred-year-old cottage industry method of manufacturing known as the Birmingham system. It was based on self-employed tradesmen known as "outworkers," or "material makers," each of whom specialized in the making of different parts of a gun. By the end of the war, there were about six hundred manufacturing companies both large and small in the London and Birmingham gun trades, employing at least ten thousand workers. Two-thirds of them worked in Birmingham, where most of the parts were made, even for guns assembled and finished in London.

The "material maker" trades were organized according to the major components of the arm: locks, stocks, barrels, furniture (such as buttplates and trigger-guard plates), and "oddworks" (such as screws, swivels, and gun tools). Most of these were further subdivided into even more specialized areas. The barrel-making trade, for example, included barrel welders, borers, grinders, filers, breech forgers, breechers, rib makers, and stampers. Among the most skilled were the straighteners, whose experienced eyes could detect even the smallest deviation in an otherwise perfectly straight barrel. Lock makers depended on dozens of workers to hand-forge the eight major parts and six screws that then had to be filed and fitted to make a complete lock. Paid by the piece according to demand, workers were often young apprentices or journeymen working at home or in small, cramped shops, sometimes in horrible conditions. The components were then delivered to the factory of the master gun maker, or "furnisher," where they were assembled, or "set up," into complete arms by another group of specialized workers. These "setters-up" adjusted, fit, and polished parts, finished stocks, engraved or stamped lockplates, and crated and shipped the finished product.

Upon leaving the factory, arms sometimes bore the name or initials of the furnisher as well as those of the major (and sometimes minor) component makers, creating an almost endless variety of markings. As seen by the examples in this section, virtually no two arms produced under the Birmingham system are identical, though all bear common characteristics. Most London furnishers placed their names on the lockplates. Birmingham furnishers often stamped their names into the stock, almost invariably using the generic mark "Tower" on the lockplate. This mark referred to the Tower of London, which for centuries served as the British national arsenal, where arms were proofed, inspected, and stored. In 1797, the British government established an inspection facility in Birmingham, and it too became known as the Tower. Although the mark implied governmental inspection—and,

The outworking system leads to the employment of a considerable number of young boys, who are employed mainly in carrying the work from one to another, as it passes through its several stages; we regret to say that many are employed in this work too young for the burdens they are called upon to bear. At any time, in the neighbourhood of St. Mary's Church, in which district of the town the gun trade has located itself, the lads may be seen, one with half-a-dozen stocked guns on his shoulder, conveying them from the stocker to the screwer; another with a tray full of locks for the polisher; a third on his way with a few barrels to the Proof-house, and so on.
—John D. Goodman, chairman of the Birmingham Small Arms Trade, 1866

Huse had agreed to receive 550 of Graysbrooks short Enfield Rifles & directed them to send down our "Viewer," prior to their being accepted. This term Viewer is equivalent to our "Inspector" and in order to meet the frauds of the gun dealers I have arranged with Messrs. S.H. & Co. to obtain the services of the Tower Viewer. To this end we have got him a sick leave of absence from the Govt. & have put him to work for the Confeds.
—Edward C. Anderson, Confederate purchasing agent, August 2, 1861

hence, superior quality—arms intended for the American market were neither inspected by representatives of the British government nor, with few exceptions, marked with the royal cipher "*VR*" (*Victoria Regina*).

They were, however, often stamped with the cryptic marks of dozens of inspectors, or "viewers," working for the Confederacy through the commission houses of William Grazebrook; S. Isaac, Campbell and Company; and Sinclair, Hamilton, and Company. These marks, along with a system of engraved inventory numbers used in 1861 and 1862, are the key to distinguishing the arms imported by the Confederate government from those imported by the Union or other countries. At the same time, some arms, especially those purchased by private speculators, were never marked at all.

The Birmingham system was a living relic of bygone methods and traditions. Its path to extinction began in 1854 with the formation of the Birmingham Small Arms Trade, a consortium of major gun makers created to regulate internal standards, control supply, set prices, and fix wages. It was unpopular with workers and also with the British government, which depended on these gun makers for military arms. A wage strike that delayed production for a crucial nine weeks during the Crimean War confirmed the British government's decision in 1854 to invest in mass-producing its own arms, using new American-made interchangeable-parts machinery installed in a refurbished Royal Small Arms Factory at Enfield. Beginning in 1857, the privately run London Armoury Company followed suit, investing in the new machinery in order to receive government contracts. In 1861, seeing the handwriting on the wall, the Birmingham Small Arms Trade began construction of its own modern arms factory at Small Heath.

The Civil War was the last hurrah of the Birmingham system. Between 1861 and 1864, Birmingham gun makers produced at least 733,000 arms for the American market, and London makers turned out another 344,000—the greatest number of arms ever produced by the system. At least forty furnishers are known to have sold arms to the Confederacy; some also sold to the Union at the same time. As long as Americans continued killing one another, workers' wages were high and profits soared. But in 1865, with the war over and the Birmingham factory completed, thousands of skilled craftsmen were suddenly out of work; those who found employment in the new factory earned only a fraction of their old wages. Thus the Birmingham system, much like the Confederate nation that had supported it, finally collapsed under pressure from the American System. The new Birmingham Small Arms Company factory fared poorly after the war, surviving into the 1970s mainly by manufacturing motorcycles.

Lockplate marks

The handwork that characterized the Birmingham system is nowhere better illustrated than in the markings on the lockplates of finished arms. Most crowns were stamped; some were engraved. Sometimes the Tower stamp was placed below the date, sometimes above it. Sometimes it appeared under the crown. Likewise, no two sets of double engraved lines on the edges of a lockplate are exactly alike. Everything depended upon the workers' skill and the extent to which the shops or furnishers enforced consistent practices.

Stock-maker and stocker marks in ramrod channels

Of approximately ten thousand workers in the gun trades of Birmingham and London, perhaps two thousand were involved in making stocks. All parts of the process were specialized. The stock maker supplied the wood and cut out the basic shape, or blank; the stocker further shaped the stock and cut cavities for the barrel, lock, and furniture; the "makers-off" completed the stock by sanding and oiling. The latter task was considered "light and not unsuitable employment" for women.[1]

The almost endless variety of names and initials stamped inside the ramrod channels of English arms gives an indication of the sheer size of the stocking trade. Yet not all the names and initials stamped there were involved in stocking: some were setters-up or finishers, who assembled the arm, thus explaining why multiple names sometimes appear in the channels. Sometimes stockers stamped their names or initials into the stock flat opposite the barrel. Typical of the decentralized Birmingham system, marking practices varied by vendor and craftsman.

Chiseled slash marks were also stamped into some ramrod channels. Intended as assembly codes, the number of strokes in the channel corresponded to the same number of strokes on the underside of the barrel, thus ensuring that these vital but noninterchangeable parts fit together.

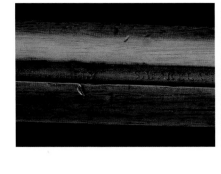
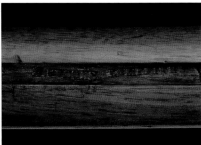

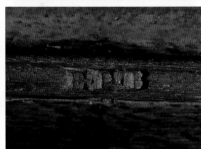

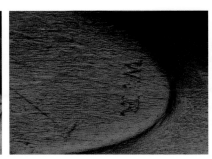

Maker marks for ramrods, barrel bands, and sights

In the Birmingham system, even the smallest parts were sometimes stamped with a maker's name. Among the makers whose work is shown here are Thomas and Charles Gilbert, "small works" makers in Birmingham; Francis Preston, a bayonet and parts manufacturer in Manchester; and Phillip Webley and Son, bullet-mold and gun-implement makers in Birmingham. Preston was one of the first to mechanize bayonet manufacture and also dabbled in artillery projectiles; Webley later became famous for the revolvers his company manufactured for the British army.

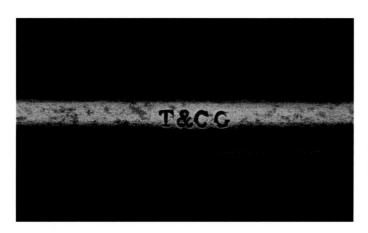

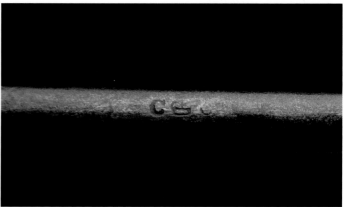

Birmingham and London commercial view and proof marks

Although Birmingham and London gun makers could afford variations in the quality of their locks, stocks, and other parts, they could not afford to take shortcuts in the quality of their barrels. All gun barrels were required by British law to undergo a series of proof tests in which the barrel was test-fired with an abnormally heavy charge to make sure it could withstand the pressure of a normal service load without bursting. Governmental inspectors at the Birmingham and London test facilities, or "proof houses," applied marks at the breech to indicate passage of each test. Each house had its own marks for commercially made arms, while arms made or contracted for by the government received the same marks at both houses. Removing, defacing, or faking view and proof marks was a serious offense, punishable by heavy fines and imprisonment.

Top, reading from bottom of photo: *The Birmingham proof house customarily applied five separate marks: a "provisional proof" applied after the barrel alone had been successfully test-fired and declared sound (a crown over the cursive letters "BP" for "Birmingham Provisional"); two "25" bore marks, indicating .577 caliber after each test; a "view" mark meaning that the completed arm had passed inspection (crossed scepters with a crown and V), and a "definitive proof," indicating that the finished barrel and lock had together been test-fired successfully (crossed scepters with a crown and B, P, and C for "Birmingham Company Proof").*

Bottom, reading from bottom of photo: *The London proof house had a slightly simpler system, omitting the bore marks: the "provisional proof" (a rampant lion over a cursive G), a "view" mark (crown over V), and a "definitive proof" (crown over an intertwined "GP" for "Gun Proof." With slight variations, the latter two marks had been in use since 1672.*

Marks of royal authority

Top: *The Royal Small Arms Factory at Enfield stamped its interchangeable Pattern 1853 rifle-muskets with distinctive marks to indicate British government ownership. Lockplates were stamped under the crown with the royal cipher "VR" as well as with a crown over a downward-pointing broad arrow. The bands, ramrods, and other parts were stamped with a crown over a letter indicating the place of manufacture and a number indicating the inspector of the part.*

Bottom: *Before interchangeable arms production began at Enfield in 1859, government-contract rifle-muskets produced under the Birmingham system bore similar (albeit often hand-engraved) marks. Stocks were marked with a broad arrow and "WD" for "War Department" (previously "BO" for "Board of Ordnance"). These examples are from the Atlanta History Center's DuBose and Traynor Collections.*

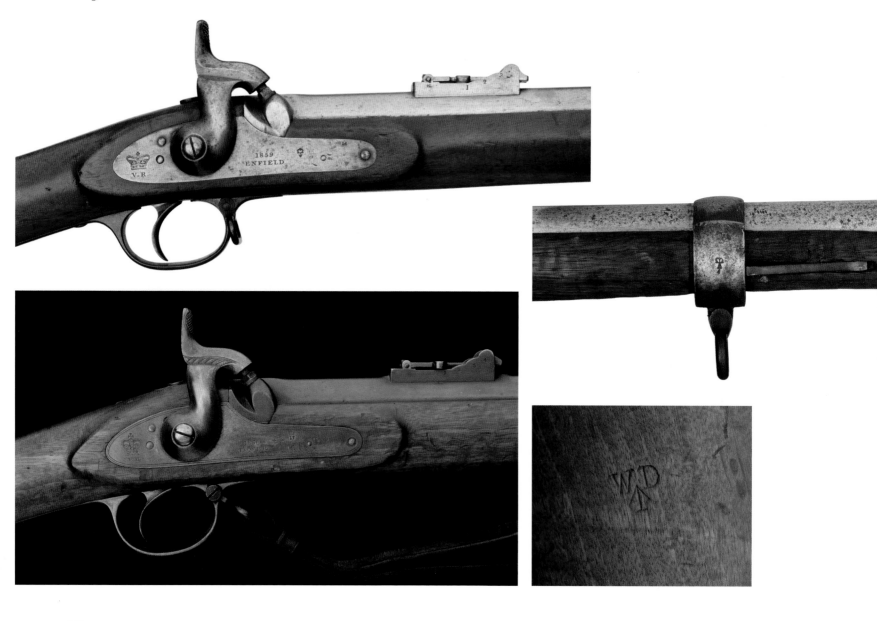

Marks of Confederate authority

Unable to personally examine all their purchases, Confederate agents needed the services of professional arms inspectors, or "viewers." Sometimes these were commercial viewers working independently or in teams of two or more; sometimes they were military viewers employed by the British War Office but moonlighting for extra pay. To avoid any possible legal or political entanglements, viewers were paid not by the Confederacy directly, but through the English commission houses hired to do the purchasing.

Like American inspectors at the U.S. armories, each viewer had a unique mark (usually his initials), which he customarily stamped into the stock. These simple and sometimes cryptic viewers' marks are often the only indication that a particular arm was the property of the Confederate States.

Top: Perhaps the most famous viewer mark indicating Confederate ownership is the "JS"-and-anchor stamp. It is thought to indicate a team of viewers headed by John Southgate, a British government viewer assigned to inspect arms at the London Armoury Company, but granted an official (and fraudulent) sick leave while he worked for Sinclair, Hamilton, and Company. The anchor-and-S mark is believed to be related, but is usually found on arms dated 1863 or 1864.

Second from top: The "IC" stamp is believed to be either the mark of furnisher and commission house S. Isaac, Campbell and Company, or the mark of Isaac Curtis, a viewer who worked for that company and J. E. Barnett and Sons. In 1863, Caleb Huse recruited Curtis and several other English viewers to work as armorers and instructors at the Fayetteville Armory.

Second from bottom: These are the marks of Sinclair, Hamilton, and Company, believed to have been awarded over the course of the war five contracts for thirty thousand rifle-muskets each, making it the Confederacy's most important arms supplier. This mark was often stamped alone or in combination with other viewer marks on the stock or, occasionally, on the barrel.

Bottom: It is estimated that two hundred to three hundred men worked as viewers in London and Birmingham, but the number who worked for the Confederacy is unknown. Nearly all their marks — including the two pictured here — are as yet unidentified.

Confederate inventory numbers and letters

There was one other marking system used to identify Confederate-purchased arms in 1861 and early 1862. This was a series of consecutive numbers applied in lots of ten thousand and engraved on buttplate tangs, ramrods, and bayonets, where they functioned as serial numbers. This system reflected the existing practice of the British army, which enabled each soldier to recognize his weapon and match it to the same numbered ramrod and bayonet. In the stock just forward of the buttplate tang, some inventoried arms were also stamped with a single block letter referring to one of the five principal furnishers with whom Sinclair, Hamilton, and Company contracted for rifle-muskets: C. W. James and W. C. Scott and Son of Birmingham, and Edward P. Bond, James Kerr, and Parker, Field, and Sons of London.

Besides a ready means of identification, inventory numbers and letters provided a measure of accounting, assuring both seller and purchaser in the Confederate trade that their products had been delivered as promised. Yet the time required to engrave each and every arm became a bottleneck just when the Confederacy was most desperate for arms. The practice was abandoned in mid-1862.

Commercial copy of British Pattern 1853 rifle-musket, third type, believed to have been furnished by Francis Preston, Manchester, Confederate inventory number 5292 (1861)

Introduced in mid-1854 at the height of the Crimean War, the Pattern 1853 rifle-musket was designed as the standard-issue arm for all line infantry regiments in the British army. Ten years later, at the height of the American Civil War, commercial copies of these weapons were standard issue for about two-thirds of the Confederate army. If any firearm could be considered typical for Confederate service, this is it.

Introduced in 1858, the third type featured a ramrod-retaining spring, or "spoon," in the channel of the stock, an improvement developed at the Royal Small Arms Factory in 1856 by the future

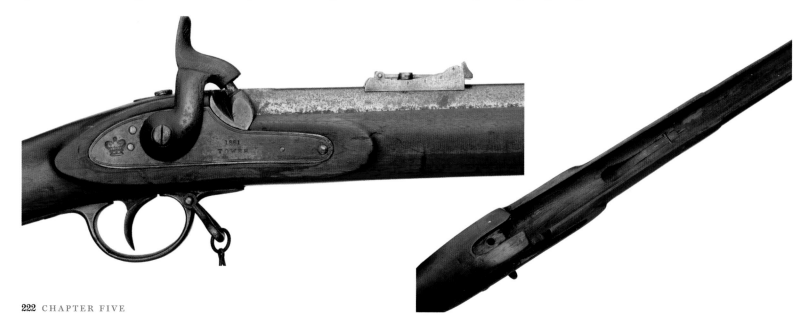

Confederate superintendent of armories James H. Burton. All English-made percussion arms were issued with a snap cap secured by a small brass chain to the stock. Introduced in 1857, it was intended to allow soldiers to practice firing without using a percussion cap, thus preventing damage to the nipple, or "cone."

As with many arms made under the Birmingham system, marks made by material makers and setters-up are everywhere in evidence. Inside the lock, "JBP" probably indicates the lock maker, while "JH" and "WS," which also appear underneath the barrel, may be the finisher and setter-up. Also under the barrel are two slash marks and the numerals "4" and "37," perhaps assembly codes or identification numbers applied when the barrels were proof-tested.

Stamped into the stock behind the trigger-guard tang is the Confederate viewer's mark, "JS," and an anchor. There is also a twice-stamped mark comprising a crown, "FP," a cursive M, an arrow, and "2." This is thought to be the furnisher's mark of Francis Preston of Manchester, and the "2" may indicate an arm of "second quality," especially since the stock has a large knot that would prevent it passing British government inspection.

On the buttplate tang and ramrod, the engraved inventory number 5292 indicates that this was probably one of the arms delivered through Sinclair, Hamilton, and Company between October 1861 and April 1862. The block letter P on the stock may also refer to the furnisher Francis Preston, who was not one of the principal furnishers included in Sinclair, Hamilton, and Company's second contract of October 1861, but perhaps sold a few guns to one of the five who was.

Commercial copy of British Pattern 1853 rifle-musket, third type, believed to have been furnished by Francis Preston, Manchester, Confederate inventory number 4281961 (1861)

This rifle-musket is nearly identical to the one pictured previously, including the "JS" and anchor and what are believed to be Francis Preston's furnisher marks near the trigger-guard tang. What makes this one unusual is the seven-digit number on the buttplate. Normally, when engravers had finished 10,000 arms, they started the sequence over again, but with the addition of the letter A or B to indicate the second or third batch. The circumstances behind the seven numbers on this arm are unknown, but the numerals "4" and "61" seem to have been added later. Was this the mistake or correction of an amateur engraver in England, or did these numbers have some other use?

**Commercial copy of British Pattern 1853 rifle-musket, third type, furnished by
J. E. Barnett and Sons, London, with Pattern 1853 socket bayonet (1862–63)**

*About a third of the commercially made Pattern 1853 rifle-muskets imported into the Confederacy
were made by London gun makers, including the brothers John and Edward Barnett, whose
great-great-uncle had been apprenticed to the trade in 1737. Working through the commission house
of S. Isaac, Campbell and Company, the Confederacy placed one of its first contracts for arms with the
Barnett brothers, who used their contacts in official circles to gather and refurbish old smoothbore arms
and surplus rifles. By 1864, Barnett had probably sold more rifle-muskets to the Confederacy than any
other London gun maker. Business was so brisk that the company (or its subcontractors) needed at least
six different name stamps for marking lockplates, three of which are pictured below.*

*Like many London-made arms, this one is undated. The lack of inventory numbers suggests that it
was shipped to the Confederacy after mid-1862, when the inventory system was discontinued. Yet the
presence of an "IC" (for S. Isaac, Campbell and Company) mark in the stock opposite the lock dates
this arm as having been made earlier than October 1863, when the company made its last Confederate
purchases. There is also a Sinclair, Hamilton, and Company mark in the stock behind the trigger guard,
indicating that one company routed its sales through the other as a subcontractor. Such practices were
common for the commission houses, which often relied on one another to help fill contracts on time.*

Commercial copies of British Pattern 1853 socket bayonet (ca. 1863)

The British Pattern 1853 rifle-musket was designed for use with a socket bayonet. Bayonet forging and finishing was yet another subspecialty in the Birmingham system, with marks as many and varied as the makers themselves.

Top: *Bayonets made under British government contract often bore the name of the maker (in this case, Francis Preston of Manchester) but invariably bore government inspection stamps: a crown over a letter indicating the place of inspection (in this case, B for Birmingham) and the number of the inspector ("47"). The socket of this example is engraved with the identification numbers of a British regiment.*

Middle: *Bayonets made for commercial sale usually had a slightly different shape at the base, often bore the name of the maker, but did not have government acceptance stamps. Two of the examples pictured here were stamped with the crowned "BSAT" insignia of the Birmingham Small Arms Trade, which inspected bayonets provided by any maker who was not a member of the trade. The larger block letters refer to the forger of the blade or the contractor who provided it.*

Bottom: *Always short of steel, the Confederacy imported steel socket blades made in England and fitted them with iron sockets in southern arsenals. The slash marks, inventory number 14, and the oddly filed slot for the front sight indicate that this was probably one of them.*

Commercial copy of British Pattern 1853 rifle-musket, third type, furnished by Parker, Field, and Sons, London (ca. 1863)

With roots in the London gun trade dating back to 1772, Parker, Field, and Sons was one of the five principal furnishers with whom Sinclair, Hamilton, and Company contracted for rifle-muskets for the Confederacy. Large enough to operate from two London addresses, Parker, Field, and Sons sold at least fifty-five hundred rifle-muskets under an 1861 contract, and probably thousands more afterward. This example bears the "ic" mark opposite the lock, indicating that it was one of the many London guns inspected by viewers working for S. Isaac, Campbell and Company.

As signified by the "lsm" stamp on the trigger guard, this gun also bears a direct connection to an aftereffect of the Civil War. In 1871, this was one of forty-five hundred Pattern 1853 rifle-muskets, most of which had been surrendered by Confederate armies, supplied by the U.S. War Department to arm the Louisiana State Militia. Made up of new volunteers as well as Confederate and Union veterans (many of the latter were black), the pro-Republican militia was headed by the former Confederate general James Longstreet. In New Orleans, it participated in a series of violent clashes before being overwhelmed in September 1874 in a street battle against white pro-Democratic paramilitary clubs armed mainly with breechloaders. This rifle-musket, once the weapon of choice for defending a slave-based republic, probably saw its last use in unsuccessful fighting against the reassertion of white supremacy.

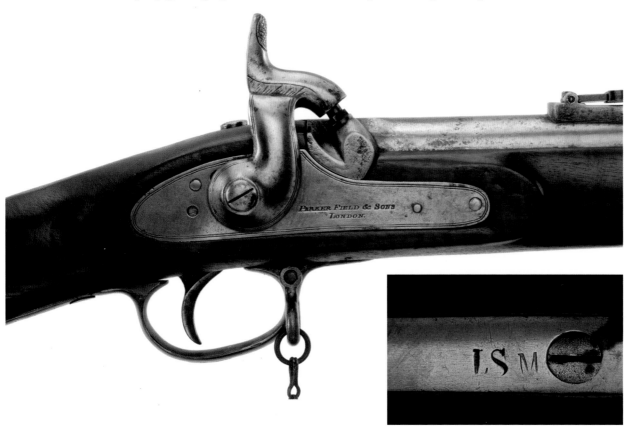

Commercial copy of British Pattern 1853 rifle-musket, third type, furnished by Edward P. Bond, London (ca. 1863)

The fourth-generation London gun maker Edward Phillip Bond was another of the five principal furnishers included in the Sinclair, Hamilton, and Company contract. Bond marked his products in three places, perhaps to distinguish them from those of his brother Eyton, who had a gun-making business in Birmingham. In addition to the "EP. Bond / London" stamp on the lockplate, the initials "EPB" appear in the ramrod channel, and "EB" under a crest is stamped on the barrel flat, just behind the carefully engraved mark lining up the breech plug and the barrel. Stamped with the Sinclair, Hamilton, and Company viewer's mark, this arm probably dates to 1863.

The .577 Pritchett bullet

Nearly all the rifled arms imported from Britain were designed to fire a .577-caliber hollow-base lead bullet designed by Robert Taylor Pritchett. It looked and functioned just like the American minié ball, but without the three grooves at the base for lubricant, which, according to British practice, was provided in the cartridge paper. English-made Pritchett bullets included a small boxwood plug in the base, designed to promote the even expansion of the hollow base into the rifling. In just fifteen months of 1863–64, 2,734,000 .577 cartridges were shipped into the Confederacy through Wilmington. Confederate arsenals made millions more, but their bullets lacked the wooden plugs.

Pritchett bullet molds

English gun makers customarily included one .577 bullet mold (right) in each case of twenty arms shipped to the Confederacy. The bullet molds ensured that soldiers would have the means of casting their own lead bullets should the regular supply of cartridges fail.

As illustrated by this southern-made mold (bottom), sometimes it did. This three-cavity mold for .577 Pritchett bullets likely was made by a blacksmith working for a local Confederate command that had run out of cartridges. The handles were fashioned from a piece of iron pipe and a section of an old octagonal gun barrel.

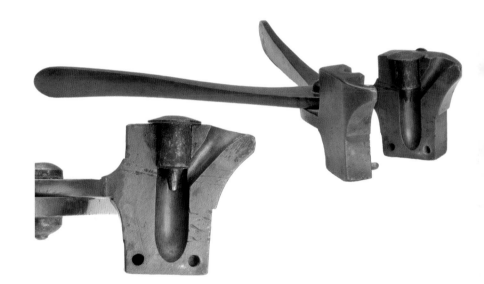

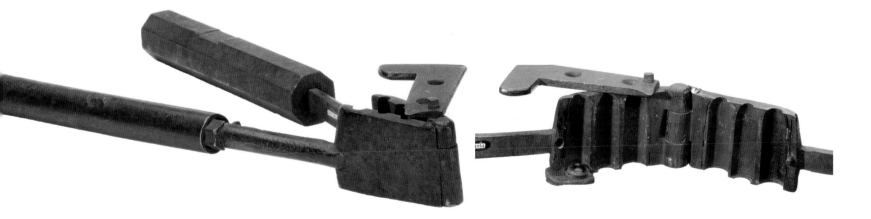

Commercial copy of British Pattern 1856 rifle, first type, furnished by Edward Brooks and Son, Birmingham, Confederate inventory number 184, with Pattern 1856 sword bayonet (1861)

Beginning in 1856, the British War Office designed a series of .577-caliber "short" rifles, all of similar pattern, for the use of special rifle regiments or sergeants of regular infantry. Confederate agents were interested in any good-quality rifled arms, regardless of pattern, because they could boost the effectiveness of armies otherwise armed with limited-range smoothbores.

These short rifles were distinguished by buttplates, trigger-guard plates, and stock tips made of iron rather than the usual brass. The 1856 pattern was further distinguished by a small guide key just forward of the bayonet stud, which fit a guide groove in the mortise of the sword bayonet. Like the U.S. Army, the British army had deemed this guide key unnecessary in 1857 and ordered studs for all new government arms to be made without it. But commercial gun makers still had the old-style studs on hand in 1861, as well as the sword bayonets that fit them, and were anxious to liquidate their old stock, especially when such small details mattered little to their customers.

As indicated by its low inventory number, this was one of the first rifles purchased by the Confederacy, probably through the commission house of William Grazebrook in May or June 1861. A few months later, it may have been aboard the Bermuda *or the* Fingal, *the first steam-powered blockade-runners to reach the South. To avoid having to engrave the hardened surface of the buttplate, workers stamped the inventory number into the underside of the stock just forward of the "JS"-and-anchor viewer's mark and the name of the furnisher, Edward Brooks and Son.*

Commercial variant of British Pattern 1856 rifle furnished by J. E. Barnett and Sons, London, Confederate inventory number 592 (1861)

The only visible difference between this rifle and the previously pictured Birmingham-made rifle bearing inventory number 184 is the lack of the small guide key forward of the bayonet stud. This rifle therefore appears to be a copy of the British Pattern 1860 and fits a Pattern 1860 sword bayonet. But the 1860 pattern incorporated a heavy and exceptionally accurate barrel with five-groove rifling, while the rifle pictured here is built around the lighter and less expensive three-groove Pattern 1856 barrel. For Confederate contracts, English gun makers often used the parts they had on hand, regardless of pattern.

Even so, this and other short rifles with sword bayonets did not come cheap: at around seventy-five shillings each (about eighteen dollars), they cost ten shillings more than an ordinary rifle-musket with a socket bayonet. This one bears the small S. Isaac, Campbell and Company "IC" viewer's mark as well as a "JS" and anchor next to the inventory number 592 on the underside of the stock. It is likely that William Grazebrook purchased this one through S. Isaac, Campbell and Company in order to fill his contract; it may have even been part of the same shipment as number 184. The Confederacy is believed to have purchased about ten thousand rifles in 1861 and 1862 before refocusing its efforts almost exclusively on rifle-muskets for the rest of the war.

Commercial copies of British Pattern 1860 sword bayonets (ca. 1861)

These heavy steel-blade bayonets with pressed-leather grips were designed to fit short rifles and artillery carbines made without the guide key forward of the bayonet stud. Many of the blades came from Solingen, Prussia, and were fitted with hilts in England. As seen by the distinctive stamp on the back of the blade, this bayonet was a product of Robert Mole and Son, the largest maker of edged weapons in Birmingham and a frequent supplier for the Confederacy.

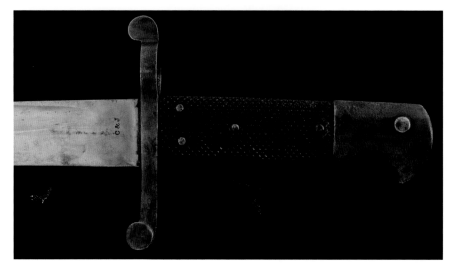

Commercial copy of British Pattern 1856 cavalry carbine furnished by J. E. Barnett and Sons, London (ca. 1863)

First introduced for service in India, these thirty-seven-inch muzzle-loading carbines were adopted by the British army in 1857 until an appropriate breech-loading design could be approved. Like previous carbines, the Pattern 1856 featured a ramrod swivel and a sling bar, but now had a rifled .577 bore. Still, these carbines were meant for short-range work: the two-leaf backsight was graduated only for two hundred and three hundred yards.

It is believed that the Confederacy imported about ten thousand commercially made copies of the Pattern 1856 carbine, mainly during the last two years of the war, when the need for cavalry weapons was especially pressing. At least twenty-five hundred and perhaps as many as five thousand were shipped from Havana, Cuba, to Galveston, Texas, between November 1864 and April 1865.

From 1870 through 1903, this example was part of the famous collection of the U.S. Cartridge Company in Massachusetts, which stamped accession number 1396 in three places on the stock. The company's 1903 sale catalogue lists this carbine as "taken from a blockade-runner captured off Cuba in 1861."[2] If this information is correct, the blockade-runner was probably the steamer Salvor, *bound from Havana for Tampa Bay, Florida, with a cargo of "200 sacks of coffee, 400,000 cigars, 400 revolvers, a number of rifles, dirks, bowie knives, a 6 pounder cannon, a quantity of felt hats, caps, shoes, 500,000 percussion caps, and a quantity of fruit."[3] On the night of October 13, 1861, the* Salvor *was captured just west of the Tortugas by the* USS Keystone State, *which towed her to Philadelphia. The ship and cargo were sold at prize court six months later. If this carbine was part of that cargo, it may not have been a C.S. Ordnance Bureau purchase, despite the "JS"-and-anchor viewer's mark. Private speculators could pay to have arms inspected just as easily as Confederate agents and their commission houses.*

Commercial copy of British Pattern 1853 artillery carbine, second type, furnished by J. E. Barnett and Sons, London (1862)

The British Army intended these forty-inch carbines to be a last-ditch weapon for artillerymen defending their batteries. Confederate agents purchased at least forty-five hundred, almost certainly for use as cavalry carbines.

This example bears a faint "IC" mark in the stock opposite the lock, indicating its purchase through S. Isaac, Campbell and Company. The only artillery carbines known to have been sold through this company were the eighty shipped to Bermuda aboard the Confederate-owned supply ship Harriett Pinckney *in August 1862. From there, their destination and distribution is unknown. Between July 1863 and November 1864, thirty-four hundred artillery carbines arrived in Wilmington, but they are thought to have been purchased through Sinclair, Hamilton, and Company.*

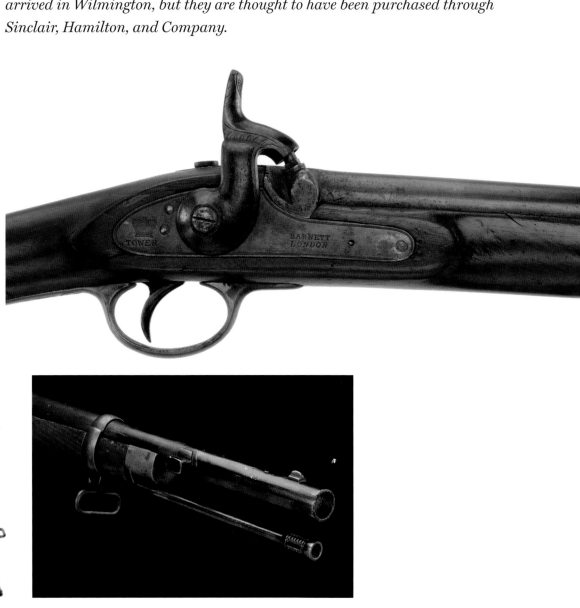

The "Little Enfield" (ca. 1890)

British Pattern 1853 rifle-muskets were so common in the late 1800s that Belgian toy makers created miniature versions, which were quite popular among Civil War veterans as gifts for their sons. At forty-two inches long and about four pounds in weight, the "Little Enfield" is a fully functioning .32-caliber gun that even came with its own (not sharpened) bayonet. Of all of the arms in his collection, this one was perhaps George Wray's favorite.

Interchangeable Arms for the Confederacy

It is well known that the manufacture of firearms, of all descriptions, has long been in a very unsatisfactory state in this country, owing mainly to the disinclination of the Birmingham manufacturers to avail themselves of any of those mechanical inventions so largely resorted to by the manufacturers of the United States. At the present time, when the Birmingham gunsmiths are performing nearly all their work by the hands of skilled and expensive workmen, Colonel Colt's revolving pistols and rifles are made at his establishment in London with greater perfection, almost entirely by self-acting machines, attended by women and boys.
—"On the Manufacture of Firearms at Manchester," *Mechanics' Magazine,* July 14, 1855

The rifles made at this establishment interchange in every part and with perfect accuracy. . . . The London Armory Company is the only establishment in Europe, excepting the Government armories, that works upon this principle. . . . If I could contract for the entire 20,000 I think I could secure them at 70 shillings, and if the Confederate Government intends to purchase a further supply, I would respectfully suggest that the great importance of interchange of parts, in a country where repairs of arms will be for many years a great expense, should be fully considered.
—C.S. Ordnance Bureau purchasing agent Caleb Huse to C.S. chief of ordnance Josiah Gorgas, May 21, 1861

Two of the exhibitions that created the biggest stir at London's Great Exhibition of 1851 (commonly known as the Crystal Palace exhibition) were those of the American gun makers and pioneers of interchangeable-parts manufacture Samuel Colt of New Haven, Connecticut, and Robbins and Lawrence of Windsor, Vermont. Although the British and French led the world in the technology of ballistics, the upstart Americans led the world in the technology of mass production. Among others, the British army's Board of Ordnance took special notice of these developments and commissioned a series of official visits to U.S. manufacturing establishments in the Connecticut River Valley, including the U.S. Armory at Springfield. Its subsequent decision to adopt the American System at a newly renovated factory at Enfield effectively shut out the private Birmingham and London gun makers, but at the same time created an opening for any new enterprise willing to make the investment in interchangeable-parts technology.

The London Armoury Company rose to the challenge. Established in 1856 to manufacture double-action Adams revolvers, the company decided instead to invest in a more lucrative product, one that seemed to foretell the future of the arms industry: interchangeable copies of the British Pattern 1853 rifle-musket. Backed by a British government contract for thirty thousand units, the London Armoury Company became Britain's first commercial gun-making venture built on the American System. By late 1859, its Bermondsey factory just south of the Thames was operating a complete set of precision machines tooled for the Pattern 1853, most of it purchased from the Ames Manufacturing Company in Massachusetts and from Greenwood and Batley of Leeds. Two years later, that machinery was turning out sixteen hundred rifle-muskets a month in addition to interchangeable .44-caliber pistols designed by the factory superintendent, James Kerr.

In May 1861, the day after his arrival in London, Caleb Huse paid a call on the London Armoury Company with the intention of contracting for ten thousand rifle-muskets. This was a chance to procure interchangeable copies of the finest long-range arms in Europe, used by the greatest military power in the world. But because of its contract with the British government, the company was unable to sign any large contracts until the following year—unless, of course, Huse could offer a better and larger deal, which he then did not have the funding to do. Fortunately for Huse, the senior director of the company was a Confederate sympathizer named Archibald Hamilton, of Sinclair, Hamilton, and Company, who arranged not only to sell Huse some of the excess production, but also to give the Confederacy priority on a long-term contract for all subsequent production. Meanwhile, Hamilton, who always put business first, was also selling excess production — perhaps four hundred to six hundred guns a month — to the United States and the State of Massachusetts, as well as to the part-time soldiers of the British Volunteer Force.

In the spring and summer of 1862, when the London Armoury Company's British contract was nearly filled, Huse tried again, proposing a contract for fifty thousand rifle-muskets. But with Confederate credit already overextended, he had no way to back the deal. As a result, many of the company's coveted interchangeable arms continued to go north instead of south. Finally, in May 1863, with the U.S. War Department having canceled its foreign arms contracts and with funds from the new Erlanger loan in hand, Huse was able to close the deal, securing most of the London Armoury Company's rifle-musket production for the rest of the war. It was perhaps the best deal the Confederacy ever made. London Armoury Company rifle-muskets were virtually identical to the best arms made for the British government. Yet, on average, each London Armoury Company gun and its bayonet cost only about ten shillings more than the sixty-five shillings the Confederacy paid for each of the noninterchangeable arms made under the Birmingham system. In June 1863, Hamilton even offered to sell the entire company and its new factory north of the Thames to the Confederate government. Josiah Gorgas initially liked the idea, but ultimately rejected the offer. Until the C.S. Armory at Macon could begin turning out Confederate copies of the Pattern 1853, the young nation would take its chances on finished arms run through the blockade rather than adding to its financial burden with a risky overseas venture.

In the end, the total number of rifle-muskets produced and sold to the Confederacy by the London Armoury Company between 1861 and 1865 is unknown, but it was at least thirty thousand and perhaps as many as seventy thousand, most of which were fabricated in 1863 and 1864. Many of the guns never made it farther than Bermuda before the fall of Wilmington in January 1865. The end of the Civil War fundamentally changed the financial prospects of the London Armoury Company. Facing the disappearance of British government contracts and a world market flooded with surplus interchangeable American-made arms, the weakened company succumbed during the Panic of 1866. It had gambled its financial future on the Confederacy and lost. Nevertheless, part of the workforce was re-formed as the London Small Arms Company, which made military arms for the British government until 1935. The rest of the workers reorganized as the London Armoury, which operated until 1991.

As first-class interchangeable arms, London Armoury Company rifle-muskets fetched good prices on the European market after the war, when thousands were gathered from captured stores and sold off by the U.S. War Department. Today they are the rarest of English-made Confederate arms. They can also be the most difficult Confederate arms to identify. British government rifle-muskets bear British government marks; U.S. government purchases usually bear inspection marks opposite the lock; even arms bought by the State of Massachusetts were often stamped in the stock. But Caleb Huse and his commission houses never subjected interchangeable London Armoury Company rifle-muskets to the same inspection, or "viewing," as they did noninterchangeable arms made under the Birmingham system. In the absence of Confederate viewer's marks or inventory numbers, establishing a southern association for any London Armoury Company rifle-musket — especially if it is dated before 1863 — is usually a matter of conjecture. The Wray Collection includes eight London Armoury Company rifle-muskets, only one of which is known beyond doubt to have seen Confederate service.

London Armoury Company lockplates

In all details of fit, finish, and quality, the London Armoury Company's products were noticeably superior to arms made by the Birmingham system. Unlike this Birmingham-made lockplate (top), the London Armoury Company equivalent (middle) dispensed with hand-engraved double lines around the lockplate and hammer. But for private customers willing to pay extra, the company could add elaborate decorative engraving on the lock and all other parts (bottom). All London Armoury Company lockplates also bore the royal cipher "VR" under the crown, indicating that the company used the same stamping die for British government and commercial contracts.

London Armoury Company stocks and lockplate-screw washers

Although all English gun makers used seasoned English or European walnut for their stocks, those made by the London Armoury Company were generally of better-grade walnut and were cut out by machine, making for a more precise fit and cleaner lines. The lockplate-screw washers, or "escutcheons," of London Armoury guns (top) *have "Enfield"-style rounded "ears" rather than the squared-off style made under the Birmingham system* (bottom). *Higher-quality stocks — usually reserved for arms meant for private sale to British Volunteer Force regiments — featured checkering on the wrist and forearm for a better grip. All stocks were stamped with a round insignia, or "roundel," containing the year of manufacture.*

London Armoury Company view, proof, and inspection marks

The London Armoury Company was subject to the same British proof laws as any other commercial gun maker. Arms sold privately were marked with standard London commercial view and proof marks (top); arms made under British governmental contract were marked with standard governmental view and proof marks (bottom), including the "TP" ("Tower Proof") under a crown. Both commercial and governmental marks were accompanied by at least two "LAC" stamps (for "London Armoury Company"), applied well clear of the all-important view and proof marks.

Most barrels, whether made for private or governmental sale, bear British government viewer's marks at the breech: a Z (for the London Armoury Company) over a crown followed by "3" (the number of the particular inspector). The "386Y" stamps are mating numbers for the barrel and breech plug, the only parts of an interchangeable rifle-musket that did not interchange.

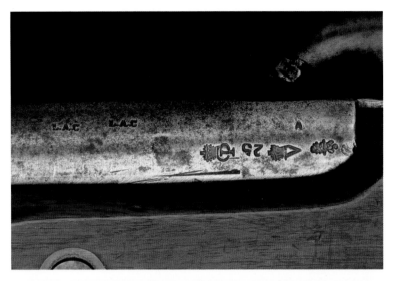

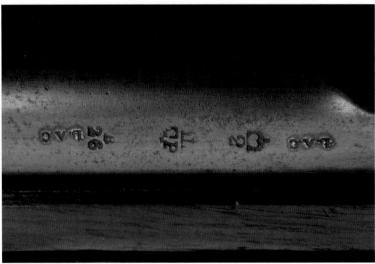

British Pattern 1853 contract rifle-musket, third type, made by the London Armoury Company (1861)

The initial success of the London Armoury Company depended upon its British government contract signed in February 1857 for thirty thousand rifle-muskets, production of which began in earnest in early 1860 and continued through mid-1862. As indicated by its plain, unchecked stock, governmental proof marks on the barrel, 1860-dated lockplate, and 1861-dated stock, this rifle-musket was probably fabricated under this contract, just before the outbreak of war in America. Unusually, it lacks the government's broad arrow inspection mark on the lockplate, indicating it may have been part of a run of excess production meant for the British Volunteer Force.

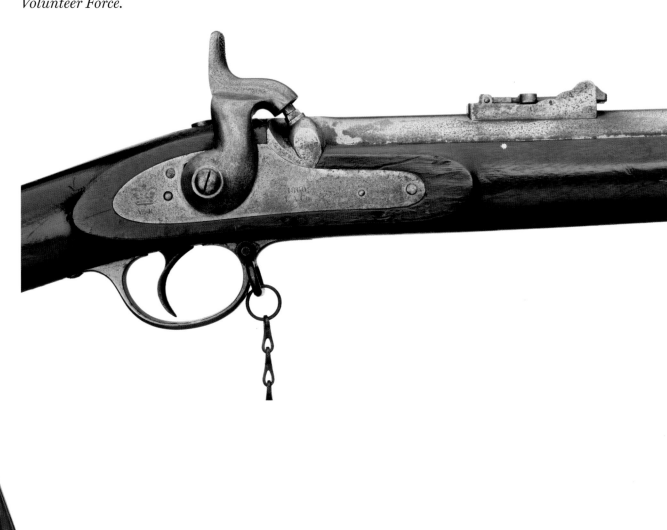

Commercial copy of British Pattern 1853 rifle-musket, third type, made by the London Armoury Company, Confederate inventory number 911 (1861)

Engraved with inventory number 911 on the buttplate tang and ramrod, this is the only London Armoury Company rifle-musket in the Wray Collection whose Confederate use is beyond doubt. It is one of only thirteen known London Armoury Company rifle-muskets with Confederate inventory numbers and one of only two with its original numbered ramrod. Purchased through Sinclair, Hamilton, and Company, it was probably shipped aboard the Bermuda, *the first large steam-powered blockade-runner to reach the South, which docked in Savannah, Georgia, on September 18, 1861. According to records in the Colin McRae papers, Caleb Huse purchased at least 3,360 rifle-muskets from the London Armoury Company through July 1862, though inventory numbers reach as high as 5816.*

Like British contract arms, this one has a plain stock, but its barrel bears London commercial view and proof marks instead of governmental marks, as befitting guns meant for private sale. Just forward of the inventory number on the buttplate is a tiny British government viewer's mark with a Z over a crown and a "4." The same mark appears on the sear inside the lock, intermixed with other parts marked "LAC." Governmental inspectors usually marked an entire batch of parts at a time, which were sometimes used randomly to assemble both private and government arms.

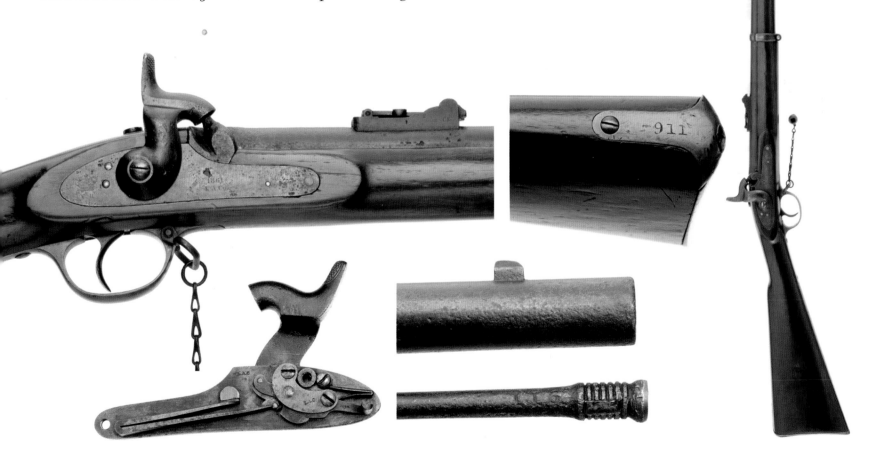

Commercial copy of British Pattern 1853 rifle-musket, third type, made by the London Armoury Company (1862)

Dated 1861 on the lockplate and 1862 on the stock, this rifle-musket was built with a finely checkered stock, marked with standard London commercial view and proof marks, and stamped on the buttplate tang with a small "LAC" rather than a governmental viewer's mark. The stock suggests that it was assembled for private sale to a member of one of the Volunteer Force regiments, perhaps for target-shooting matches. But given that the London Armoury Company was selling such a large portion of its excess production to the Confederacy in 1861 — and that other rifle-muskets with checkered stocks are known to have reached the South — it is possible that this one did too. If so, it was surely the finest arm a Confederate soldier could have hoped to own.

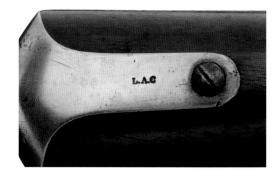

Commercial copy of British Pattern 1853 rifle-musket, third type, made by the London Armoury Company (1862)

Dated 1862 on both the lockplate and the stock, this well-worn rifle-musket is built around a plain, unchecked stock and a barrel with London commercial view and proof marks. Inside the lock, there are no governmental viewer's marks, only the company's private "LAC" stamp. Given the absence of any U.S. inspection or Massachusetts ownership markings in the stock, the features and markings of this rifle-musket strongly suggest private sale to the Confederacy. The most convincing evidence is the carved remains of a soldier's name in the stock opposite the lock, a common (though technically illegal) practice among Confederate soldiers.

To save time, the London Armoury Company used a single date stamp for all stocks, which bore only the first three digits of the year ("186_"). Later, when the arm was finished, the last number of the year was applied. In this case, the stamps were applied twice and obviously in a hurry: the one on the left is unfinished, but the one on the right has a barely legible "1862."

Commercial copy of British Pattern 1853 contract rifle-musket, third type, made by the London Armoury Company (1862)

The checkering on this 1862-dated rifle-musket suggests that the stock was meant for private sale, while the crown-and-broad-arrow viewer's mark on the lockplate indicates governmental inspection and ownership. Although these features suggest an arm fabricated for the British army or Volunteer Force, the barrel tells a different story.

Incredibly, the British government proof marks have been overstamped with "LAC" marks, including what appears to be a reapplied broad arrow directly over the original definitive, or "Tower Proof," mark. According to the Gun Barrel Proof Act of 1855, barrels with proof marks removed or defaced were to be considered unproved, hence illegal to sell, with a fine of up to £20 (nearly $2,000 today) for each offense. Such a violation would hardly go unnoticed in England, but would not matter in America, especially in the Confederacy.

Why anyone associated with the London Armoury Company would take such a risk is unknown. Selling government-marked arms to either side in the Civil War would have been a serious violation of British neutrality laws, an even graver offense than violating proof laws. Hence, such arms had to be assembled from rejected parts — or at least be made to appear that way to unknowing customs officers. The government's condemnation, or "sold out of service," stamp was an S and two point-to-point broad arrows struck directly over the definitive proof mark. Perhaps sympathetic (or bribed) government inspectors did not have these stamps on hand and simply had the London Armoury Company apply its "LAC" mark instead, thus making the arm technically "legal." It is also possible that the managing director, James Kerr, who was one of the five principal furnishers of noninterchangeable arms for Sinclair, Hamilton, and Company, absconded with parts (or even entire guns) from the London Armoury Company factory in order to fill a rush order for his other arms business. The answer will probably never be known.

Commercial copy of British Pattern 1853 rifle-musket, fourth type, made by the London Armoury Company (1863)

In June 1861, the British War Office adopted a fourth and final configuration of the Pattern 1853 rifle-musket, distinguished by barrel bands with recessed screw heads to prevent snagging on a soldier's clothing or equipment. Following the War Office's lead, the London Armoury Company began manufacturing the new bands in late 1862. Even though it had already completed its British government contract several months earlier, the company wanted to be the only commercial arms maker offering exact duplicates of the current government pattern.

Bearing an 1863 date on both stock and lockplate, this rifle-musket could have been fabricated in the last six months of the year, when most of the London Armoury Company's production is believed to have been sold to the Confederacy. Indeed, the homemade checkering pattern carved into the wrist is strongly reminiscent of Confederate soldiers carving their names into the stocks.

But as with many London Armoury Company rifle-muskets, appearances can be deceiving: this one undoubtedly went to the British Volunteer Force. It is stamped with governmental view and proof marks (with the "LAC" marks where they should be), as well as a "crown-over-1 and L" stamp on the top of the barrel, signifying that it was officially certified by a British government inspector for use in volunteer target-shooting matches, probably several years after 1863.

Stamped into the stock just behind the trigger-guard tang is the "J Smiles" mark of James Smiles, an employee (probably a viewer) of the London Armoury Company. For some time it was thought that Smiles was the viewer associated with the Confederate "JS"-and-anchor mark, but there is no firm evidence of any Confederate association except that his name appears on London Armoury Company rifle-muskets made in 1863 and 1864.

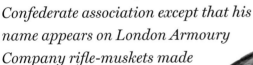

Kerr patent revolvers, third type, made by the London Armoury Company, serial numbers 3398 and 3418 (ca. 1861–62)

Among the founders of the London Armoury Company was Robert Adams, who intended it to focus on manufacturing the double-action revolver that bore his name. But when the firm decided to manufacture rifle-muskets, Adams left, and his fellow shareholder James Kerr became manager. Kerr not only oversaw the manufacture of rifle-muskets, but also put into production his own patented side-hammer revolver in place of the Adams.

Between 1859 and 1866, the London Armoury Company produced approximately 11,500 Kerr revolvers, of which 9,000 went to the Confederate army and navy under three contracts. They were among the best arms used by the Confederacy, second only in quality and quantity to northern-made Colt and Remington revolvers purchased before the war or captured on the battlefield. Indeed, the number of Kerr revolvers imported into the Confederacy was only slightly less than the combined total production of revolvers by all southern manufacturers during the war.

These nearly identical 54 bore (.442-caliber) five-shot revolvers feature finely checkered wooden grips and are stamped with London commercial proof marks on the barrels and cylinders. Most important, both bear the faint remains of "JS"-and-anchor stamps at the base of the grips, believed to indicate inspection by the British government inspector John Southgate and his team of viewers. Kerr revolvers are the only London Armoury Company guns so marked. Because these revolvers were produced only for private sale, there was no conflict of interest for Southgate, especially since he was technically on sick leave from his London Armoury Company assignment while he moonlighted for Sinclair, Hamilton, and Company in Birmingham.

A Scramble for Armaments

Although Caleb Huse was the key purchasing agent in Britain, he was by no means the only American to buy arms there. Union agents were buying up all the European firearms they could get their hands on until rifle-musket production in the North could catch up with demand. It was a sort of cold war, with each side actively spying on the other, cajoling, threatening, and bribing as needed. Almost immediately, Huse gained a huge advantage by striking up partnerships with three commission houses that would do most of the actual purchasing: William J. Grazebrook; Sinclair, Hamilton, and Company; and S. Isaac, Campbell and Company. Although these firms charged considerable fees for their services, their inside knowledge of the gun trade often enabled them to outmaneuver Union agents and secure the best-quality English rifled arms, leaving their competitors with third- or even fourth-class smoothbore arms from the Continent. In early July 1861, a Union purchasing agent named William McFarland arranged a deal with London gun makers to procure their output for the next six months, but missed the deadline for making the required down payment. The timely intervention of Samuel Isaac and a large down payment of £10,000 from Huse meant that the guns instead went to the Confederacy. So successful were Huse's efforts that when the Confederate garrison at Vicksburg, Mississippi, surrendered in July 1863, several Union regiments exchanged their old .69-caliber European muskets for their prisoners' new .577-caliber English rifle-muskets.

Besides Union agents such as McFarland, Huse competed against purchasing agents from his own country. North Carolina, South Carolina, Georgia, and Louisiana sent their own representatives to Britain, usually with a letter of introduction requesting Huse, already overburdened, to render assistance and provide shipping. All told, southern state agents purchased at least twenty thousand rifles and rifle-muskets as well as artillery pieces, accoutrements, shoes, cloth, and other supplies. Southern state agents in turn competed against northern state agents from New York, Massachusetts, and possibly other states, while private individuals and profiteering speculators from both sections scavenged all manner of weapons through arms merchants in Britain and throughout Europe. Meanwhile, all parties vied with 170,000 Englishmen who were busy arming themselves as volunteer regiments for home defense against an overblown threat of attack from France. The intense competition drove up prices for all concerned, generating immense profits for gun makers and dealers alike.

In 1862, the C.S. Ordnance Bureau managed to rein in state purchasing, usually by mutual consent, occasionally by force: in the first year of the war, its officers

About 4,300 of the excellent Enfield rifles which were imported by the State at great risk and expense, have been seized at the different ports where they landed, by officers of the Confederate Government. . . . While my remonstrances have been met with respectful language by those in authority, and the act generally apologised for as a mistake, they have neglected to restore the property seized, and have, after my remonstrance, repeated the seizure on the arrival of other arms. As the rights of the State were disregarded by the Confederate authorities, I thought it unwise to send more money to Europe to invest in other arms to be lost at sea or seized.

—Governor Joseph E. Brown of Georgia in his report to the Georgia Legislature, November 1862

seized thousands of state-purchased arms when they arrived on the docks. The resulting disputes reached President Jefferson Davis, who had to carefully apportion the cargoes of the first blockade-runners among governors, generals, and political interests. Private speculation continued throughout the war, resulting in unknown thousands of foreign arms pouring into the South for both military and civilian use. Fortunately for the Confederacy, the U.S. War Department, confident that domestic arms production would meet future demand, canceled its foreign contracts in late 1862. Although the field was abandoned to the Confederacy, northern agents had done their share of harm. Among the 1.3 million European arms shipped to the North before deliveries ended in July 1863 were about 500,000 London- or Birmingham-made commercial copies of British Pattern 1853 rifle-muskets, some of which had been purchased as much to keep them out of Confederate hands as to equip Union soldiers.

Over the course of the war, Caleb Huse spent some $12 million, more than any other Confederate agent abroad. Close to $5 million of that went to S. Isaac, Campbell and Company, once a major supplier of quartermaster stores to the British Army, but disgraced by a bribery scandal in 1858 and banned from receiving British government contracts. Yet the company remained a powerful force in the military-equipment business and lavished every possible courtesy on its new and best client, including the extension of at least $2 million worth of credit. In addition to arms, the company provided swords, leather accoutrements, knapsacks, buttons, shoes, and a host of other items, all from a variety of makers or surplus dealers. It also took care of vital details such as storage, transportation, insurance, and customs fees. For Huse, it was an expensive arrangement, but one that centralized and streamlined purchasing as much as possible. He needed arms and equipment, and he needed them fast; cost and quality were less important than delivery and quantity.

At first, Huse purchased not only for the C.S. Ordnance Bureau but also for the Quartermaster Bureau and the Medical Department. The only entity for which he did not purchase was the C.S. Navy, which was represented by its own agent, thirty-eight-year-old Commander James Dunwoody Bulloch. Huse was able to ship his purchases with the aid of Fraser, Trenholm, and Company in London and its two sister companies in Charleston and Bermuda, which served as financial clearing-houses and shipping companies for the Confederate army and navy. By mid-1863, the situation had grown more complex. The C.S. Quartermaster Bureau, which had sent a dozen or so of its own purchasing agents to Canada and Europe, entered into a partnership with the C.S. Navy and an English shipping company to transport quartermaster stores, naval ordnance, and any other military cargoes it could find. Uninformed of the scheme, and with Ordnance Bureau blockade-runners already in operation, Huse was stunned to find the new company demanding to ship arms for its own profit.

In the bureaucratic turf war between the Ordnance and Quartermaster Bureaus that followed, Huse was accused of malfeasance by his new Confederate competitors. An official inquiry led by Colin McCrae cleared Huse of all charges in 1864, but was not so kind to Samuel Isaac's company. In the course of the investigation, it was discovered that the commission house had been keeping a double set of books, consistently overcharging the Confederate government and engaging in other questionable practices. Its official partnership with the Confederacy soon came to an abrupt halt. After July 1863, Confederate purchasing agents worked under the direct supervision of McRae, who, because he held the purse strings, dictated operations. The items presented in this section represent the wide variety of weapons and accoutrements purchased by Huse and his competitors during the two turbulent years before McRae's appointment as chief financial agent.

Commercial copy of British Pattern 1853 artillery carbine, first type, assembled from parts by an unknown Birmingham furnisher, Confederate inventory number 242 (1861)

The desperation of English arms merchants in 1861 to fill rush orders for southern customers is nowhere better illustrated than in this ersatz artillery carbine. It is built around a Liège-made barrel with an early-style bayonet stud and guide key and stamped with both Belgian and British government proof marks, indicating that the barrel was made under contract in Belgium and probably used during the Crimean War. In 1860, English gun makers relieved the British War Office of tens of thousands of surplus Crimean War arms, many of which were later stripped for parts and "made up" into new arms for the American market.

As indicated by the "LAC" stamp on the underside, the barrel then passed through the hands of the London Armoury Company. At that time it was still legal to resell the former government-owned barrel without re-proving it, but as a result of such questionable marriages of parts, the practice was outlawed in 1868. The London Armoury Company also provided the lock, which is one of the company's early patterns, with an engraved double-line border, probably dating to 1859 or early 1860. It seems apparent that James Kerr and Archibald Hamilton used their positions in the London Armoury Company to acquire such surplus parts for their other arms businesses in London and Birmingham.

All other extant artillery carbines bearing the "JS"-and-anchor viewer's mark on the underside of the stock, along with engraved numbers on the buttplate, were made in Birmingham, suggesting this one was assembled there too, probably by or for William and Charles Scott and Son. Given its low inventory number, it was almost certainly among the very first shipments to the Confederacy and clearly saw its share of use during the war. The ramrod is a replacement.

Commercial variant of British Pattern 1856 rifle, made by an unknown Birmingham furnisher, Confederate inventory number 1846 (1861)

Among the many products of the London and Birmingham gun trades were military-style arms cosmetically similar to official British patterns but not intended for governmental inspection or use. Instead, such arms were meant for police, prison guards, English or colonial volunteer regiments, or anyone else who could afford to buy them.

This Birmingham-made rifle was based on the British Pattern 1856, but with a few minor differences: the buttplate, trigger-guard plate, and stock tip are made of brass, there is no guide key forward of the bayonet stud, and the rear sling swivel screwed directly into the stock instead of through the trigger-guard tang. As indicated by the inventory number on the buttplate and the "JS"-and-anchor viewer's mark, this unusual rifle was sold to the Confederacy, probably in the summer or fall of 1861.

It was "made up" in a hurry. Unusually, the lockplate has the royal cipher "VR" stamped below the crown, indicating that it was originally intended for a government-contract arm. Most unusually (indeed, almost unheard of), the barrel bears London proof marks, meaning a London barrel was mated with a Birmingham lock and stock. While normally such a mismatch is evidence of modern tampering, in this case it is believed to be a genuine example of furnishers rushing to fill a lucrative Confederate contract. In a pinch, barrels could be purchased on the open market, and setters-up could pull out government-inspected locks from their parts bins. Such was the nature of doing business with a wealthy customer who needed a lot of guns quickly.

Commercial variant of British Pattern 1853 rifle-musket, made by an unknown Birmingham furnisher, purchased by the State of South Carolina, inventory number 742 (1862)

At forty inches in length, the barrel of this rifle-musket is one inch longer than the British Pattern 1853, while its breech has an unusual octagonal shape. Between the standard Birmingham proof marks is a C inside a diamond as well as a bore stamp of "24," indicating a caliber of .58 instead of the normal .577. This appears to be a rough copy of the forty-inch .58-caliber U.S. Model 1855 barrel, three thousand of which were fitted to English-made rifle-muskets offered for sale to the U.S. War Department by the arms baron Samuel Colt in March 1862.

Barrels of the same dimensions were also fabricated by Birmingham gun makers under a contract with the government of Spain, which, in 1857, had adopted a series of arms based on the British Pattern 1853. These barrels may have been diverted from the Spanish contract for the more lucrative American market. Although several thousand rifle-muskets built around these .58-caliber barrels were sold to both North and South, English gun makers understood that no more need be made, since American buyers were satisfied with the usual .577-caliber arms, which, if necessary, could fire .58-caliber ammunition.

This example has an unquestionable southern provenance. It bears the "JS"-over-anchor viewer's mark on the underside of the stock, the engraved inventory number 742 on the buttplate tang, and the block letters "SC" stamped into the butt, indicating its purchase by the State of South Carolina. In late March 1862, the state sent an agent to London with authorization to spend $60,000 for arms, ammunition, and medicine for South Carolina. It is believed that the first one thousand of the three thousand rifle-muskets eventually acquired by the state were built with these .58-caliber barrels. This one was probably delivered to South Carolina in the summer of 1862. Ironically, many of these state-purchased arms ended up gathering dust in the state arsenal in Columbia, where they were burned by Sherman's troops in 1865.

Commercial copy of British Pattern 1853 rifle-musket furnished by Henry Beckwith, London, purchased by the State of Georgia, inventory number 3885 (1861)

In June 1861, the former U.S. Navy officer and Savannah mayor Edward C. Anderson was dispatched by his friend Jefferson Davis to London, where he was to assist Caleb Huse while making sure the young northern-born officer was doing his job. Meanwhile, Anderson had also been asked to buy guns for his native state by Georgia governor Joseph E. Brown. There seemed to be no conflict of interest as long as both parties could get what they wanted, which, in the case of Governor Brown, was 4,700 rifle-muskets and 800 rifles. Anderson acquired them in September 1861 from Sinclair, Hamilton, and Company.

To prevent any possible confusion with Confederate government arms, the Georgia guns were stamped with a prominent G on the stock and assigned their own inventory numbers — one series for rifles and another for rifle-muskets — on the buttplate tang. Yet these carefully applied markings were ignored by the C.S. War Department, which seized the first two shipments of 2,580 Georgia arms at their ports of entry in the fall of 1861 and promptly distributed them wherever it felt they were needed most. When informed by an apologetic Confederate secretary of state that "your arms had been so dispersed that it was impossible to recover them," Governor Brown threatened to seize Confederate arms in retaliation.[4] He was only partly mollified when the War Department assured him that some of the state's arms had in fact been issued to Georgia troops in Confederate service.

Georgia rifle-musket number 3885 was almost certainly shipped on Fraser, Trenholm, and Company's steamer the Economist, *which arrived in Charleston on March 14, 1862. By then the initial rush for arms had subsided, and this gun, along with another 1,700 purchased by the state through Caleb Huse the previous month, probably made it to Georgia. It was assembled in a small shop headed by the second-generation London gunsmith Henry Beckwith. But the block letter B on the stock signifies not Beckwith but the larger London gun maker Edward P. Bond, who, as one of the principal furnishers for Sinclair, Hamilton, and Company, acted as the middleman in this transaction, no doubt for a surcharge. In the end, despite all the expense, trouble, and blustering, Brown managed to retain at least 3,000 rifle-muskets, sufficient for the state troops he wanted to maintain.*

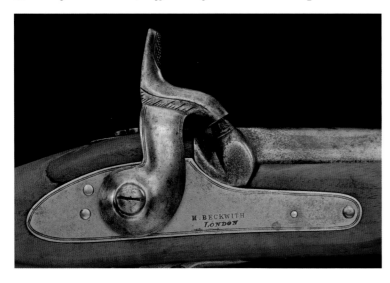

Commercial copy of British Pattern 1853 enlisted man's cavalry sword furnished by S. Isaac, Campbell and Company, London, purchased by the State of Georgia (1861)

Although the manufacture of swords and sabers was a relatively easy and low-tech undertaking, time, labor, and material shortages required the South to purchase as many as possible abroad. Over the course of the war, Caleb Huse bought at least twenty-five thousand English-made swords or sabers for the Confederacy, and private speculators bought thousands more.

The most common of these was the straight-bladed 1853 pattern cavalry trooper's sword, which had a characteristic pressed-leather grip. This one bears the "Isaac & Co." mark of S. Isaac, Campbell and Company on the back of the blade as well as a stamped G at the ricasso, indicating purchase by the State of Georgia. It is probably one of the one thousand swords acquired by Edward C. Anderson and shipped aboard the Fingal, *which arrived in Savannah on November 13, 1861. Believing his mission successfully completed, Anderson returned on the same ship, personally accompanying these swords as well as the first lot of 1,100 rifle-muskets he had purchased for the State of Georgia. Unlike the rifle-muskets, these swords probably went directly to Georgia commands.*

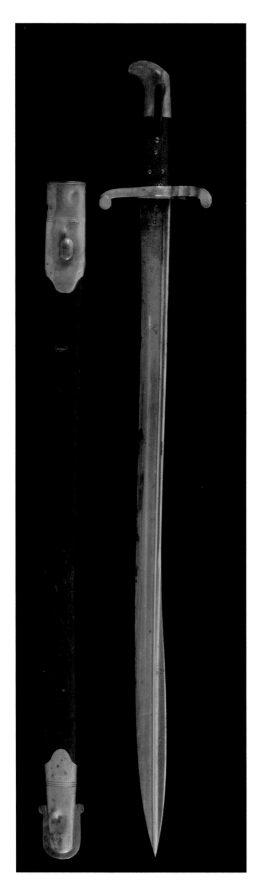

Commercial copy of British Pattern 1855 Lancaster sword bayonet believed to have been purchased by State of North Carolina (1862)

Originally designed for the experimental Lancaster rifle, this distinctive brass-mounted sword bayonet bears a tiny "NC" stamp on the quillon at the tip of the guard, suggesting that it may have been purchased by the State of North Carolina. If so, it may be the only one in existence.

It is stamped on the ricasso with the knight's-head maker's mark of C. R. Kirschbaum and Company of Solingen, Prussia, as well as the inspection stamp of the Birmingham Small Arms Trade, indicating that it was meant for private sale. With a guide groove extending forward of the mortise, the Lancaster-pattern bayonet fit most of the British pattern rifles and artillery carbines of the late 1850s. It would not, however, fit the two thousand rifle-muskets procured by North Carolina's agent in London and delivered to Wilmington in April 1862. Today there are four surviving rifle-muskets believed to have been part of that shipment, two of which bear small "NC" state acceptance marks closely resembling the "NC" on the guard of this bayonet.

Another shipment of twelve hundred arms identified only as "Enfield rifles" arrived in Wilmington in September 1863 aboard North Carolina's own blockade-runner, the Advance, *but they are recorded as having been subsequently sold to the C.S. Ordnance Bureau. It is possible that there were some English-made rifles and bayonets in the cargo that remained state property. Yet given that Lancaster bayonets were quite popular among the British Volunteer Force, it is also possible that the "NC" mark has nothing to do with North Carolina at all.*

Commercial copy of British Pattern 1858 rifle furnished by Potts and Hunt, London (1861)

Popularly known as the "bar on band" rifle, this pattern was developed by the British War Office because it was feared that the barrel might be weakened by having a bayonet stud brazed directly to a dovetailed slot at the muzzle. Hence, the stud was instead attached to the upper barrel band, giving the rifle its distinctive "snub-nosed" look. Like all British pattern arms, these rifles were sold to both sides in the Civil War.

This one was made by the second-generation firm of Thomas A. Potts and Thomas Hunt in the Minories gun-making quarter near the Tower of London. It is believed to have been among 1,940 rifles delivered to New York in August 1861 under contract with the Colt Firearms Manufacturing Company of New Haven, Connecticut. Lacking any prior arrangement, a Colt representative called on the U.S. War Department's purchasing agent and arranged their sale at twenty-five dollars each, including bayonets, thus salvaging a small profit in a very speculative enterprise. The War Department is thought to have purchased around 9,400 British pattern rifles, while the State of New York bought another 4,000.

Commercial copy of French Pattern 1842 musket, made in Liège, Belgium (ca. 1850)

When their initial efforts in England were largely thwarted by Confederate agents, northern buyers turned instead to Continental Europe, where they nearly cleaned out the arsenals of Belgium, France, Austria, and the German states. Among an estimated 800,000 surplus arms purchased on the Continent were at least 147,000 of these smoothbore .71-caliber French-pattern muskets made in the great arms-making center of Liège. Many were acquired for the U.S. War Department by Herman Boker and Company, an import-export firm with offices in New York, Birmingham, and Liège.

Derisively termed "pumpkin slingers" by the soldiers to whom they were issued, these old muskets were nevertheless sturdy and reliable. Though none are known to have been purchased by the Confederacy, many were listed in the inventories of Confederate arsenals, probably as the result of battlefield capture. Many saw service with state reserve or militia units in 1864. At the Atlanta Arsenal, there were enough "Belgian muskets" on hand to justify the construction of a gang mold for casting .71-caliber bullets; this mold is now part of the DuBose Collection.

Thomas Wilson–patented breech-loading rifle, serial number A29 (1860)

This patented breech-loading military rifle was one of the most technologically advanced arms imported into the Confederacy. Today it is also one of the rarest, with only seven examples known to survive. It was the work of Thomas Wilson, a mechanical engineer and arms inventor in Birmingham who held at least twenty-five patents in his lifetime. Covered under British patent numbers 1318 (May 28, 1859) and 685 (March 15, 1860), this design used a normal percussion-ignited paper cartridge inserted into the breech under a sliding door secured in place by a transverse sliding wedge. In 1860, the British army tested Wilson's simple design as a means of converting its Pattern 1853 muzzle-loading arms into breechloaders. His design was rejected, but only because of inaccuracy caused by improperly sealed cartridges.

Failing to secure a War Office contract, Wilson sought other markets, including the newly formed Confederacy. In mid-1863, a small number of Wilson's rifles are believed to have been procured for the C.S. Navy through the Charleston import-export firm of Courtney, Tennent, and Company. Further evidence for Confederate use is fragmentary, but there is a report of Wilson rifles having been in use at Charleston in 1864.

Thought to represent the earliest configuration, this example is configured after the British Pattern 1860 rifle. With six broad lands and six narrow grooves, the barrel is made in 30 bore, or .54 caliber, one of at least three calibers that Wilson used in an attempt to perfect the rifle's accuracy. Though it never saw Confederate service, this example is essentially of the same configuration as those that did. In 1957, the arms historian William B. Edwards purchased this gun in a sale from a firearms museum in Liège, where it had been deposited as a model arm to protect Wilson's Belgian patent. Nevertheless, as indicated by the replaced ramrod and breech door (a modern restoration), the cracked stock, and numerous nicks in the stock, it saw significant use.

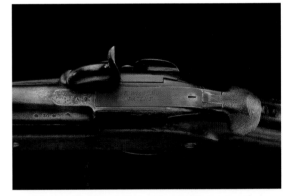

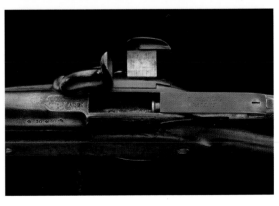

Girard-LeMat revolver, "transitional" type, assembled in Paris, serial number 658 (1862)

Today the LeMat "grapeshot" revolver is easily the most famous and distinctive of all Confederate firearms, all the more so because of its colorful inventor, who insisted on having his name stamped on every weapon made under his patent. The massive revolver packed a powerful punch: a nine-shot .42-caliber cylinder rotating around an 18-gauge shotgun barrel. Switching from one to the other was as simple as pivoting a small lever on the hammer.

It was the brainchild of the physician, entrepreneur, and honorary colonel Jean François Alexandre LeMat, a French émigré who settled in New Orleans in 1844, where he filed the first patent for his soon-to-be-famous revolver in 1856. Seeking to have his revolvers manufactured in quantity, three years later he formed a partnership with the future Confederate general (and his cousin by marriage) Pierre Gustave Toutant Beauregard. But the partners found no takers among northern manufacturers, the U.S. Army, or gun makers in Europe, where LeMat wisely patented his design anyway.

The coming of war in 1861 revived LeMat's fortunes. With a new partner, Charles Girard, a noted botanist (and skilled Confederate propagandist), LeMat obtained contracts for five thousand revolvers for the C.S. army and three thousand for the navy in the summer of 1861. The partners considered domestic manufacture (including Cook and Brother in New Orleans) but instead established a factory in Paris. There they turned out twenty-five hundred revolvers, about eighteen hundred of which are believed to have been slipped past the blockade into the Confederacy. Another thousand were assembled under contract in Birmingham in early 1865, though none reached the South.

Although the first four hundred revolvers were shipped directly from Paris in the summer of 1862, the next lot of five hundred, including the example pictured here, were to be delivered through Caleb Huse in London. At first Huse refused to accept them, considering the bulky hybrid revolvers unreliable and overpriced, especially compared with the London Armoury Company's sleek and interchangeable Kerr revolvers. Political pressures in Richmond finally forced Huse to relent, and the five hundred LeMat revolvers began arriving in southern ports in January 1863. The provenance of this gun after it reached the South is unknown.

Engraved on the top of the barrel is a French government legal notice. After "Colonel" LeMat's name is the abbreviation "Bte" for "Breveté" ("patented"), followed by "s.g.d.g." ("sans garantie du gouvernement," "without the guarantee of the government"). Stamped next to the serial number is "LM" under a star, believed to be the mark of Lejay and Massiaux, a manufacturing firm near the Belgian border that supplied the Paris factory with barrels under a cottage industry system much like the Birmingham system.

Girard-LeMat carbine assembled in Paris, serial number 31 (ca. 1863)

This carbine version of the famous LeMat grapeshot revolver is one of the great rarities in Confederate collecting: there are only eighteen surviving examples, the highest-known serial number being 112. The carbines were simply elongated versions of the revolver, with the same .42-caliber cylinder and upper barrel, but a rifled .48-caliber lower barrel. Some were in Confederate service as early as May 1863, when the Richmond Arsenal was providing cartridges for them. This well-worn example has been incorrectly restored with a smoothbore lower barrel and a loading lever taken from one of the revolvers.

As demonstrated by these restorations, LeMat arms did not hold up well in the field. Today, many surviving examples have missing loading levers, repaired hammers, or faulty cylinders (misaligned, unable to rotate or lock). Many of the loading levers may have been discarded by soldiers who found them too awkward to use. Additionally, production was slow, and there was the problem of making and supplying odd-caliber ammunition, not to mention the difficulties in running completed arms through the blockade. Although many of the mechanical problems were resolved in later production (especially in England), Caleb Huse, James D. Bulloch, and others were probably justified in their view that no matter how ferocious, LeMat's guns were simply not worth the effort. Yet with Girard and LeMat's tireless promotion (including the presentation of revolvers to J. E. B. Stuart, Braxton Bragg, P. G. T. Beauregard, and Jefferson Davis), Confederate contracts were renewed and deliveries continued through the closing of Wilmington in January 1865.

After the war ended and his primary customer was no longer in business, Charles Girard struggled to keep the Paris factory open, taking orders from Japan, Russia, and Egypt. After a failed attempt to sell the patent rights and remaining guns to the Colt Firearms Manufacturing Company, the LeMat factory closed in May 1866. LeMat himself continued his tinkering long after the war, patenting center-fire versions of his revolver, working on ship and dirigible designs, and even volunteering to fight in the Franco-Prussian war in 1870–71. He returned to France in 1868 and died there in 1895.

Commercial copy of British Pattern 1860 cartridge pouch, made by Alexander Ross and Company, London (1861)

Along with firearms, Confederate agents in Britain purchased vast quantities of the leather accoutrements used to carry ammunition. Unlike its forty-round American cousin, the British army cartridge box of 1860 (called a "pouch") was designed to carry fifty rounds, wrapped ten to a bundle. This copy of the British Pattern 1860 Sergeant of Guards pouch was made by Alexander Ross and Company, whose stamp "A. Ross & Co. / c&m 1861" appears on the inside edge of the outer flap.

In 1861, Ross had been in business for just over one hundred years and, as indicated by the "c&m" stamp ("contractor and manufacturer"), was still on the approved list of contractors for the British army. With governmental business at stake, the company maintained the highest-quality standards even for commercial work, although it could have used cheaper leather and leather dyes—a matter of little consequence for Confederate purchasers. This example may have been among the £10,000 worth of accoutrements purchased by Edward C. Anderson from Alexander Ross in September 1861 and shipped aboard the Fingal the next month.

Commercial copy of British Pattern 1860 cartridge pouch, made for S. Isaac, Campbell and Company, London, with Confederate-made sling (ca. 1863)

S. Isaac, Campbell and Company had few qualms about taking shortcuts in the goods it sold to the Confederacy. Compared to the previously pictured cartridge pouch made by Ross, the stitching on this example is noticeably sloppier, the quality of leather and finish is poorer, and the iron sling buckles lack the usual tin or enamel coating to protect them from rust. Although bearing the familiar company stamp with its London address, 71 Jermyn Street, this pouch was almost certainly made by a subcontractor, probably at one of many leather works in the Bermondsey area of London. It undoubtedly saw Confederate use, its leather sling having been replaced with a machine-sewn linen sling similar to gun slings made in Richmond.

Commercial copy of British Pattern 1861 ball bag for rifle regiments, maker unknown (ca. 1863)

The Pattern 1861 ball bag was the British army's latest piece of equipment for the Pattern 1853 rifle-musket. Worn on a soldier's waist belt, it was meant to hold loose cartridges unwrapped from bundles in the cartridge pouch. Confederate troops, accustomed to the American system of taking cartridges directly from their cartridge boxes, found the ball bags pointless. In 1863 and 1864, at least four thousand of them were classified as scrap leather and turned in to the Richmond Arsenal, where the leather was reused to make American-style cap pouches. This one is unmarked, but its superior quality suggests manufacture by Alexander Ross or a similarly established company.

Soldiers' bootees, believed to have been made in England (ca. 1864)

If Confederate soldiers ever lacked shoes, it was not for want of effort on the part of C.S. Quartermaster Bureau agents working in England, who, in 1864 alone, shipped 545,000 pairs of shoes to the Confederacy, most of them high-top military-style bootees or brogans. Many were made in Northampton, the center of the shoe-making industry in England. S. Isaac, Campbell and Company set up the first mechanized shoe factory there in 1859, much to the displeasure of thousands of workers used to the traditional craft system. By 1862, the factory was making 100,000 pairs of shoes a year, many of which were sold to the Confederacy.

Featuring pull tabs and brass eyelets, these bootees were approximate copies of "Blutcher" shoes made for the British army, but have pegged soles, which were less expensive than sturdier hand-sewn ones. They have been repaired with the addition of a half sole.

Confederate naval officer's sword made by Robert Mole and Son, Birmingham, retailed by Courtney, Tennent, and Company, Charleston, South Carolina (ca. 1863)

Based on the British Pattern 1827 naval officer's sword, these rare and elegant weapons are believed to have been designed for the C.S. Navy by Commander George T. Sinclair, once captain of the ironclad css Atlanta *(converted from the blockade-runner* Fingal*) and one of the navy's purchasing agents in England beginning in 1862. Perhaps only a few hundred of these swords were ever made, making surviving examples extremely rare.*

They were embellished with traditional naval motifs, including the head of a mythical sea serpent at the pommel, intertwined serpents on the drag of the leather scabbard, and coils of rope for the ring bands. Cast into the guard is a fouled anchor over crossed cannon, the insignia of the C.S. Navy, on either side of which are tobacco leaves and cotton plants, symbolizing the commercial wealth of the South. Meanwhile, blades were etched with the same symbols as well as a Confederate first national-pattern flag.

This example was made by Robert Mole and Son, high-quality cutlery makers in Birmingham, but marked for retail sale with the stamp of Courtney, Tennent, and Company of Charleston. William C. Courtney lived in London for most of the war while his company served as the Confederate navy's commission house in England, not unlike Sinclair, Hamilton, and Company for the army.

Blakely 2.9-inch mountain rifle (ca. 1862)

Along with small arms and accoutrements, the Confederacy badly needed rifled artillery. In the first twenty-one months of the war, Caleb Huse spent nearly £97,000 purchasing 129 cannons, from the smallest field pieces to the largest coastal guns. He was able to pick and choose from among a new generation of lighter, stronger, and more accurate rifled guns made of iron and steel instead of heavy bronze.

One of the most promising of these new guns was the invention of a young Irish-born Royal Artillery captain named T. Alexander Blakely, who had tried unsuccessfully to interest the British army in his method of constructing gun barrels reinforced with wrought-iron or steel bands. But when his design was rejected and his rival Sir William Armstrong was made superintendent of the Royal Arsenal at Woolwich, Blakely left the army to found his own gun-manufacturing business. Using five foundries — including his own Blakely Ordnance Company in London — Blakely eventually constructed about four hundred guns in thirteen calibers ranging from 2.5 inches to a massive 12.75 inches. He sold his guns all over the world, including Russia, Peru, Morocco, Japan, and, of course, both belligerent nations in America.

Blakely's best customer turned out to be the Confederacy, which purchased a large number of his lightweight, 3.5-inch field rifles, some of which became famous in the hands of General J. E. B. Stuart's horse artillery in the Army of Northern Virginia. This smaller, 2.9-inch version was designed as a mountain gun for rough or inaccessible terrain, but its battlefield history is unknown. Measuring thirty-seven inches long and rifled with six distinctive sawtooth, or "hook-slant," grooves, it is believed to be one of only four guns of this size and configuration to make it into a southern port. George Wray purchased it in 1977 from an antiques dealer in Exton, Pennsylvania. This gun may not have been cast — and certainly was not marked — in the inventor's presence: on the right trunnion, "Blakely" is misspelled "Blakeley."

6. Southern Ingenuity

It was not that the South lacked its share of brains, imagination, or optimistic inventors. Gabriel J. Rains invented a pressure-activated fuse that allowed ordinary artillery shells to be turned into land mines. The Confederate navy developed floating, electrically detonated mines, ironclad warships, and the first submarine to sink an enemy ship. A Kentucky captain named D. R. Williams came up with a breech-loading cannon capable of firing at least fifteen 1.57-inch rounds per minute. During the war, the Confederate States issued 274 patents, about one-third of which had military applications, including thirteen patents for breech-loading or revolving firearms and cannon. Unfortunately, because the C.S. Patent Office records were destroyed by fire in 1865, historians will never know precisely how these inventions worked. But it is clear that what the South lacked was not inventiveness, but the industrial infrastructure and skilled labor to put inventions into production. Despite a few noteworthy successes, southern ingenuity simply could not offset northern technology, manpower, and industry.

Nowhere was this disparity more apparent than in the emergence of breech-loading arms during the war. Nearly all infantrymen on both sides were armed with muzzle-loading rifle-muskets, but after 1862 Union cavalrymen were usually armed with breech-loading rifled carbines, much easier to load on horseback and capable of firing at least nine times a minute, three times as fast as a muzzle-loader. From 1861 through 1865, northern manufacturers turned out close to 470,000 breech-loading carbines and rifles of at least sixteen different designs. Among them were the devastatingly effective magazine-fed repeaters developed by Benjamin Tyler Henry and Christian Spencer, the most successful and technologically advanced firearms of the era. Meanwhile, southern manufacturers managed to produce only about 7,200 breech-loading arms of five different designs, all carbines and none of them repeating, and about 5,500 of these were copies of the northern-made Sharps carbine.

In 1861, as thousands of volunteers flocked to join the U.S. Army, its newly appointed chief of ordnance, James W. Ripley, wisely focused on supplying the infantry (three-fourths of the Union army) with muzzle-loading weapons, deeming

I think it may be fairly asserted, now, that the highest efficiency of a body of men with fire-arms can only be secured by putting in their hands the best breech-loading arm. The long habit of using muzzle loading arms will resist what seems to be so great an innovation, and ignorance may condemn; but as certainly as the percussion cap has superseded flint and steel, so surely will the breech-loading gun drive out of use those that load at the muzzle.
—Secretary of War John B. Floyd, December 3, 1860

them the most expedient and cost-effective way to arm the greatest number of soldiers. Neither the Springfield Armory nor its contractors had time to select breech-loading infantry or cavalry arms and tool up for their production. Meanwhile, although Ripley was convinced of the value of breech-loading carbines for the cavalry, he was nearly overwhelmed with inventors and manufacturers seeking contracts for a bewildering array of patented breech-loading designs, most of them already available on the private market. Because each design required a unique cartridge in its own caliber as well as a unique set of replacement parts, adopting any of them would create major problems of supply and maintenance. Yet Ripley faced a bigger problem: the Sharps Rifle Manufacturing Company, the largest maker of breechloaders in the world, was not yet able to produce enough carbines for all the volunteer cavalry units then being formed. Thus the U.S. Ordnance Department was forced to dramatically expand its previously limited horizons, contracting for huge numbers of largely untried designs. For arms makers and inventors in the North, the economic incentive of governmental contracts, combined with the industrial infrastructure and mechanical know-how born of the Industrial Revolution, allowed them to mass-produce breech-loading weapons on a theretofore-unimaginable scale.

At first, Confederate chief of ordnance Josiah Gorgas faced similar challenges: offered all sorts of exotic breech-loading weapons, he also wisely chose to concentrate his limited resources on procuring the largest possible number of muzzle-loading arms — in his case, mostly British rifle-muskets imported through the blockade. But there the similarities ended. Other than about thirty-five hundred Sharps and Maynard carbines purchased on the eve of war by southern state agents working in the North, there were simply no breech-loading arms to be had in any quantity in the South, nor were there any reliable designs available for sale in Europe. Worse, only in Richmond did the industrial infrastructure exist to support the production of breech-loading arms in significant numbers. So it was there that the Confederacy made its best effort at producing breechloaders: about fifty-five hundred copies of the Sharps carbine. The cold reality was that the Confederacy barely had the capacity to manufacture a proven breech-loading design such as the Sharps, let alone new and untried inventions.

There was only one truly original and technologically advanced breech-loading design manufactured in the Confederacy. It was the work of a brilliant New Hampshire-born engineer and mechanic named George W. Morse, who gave up his promising (and lucrative) work for the U.S. Army on the eve of the war in favor of his adopted homeland, offering his considerable skill and experience to the

Confederacy. But Morse's self-priming center-fire cartridge and the brass-framed carbines designed to shoot them found a cool reception in the South. Never trusted by Jefferson Davis nor adopted by the Confederate government, Morse's design was put into production only on a small scale by the State of South Carolina, which fabricated just over a thousand carbines under his supervision from October 1863 through the end of the war.

All other efforts to make breech-loading arms in the Confederacy had been abandoned by May 1863. The C.S. Ordnance Bureau as well as private manufacturers had reached the same conclusion: breechloaders required too great an expenditure in time and materials for too little return. In the final two years of the war, the Confederacy concentrated its few resources on producing as many muzzle-loaders as possible, hoping that their superior range and reliability might offset the northern breechloaders' rapidity of fire. By January 1865, the Ordnance Bureau was trying desperately to turn out a few hundred copies of an obsolete British muzzle-loading cavalry carbine at a newly established factory in Tallassee, Alabama. At the same time, U.S. Army officers at the Springfield Armory in Massachusetts were selecting the next generation of infantry and cavalry arms from among forty-eight breech-loading designs, both single-shot and repeating, most of them developed during the war. Erskine S. Allin, master armorer at the Springfield Armory, was well on his way to developing his center-fire cartridge and "trapdoor" system for altering muzzle-loading rifle-muskets into breechloaders — a system that would lead to a retooling of the national armory after the war and draw a patent infringement suit by George Morse.

Even in the North, the complexity and expense of producing breech-loading arms limited their production and battlefield impact relative to more than 2.7 million muzzle-loading muskets or rifle-muskets used by Union armies. But as the war drew to a close, the widening technological gap between North and South began to play a critical role on the battlefield. Encounters between Union cavalry armed with seven-shot repeating Spencer carbines (or even infantry bearing fifteen-shot Henry rifles) and Confederate troops using single-shot muzzle-loaders were increasingly common. Had the war lasted another year, the rising tide of Yankee breechloaders might have finished off the last Confederate armies as quickly as General James H. Wilson's thirteen thousand Spencer-armed troopers sacked the southern manufacturing centers of Selma, Columbus, and Macon in April 1865. Thus, for the Union, the Civil War put an end to the muzzle-loader; for the Confederacy, it put an end to the breechloader. The practical limitations of southern ingenuity in a largely preindustrial economy formed a lesson the Confederacy learned the hard way.

Breechloaders and Failures

In 1861, the idea of breech-loading arms was hardly new: in its day, John H. Hall's Model 1819 flintlock rifle, today famous as the world's first interchangeable-parts firearm, was equally as famous (or infamous) as a breechloader. The Hall system suffered from a serious design flaw, one that would plague nearly all breech-loading systems of the era: an insufficient seal where the tilting breech door joined the barrel. Without a tight seal, the hot gases created by the ignition of gunpowder leaked from the joint, diminishing the velocity of the bullet and limiting the gun's range and accuracy.

A host of new breech-loading designs patented in the 1850s not only seemed to solve the gas-seal problem with new kinds of linen, tin, or brass cartridge ammunition, but also promised to greatly increase the rate of fire. Yet with some justification, the old guard in the U.S. Army establishment feared that more firepower would require more ammunition than an army supply train could carry. Some officers even wondered whether ordinary soldiers could be trained to load, fire, and properly maintain the newfangled devices. In 1854, the U.S. Congress appropriated $90,000 for the Army to select from the many new designs competing for business in the private arms market a breech-loading replacement for the old Hall arms. U.S. secretary of war and future Confederate president Jefferson Davis frustrated the effort by declining to expend the allocated funds for the remainder of his term of office. Davis felt that the War Department's first priority should be to perfect the techniques of interchangeability of proven muzzle-loading designs at the national armories; it could ill afford to waste resources on unproven, expensive new breech-loading designs that would be difficult to mass-produce.

Davis's successor was the future Confederate general John B. Floyd, who had a much more favorable view of the rapidly evolving breech-loading technology. Under Floyd's watch, the U.S. Army conducted a series of firing trials beginning in 1857 and 1858, testing at least twenty different breech-loading carbine designs. As a result, the Ordnance Department began purchasing small numbers of breech-loading carbines for field-testing, including the Burnside, Greene, and Joslyn as well as the Colt revolving carbine. One of the most promising designs was that of Dr. Edward Maynard, the dentist made famous (and wealthy) by his tape primer system adopted by the U.S. Army for its Model 1855 series of arms. Maynard's breechloaders featured a barrel that tilted downward to accept a brass cartridge with a vent in the base to admit a spark. The wide base of the cartridge served as its own gas seal: ignition forced it snugly against the rear face of the barrel, where it also served as a convenient means of extracting the cartridge after firing. The army

They feel it their duty to state that they have seen nothing in these trials to lead them to think that a breech-loading arm has yet been invented which is suited to replace the muzzle-loading gun for foot troops; on the contrary, they have seen much to impress them with an opinion unfavorable to the use of a breech-loading gun for general military purposes.
— Report of the U.S. Army Ordnance Board, June 1857

Out of a lot of 60 carbines received from the Richmond Arsenal about three weeks ago and manufactured by Mr. S. C. Robinson — 40 out of the 60 have been tested and condemned as unfit for the service — The great fault about them is that after they are fired two or three times that part of the stock of the gun just under the breech bursts and splits. Many of them will not burst a cap until the second trial.
— Ordnance officer Charles Mennigerode, Fitzhugh Lee's cavalry brigade, to chief of ordnance Josiah Gorgas, March 23, 1863

was sufficiently impressed with the accuracy and reliability of Maynard's invention that it ordered four hundred for field-testing in December 1857. Southern states were sufficiently in need of breechloaders at the beginning of the war to purchase most of Maynard's prewar production, and at least two private manufacturers in the Confederacy attempted to copy the thin and compact Maynard design during the war.

But it was the Sharps, the oldest of these designs, that stood out above the others. Developed by Christian Sharps, a former protégé of John H. Hall, the simple dropping-block breech system had been improved through six models since its introduction in 1849, including a more accurate rifle-length version. Though the .52-caliber Sharps used a traditional paper cartridge, the patented Conant and Lawrence gas checks incorporated into the breech block in the late 1850s effectively addressed the problem of sealing the breech. Most important, its successful use by mounted troops on the western frontier silenced most of the skeptics, including Jefferson Davis. Between 1857 and 1860, the army purchased more than seventy-one hundred Sharps carbines, making it the obvious first choice for arming Union cavalry regiments when the time came in 1861. It was also the obvious first choice for a Confederacy badly in need of a reliable and easily copied breech-loading carbine.

Among twenty-four thousand Sharps arms produced before the war were six thousand carbines sold in 1855 to the government of Great Britain. Between 1855 and 1860, James H. Burton, the future Confederate superintendent of armories, thoroughly familiarized himself with the Sharps and experimented on improving it while serving as chief engineer at the Royal Small Arms Factory at Enfield. Having returned to his native Virginia in 1861, Burton recommended the Sharps as the best and easiest-to-produce breech-loading carbine for the young Confederacy. Early in the following year, the C.S. Ordnance Bureau contracted for copies of the famous breechloader with the Richmond-based lumber magnate Samuel C. Robinson and his silent partner, the Connecticut-born machinery manufacturer John H. Lester. Lester had been the driving force behind the incongruously named Union Manufacturing Company, which made sewing machines and altered flintlock muskets to the percussion system for the State of Virginia. Aided by a $45,000 advance from the Confederate government, Robinson and Lester began assembling the machinery, tools, and patterns for manufacturing their faux Sharps, with production generously estimated at six hundred a month.

Meanwhile, a thirty-two-year-old Virginia artist and inventor named Charles W.

Alexander approached Burton with a homemade carbine featuring a pivoting breech, a design he had patented in 1858. Burton believed that the basic idea was sound and that with a few modifications — including the addition of a Lawrence gas check — Alexander's breechloader could be of potential military service. At the C.S. Armory in Richmond, Burton assigned to Alexander the space, tools, and workmen needed to fabricate a prototype carbine with the appropriate gas check in the breech. Burton hoped to be able to introduce the resulting arm into Confederate service, for which he was to be paid a substantial share of the profits in exchange for his technical advice and personal influence, much like the arrangement for manufacturing the so-called Spiller and Burr revolvers (see chapter 4). In April 1862, the Ordnance Bureau contracted for twenty thousand carbines "of the Alexander or Sharps design" with a self-described mechanical engineer and entrepreneur named Thomas E. McNeill and his business partner, Alabama quartermaster general Duff C. Green, principals of the newly founded Alabama Arms Manufacturing Company.[1] Again, Burton was to be awarded a share of the profits.

Almost immediately, things began to go wrong. On the delicate point of financial compensation, Burton was reminded by his boss, Josiah Gorgas, "It is by no means proper that you should make your influence with me enter into the stipulations of a contract"; the Spiller and Burr arrangement was "an exception and must not be permitted to pass into a rule."[2] Meanwhile, McNeill and Green turned out to be unscrupulous (or at least incompetent) businessmen who never produced a single new arm. By the summer of 1862, Alexander had absconded with the prototype, probably looking to start his own lucrative venture in the firearms business. Neither the carbine nor its supposed inventor could be located by police or the Confederate provost marshal, even after Alexander was granted a Confederate patent on April 18, 1863, which credited him for the design perfected by Burton and his workmen at governmental expense. Thus, in addition to the mountain of problems inherent in mobilizing an agrarian economy for war, Gorgas also had to wrestle with greedy inventors and less than patriotic contractors — a problem his northern counterparts knew only too well.

In November 1862, the Confederacy's other major investment in breech-loading technology began to bear fruit: the S. C. Robinson Company began deliveries of their pseudo-Sharps carbines to the Richmond Arsenal. The first batch of arms soon gained a poor reputation in the newspapers for weak hammers and burst stocks, causing no less an authority than General Robert E. Lee to claim that they were "so defective as to be demoralizing to our men."[3] As it turned out, the problems were minor and easily rectified; with proper training in loading and maintenance, Confederate cavalrymen found their ersatz Sharps carbines almost as good as the real thing. But as early as December 1862, Robinson and Lester were considering selling the business to the Confederate government. Chronic shortages of men and materials on top of the incredible expense of outfitting a modern arms factory made profitability virtually impossible. In March 1863, the partners wisely cut their losses and sold off the carbine factory to the Confederate government, recouping about $310,000 of their investment. The factory operated under Confederate control through April 1864, when the threat of Union armies advancing on Richmond convinced Burton to rethink his options.

In the summer of 1864, the C.S. Ordnance Bureau began to move the machinery in Richmond for making both breech-loading and muzzle-loading carbines to a new armory safely tucked away in Tallassee, Alabama, about thirty miles east of Montgomery. There, the machinery could be put to work producing a simple .58-caliber muzzle-loading carbine based on the British Pattern 1856 cavalry carbine. Production began in February 1865, and about five hundred carbines were nearing completion when the war ended. Given the dire circumstances of the Confederacy's final months, producing even obsolescent arms was still an extraordinary logistical feat.

U.S. Model 1819 Hall breech-loading rifle made by the U.S. Armory at Harpers Ferry (ca. 1836), believed to have been altered to percussion at the **C.S. Armory at Holly Springs, Mississippi** (1862)

At the time of its introduction, John H. Hall's Model 1819 rifle was the most technologically advanced firearm in the world, an innovative new breech-loading gun that also ushered in the Industrial Revolution in the United States. By 1861, Hall's breech-loading flintlock ignition system was not only obsolete, but was often considered dangerous because of hot gases leaking from the breech joint a few inches from the shooter's face.

Nevertheless, at the beginning of the war, the Confederacy had to make do with what it had: at least ten thousand Hall flintlock rifles had been issued to the southern states under the Militia Act of 1808, seized from U.S. arsenals in 1861, or purchased as surplus through private arms dealers on the eve of the war. For the moment, the best that could be done was to alter their flintlocks into percussion locks, thus giving the cavalry a slightly longer-range alternative to civilian shotguns.

Bearing assembly number 31 on the left side of the breechblock, this rifle is believed to have been among sixty-eight altered to percussion in April and May 1862 at the Holly Springs Armory in Mississippi. These arms had been issued in their original flintlock configuration, but were turned in to the armory after the Battle of Shiloh as soon as other arms became available. Although the name and date stamp were ground off at the time of alteration, the pin-fastened bands indicate that this arm was produced at the Harpers Ferry Armory between 1832 and 1840. Given its good condition, it may not have been reissued after being altered.

New Model 1859 breech-loading carbine made by the Sharps Rifle Manufacturing Company, New Haven, Connecticut, serial number 33101, believed to have been purchased by the State of Georgia (1860–61)

The Sharps carbine was the most trusted and widely produced single-shot breech-loading carbine of the Civil War — for both the Union and the Confederacy. Already selling briskly on the civilian market before the war, Model 1853 Sharps carbines were so popular among Free State agitators in Kansas that they gained the nickname "Beecher's Bibles" (for the abolitionist minister Henry Ward Beecher), a perception only strengthened when John Brown's men used them in his 1859 raid on Harpers Ferry.

Proslavery southerners were just as keen to get their hands on the famous Yankee breechloaders. By November 17, 1860, eleven days after Lincoln's election, Georgia governor Joseph E. Brown had already ordered two thousand Sharps breechloaders for the state's defense, much to the delight of the state senate, which authorized him to buy as many as five thousand. The defiant but parsimonious governor stuck to his more fiscally responsible original order, and in February 1861, sent his aide-de-camp Henry R. Jackson to the Sharps factory with $25,000 in state bonds in partial payment. The company could provide him only sixteen hundred New Model 1859 carbines, but the delivery of an additional four hundred rifles was arranged through William J. Syms and Brother, a private arms dealer in New York.

Distinguished by its lack of U.S. inspection marks, this is believed to be one of Governor Brown's carbines. Like all New Model 1859 carbines, it featured a pellet primer, a tubular feed system that automatically inserted a small copper disc filled with fulminate of mercury onto the nipple each time the hammer was cocked. Yet it is one of only about three thousand New Model 1859s fitted with brass buttplates, implement compartments, and barrel bands, most of which were sold to Georgia, and nearly all the rest to the U.S. War Department. It is believed that Georgia's carbines eventually saw service with the First and Fifth Georgia Cavalry, the Fifty-Seventh Infantry, and the Second Georgia State Troops.

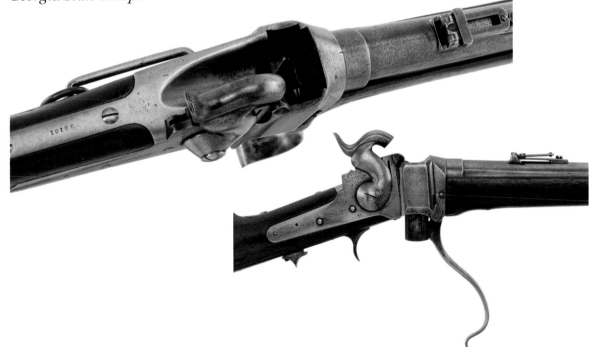

U.S. Patent Office model for Charles W. Alexander's breech-loading design, patent number 20,315 (1858)

This is the model that Charles W. Alexander provided the U.S. Patent Office to accompany his patent application (dated May 25, 1858) for an "improvement in breech-loading rifles." His was an unsophisticated system, using a laterally pivoting breech piece into which the operator placed loose powder and a patched round ball before closing it with a thumb latch. In essence, it was Hall's system with all its imperfections, but with a laterally opening instead of a vertically slanting breech.

In the 1863 investigation undertaken by the C.S. Patent Office into Alexander's claim for an "improved" design, James H. Burton filed an affidavit stating that Alexander had first approached him in the spring of 1861, seeking an opinion of his breech-loading design. Burton described Alexander's gun and its pivoting breech in precise detail, recalling that its design was substantially the same as that patented in Great Britain by the Birmingham gun maker James Leetch in 1853. Yet according to Burton, it was "a rough specimen having been made in a blacksmith's shop in the mountains," with a primitive gas check entirely too fragile for military service. Burton suggested to Alexander that the gun should have a "shorter breech piece without any chamber for the cartridge and to be used simply for the purpose of closing the breech of the barrel."[4]

Protoype breech-loading carbine believed to have been made by Charles W. Alexander at the C.S. Armory in Richmond (1862)

Six months after presenting his first design, Alexander approached Burton with a second arm. Burton recalled that it was built with "a solid revolving breech piece with some device not clearly recollected by the deponent," but in any event lacking an adequate gas check. According to his affidavit, Burton not only suggested the addition of a gas check "similar in construction and application" to that patented by Richard S. Lawrence but also provided Alexander with a Sharps carbine from which to copy it.[5] Pictured here is the .32-caliber prototype that Alexander built at the C.S. Armory in Richmond in January and February 1862 in response to Burton's suggestions for the second arm. It is easily the greatest rarity in the Wray Collection and, with its two-piece breech and pellet-primer device, easily the greatest oddity as well.

In keeping with Burton's wishes, the arm no longer has a chambered breech piece into which a charge was inserted, but instead relies on a solid, laterally pivoting latch to close the breech. Likewise, the remnant of a brass gas-check plate over the vent hole in the pivoting upper breech piece seems to bear Burton's technical thumbprint, as does the center-mounted hammer, which strikes the nipple by way of a spring-mounted pin, a feature that Burton had already considered in his experiments with Sharps carbines at Enfield.

And yet this carbine is clearly not suitable for military use: its caliber is odd, its stock is decidedly civilian in appearance, and it is smaller and lighter than a Maynard carbine. Even with improvements, its breech-loading mechanism was delicate, and its pellet-priming system was unique among Confederate-made arms (indeed, the pellet primer was the first feature eliminated on Confederate copies of Sharps carbines). Why would Burton, one of the world's foremost authorities on firearms, consider this arm a worthy alternative to the Sharps or

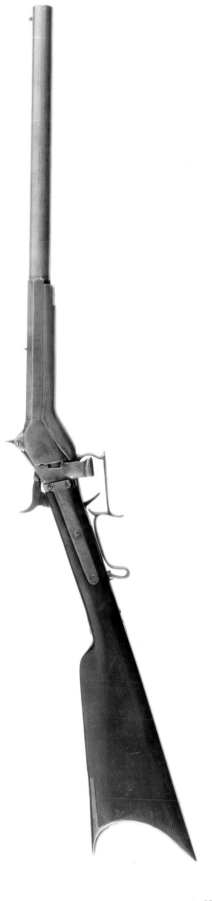

even the Maynard carbine? Perhaps he did not. It is possible that this is Alexander's second gun and not the third and final version built at Richmond, which perhaps more closely resembled a Sharps carbine. If so, that could explain why Alexander felt the gun to be his property, despite the unusually prominent "C*S" government ownership mark on the left side of the breech.

While Confederate authorities sought his return and Alexander submitted his patent claim, he seems to have moved around frequently: fragmentary records show him in Memphis in March 1862 and in Alabama and Georgia in 1864 and 1865, possibly affiliated with Thomas McNeill and Duff Green. In October 1865, Alexander took the oath of allegiance to the United States and applied for a passport, perhaps intending to travel abroad before returning to his hometown of Moorefield, West Virginia, where he died in 1910.

For many years, Alexander's breech-loading carbine was presumed lost, its existence known only through a few scattered references in the footnotes of firearms history. For reasons still unknown, it surfaced in a Nevada collection in 1980, whereupon George Wray recognized its importance, having already purchased Alexander's 1856 patent model. Today it is one of the great treasures of Confederate history.

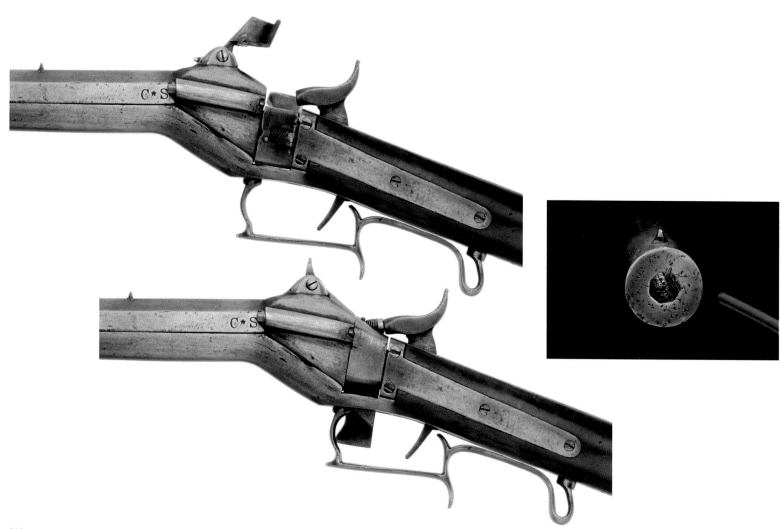

Lawrence gas check

Possibly the most important component of the New Model 1859 Sharps carbine was Richard S. Lawrence's patented gas check (top), which assured a tight seal between the dropping breechblock and the barrel. Built into the breechblock, the gas check relied on a thin expandable ring that fit over a hollow chamber under the nipple. When a powder charge was ignited, hot gas from the explosion filled the chamber and drove the ring firmly against the rear face of the barrel, sealing it securely.

It was this small but crucial feature that James Burton insisted be built into the upper breech piece of Alexander's breechloader (middle right and bottom). This piece, which also contained the nipple, was in turn held in place by a laterally pivoting latch with grooves for seating the tiny pellet primers (middle left).

Confederate contract copy of Sharps New Model 1859 carbine made by Samuel C. Robinson and Company, Richmond, serial number 531 (1862)

Between November 1862 and the end of February 1863, S. C. Robinson and Company delivered 1,900 of their .52-caliber Sharps copies, or about 475 units a month. This enviable rate of production (at least for the Confederacy) was aided in large measure by several commonsense shortcuts, including replacing the adjustable leaf rear sight with a simple block sight, and eliminating the implement compartment. Most important, Robinson did away with the delicate pellet-primer device, preferring instead to rely on simple and easily mass-produced percussion caps.

At the same time, initial production was plagued by quality-control problems. In December 1862, an ordnance officer at the Richmond Arsenal reported weak hammers that failed to ignite a cap or else fell at half cock and, in one instance, a nipple, or "cone," with an undrilled vent hole. Such problems undoubtedly reflected the manufacturer's inexperience but could have been prevented by more vigilant Ordnance Bureau inspection. When his first arms were ready for delivery on November 29, 1862, Robinson had to write to Josiah Gorgas and request that master armorer Salmon Adams be sent over to his factory to inspect them and make suggestions for their improvement.

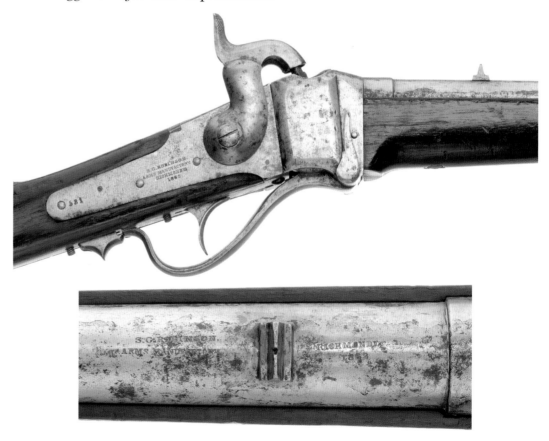

Copy of Sharps New Model 1859 breech-loading carbine made by the C.S. Armory at Richmond, serial number 3526 (1863)

When the Confederate government bought out Robinson and Lester on March 1, 1863, operations at their factory continued seamlessly with the same machinery, the same workers, the same serial-number range, and some of the same problems. Although lock defects were soon corrected, it took more time to remedy the worst problem, the one complained of by General Lee himself: stocks that burst just forward of the breech.

As it turned out, the problem was not the gun, but its Confederate-made paper cartridges. When the closing breech sheared off the paper tail of the cartridge to expose the powder for ignition, loose powder dropped into the small gap around the lever hinge at the base of the breech, causing a small but unnerving explosion when ignited. The Sharps Rifle Manufacturing Company, which had noted the problem in 1859, quietly solved it by introducing sturdier, slightly shorter linen cartridges. The Confederacy solved the problem by milling a small crescent-shaped opening in the base of the stock, which allowed any loose powder to fall out. Yet as seen by the example pictured here, that simple modification did not always prevent small chunks of the stock from being blown out anyway.

Between March 1863 and April 1864, the former S. C. Robinson factory operated as the C.S. Carbine Factory, fabricating another thirty-five hundred arms. Bearing serial number 3526, this one probably dates to the late summer of 1863. It is assembled in part from U.S.-made parts scavenged from the battlefield, including the buttplate, barrel band, and several internal lock parts. The breechblock bears serial number 3728, suggesting that it was replaced because of wear or damage from the same explosion that chipped the stock.

Maynard breech-loading carbine, first type, made by the Massachusetts Arms Company, Chicopee Falls, Massachusetts, serial number 3230, believed to have been purchased by a southern state (1861)

Aside from their breech-loading system and patented tape-primer devices, Edward Maynard's .35- and .50-caliber guns were known for their light weight, diminutive size, and tang-mounted rear sight, all of which made them unlikely candidates for military service. Carbines had twenty-inch barrels, and rifles were only six inches longer; both were only about an inch wide and lacked a heat-shielding fore stock. Fortunately for Maynard, the U.S. Army's order for four hundred carbines gave him the high-profile endorsement he needed to begin marketing his small but powerful breechloaders. In the spring of 1857, Maynard optimistically contracted with the Massachusetts Arms Company to produce five thousand arms for the civilian market, but since the gun did not enjoy the reputation of the Sharps carbine, sales lagged. By October 1860, the company had sold only about fourteen hundred units.

Lincoln's election the next month changed everything. Over the next six months, the Massachusetts Arms Company disposed of 90 percent of its Maynard breechloaders to the future states of the Confederacy, including orders for Georgia (650), Florida (1,000), and Mississippi (800), plus smaller orders from volunteer companies in Louisiana and South Carolina. Most of the arms were sold through the New York retailer William J. Syms and Brother, which in early January 1861 bypassed a local restriction on sales to the southern states by having the guns shipped from Washington, D.C. The specific provenance of this well-worn .50-caliber carbine is unknown, but it was the most common configuration sold, with 325 going to Mississippi and 620 to Georgia.

The Massachusetts Arms Company's rapidly rising fortunes were cut short on the night of January 18, 1861, when the factory was destroyed by fire, though its remaining inventory was saved by being passed out of a second-story window. The company rebuilt in 1862 and manufactured improved versions of Maynard's arm through the 1890s.

Confederate contract breech-loading carbine made by Keen, Walker, and Company, Danville, Virginia, based on the Maynard design (1862)

In the fall of 1861, Elisha F. Keen, a wealthy tobacco merchant and onetime colonel of the Fifty-Seventh Virginia Infantry, formed a partnership with James M. Walker, the mayor of Danville, to manufacture approximations of the Maynard carbine. With its thin stock, lack of a forearm, and toggle lever under the breech, Keen, Walker, and Company's faux Maynard differed mainly in its internal mechanism: instead of tilting the entire barrel upward so that a brass cartridge could be inserted into the breech, the lever tilted an iron breechblock upward so that a paper cartridge could be inserted into its chamber, much like the old Hall system. The forward lip of the chamber was lined with bronze in an attempt to provide an expanding gas seal at the breech.

There are no identifying marks on this example, except for the P *("proved") inspection mark applied to the barrel at the C.S. Arsenal at Danville. Rifled with seven lands and grooves, its .52-caliber barrel may have been taken from a U.S. Model 1841 Hall breech-loading rifle.*

After turning out only 282 breech-loading carbines, Keen, Walker, and Company ceased production at the end of 1862, probably to use its few resources for a contract from the State of Virginia for altering breech-loading Hall rifles into muzzle-loaders. It was an ironic but all too typical outcome for the handful of private firms in the South that attempted to manufacture breechloaders.

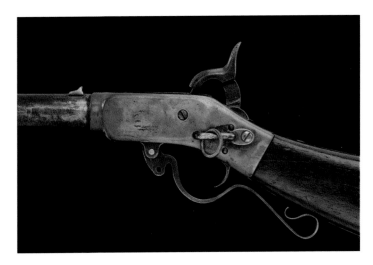

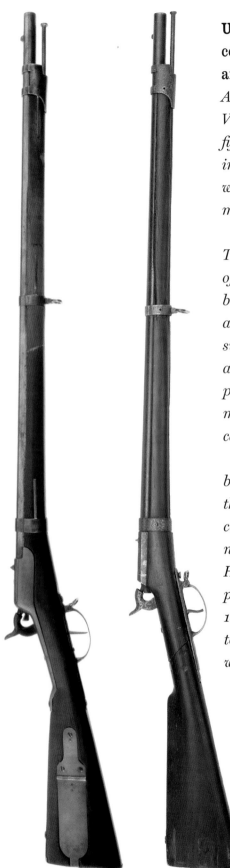

U.S. Model 1819 Hall breech-loading rifles altered to muzzle-loading configurations for the State of Virginia by Thomas N. Read and John T. Watson, Danville, Virginia (1862–63)

Although understanding the unpopularity of Hall's breechloaders, Virginia's adjutant general still wanted to make some use of the fifteen hundred Hall rifles and carbines that the state had in storage in the spring of 1862. The result was the only known instance in which breech-loading firearms were altered into muzzle-loaders for military use.

Credit for this dubious feat belongs to the Danville mechanics Thomas N. Read and John T. Watson, men who were hardly ignorant of breech-loading systems but who resorted to this technological leap backward as the quickest and most practical solution to the problem at hand. Read was the Keen, Walker, and Company foreman who supervised the manufacture of the company's breech-loading carbines, and was later granted a Confederate patent for a breech-loading arm, perhaps an improvement on the carbines he had been building. He may also have been involved in making a handful of Sharps-like carbines designed by Captain G. Thomas Getty.

Read and Watson's method was simple: remove the Hall tilting breechblock and cut off the frame, leaving only an open-breech barrel, then insert a stationary brass receiver with its own vent, nipple, and centrally hung hammer. The resulting muzzle-loader then needed a new stock, though Read and Watson recycled the forward portion from Hall's rifles and attached the two sections with an iron staple. They put together about nine hundred rifles in this way from the spring of 1862 through the fall of 1863. Many are thought to have been issued to the Virginia State Line, a reserve unit formed in 1862 to guard the western part of the state.

What is thought to be the earlier version (bottom) *features a smaller brass breech piece and bears the mark "H 76" stamped into the stock. The later-type alteration* (top) *has a larger and bulkier receiver with a thick brass tang extending rearward. It has no discernible marks other than hand-assembly marks IV, XIX, and 41 inside the receiver and stock. Obviously, all semblance of interchangeability was lost. Because they were made with two-piece stocks, these guns were easily damaged and just as easily converted into sporting rifles or shotguns after the war. This example had its original forearm removed, probably at the same time it was fitted with an implement compartment taken from a U.S. Model 1841 rifle. The forearm was later restored, presumably to boost its value on the collector's market.*

Confederate contract copy of U.S. Model 1855 carbine made by Bilharz, Hall, and Company, Pittsylvania Court House, Virginia (1863)

In 1861, a German-born harness maker, mechanic, and distiller named Candidus Bilharz formed a company for producing breech-loading firearms in partnership with George W. Hall and Colonel L. D. Bennett. Located about twenty miles north of Danville, Virginia, in Pittsylvania Court House (today known as Chatham), the company produced one of only a handful of original breech-loading designs originating in the South. Though solidly built, their unique "rising breech" system suffered from a familiar problem: an insufficient gas seal between barrel and breech. By September 1862, Bilharz, Hall, and Company had manufactured one hundred breech-loading carbines for the C.S. Ordnance Bureau at forty-five dollars each. It is believed that none were ever issued.

In the spring of 1863, Bilharz, Hall, and Company set technological ambitions aside and turned to copying the simple, .58-caliber U.S. Model 1855 muzzle-loading carbine. Over the next year, the company managed to deliver an estimated 750 carbines to the C.S. Armory at Richmond, but it appears that the armory had to supply many of the parts and some of the materials. Already functioning as a virtual subsection of the Richmond Armory, the private company went out of business in the summer of 1864 as the Confederacy began moving its carbine manufacturing to the safer confines of Tallassee, Alabama.

The "pinched"-style front sight of this example suggests that both sight and barrel originated in Richmond, yet as seen by the P and "csa" stamps at the breech, the barrel was proved at the C.S. Arsenal in Danville. Likewise, the Richmond Armory probably provided the hammer, which originated on a U.S. Model 1841 rifle. Unusually, this carbine bears no serial number, and is marked internally only with mating number "E7," suggesting that it was one of the earliest arms made.

George W. Morse and the Quest for a Better Breechloader

While the U.S. Army was conducting trials to select a breech-loading carbine design for the cavalry, it also began considering ways to alter existing muzzle-loading muskets into breechloaders for the infantry. The potential cost savings of modernizing obsolete but otherwise perfectly serviceable arms was huge: in 1859, the national arsenals housed some 520,000 .69-caliber muskets, of which 33,000 had already been rifled, making them prime candidates for further improvement. In July 1858, a board of ordnance officers met at West Point, New York, to conduct tests on three designs for accomplishing breech-loading alterations. The most promising was that of George Woodward Morse, who had developed the first internally primed center-fire metallic cartridge as well as a "trapdoor" breech system designed to fire it. His system was years ahead of its time and remains the technological foundation for all modern firearms, from simple .38-caliber revolvers to magazine-fed military assault rifles. But Morse's pioneering technological achievement was soon overshadowed by his biggest professional mistake: siding with the Confederacy in 1861.

Morse was possibly the most important yet least known firearms inventor of the nineteenth century. Born in 1812 in Haverhill, New Hampshire, he demonstrated his mechanical skill from an early age: in 1831, a local newspaper reported that he had invented a gun with an internally housed lock "so constructed as to discharge the gun sixty times with once [one] priming."[6] Morse moved to Boston, where he worked and trained as a machinist before moving to Louisiana in the late 1830s. Following in the footsteps of his successful older brother, the young George Morse worked as an engineer and a deputy U.S. land surveyor. In 1852, he was appointed state engineer of Louisiana, charged with removing obstructions and building levees along the Mississippi River. Through work and marriage, Morse acquired three large tracts of land in the Natchitoches area, including a plantation that he named Londonderry. In a departure from the ways of his abolitionist father, he and his wife also owned at least fifteen enslaved people, with a half-share interest in seventeen more.

Even while working as an engineer and a planter, Morse retained an active interest in the latest firearms technology, especially in the quest to solve the greatest challenge of the day: a reliable breech-loading system. Though he is best known today for his breech-loading design, Morse's real technological breakthrough came in the cartridges. Because nearly all breech-loading designs of the time used cartridges that had to be ignited externally by a percussion cap, the action of affixing a cap for each shot increased loading time. Furthermore, the paper or linen compo-

The opposition to breech loading is short-lived; the day is near at hand when ramrods will be as obsolete as matchlocks.
—George W. Morse, June 8, 1858

His inventions were so far in advance of the state of the art at that time, that he was obliged to wait for the public to be educated up to his standpoint, and overcome the great prejudice existing in the army, as well as everywhere else, against breech-loading guns of every kind, but especially against one which used special ammunition. . . . He lives to see his plans adopted by the whole world; while he is ignored and poor in his declining years, and those who have adopted his inventions without remunerating him are rolling in wealth.
—Report of the Committee on Patents, U.S. House of Representatives, 1878

sition of most breech-loading cartridges still allowed some ignition gas to escape, even with a Lawrence gas check in place. Gutta-percha (a natural latex), rubber, and tin were improvements, but the problem persisted. The best of the new cartridge designs—such as the Maynard or Burnside—used a brass casing to guard against gas leakage, but still had to be primed externally. Complicating the problem was the matter of military use: although machinery of the day could easily produce the fine tolerances needed to reduce the gap between breech and barrel, military arms required looser tolerances so that dirt, dust, and powder residue would not clog the mechanism.

For Morse, the solution was obvious: combine a brass casing with an internal priming system. Such a cartridge would eliminate the need to cap the arm and would make possible a more rapid repeating action. Most important, a self-contained cartridge would hold the ignition gases inside itself and inside the breech, thus solving the problem of gas leakage; it would also enjoy the distinct advantage of being waterproof. Morse was hardly alone in having this idea. In the late 1850s, Benjamin Tyler Henry perfected an internally primed brass rimfire cartridge for use in the new repeating rifle that bore his name—the direct descendant of the Volition or Volcanic rifle and the direct ancestor of the famous Winchester. In 1860, Horace Smith and Daniel Wesson essentially perfected the design. But unlike the rimfire cartridge, which contained fulminate of mercury spun into the rim of the base, Morse's center-fire cartridge placed the ignition point in the center of the base. This singular feature enabled the external walls of Morse's cartridge to be thicker and sturdier, thus able to withstand higher pressures and provide greater velocity to the bullet than a thin rimfire cartridge. Although rimfire cartridges made possible the Henry and Spencer repeating arms, it was Morse's center-fire cartridges that made possible modern automatic and semiautomatic rifles.

Patented in October 1856, the first version of Morse's cartridge had a central vent hole in its base over which was placed a removable fulminate of mercury primer contained under a soft metal (usually tin) cap that was intended to expand and seal the breech at firing. The key feature of the patented arm designed to fire the cartridge was a pivoting breech door, or "cover," on top of the barrel; the door attached to a sliding breechblock, through which ran a firing pin. "Throw the gun in the water, take it out or fire it under water, and it makes no difference," Morse noted proudly in his patent description.[7] In the carbine trials of 1857, the U.S. Army rejected this innovative but complex system in favor of a simpler one using externally primed brass cartridges invented by the future Union general Ambrose Burnside. Likewise, Morse's design was tested but not adopted by the U.S. Navy. But Morse was far from finished. His next three patents, granted in May and June 1858, were major improvements on his earlier designs and formed the basis for his subsequent military work. Two of the patents, numbers 20,214, and 20,727, describe a brass cartridge with an internal *tige*, or anvil, against which an ordinary percussion cap would be ignited when struck by the firing pin. The cartridge was sealed at the base by a rubber gasket. The third patent, number 20,503, improved on his idea for a pivoting breech door and firing pin and was intended specifically for altering muzzle-loading military arms. Morse repurposed the existing military lock, turning the hammer into a lever for drawing back the firing pin, which was then released by pulling the trigger.

It was this design that the West Point board of ordnance officers enthusiastically recommended in July 1858 for altering the army's vast stores of muzzle-loaders into breechloaders. They chose Morse's system over those of his fellow inventors William Montgomery Storm and James H. Merrill because of its reliability, accuracy, and economy. In his report to Congress, Major William H. Bell noted that because the cap of Morse's cartridge was in direct contact with the powder charge, "the certainty of fire is greater than that of any other breech- or muzzle-loading arm," while the sealed breech of his alteration meant that "the whole effect . . . of the cap and of the charge of powder goes to move the ball" instead of being wasted through vent discharge. Furthermore, while the paper cartridge of a muzzle-loader "might spoil in a few days' rainy weather," Morse's cartridge "would not be affected for years," thus saving the army a lot of money on ammunition, at least in the long run.[8]

The following September, the U.S. War Department negotiated with Morse for the right to alter two thousand rifled and percussion-altered U.S. Model 1816 muskets as well as additional U.S. Model 1841 rifles for field testing, the final step before alterations could begin on a large scale. The resulting $10,000 contract, which paid Morse five dollars per gun altered, was the largest arms-related royalty payment the U.S. government had ever made. In February 1860, the War Department agreed to pay Morse a further $3,000 for the right to alter one thousand muzzle-loading carbines. Hedging its bets, the department agreed to pay Morse's runner-up, William Montgomery Storm, for the right to alter two thousand arms to his breech-loading system, but only for a modest $2,500; likewise, it paid gun maker James H.

Merrill $3,000 to alter three hundred arms. Such spending appeared extravagant and even frivolous to some in Congress, especially Mississippi senator and former secretary of war Jefferson Davis. Hence, before enough arms could be altered to a breech-loading configuration for the requisite field testing, funding for the entire project ran out and was not renewed. Once on the verge of the greatest business deal of his life, Morse was left without his only customer, while the U.S. Army was left without a proven breech-loading infantry arm on the eve of its greatest national crisis.

And yet in its slow but methodical way, the prewar army was clearly moving in the direction of adopting breech-loading arms for all branches of the service, despite congressional skepticism. In late 1860, Secretary of War John B. Floyd approved the Ordnance Department's recommendation that Morse's .54-caliber cartridges be manufactured by the U.S. Arsenal at Frankford (near Philadelphia) rather than a private company. Morse later claimed that the Ordnance Department was negotiating for the right to alter a hundred thousand more muzzle-loaders when the war broke out. Morse's system received similarly glowing endorsements from the professionals at the Springfield Armory, including its soon-to-be-famous master armorer Erskine Allin, who commented, "For accuracy, rapidity of firing, penetration, and safety [Morse's altered carbines] are not to be equaled by any breech-loading carbine that has yet been made for the public service."[9] Had the Civil War not intervened and had Morse not chosen to side with the Confederacy, it is likely that he, not Erskine Allin, would be remembered as the father of modern breech-loading rifles in the U.S. Army and beyond. Instead, the name *Morse* is associated today mainly with the inventor of the telegraph, Samuel F. B. Morse, to whom George Morse was only very distantly related.

Aside from the collection of Morse prototypes at the Springfield Armory Museum, the Wray Collection at the Atlanta History Center contains the most complete representation of George W. Morse's work. These artifacts tell one of the great cautionary tales in the history of technology: no matter how brilliant or far reaching, an invention must come along at the right time and place in order to have significant impact. For Morse, the late 1850s seemed to be that time, and the United States should have been that place. But with the outbreak of war in 1861, the U.S. government put on hold its plans for breech-loading infantry arms, choosing instead to mass-produce overwhelming numbers of proven muzzle-loading rifle-muskets. Only after the crisis had passed did the government resume upgrading its armaments, by which time technological developments had left George Morse behind. Meanwhile, Morse put political conviction over personal profit and threw in his lot with a new nation that lacked even the capacity to mass-produce muzzle-loading arms, let alone breechloaders. It was a decision that would undeservedly relegate him to a footnote in American history.

Daguerreotype of George W. Morse and family in Louisiana (1853)

Left to right: Morse with his daughter, Lelia Everiste; wife, Marianne; and son, Peabody Atkinson, who was named for Morse's older brother. A second son, Bryant H. Morse, was born after the image was taken. During the Civil War, it is believed that Peabody Atkinson Morse served briefly in Company A of the Second Louisiana Cavalry.

Center-fire cartridges for Morse's breech-loading arms (1859–64)

The world's first self-priming center-fire metallic cartridge was relatively simple in concept: soldered inside a rolled brass cartridge were metal straps forming an anvil on which an ordinary percussion cap was mounted. The only difficulty lay in the new tools and precision machinery required for mass-producing them — hardly a problem in the North, but quite a problem in the South.

Left to right: *Two exceedingly rare .54-caliber cartridges made by the Frankford Arsenal for the U.S. Model 1841 alterations (with remains of their rubber gaskets intact), a .50-caliber cartridge made by the State Military Works in South Carolina, a .56-caliber cartridge made by Muzzy and Company (Worcester, Massachusetts), and a .58-caliber cartridge of unknown origins.*

Morse-Muzzy cased sporting arms sets, serial numbers 7 and 94 (ca. 1858–59)

With his patents issued on October 28, 1856, as well as a British patent granted in May 1857, George Morse lost no time in testing his invention and trying to make it profitable. In 1857, he contracted with Nathan M. Muzzy and Company in Worcester, Massachusetts, to manufacture one hundred cased sets of sporting arms. Each set included an elaborately engraved breech-loading receiver and three precisely milled interchangeable barrels: two rifled barrels in carbine and rifle lengths (.52 to .54 caliber), and a 14-gauge (about .70-caliber) smoothbore shotgun barrel. Forty-nine reloadable brass cartridge cases were included, along with bullet molds, powder measures, punches to make the India rubber gasket for the base of the cartridge case, and a tool for seating the bullet in the cartridge.

Morse designed his first breech-loading mechanism so that the action of opening the breech door also cocked the side-mounted firing lever. At the same time, the sliding breechblock (with twin arms, or "limbs," connecting it to the breech door) automatically retracted the spent cartridge by using two metal "nippers" that grasped the lower edge of the cartridge and dropped it downward through a small swinging door under the open breech. Morse's first attempt at applying his breech-loading system was surprisingly modern in concept, but faulty in execution. Its many moving parts made the entire mechanism prone to jam, especially if clogged with dirt or dust.

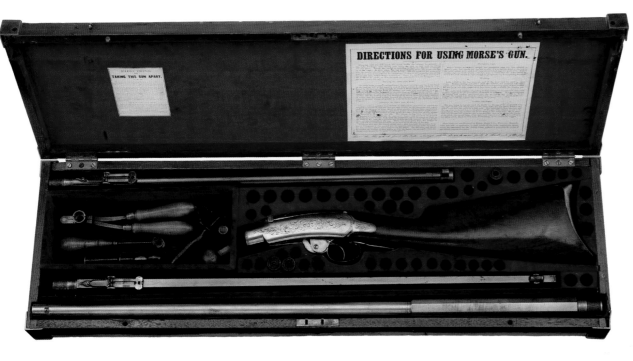

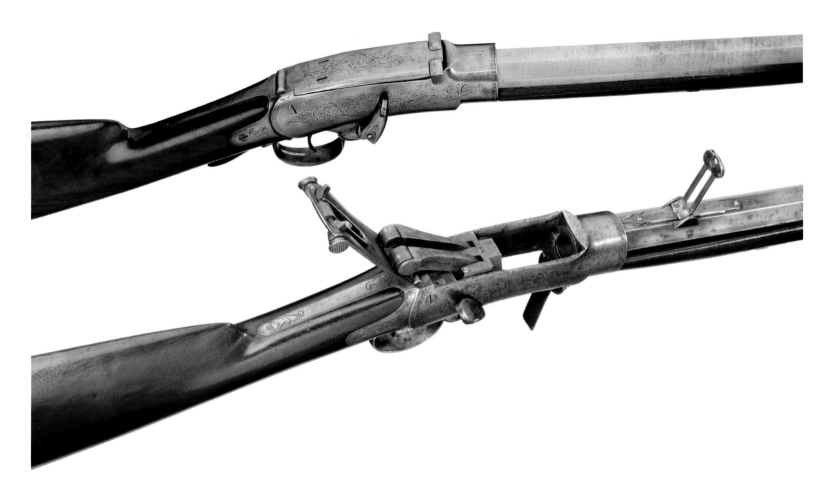

Muzzy and Company's cased sets were never popular on the commercial
market, where their novel breech-loading system did not appeal to sportsmen used
to more familiar muzzle-loaders. Even as the sets were being produced, Morse
realized that his best market would be the U.S. Army, where his system's high rate
of fire and durable, waterproof ammunition would be more highly valued.

According to a note found inside the case of gun number 7 (top), it belonged
to Robert Crenshaw, a veteran of the Seminole and Mexican Wars and captain
of Company F, Second Mississippi Cavalry. Crenshaw was mortally wounded
on July 7, 1864, near Clinton, Mississippi. Given his Morse breechloader's fine
condition, it is unlikely he ever used it in combat. The receiver of this arm bears
a misprint: the date of Morse's patent is given incorrectly as October 20.

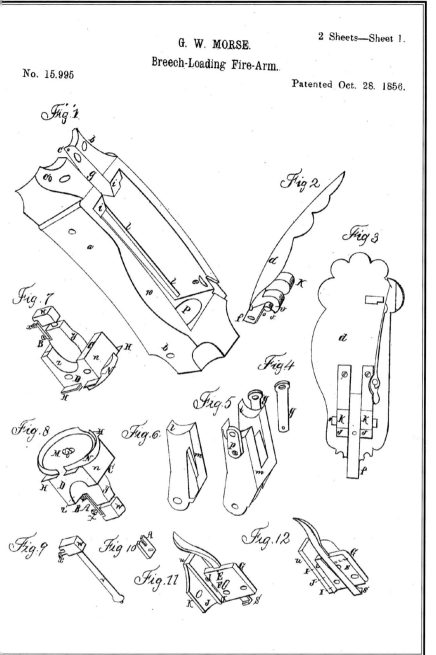

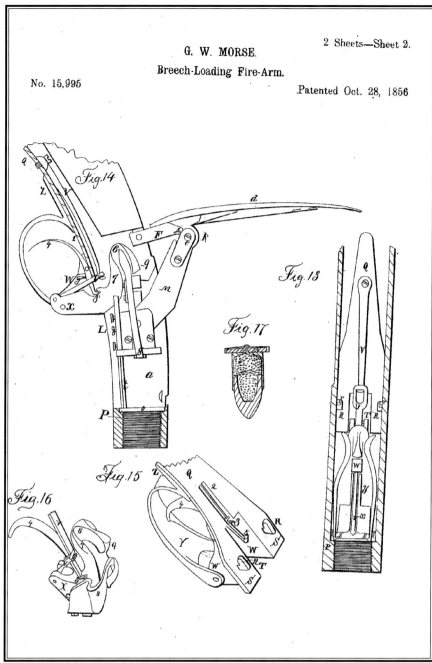

U.S. Patent Office model for George W. Morse's breech-loading design, patent number 20,503 (1858)

On June 8, 1858, Morse was granted U.S. patent number 20,503 for what would become his signature breech-loading design and the foundation for all his subsequent work, both for the U.S. government and the State of South Carolina. Morse's handmade wooden model still bears the original U.S. Patent Office tag, attached with the proverbial red tape. The iron hammer and trigger guard are rough castings probably provided by the Springfield Armory.

As reflected by this model, Morse improved and simplified the basic design of the Muzzy and Company arms. He introduced a heavy fixed block around the firing pin under the pivoting breech door to seal the breech, thus eliminating the sliding breechblock of his previous patent. He replaced the extraction nippers with a hand-operated lever under the breech chamber that pushed the spent cartridges upward, making them easier to pull out by hand.

It was on the basis of this patent — specifically, the extraction lever and the latch device that secured the forward end of the breech door to the barrel — that Morse unsuccessfully launched his second patent infringement suit against the U.S. government in 1884.

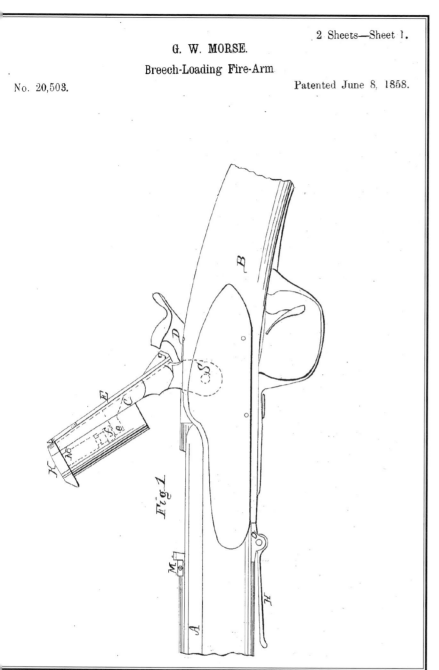

G. W. MORSE.

Breech-Loading Fire-Arm.

No. 20,503.

Patented June 8, 1858.

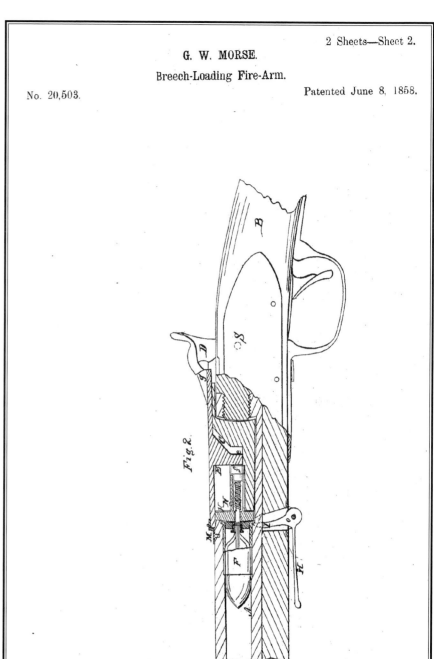

G. W. MORSE.

Breech-Loading Fire-Arm.

No. 20,503.

Patented June 8, 1858.

U.S. Model 1816 musket made at the U.S. Armory at Springfield (1839), altered to percussion, rifled and sighted (ca. 1857), altered to Morse's breech-loading system, serial number 19 (1859)

In March 1859, the U.S. Armory at Springfield began the breech-loading alteration of one thousand rifled muskets according to Morse's U.S. Patent 20,503. Morse himself was directly involved in the work, tinkering with the design as the first few altered arms were completed. He eliminated the extraction lever described in his 1858 patent, but revived the sliding breechblock (with its distinctive arms, or "limbs") from his 1856 patent and the Muzzy and Company arms, but without the cumbersome extraction nippers. The arms so altered were the first internally primed breech-loading guns adopted and produced by the U.S. Army. They were also the basic model for the carbines produced by the State of South Carolina four years later.

This example bears the number "4" stamped onto the brass plug that replaced the frizzen pan in the alteration to percussion, while the number "36" is lightly stamped into the barrel just above. The number "19" stamped onto internal parts is believed to be a serial number, thus indicating the nineteenth arm altered to Morse's system. In January 1860, only fifty-six muskets were finished, and another 544 were in progress, when the appropriated funding ran out and work ceased. So far as is known, all remained in the Washington Arsenal and were never issued for field testing, though Muzzy and Company had been contracted to make ten thousand .69-caliber Morse cartridges.

When this musket was fabricated in 1839, its smoothbore barrel and flintlock ignition system represented a technology essentially unchanged since the Revolutionary War. Between 1855 and 1859, it was altered to percussion, rifled, sighted, and prepared to fire a minié ball, in accordance with the latest muzzle-loading technology. Within a year or two, it was modernized yet again into a breechloader, foreshadowing the Allin system used by the U.S. Army through the Spanish-American War (1898) and the internally primed cartridges used through the present day. Such was the rapid pace of firearms technology in the Civil War era, which is represented so well by this single artifact.

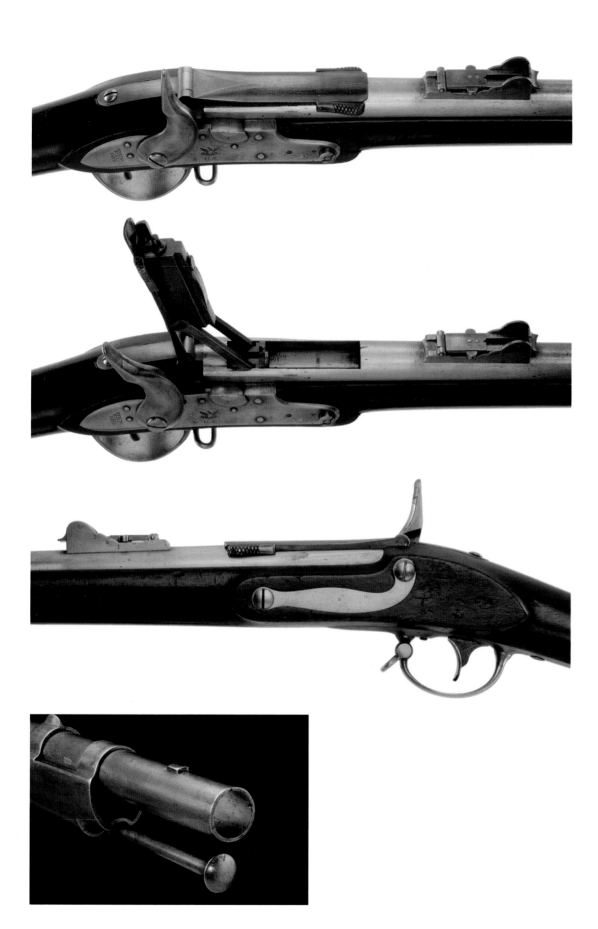

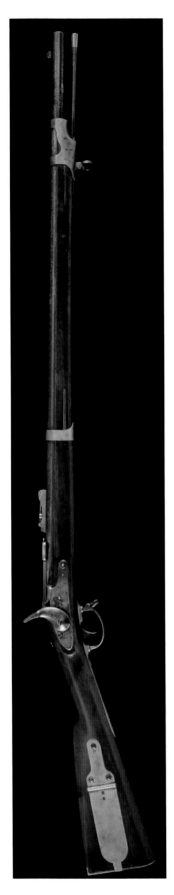

U.S. Model 1841 rifle made at the U.S. Armory at Harpers Ferry (1851), altered to Morse's breech-loading system, marked *E* (1859)

Between June and September 1859, the Springfield Armory altered four U.S. Model 1841 rifles according to Morse's 1858 patent as model arms for the potential modernizing of forty-three thousand "Mississippi" rifles held in the national arsenals. Three of the four model arms were sent to the Washington Arsenal in December, there to be fitted with bayonet studs. The fourth model arm and the machinery built for altering it were transferred to the Harpers Ferry Armory, where alterations continued into the latter half of 1860, though it is unknown how many rifles were completed.

Well aware of the value of these Morse-altered rifles for the potential defense of his native South, U.S. secretary of war John B. Floyd urged that they be finished as soon as possible for shipment to the U.S. Arsenal at San Antonio, Texas, where state officials had already expressed their interest in the arms. But all the newly altered rifles — along with all the arms altered to the William Montgomery Storm breech-loading system — were destroyed on the night of April 18, 1861, when U.S. troops burned the arsenal buildings at Harpers Ferry to prevent their contents from falling into the hands of Virginia troops.

Only the three Morse-altered model arms sent to the Washington Arsenal survived. This one, marked only with the identification letter E on its internal parts and never fitted with a bayonet stud, is believed to have been sent to the Frankford Arsenal as a reference for manufacturing the necessary .54-caliber cartridges. Perhaps more than any other arm in the Wray Collection, this rifle is a true national treasure: a milestone in American industrial technology and the direct ancestor of virtually all firearms produced since the Civil War.

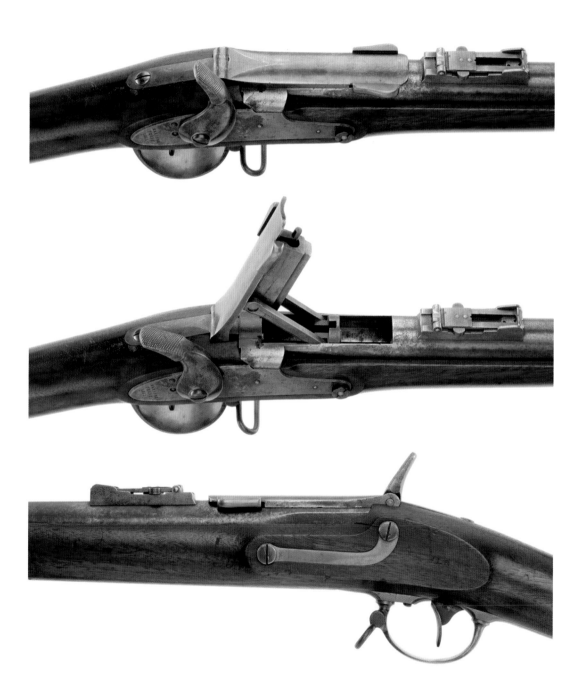

U.S. Model 1841 rifle made at the U.S. Armory at Harpers Ferry (1851), altered to the Merrill breech-loading system by the Merrill Patent Fire Arm Manufacturing Company, Baltimore, Maryland (1860)

One of the other two breech-loading systems tested against Morse's design in the 1858 trials was that of the Baltimore gun maker James H. Merrill, who had first patented a vertically pivoting breech door in 1856. Unlike Morse's invention, Merrill's system still relied on a paper cartridge (albeit one with a "waterproof" coating) and an ordinary percussion cap.

Although Merrill's proposed design was not as favorably received as Morse's, in April 1859 the U.S. War Department placed an order with Merrill for the alteration of three hundred U.S. Model 1841 rifles, Model 1842 rifled muskets, and Model 1847 musketoons, at ten dollars each. The altered Model 1841 rifles, which were also rebored to .58 caliber, were intended for field trials by infantrymen at Fort Randall, in present-day Gregory County, South Dakota.

This is one of the eighty-six rifles Merrill delivered in September 1860 (the remaining fourteen were "spoiled" during alteration). Although Merrill was never again asked to alter U.S.-made arms, he went on to produce about 15,500 carbines and 800 rifles of this design during the war.

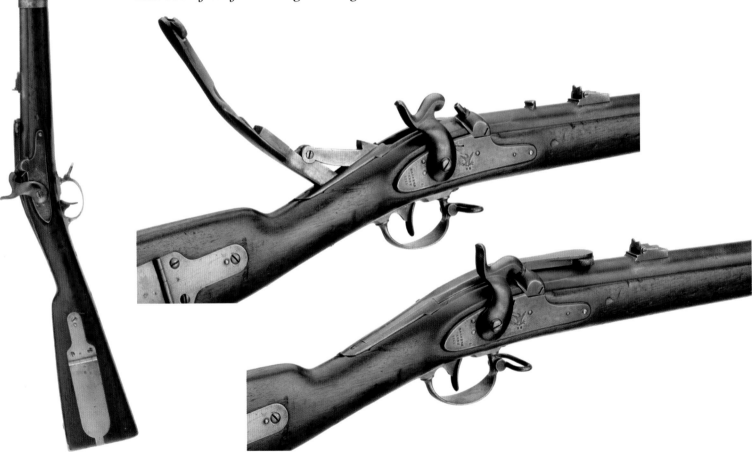

U.S. Model 1841 contract rifle made by Robbins and Lawrence, Windsor, Vermont (1849), altered to the Linder breech-loading system by Enos G. Allen and Andrew J. Morse, Boston, Massachusetts, serial number 47 (1861)

Although the German-born inventor Edward Linder did not submit a sample arm for the U.S. Army trials in 1858, his was one of the more creative breech-loading solutions of the day. As originally envisioned in his 1856 patent, each altered muzzle-loader included under the barrel a lever that would be pressed downward as the shot passed by, automatically opening the breech for the next shot. Another version had a piston under the barrel that used the explosion created by ignition to open the breech, not unlike a modern semiautomatic firearm. Though Linder relied on a traditional paper cartridge and percussion cap, his self-actuating breech was supposed to allow air to flow freely through the barrel, thus burning away powder residue and making cleaning unnecessary.

This is one of one hundred U.S. Model 1841 rifles altered to Linder's system for the State of Massachusetts between late September and mid-November 1861, by the gunsmith and steam-gauge manufacturer Enos Allen in partnership with the brass foundry of Andrew Morse. At the same time, Benjamin F. Butler, a politician turned general, purchased another two hundred similarly altered rifles on behalf of the U.S. Army. As built, Linder's alteration used a simple leaf spring to open the breech when the sleeve covering it was moved to the side, thus wisely eliminating the complicated, automatically opening breech. Linder's design was later applied to sixty-five hundred carbines manufactured by the Amoskeag Manufacturing Company in Manchester, New Hampshire.

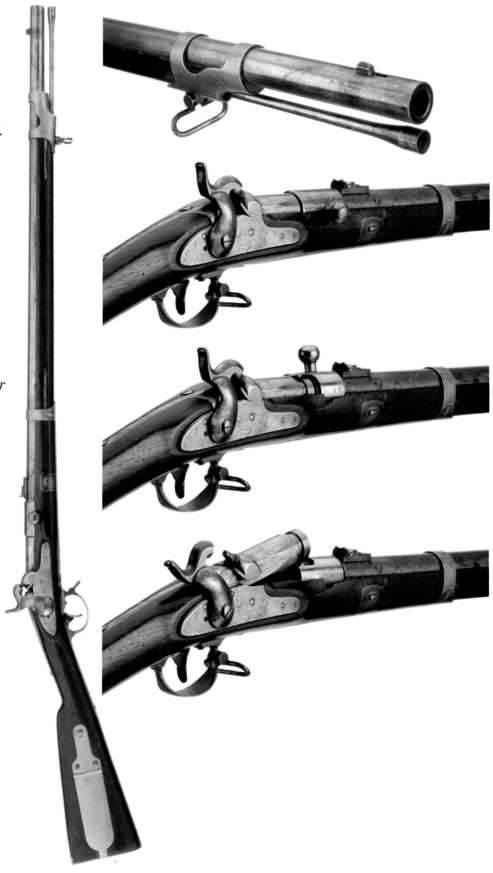

"The Best of the Lot": The Palmetto State's Morse Carbines

I am aware that the President does not like breech-loading guns, but still I know that he considers mine the best of the lot. . . . If Gen'l Lee had a few men armed with these guns in the trenches, no amount of force could take them.
—George W. Morse to South Carolina adjutant and inspector general Albert C. Garlington, November 7, 1864

These works carried on as they are now would prove ruinous to any private individual without unlimited capital in less than six months; carried on by the State, they will add unnecessarily to the burden of the war without producing any adequate results.
—Report of William S. Downer, superintendent of the C.S. Armory at Richmond, on South Carolina's State Military Works, October 5, 1863

With the coming of war in 1861, there was never any doubt about which side George W. Morse would be on. For more than twenty years, he had lived in Louisiana, raised a family, and made a fortune in land and slaves. Well before the first shots at Fort Sumter, Morse was trying to interest the newly formed Confederate government in his breech-loading design. "These arms can be manufactured in Europe or anywhere else at about the same cost as those of the ordinary kind," Morse wrote to the Confederate secretary of war in March 1861. "It seems to me that the adoption of a single plan of breechloader, with one caliber, for both the army and navy, would be advantageous."[10] Amid the flood of similar offers coming in from inventors all over the South, the Confederacy ignored Morse's initial overtures. Fully aware of Texas's previous interest in his breech-loading design, Morse sought a contract with the state for manufacturing one thousand of his breech-loading arms in Europe, but this effort also came to naught.

At the same time, Morse and his work were well known. In early March 1861, Confederate president Jefferson Davis sent him to Washington, D.C., to procure machinery for producing muzzle-loading arms. After the secession of Virginia in April, the machinery originally built for Morse's breech-loading alterations at the Springfield Armory and subsequently moved to Harpers Ferry fell into the South's hands. Ironically—and perhaps in part because of Jefferson Davis's influence—the Confederate government did not want the Morse machinery. Instead, upon Morse's request it was sent to the Tennessee State Armory in Nashville, where he had been hired as superintendent. In his new post, Morse was under intense pressure to provide arms of any kind as quickly as possible, reducing the alteration of breech-loading arms to second priority. Morse's machinery was not yet in operation in February 1862, when the Union advance on Nashville forced the armory (since taken over by the Confederate government) to relocate to Atlanta.

The machinery remained in storage there through April 1862, when David Lopez, general superintendent of South Carolina's State Military Works, approached Tennessee governor Isham Harris regarding its purchase or loan. South Carolina had established a temporary state armory in Columbia earlier that year and was planning the construction of a permanent facility in the small upstate town of Greenville. It seemed the perfect location: remote from possible Union advances, connected to the rest of the state by a railroad, close to sources of iron, and, most important, the site of a twenty-acre tract of land donated especially for the purpose. Harris agreed to lend South Carolina the idle Tennessee machinery, even though some of it technically still belonged to Virginia (which claimed the spoils of Harpers Ferry) and was also claimed by the Confederate government. As the brains behind the machinery, Morse came with the deal. For the next three years, he worked for the State of South Carolina, supervising the production of brass-framed .50-caliber carbines based on his patented breech-loading design.

An article in the *Atlanta Intelligencer* (December 19, 1862) describes in great detail one of the first prototypes of Morse's newly designed carbine, stating that it was made in Atlanta at the firm of Hammond Marshall and Company. "We were struck with the simplicity of its construction and its power of execution," noted the newspaper. "In all probability we shall soon see manufactured here a large quantity of this valuable arm for the defense of our homes and firesides, with which to drive the enemy from Southern Soil."[11] Marshall, a dentist and engraver by trade, was a retailer of arms (especially swords), but lacked the facilities for full-scale firearms production. The prototype was probably fabricated at Morse's own expense at the State Military Works in Greenville, where Lopez had managed to get the first shops operational in the fall of 1862. Morse, as superintendent of small arms, was drawing a handsome salary of $750 every three months but still had the right to manufacture and sell his design privately. In addition to Marshall and Company, Morse shopped his prototype to the C.S. Ordnance Bureau in Richmond. In a report to Josiah Gorgas in February 1863, Major William S. Downer called Morse's carbine "a clean, accurate, and pleasant weapon to shoot," but was worried mainly about the design of the brass cartridges and the technical difficulties in manufacturing them, concluding that unless those difficulties were addressed, "it cannot prove a reliable arm in the service."[12]

Meanwhile, Lopez had sent a prototype Morse carbine as well as a sample Burnside carbine to South Carolina governor Milledge L. Bonham, recommending Morse's design as the best choice for the state. (Morse must have been pleased with this reversal of the U.S. War Department's rejection of his design in favor of Burnside's in 1857.) In February 1863, the South Carolina legislature appropriated $15,000 for the manufacture of one thousand Morse carbines at the State Military Works. For the next seven months, Morse and his mechanics labored to modify the former Springfield–Harpers Ferry alteration machinery for the production of his breech-loading carbine. Among many technical challenges, Morse needed some entirely new equipment, including a rolling machine for making the all-important brass cartridges, a task he had previously been able to delegate to Muzzy and Company (in the case of his Model 1816 alterations) or the Frankford Arsenal (for his Model 1841 rifle alterations). Parts production began over the summer, but it was not until the end of September 1863 that the first carbines were ready. Over the next seventeen months, South Carolina's state armory turned out at least 1,032 of the most technologically advanced firearms in the Confederacy, but they were strictly reserved for state troops.

It was an endeavor that often pushed the available human and material resources to the limit. Despite the usual bureaucratic battles with Confederate authorities, the State Military Works managed to retain most of its skilled labor through 1865, including about seventeen white machinists in the small arms shop that did most of the work fabricating carbines. Another fifty or so white men worked in the office, machine shop, foundry, blacksmith shop, carpentry shop, and gun repair shop, where they were joined by several free black men, including a gun stocker and pattern maker. Even so, at peak production in 1864 about a third of the workforce was made up of enslaved laborers, many of whom were unskilled. Others served as blacksmiths, firemen, teamsters, and carpenters, including a thirty-year-old carpenter named Nat, who belonged to Morse's wife. Some of these men were voluntarily hired out by their owners at eleven dollars a month (payable to the owner), but by the end of 1864 the state had the authority to impress whatever slave labor it needed, whether slaveholders liked it or not.

Despite the State Military Works' success at putting Morse's innovative design into production, the start-up, operating, and transportation costs were rapidly turning the factory into a financial disaster. Instead of being located alongside one of the state's many sources of waterpower, the factory's workshops were powered by steam engines, which ran on expensive coal transported along a single, overburdened railroad. In the fall of 1863, Governor Bonham began looking for a way out, starting with the ever-acquisitive C.S. Ordnance Bureau. After a site inspection in October 1863, Richmond Armory superintendent William S. Downer concluded that the layout and operations of the shops were so inefficient as to be "entirely unpracticable for our purposes."[13] In December 1863, the state legislature authorized Governor Bonham to dispose of the works by private sale, but no buyer could be found. Eleven months later, the governor scheduled the works to be sold at public auction, but opposition forced him to postpone the sale. Morse, desperate to continue manufacturing and selling his carbines, suggested that the factory expand its product line to include agricultural and domestic implements.

In December 1864, a new governor took office. Determined to make the State Military Works profitable after all, he took Morse up on his suggestion. An optimistic state legislature even placed an order for another fifteen hundred Morse carbines in early 1865. It was too little, too late. Nevertheless, unlike nearly all other state or private arms manufactories, South Carolina's State Military Works had beaten the odds: it was still operating at the close of the war, and was never destroyed by Union troops. In 1866, the state sold the factory to a company planning to build a cotton mill; some of the machinery was sold to former superintendent J. Ralph Smith for his iron and machine works business in Charleston. From there, the fate of the machinery used to make the first center-fire breechloaders in American history is unknown.

Morse's loyalty to the Confederacy had cost him dearly: though his land holdings in Louisiana remained, his slave property was gone and his future as an arms inventor lay buried in the ruins of his adopted homeland. But he still had his 1856 and 1858 patents. In 1872, he moved to Washington, D.C., where he worked as a civil engineer while taking up a series of patent infringement claims against the U.S. government and the Winchester Repeating Arms Company. Morse well understood (at least in retrospect) how his center-fire cartridge and breech-loading system had changed forever the nature of warfare: "Instead of placing men in battle array, shoulder to shoulder, as of old, they are now more effective than before, when placed fifteen to thirty feet apart, and a new system of army tactics must be adopted in consequence." The new weapon "can tear down or build up Empires [and] by its use we easily subdue all uncivilized nations, and introduce the railroad, the telegraph, and the Bible." [14] Morse likewise understood that he had to downplay his wartime allegiance, thereafter maintaining that his work had only been for the States of Tennessee and South Carolina and never for the Confederacy itself.

In his most ambitious action, Morse sued for $891,000 in 1874, claiming royalties of five dollars for each of the 178,200 breech-loading center-fire-cartridge arms produced, altered, or purchased by the U.S. Government during the previous nine years, including the Allin, Sharps, and Remington systems. Four years later, Morse petitioned the U.S. Senate to formally recognize him as the inventor of the "modern centre-fire cartridge system of breech-loading fire-arms." The Senate Committee on Patents enthusiastically agreed, and proposed a bill to compensate Morse for his "services and expenses" in the amount of $25,000. [15] But the following year, after specifically mentioning Morse's Confederate past, the committee reversed itself, concluding that "there is very trifling, if any, originality in the Morse patent" and that all its elements had been anticipated by other American and European inventions. [16] Meanwhile, after an initial settlement with Morse for $10,000 in 1872, the Winchester Repeating Arms Company avoided an additional $15,000 payment by arguing successfully that it had manufactured its cartridges not according to Morse's patents, but according to the Smith and Wesson patents with Benjamin Tyler Henry's improvements. Ultimately, all of Morse's suits failed because the courts ruled strictly on what was specified in his patents rather than on what was implied by their principles and ultimate applications. In truth, these legal decisions were probably justified, especially since other inventors had been working on the same basic idea and several of Morse's patents had already expired. At the same time, it seems apparent that no one wanted to pay a former rebel for inventing anything, especially in the highly profitable firearms business.

Even so, Morse continued his work on internally primed cartridges. He was granted two final U.S. patents in 1886 and 1887, which were, ironically enough, for work prompted by the U.S. Ordnance Department, which wanted to adapt Morse's 1856 and 1858 cartridge patents for the longer cartridge cases then being used in smaller-bore military rifles. The Frankford Arsenal manufactured one million tinned-brass .45-caliber 70-grain Morse Model 1886 Movable Base Cartridges for testing. Ultimately, they were rejected for service use. Morse was working on them in Washington when he died in March 1888, still having seen virtually no reward or recognition for his efforts in developing the basic system that made modern firearms possible.

Morse breech-loading carbines made by the South Carolina State Military Works, Greenville, first type, serial numbers 126 and 141 (1863)

The carbine designed by George W. Morse for the State of South Carolina was an extraordinary departure from any other military firearm produced in the Confederacy. Although its breech-loading system was essentially unchanged from the one he developed for the Springfield Armory alterations, Morse made a much more compact arm for South Carolina, with a hammer or firing lever mounted inside the frame. At about six and a half pounds in weight and forty inches in length, his .50-caliber breech-loading carbine was three or four pounds lighter and about sixteen inches shorter than an ordinary .577- or .58-caliber muzzle-loading rifle-musket, but, theoretically at least, just as accurate and powerful. Symbolic of the shift from nineteenth- to twentieth-century technology, where once there had been a ramrod under the barrel, now there was only a cleaning rod, which was meant to be used with a cleaning jag stored in the buttplate.

Nevertheless, the first two hundred or so carbines produced in the fall of 1863 suffered from two serious defects: the solid block around the firing pin under the breech door was quite heavy, and the latching device at the forward end of the door was much too weak.

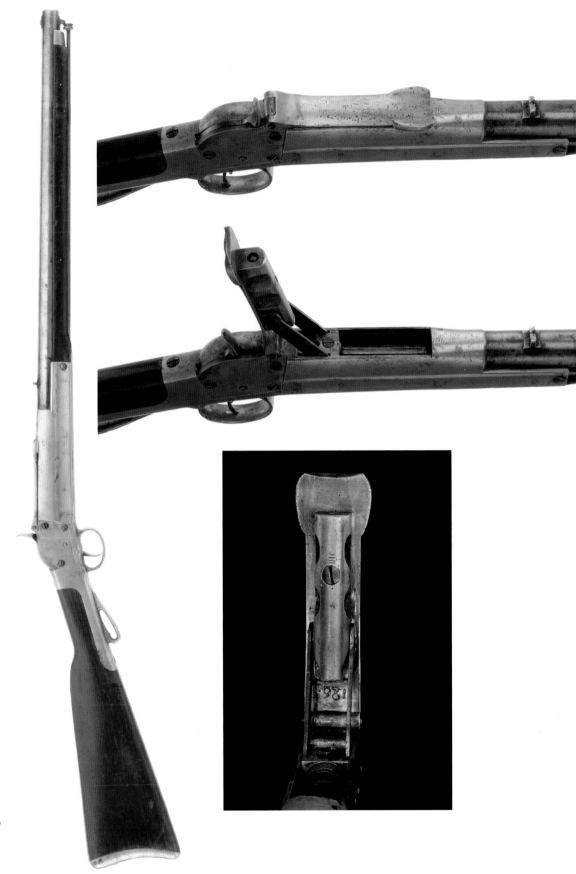

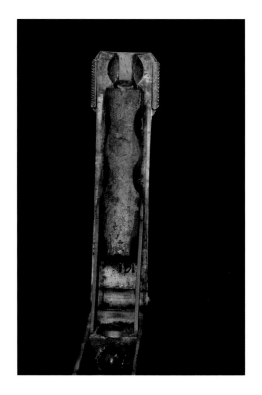

As William S. Downer noted in his negative report on Morse's carbine, when the weapon was cocked and held up at an angle, the breech door tended to flip open, thus allowing the chambered cartridge to fall out. At first, Morse tried to lighten the block by milling out three oval slots on each side of it.

Morse finally solved the problem by attaching a spring-loaded iron latch to the end of the breech door, a feature retrofitted onto existing first-type arms, such as carbine number 141, in late 1863 or early 1864 (left). For reasons unknown, the first two-and-a-half inches of the barrel on this carbine are octagonal rather than round, a possible indication that mechanics were reworking old barrels in addition to making new ones. All Morse carbines featured a sling or carrying loop cast into the receiver at the rear of the trigger guard. Though it resembles a lever action, this solid loop had nothing to do with operating the carbine.

Morse breech-loading carbines made by the South Carolina State Military Works, Greenville, second type, serial numbers 230 and 309 (1863–64)

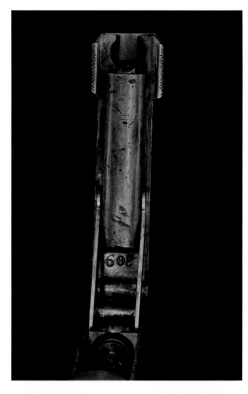

By the end of 1863, the breech doors of Morse's improved carbines were being built with the new spring-loaded latch at the forward end, which was opened by grasping the two knurled outer edges and pulling backward. When closed, the spring-loaded latch tab fit snugly under the head of an enlarged screw attached to the top of the movable breechblock, thus securely closing and sealing the breech. The new closure eliminated the need to lighten the block under the breech door by milling out slots.

It is believed that nearly all State Military Works carbines were made in .50 caliber with three lands and grooves, though a handful are known in .54 and .58 calibers, perhaps the result of postwar alterations. Four hundred Morse carbines stored in the state's arsenal in Columbia were destroyed by General William T. Sherman's troops in February 1865. Some of the remaining six hundred evidently saw civilian use after the war. Since Morse center-fire ammunition was no longer available, the firing pin of carbine number 230 (middle right) *was altered to ignite a .50-caliber rimfire cartridge, perhaps one made by Remington or Sharps.*

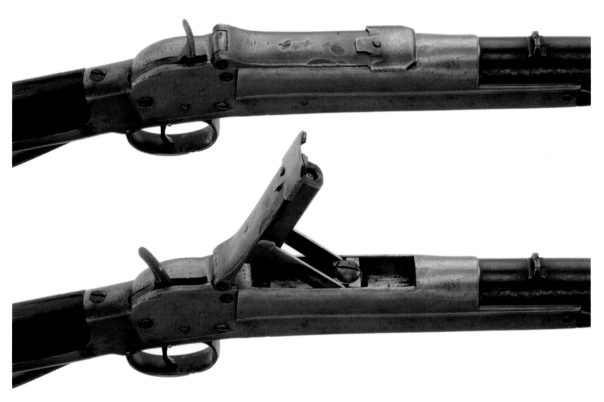

Morse breech-loading shotgun, made by the South Carolina State Military Works, Greenville (ca. 1864)

Morse was an inveterate tinkerer, not only working constantly to improve his carbines, but also experimenting with different configurations. Bearing an unnumbered receiver and a long, smoothbore, 24-gauge (about .58-caliber) barrel, this breech-loading shotgun was probably made for a private customer. It was built around a second-type receiver and has no cleaning rod or jag. It is the only example known.

Morse breech-loading carbines made by the South Carolina State Military Works, Greenville, third type, serial numbers 666 (1864) and 966 (1865)

In early 1864, Morse made a third and final improvement to his carbine's breech door. The large screw atop the sliding brass breechblock of the second type was superseded by a stronger steel bar with a slot cut into its rear surface atop a sliding steel block. When closed, the spring-loaded latch tab of the breech door fit neatly under the bar, which then bridged the gap between breech and barrel, creating the most secure seal yet on a Morse arm.

Even so, Morse's carbines still suffered from some inherent weaknesses. The frame and interior of the breech door were made of brass, which less-skilled mechanics found easier to work with, but being softer than steel, did not hold up well under the pressure of repeated firing. As seen by carbine number 966 (which bears "Morse" stamped on the right side of the receiver), the brass breech door was prone to cracking at the weak point near the rear hinge. Additionally, the thin stock, secured to the receiver by only two screws, was hard-pressed to hold up under the shock of recoil, especially when other woods were substituted in place of the usual walnut.

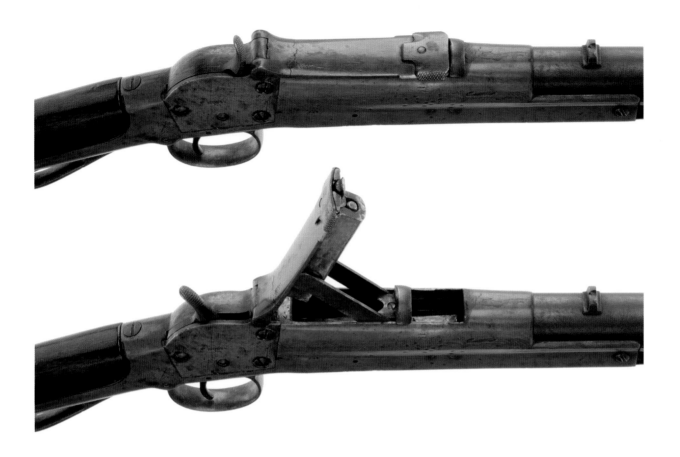

In the fall of 1863 or early 1864, the two companies of Edward M. Boykin's state cavalry squadron were the first to be issued Morse carbines. Because Governor Bonham had forbidden the use of the carbines by anyone except soldiers in the service of South Carolina, when Boykin's companies were called into Confederate service, they had to return their Morse carbines to the state arsenal and accept Confederate-issued rifle-muskets instead. At least four other companies of cavalry raised for state defense in late 1864 and early 1865 were armed with Morse carbines, and a few spent cartridges have been recovered at the sites of 1865 skirmishes across the state. Remnants of a carbine were recovered from an area in which General Wade Hampton's Confederate cavalry fought at the Battle of Bentonville, North Carolina, in March 1865.

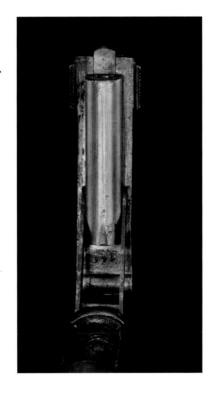

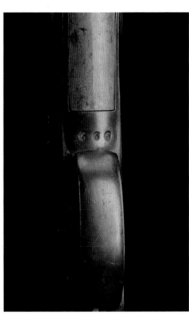

Cartridge pouches for Morse breech-loading carbines made by or for the South Carolina State Military Works, Greenville (ca. 1864–65)

Morse's breech-loading carbine required a new means of carrying its .50-caliber brass cartridge ammunition. It is unknown whether Morse or someone else at the State Military Works designed these leather cartridge pouches and their cotton-webbing waist belt, which resemble pouch designs of the later nineteenth and early twentieth centuries. Each pair of pouches contained twenty-four tin tubes for cartridges, an inexplicably small number given a potential rate of fire of about eight rounds a minute.

U.S. Model 1866 breech-loading "trapdoor" rifle, made and altered to the Allin system at the U.S. Armory at Springfield, serial number 700 (1865–66)

In 1865, the U.S. Army returned to the task of altering obsolete muzzle-loaders into breechloaders, this time using Morse's basic idea but not his name. The "new" system relied on two features: an improved center-fire cartridge developed by the future U.S. chief of ordnance Stephen V. Benét (grandfather and namesake of the famous writer) at the Frankford Arsenal, and a breech-door mechanism that hinged toward the muzzle instead of the breech, a refinement patented by Springfield's master armorer Erskine Allin. Fitted with .50-caliber sleeved or newly made barrels, the altered rifle-muskets became known as the U.S. Models of 1866, 1868, and 1870.

Both Benet and Allin were well aware of Morse's system; Allin had written an endorsement of it in 1860, which Morse cited in his 1878 petition to Congress. Yet their designs were indeed improvements of Morse's, at least enough to skirt his patent-infringement claims. Better yet for the U.S. government, because Benet and Allin were Ordnance Department employees, their designs were available for use without expensive and legally cumbersome royalty payments.

By 1872, the Springfield Armory had altered at least one hundred thousand rifle-muskets to accommodate Benet's cartridge and Allin's now-famous "trapdoor." Another half a million newly made arms using the same system were used by the U.S. Army and state militias through the Spanish-American War and beyond. Had it not been for the Civil War, these arms might have borne the name of George W. Morse.

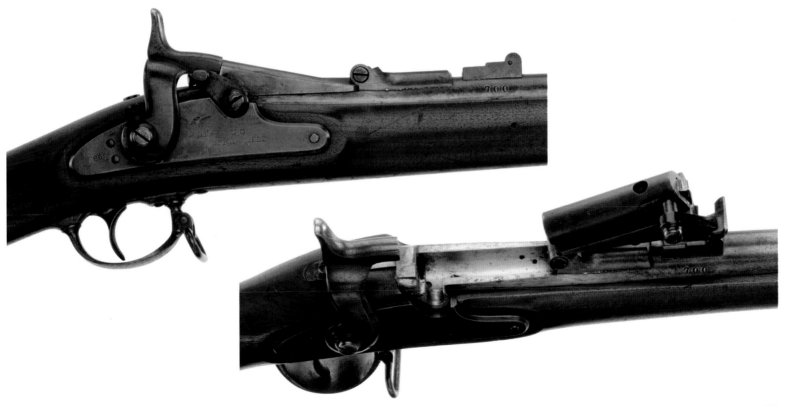

Whitney-Burgess-Morse repeating rifle, sporting model, made by the Whitney Arms Company, New Haven, Connecticut, serial number 1709 (ca. 1880)

Although the U.S. government was in no mood to recognize George Morse's patent claims, one private company did. In 1878, in the midst of Morse's legal action against the Winchester Repeating Arms Company, the Whitney Arms Company entered into a license agreement with Morse for the use of his cartridge patent dated October 28, 1856. Whitney was manufacturing a .45-caliber lever-action repeating rifle designed by Andrew Burgess to compete against Winchester in the lucrative sporting-arms market.

This is the only instance in which Morse received commercial acknowledgment for the use of his prewar patents, but he probably received very little in the way of financial compensation. The repeating rifle was never successful, and only about three thousand were ever made.

**Morse "inside lock" musket made by the South Carolina State Military Works,
Greenville, serial number 70 (1863)**

*In 1862 and 1863, the State Military Works devoted much of its time to altering South Carolina's
flintlock muskets into more reliable percussion-lock weapons, using the traditional method of placing
a new bolster over the vent hole and attaching a percussion hammer. Morse had a better idea, one that
would render the centuries-old side-mounted lock arrangement unnecessary and obsolete. His "inside
lock" mechanism used a horizontal pin inside the stock as the axis for the hammer, while a simple,
one-piece internal lock frame held the main- and trigger springs. Although requiring a new stock, the
"inside lock" meant that less wood needed to be cut from it, thus making for a stronger weapon.*

*Bearing serial number 70, this example was one of 140 muskets and rifles altered to the inside-lock
system in the fall of 1863. "We are also manufacturing a new musket lock of my invention," Morse
wrote to the South Carolina legislature, "for which I shall have the right to claim some consideration,
as it is admitted to be vastly superior to the old lock, and made with less than one half of the machinery
required in the manufacture of a gun lock of the old style, and at about one half its cost."[17] Thus, the
inventor made sure that "MORSE'S LOCK" was stamped into the trigger guard of each and every arm,
along with the date and the place of manufacture.*

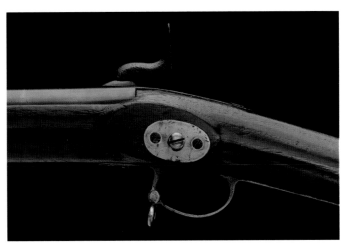

Morse experimental inside-lock rifle believed to have been made at the Tennessee State Armory, Nashville, Tennessee (ca. 1861)

While its inside-lock mechanism is virtually identical to those fabricated at South Carolina's State Military Works, this completely unmarked arm bears none of the other characteristics of rifles and muskets altered there. As required for arms fitted with the inside lock, its stock is newly made, but was cut out for a traditional side-mounted lock cavity and then filled in with a piece of sheet brass, suggesting that the inside-lock alteration was an afterthought. With the possible exception of the barrel bands, all of the U.S. Model 1841–style furniture is also newly made.

South Carolina was not making Model 1841–style rifles in 1863, and it seems unlikely that Morse would have gone to the trouble of having a new one built when there were plenty of old ones on hand. Additionally, as indicated by the long breech tang with two screw holes instead of one, the barrel appears to have been adapted from a heavier, Kentucky-style barrel. The exterior has been milled down to a smaller diameter, with only the breech retaining its original thickness, while the interior was probably rebored from a smaller caliber to achieve its seven-groove .54-caliber configuration.

Hence, this rifle seems to have much more in common with the U.S. Model 1841 copies and altered Kentucky rifles made for the State of Tennessee when Morse was superintendent of the state armory at Nashville. While the state was trying desperately to arm its new regiments in 1861 and 1862, Morse may have been trying desperately to save time, money, and materials by inventing the muzzle-loading equivalent of a better mousetrap. Morse's inside lock was indeed more efficient than any other percussion lock, yet it was another case of too little, too late: as he well knew, the era of the muzzle-loader was drawing rapidly to a close. Today, this one-of-a-kind prototype is one of the great stories of the Wray Collection and, like Morse's breech-loading carbines, a brilliant invention applied at the wrong time and the wrong place.

7. The Specialists

The American Civil War was the first conflict in history in which soldiers were specifically selected and trained as snipers. Often working in pairs, snipers—then known as "sharpshooters"—operated with near autonomy at or beyond the front lines. Here, using available cover and specially constructed "hides," they dealt death to officers, artillerymen, or other unsuspecting targets, sometimes at ranges of a thousand yards or more. Such men often stood apart as cold and calculating loners, more akin to hunters than soldiers—indeed, many were, especially in the western armies. Theirs was a war of inches, governed by patience, cunning, and precisely sighted killing tools.

These tools were as specialized as the men who used them. In the 1840s, the advent of the percussion lock created a more stable firing platform than the flintlock and gave rise to the sport of target shooting as well as a variety of specialized rifles designed specifically for shooting competitions. In the Northeast and Midwest especially, German and Swiss émigrés reestablished their traditional *schuetzen* clubs, while many native-born Americans, fearing "foreign" dominance, established their own shooting clubs in response. Competition rifles usually featured thick, heavy barrels designed to hold a large powder charge, precisely rifled bores in .40 to .50 caliber with six or eight deep grooves, double or set triggers, and finely tuned front, rear, and tang sights. At the same time, advances in the science of optics allowed John R. Chapman, a British engineer, and Morgan James, a New York gunsmith, to begin producing the first practical telescopic sights in the 1840s. By the mid-1850s, American inventors led the world in the development of adjustable telescopic rifle sights that magnified up to twenty times and were still stable enough to withstand the shock of repeated firing. The resulting telescopic rifles were expensive, finely crafted instruments weighing up to fifty pounds and capable of hitting targets accurately at three-quarters of a mile.

During the Civil War, sharpshooting evolved from skirmishing. Instead of the shoulder-to-shoulder linear tactics used by the main body of infantrymen, skirmishing involved open formations and made maximum use of cover to screen the main battle lines while probing and harassing those of the enemy. Early in the war,

Some of those Yankee sharpshooters were marvelous. They had little telescopes on their rifles that would fetch a man up close until he seemed to be only about 100 yards away from the muzzle. I've seen them pick a man off who was a mile away. . . . You wouldn't have any idea anybody was in sight of you, and all of a sudden, with everything as silent as the grave and not a sound of a gun, here would come skipping along one of those "forced" balls and cut a hole clear through you.
—Confederate veteran of Pickett's Division, quoted in the *Baltimore Herald*, November 3, 1886

both sides formed elite units drilled especially in skirmish tactics and armed with the best rifle-muskets as well as a few heavy target rifles. Theirs was the type of combat that made the best use of rifled weapons, and its success forced armies into ever deeper and more elaborate earthen defenses as the war dragged on. Although it never replaced linear tactics, skirmishing proved an effective means of gathering intelligence, scouting for weak spots, and creating diversions. By 1864 and 1865, nearly all infantrymen, not just those in the elite units, had become proficient in skirmish tactics; their skillful use of rifle-muskets had helped create a war of constant engagement and slow attrition, especially in the trenches around Atlanta, Petersburg, and Richmond.

Meanwhile, sharpshooting, or sniping in the modern sense, emerged as a distinct specialty above and beyond skirmishing. Small squads of men handpicked for their nerve, endurance, and marksmanship were organized and armed exclusively with the best target rifles money could buy, including, in the case of Confederate sharpshooters, lightweight but deadly accurate Whitworth rifles. Their job was to go beyond the skirmish line to inflict not only physical but psychological harm — in effect, blinding their enemies by forcing them to keep low in the trenches. Where sharpshooters were at work, no enemy ever felt safe.

George Wray had a particular fascination with Civil War sharpshooters and their specialized rifles. Only in this area did he collect beyond the Confederacy, expanding his holdings to include northern- and English-made target rifles, especially Whitworths. His fourteen Whitworth rifles represent the full range of 1860s civilian and military production and include five cased sets. Of these, only the four with positive or possible Confederate associations are highlighted in this book. Perhaps the most remarkable arms in the Wray Collection are two sharpshooter rifles made in Macon by the Yankee-turned-Confederate gunsmith Thomas Morse (no relation to George W. Morse). These unique arms tell one of the most fascinating stories in the Wray Collection, one that challenges all our assumptions about sectional loyalty during the Civil War. George Wray acquired the lighter breech-loading rifle in the mid-1970s and then spent the next thirty years searching out Morse's story. The heavy target rifle was the culmination of his efforts, purchased just weeks before his death. It was the last of more than 200 firearms in his extensive collection.

THE ARMY OF THE POTOMAC—A SHARP-SHOOTER ON PICKET DUTY.—[FROM A PAINTING BY W. HOMER, ESQ.]

Winslow Homer served as a combat artist for Harper's Weekly *magazine during the 1862 Peninsula Campaign, where he sketched this Union sharpshooter at work with a heavy civilian target rifle.*

Colonel Berdan's Sharpshooters

In 1861, a thirty-seven-year-old New Yorker named Hiram Berdan—inventor, entrepreneur, and one of the nation's most celebrated competition shooters—had an idea for creating a new kind of regiment. Instead of recruiting ordinary volunteers from a particular state or region, many with no firearms experience whatsoever, Berdan sought only the best marksmen from all the northern states to form an elite unit of sharpshooters. To qualify for membership, an applicant had to place ten consecutive shots within five inches of a bull's-eye from a distance of two hundred yards. Because of promises of extra pay, special uniforms, and, above all else, specially made Sharps rifles, Berdan's regiment attracted a flood of prospective recruits, making him a national celebrity. Company A was made up of Swiss and German émigrés experienced with *schuetzen* target rifles and was headed by Caspar Trepp, a Swiss soldier of fortune who had fought with the British army in the Crimean War. By October 1861, with eighteen companies raised in eight states, Berdan had enough men for two regiments, which were mustered into service as the First and Second Regiment, U.S. Sharpshooters.

Despite the fanfare surrounding their formation, the Sharpshooters lay idle for the next seven months, encamped near Washington and frustrated at promises unfulfilled. Only two companies of men were armed, and that with their own target rifles, for which they were never paid the promised bounty of sixty dollars each. Even more maddening was Berdan's failure to deliver on his promise of Sharps rifles, a promise he had made without first consulting U.S. Army chief of ordnance James W. Ripley. Even after enduring months of political badgering, the strong-willed Ripley refused to interrupt the Sharps Rifle Manufacturing Company's production of badly needed cavalry carbines for a mere two thousand special-purpose rifles. In January 1862, the matter reached all the way to President Abraham Lincoln, who finally compelled Ripley to order the two thousand rifles, thus saving Berdan from the wrath of his own men. Until the arms could be delivered, Berdan's Sharpshooters were armed with less than satisfactory Colt revolving rifle-muskets. Finally, in May and June 1862, Berdan's men received their coveted Sharps rifles, just in time for the Peninsula Campaign in Virginia.

The long wait for the rifles proved to be worth it. Civilian target rifles made for excellent long-range sniping, but their excessive weight and slow rate of fire made them impractical for skirmishing at two hundred yards or less. At that range, the accuracy and firepower of Sharps rifles (capable of firing eight to ten rounds a minute) overwhelmed muzzle-loading Confederate arms, especially smoothbore muskets. In the maelstrom of the cornfield at the Battle of Antietam, ranges often closed to ten or twenty yards. There the Second U.S. Sharpshooters probably accounted for at least 225 Confederate casualties in little more than half an hour, but at the cost of sixty-six of their own — about half their active strength. Meanwhile, a few men of the First Company of Andrew's Sharpshooters from Massachusetts still carried their heavy target rifles when they fought at similar ranges in the West Woods, "where rapid loading and quick shooting with them was out of the question, their guns being little better in that affair than clubs."[1] Soon after, the Andrew's Sharpshooters requested and received some of the Berdan pattern Sharps rifles. Nevertheless, most sharpshooter units, including Berdan's, always kept on hand a small number of civilian muzzle-loading target rifles for long-range sniping.

The First and Second U.S. Sharpshooters served in virtually every battle fought by the Army of the Potomac until late 1864, when their three-year term of service expired. Of the 106 men who had formed Company A of the First Regiment in 1861, only twelve remained to muster out in August 1864. Colonel Berdan himself had long since departed. Conspicuously absent from the front lines of every engagement, the controversial colonel resigned in late 1863, but only after attempting to silence Caspar Trepp and other senior officers who had complained about his lack of personal courage and leadership. Berdan went on to a successful and lucrative postwar career as a mechanical engineer working in weapons development. He patented an internally primed center-fire metallic cartridge in 1866 and two designs for bolt-action firearms in 1868 and 1870 (both of which were adopted by the Russian government). He worked with torpedo boats, range finders, time fuses, and other devices before his death in 1893.

Half-stock target rifle made by George O. Leonard, Keene, New Hampshire (ca. 1860)

In 1859, the Vermont-born gunsmith George O. Leonard set up shop in the small town of Keene, New Hampshire, where his target rifles gained a reputation for extraordinary quality and accuracy. The following year, working virtually on his own, he turned out thirty rifles. With the coming of war in 1861, Leonard's target rifles were suddenly in great demand, and he hired additional gunsmiths to help him fill orders from at least one of the New Hampshire companies of Berdan's Sharpshooters.

This half-stock target rifle was built around an octagonal cast steel barrel rifled in .40 caliber with seven lands and grooves. The barrel has been fitted with a "lollipop"-type round sight on the barrel tang, a graduated rear sight forward of the breech, and a hooded globe sight just behind the muzzle. The forward-action lock with double-set triggers features elaborate engraving, as does the German silver implement compartment, the forward end of which is made in the shape of an American eagle with a shield on its chest.

Given the elaborate decoration on this arm and its lack of a telescopic sight, it is probably one of the thirty rifles Leonard crafted before the outbreak of war, though it easily could have been used in combat afterward. A plainer and much heavier Leonard target rifle, mounted with a telescopic tube sight, was recovered at the Devil's Den at Gettysburg, where it was dropped by a wounded Texas sniper.

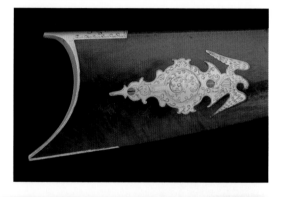

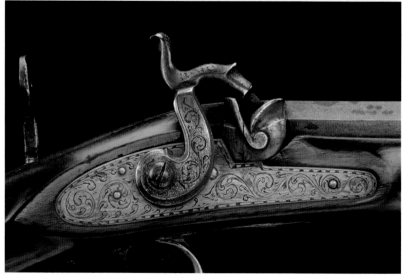

**Half-stock target rifle made by Nelson Lewis, Troy, New York, with a
telescopic sight made by Riley Haskell, Painesville, Ohio (ca. 1861)**

*At the beginning of the war, two companies of Berdan's Sharpshooters (one recruited in Michigan
and the other in New Hampshire) were armed entirely with their own target rifles, as were
Andrew's Sharpshooters of Massachusetts and a number of similar companies. Some of the arms
were crafted by the expert gun maker Nelson Lewis of Troy, New York. Like most small-town gun
makers of his day, Lewis did not make all parts from scratch; rather, he ordered the needed barrels,
locks, or furniture (sometimes in an unfinished state) from larger gun makers. Nelson Lewis and
his son William stocked and finished the arm themselves, sometimes adding custom-made sights or
other accessories as requested by customers.*

*Lewis built this 13½-pound target rifle around an octagonal cast-steel barrel fabricated by
E. Remington and Sons of Ilion, New York. He then rifled the barrel in .45 caliber with eight deep
lands and grooves; the side-mounted ramrod is made of wood so as not to scrape or wear down
the rifling. Meanwhile, the detachable "false muzzle" and brass plunger-type ball starter enabled a
conical bullet to be seated evenly in the bore so that it would take the rifling perfectly. Lewis gave
this rifle a back-action lock with a double-set trigger mechanism. By pulling the rear trigger, the
shooter set the forward "hair" trigger so that even the slightest pressure would release the hammer,
thus reducing any motion that could throw off the aim.*

*Finally, Lewis fitted this target rifle with a telescopic tube sight made by or for the gun maker
Riley Haskell of Painesville, Ohio, famous today as the inventor of the "Haskell Minnow," one of
the first artificial fishing lures. Given the relatively plain finish of this rifle as well as its telescopic
sight, it was probably fitted out specifically for military sharpshooters at the beginning of the war.*

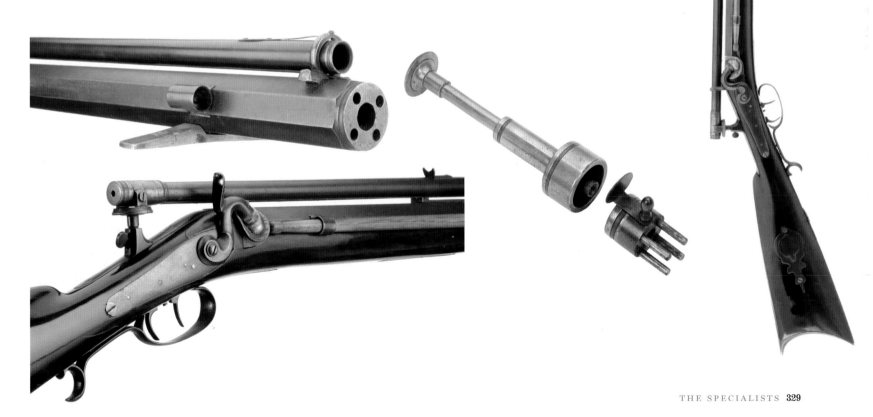

New Model 1859 Sharps breech-loading rifle, Berdan pattern, serial number 57192, made by the Sharps Rifle Manufacturing Company, Hartford, Connecticut (1862)

The two thousand Sharps rifles made in April and May 1862 according to Colonel Berdan's special order were the standard production .52-caliber New Model 1859 rifle but fitted for a socket bayonet and equipped with a double-set trigger mechanism. These rifles had been selected from among other competing designs in informal trials at the Sharpshooters' camp in October 1861. Sighted up to eight hundred yards, they proved to be accurate, reliable, and extremely popular, suffering from only minor problems: the double-set trigger mechanism frequently needed repair, while the .52-caliber linen cartridges often ran short in an army supplied overwhelmingly with .58-caliber paper cartridges.

By the time Berdan finally got his 2,000 Sharps rifles in May and June 1862, his ranks had dwindled to only about half that number. The remaining 1,000 rifles were stored at the Washington Arsenal, specifically reserved for new recruits or as replacements for damaged arms. Yet the pressure on U.S. Ordnance officers to issue these highly desirable rifles to other troops was overwhelming. In early September 1862, 180 were issued to the Forty-Second Pennsylvania "Bucktails," much to the chagrin of Berdan, who had only recently managed to reclaim 300 from the Sixteenth Michigan but had lost perhaps 100 others when Company L of the Second U.S. Sharpshooters joined the First Minnesota earlier that year. About 200 other rifles went to the flank companies of the Fifty-Fourth New York. In early 1863, many of the remaining Sharps rifles at the Washington Arsenal were issued to Berdan's men to replace worn-out arms, while others were turned in for repair and later reissued. Ultimately, all 2,000 of Berdan's Sharps rifles saw hard service, but not just in the hands of his famous sharpshooters.

This example bears serial number 57192 on the barrel tang and under the barrel, placing it well within the range of rifles manufactured for Berdan's men. The usual "JT" mark in the stock (for U.S. inspector John Taylor) is no longer visible, but the barrel breech bears the small stamp "OWR" for Orville W. Ainsworth, a civilian inspector borrowed from the Colt Firearms Manufacturing Company to help examine Berdan's rifles. Given its relatively good condition, this rifle was probably refurbished near the end of the war, which might explain how the "JT" mark went missing. One of the screws in the tang is a civilian type decorated with floral engraving, suggesting either a field repair or postwar use.

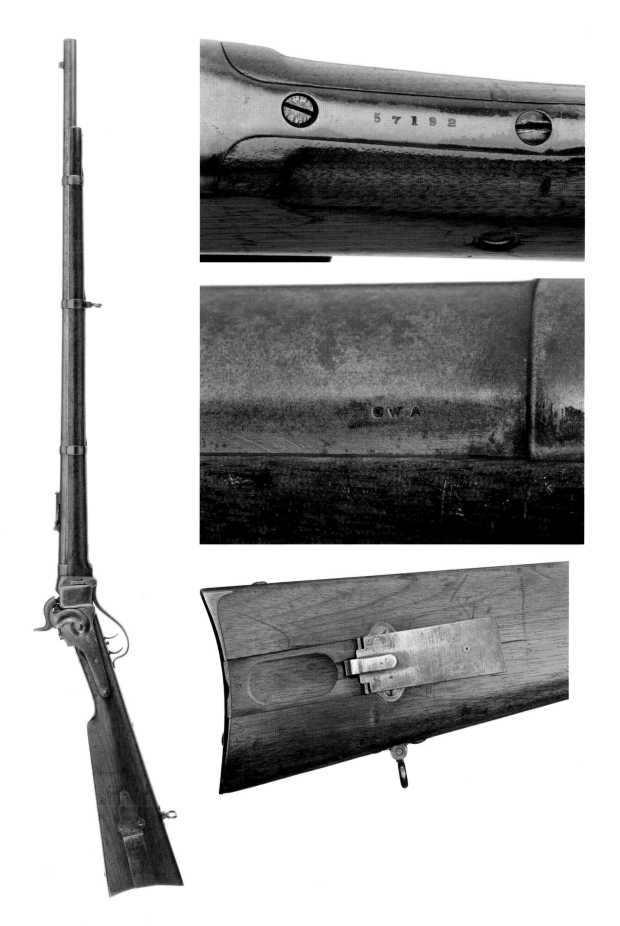

Southern Marksmen

In April 1862, when the C.S. Congress authorized conscription, it also authorized the organization of specialized sharpshooter units. Over the next year, southern states formed some twenty-three independent sharpshooter battalions or regiments for Confederate service. Like similar units in the Union army, the Confederate sharpshooters usually served as regular line infantrymen, only occasionally being called on to operate as skirmishers or scouts. Few Confederate sharpshooters approached the level of training or marksmanship of Berdan's men until 1863, when both the Army of Tennessee and the Army of Northern Virginia began forming their own sharpshooting companies from within existing brigades or divisions. Unlike the independent battalions, the new units were composed of veterans who had been selected especially for their marksmanship and then trained in skirmish tactics, distance estimation, and target shooting at ranges in excess of a thousand yards. They played an increasingly effective (and deadly) role on the battlefield in the last two years of the war.

Most Confederate sharpshooters conducted their skirmishing operations with ordinary rifle-muskets, though many preferred British-pattern short rifles, which were lighter, easier to handle, and often more accurate than their longer counterparts. At the same time, specialized long-range target rifles were extremely scarce in the South, a problem that Chief of Ordnance Josiah Gorgas addressed in May 1862. "It is highly desirable to get up some Telescopic Rifles for Sharpshooters," he wrote to Captain Richard M. Cuyler at the C.S. Arsenal at Macon. "If you can find any ingenious workmen to undertake them, do so. Let the barrel be 26 inches, bore .577, and twist one turn in 30 inches. The heavy barrels of country rifles will do."[2] Cuyler then turned to Walter C. Hodgkins, an accomplished gun maker whose father, Daniel, had leased his entire gun manufactory in Macon to the Confederate government just a few months before. For maximum accuracy and minimum recoil, Walter Hodgkins recommended .48 as the usual caliber for such arms, but Gorgas insisted on the Confederate standard of .577 instead.

Over the next eighteen months, Cuyler and Hodgkins spearheaded the Confederacy's attempt to provide accurate weapons for its sharpshooter units, producing heavy telescopic "sharpshooter rifles" as well as lighter, globe-sighted "scouting rifles," many of which were adapted from sporting rifles. Apparently, all such rifles differed slightly in dimensions and details but shared the same caliber. In August 1863, Cuyler reported that he had on hand fifteen rifles of both kinds, with components for fifty more, including 170 telescopic sights imported through the blockade. The main holdup came from trying to find good barrels as well as skilled labor—

Sharpshooters, like fiddlers, are born and not made.
—Attributed to Confederate general Ambrose Powell Hill by one of his sharpshooters, 1895

The public may not be aware that we have in Macon one of the best makers of Rifles and Pistols in this country—I believe in the world. . . . In addition to this he is one of the finest living shots himself. . . . He has also discovered an easy method of loading five to six times a minute at the muzzle. . . . One object in this note is to inquire if Mr. Morse's great talents in this way could not be made use of more profitably to the community and the Confederate States, than by the slow process of making one rifle at a time, although one that could hit a dollar every time at 500 yards.
—"Morse's Rifles and Pistols,"
Weekly Georgia Telegraph, June 21, 1861

some of his best mechanics had defected to the Georgia Armory in Milledgeville, which was paying higher wages. Nevertheless, Cuyler managed to build or acquire several dozen more "Macon" rifles, as indicated by records of their use by state-raised sharpshooter battalions and brigade-based sharpshooter companies in the Army of Tennessee through 1864. Although English-made Whitworth sharpshooter rifles are today more famous and survive in greater numbers, Macon-made sharpshooter rifles were probably more numerous during the war, although it is believed that only one example survives.

Confederate contract target rifle made by Thomas Morse, Macon, Georgia (ca. 1862)

At just over thirty pounds, this is the largest and heaviest rifle in the Wray Collection. It is also believed to be the only Macon sharpshooter rifle in existence. In most respects, it is typical of northern-made target rifles, and for good reason: its maker, Thomas Morse, spent his first twenty-five years as a gunsmith in Lancaster, New Hampshire, where he was known for his finely made sporting rifles stocked in bird's-eye maple.

Perhaps attracted by the town's booming business climate, the forty-six-year-old Morse relocated to Macon in 1858, where he went to work for Daniel C. Hodgkins and his son Walter before forming his own business at the corner of Mulberry and Third Streets. When war broke out in 1861, he sided with his adopted state, where his skills were probably well known to Walter C. Hodgkins.

Unlike virtually all civilian or northern target rifles of the period, this one is bored to the Confederate standard caliber of .577, a certain indication of wartime manufacture. Typical of civilian rifles, however, its massive one-and-a-quarter-inch-thick octagonal barrel was made to be unscrewed from the stock so that the gun could be broken down and carried in a wooden case along with a false muzzle, brass ball starter, bullet former, and other tools. But unlike the finely crafted, velvet-lined gun cases made in peacetime, this one was clearly meant to be more functional than elegant, its cheap pine once covered by black oilcloth, the remains of which still cling to outlying nails. Although this rifle is missing its tang-mounted lollipop sight behind the hammer, features including its adjustable rear sight, hooded globe-type front sight, and distinctive high-arch rifling of thirteen lands and grooves probably made it a highly accurate and deadly weapon.

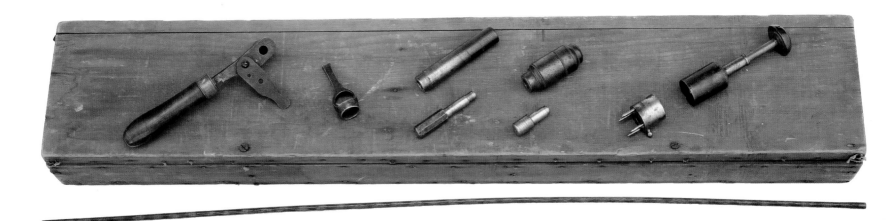

Despite its southern origin, this rifle still bears all the hallmarks of Morse's New Hampshire–made arms, including a half-circular flare around the bolster and a slotted hammer nut. Furthermore, the broken left inside leg of the letter M on the die stamp "T. MORSE" matches precisely the same flaw on a Morse rifle known to have been made in New Hampshire, indicating that he brought his name die with him to Macon. As would be expected, the "MACON, Ga" stamp below was made with a different die.

Half-stock breech-loading sharpshooter or scouting rifle made by Thomas Morse, Macon, Georgia (1863)

The destruction of the Confederate Patent Office records in 1865 is especially tragic for anyone attempting to assess the origins of this unique rifle, which very well could be the "Breech Loading Firearm" for which Thomas Morse was issued Patent Number 199 on September 10, 1863. Beautifully stocked in bird's-eye maple, this unique and virtually pristine rifle features what appears to be a double-set trigger. But pressing the rear trigger and twisting the barrel to the left in fact serves to open the breech, exposing a recessed chamber for an oversized (possibly metallic) cartridge — a design very much on the cutting edge of firearms technology in the 1860s. An article in the Weekly Georgia Telegraph *("Morse's Rifles and Pistols," June 21, 1861) boasted of Morse's mechanical ingenuity and personal marksmanship, claiming that Morse had "discovered an easy method of loading five to six times a minute at the muzzle" and that his rifles were made on an "entirely new plan." Perhaps the writer, confusing muzzle with breech, was describing this rifle (or a previous version), which indeed might have been loaded five or six times a minute.*

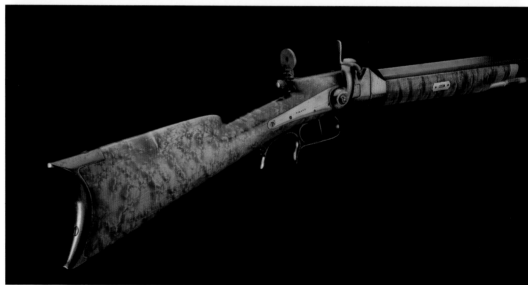

Rifled with ten lands and grooves at .40 caliber, this rifle was not made to Gorgas's specifications but was nonetheless meant for long-range shooting. It features a hooded globe-type front sight similar to that of Morse's heavier target rifle, as well as an adjustable lollipop tang sight. The name "T. MORSE 1863" on the left breech and the misspelled "T. MORS" on the right are of the same style and size as letters used on Morse's heavier target rifle but stamped individually, perhaps an indication that his prewar solid name stamp (with the broken M) had by then deteriorated beyond use. Although Morse probably made both rifles in Macon, this one is almost certainly the later of the two.

As soon as the war was over, Thomas Morse moved back to Lancaster, New Hampshire, where he resumed work as a gunsmith, apparently as if the war had never happened. In the late 1870s, some local veterans were discussing coming under fire from a Confederate sharpshooter just before the Battle of Fredericksburg in December 1862. Morse, who had been quietly listening to the story, spoke up and "admitted that it was he who did the firing from the house; but he recognized the Lancaster men through his lens and took care not to hit his former friends."[3]

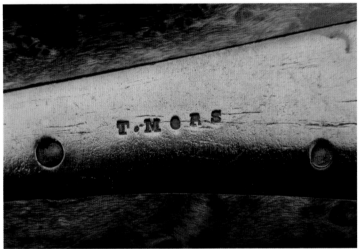

Truth or tall tale? There is no evidence that Morse ever joined the Confederate army (at age forty-nine in 1861, he was too old). Yet when Morse's patent was granted in September 1863, he was listed as a resident of Richmond. Perhaps he did indeed make the short trip from Richmond to Fredericksburg in December 1862 to try out one of his rifles by taking a few shots across the river, with or without any formal military association or permission. There were many northerners who sided with the South (Josiah Gorgas, for example) and vice versa, but most of them ended up staying in their region of choice after the war. Why would this Yankee turned Confederate return to his Yankee hometown, especially if his Confederate past was so well known? Does simple economic opportunity explain Morse's shifting loyalties, or was there something else? In any event, it seems that Thomas Morse felt no need to hide anything about his Confederate past.

Half-stock sharpshooter or scouting rifle made by Dickson, Nelson, and Company, Adairsville or Macon, Georgia (1863)

In 1862 and 1863, states that had raised their own sharpshooter battalions were trying to acquire the specialized weapons they needed. Built for the state of Alabama by Dickson, Nelson, and Company, this rifle combined the civilian features of a hunting rifle with the military features of the U.S. Model 1841–style rifles the company produced between 1863 and 1865. It is the only known Dickson, Nelson, and Company rifle in this configuration, and one of only two or three bearing an "1863" date on the lockplate.

This arm was built around a military barrel rifled in .54 caliber with seven lands and grooves but half-stocked in civilian style with a crescent-shaped buttplate, decorative implement compartment, and finger spurs on the trigger guard. The lock is identical to those produced for other Dickson, Nelson, and Company rifles but features a double-set trigger. Although the barrel bears a faint P proof mark, it lacks the usual Alabama state inspection marks—it may have been produced before they were put into use.

Strangely, the front and rear sights are of the same block type found on ordinary "Mississippi" rifles, suggesting that this lightweight rifle was meant only for medium-range skirmishing. If so, it may have been intended for the Seventeenth or Twenty-Third Battalion, Alabama Sharpshooters. The fanciful engraving of a Confederate battle flag and "1st AVC" on the implement compartment is almost certainly a modern imposition: the Alabama Volunteer Corps ceased to exist in 1861.

Sir Joseph Whitworth's Rifles

At just under ten pounds, Sir Joseph Whitworth's telescopically sighted hexagonal-bore rifles were the lightest, handiest, and most accurate sharpshooter arms the world had seen, easily capable of scoring hits on targets up to fifteen hundred yards away, and occasionally even farther. These finely crafted instruments of war—the superweapons of their day—made their first combat appearance during the Civil War in the hands of a very few highly skilled Confederate sharpshooters.

In 1861, Joseph Whitworth was Britain's foremost mechanical engineer, well known for developing the gauges and other measuring tools that made precision-tolerance machinery and interchangeable parts possible. Whitworth was probably most famous for introducing the first standard measurement for screw threads, known as the British Standard Whitworth, which is still in use today. In 1854, the British Board of Ordnance sought Whitworth's advice on designing interchangeable-parts machinery for the Royal Small Arms Factory at Enfield, a task that then led to the question of designing the most efficient system of rifling. At governmental expense, Whitworth had a covered five-hundred-yard range built at his country home for a series of careful, systematic ballistic experiments.

After concluding that relying on spiral grooves to spin a bullet was mechanically inefficient, he revived the old idea of a polygonal bore within which slightly twisting planes "preguided" a projectile made in precisely the same shape, not unlike a screw threading a nut. Settling on a .451-caliber hexagonal bore with a pitch of one turn in twenty inches (as opposed to the then-standard .577-caliber land-and-groove system with one turn in seventy-eight inches), Whitworth's system proved to be about six times as accurate as the Pattern 1853 rifle-musket. Yet its salient feature was also its chief drawback. With an extraordinarily fine tolerance between bore and projectile, the bore was easily fouled with powder residue and therefore had to be cleaned after only a few shots. That problem, combined with the exorbitant expense of their manufacture, meant that the British government eventually deemed Whitworth rifles unsuitable as standard-issue infantry weapons. It produced only about eighty-two hundred at the Royal Small Arms Factory.

Meanwhile, Whitworth enjoyed considerable success in the private market. In 1857 he began having his rifles manufactured and in 1860 established his own Whitworth Rifle Company in Manchester (reorganized in May 1862 as the Manchester Ordnance and Rifle Company). Between 1857 and 1865, at least five thousand Whitworth rifles were fabricated in sporting, target, and military models, along with experimental or special-order rifles with custom-made features. Many of the military-pattern arms became instant favorites at target-shooting competitions

What! What! Men dodging this way for single bullets! . . . I am ashamed of you. They couldn't hit an elephant at this distance.
—Last words of Union major general John Sedgwick, May 9, 1864

Elias Burns sang out, "The rebel bullet is not yet made, that is to kill me." At that, he jumped up and fell down the same instant with a bullet in his brain. He fell across my lap—I was still sitting—and his brains and blood ran into my haversack, spoiling my rations. So I took his.
—Private Robert H. Strong, 105th Illinois, during the Atlanta Campaign, 1864

between companies of the British Volunteer Force, which often awarded Whitworth cased sets as prizes. Strangely enough, none of these commercially made arms were interchangeable, but since all were fabricated by some of the best craftsmen in the gun-making industry, they were the most accurate, highest-quality arms of the muzzle-loading era.

In 1858, Whitworth purchased the rights to a new telescopic sight developed especially for rifles by an avid hunter and former East India Company officer named David Davidson. His lightweight detachable sight could be easily focused and adjusted for elevation, creating a method of sighting by which, according to his 1862 patent, "error of aim is, practically speaking, annihilated."[4] Gaining control of Davidson's telescopic sight was a business coup for Whitworth, forestalling the use of this obviously valuable device by his many competitors, including the London Armoury Company, which was marketing James Kerr's patented target rifles.

Based on the reputation of Whitworth's rifles, the Confederate agent Edward C. Anderson purchased two of them from the factory in Manchester soon after he arrived in England in 1861, commenting, "He asks enormously for them."[5] The already-expensive guns were made even more so by Confederate currency inflation; by 1863, one Whitworth rifle and a thousand rounds of ammunition cost the C.S. Ordnance Bureau $1,000 — and it is unclear whether that price included the Davidson sight. But the Confederacy badly needed sharpshooter rifles, and Whitworth's rifles were well beyond the quality of anything that could be produced at the Macon Arsenal.

The first few dozen Confederate-purchased Whitworth rifles began arriving in the South in the spring of 1863, and Confederate ordnance chief Josiah Gorgas personally divvied them up between the Army of Northern Virginia, the Army of Tennessee, and General P. G. T. Beauregard's forces defending Charleston. "These arms are reported to be very effective at 1,200 yards," Gorgas wrote to General Braxton Bragg. "I have the honor to request that they may be placed in the hands of careful and reliable men only as they are very costly, so costly indeed that it is not deemed expedient to increase the number already brought in."[6] Confederate field commanders took Gorgas at his word and often organized shooting competitions among regiments, brigades, and divisions so that only the best shots received use of the coveted weapons. The winners were then organized into special sharpshooter squads, excused from normal camp duties, and sent on the hunt for enemy pickets, officers, artillerymen, or other sharpshooters. The most famous Whitworth kill occurred on May 9, 1864, at the beginning of the Battle of Spotsylvania Court

House, Virginia, when Major General John Sedgwick was shot through the head at a distance of about eight hundred yards. He was the most senior Union officer killed in the war. At least five Confederate sharpshooters later claimed credit for the fatal shot.

In the Army of Tennessee, General Patrick Cleburne became famous for organizing and training one of the Confederacy's first Whitworth-armed sharpshooter squads. The snipers had their own wagon and reported directly to division headquarters. Each day they were assigned to a particularly hot portion of the line, sometimes silencing troublesome Union batteries by picking off the gunners, thus compensating for the Confederacy's lack of long-range rifled artillery. But the job was not without risk. Cleburne's squad lost 60 percent of its men during the Atlanta Campaign of 1864. In Joseph H. Lewis's Kentucky ("orphan") brigade, half the original members of its sharpshooter squad were killed and most of the rest wounded; counting replacements, there were only seventeen men in the squad during the entire war.

Today, Whitworth rifles are among the most collectible of nineteenth-century English arms, in part because of the large number of surviving examples in so many varieties and configurations. Yet only a tiny fraction of these rifles ever saw Confederate service. Documentary evidence indicates that the C.S. Ordnance Bureau purchased no more than fifty, though oral testimony and field recoveries of spent bullets suggest a slightly higher number, perhaps reflecting additional purchases by private speculators. The largest recorded number of Whitworth rifles in any Confederate army was thirty-two in the Army of Tennessee in June 1864. Today only about twenty Whitworth rifles of the type purchased by the Confederacy survive, making them among the rarest and most valuable of all Confederate arms.

Whitworth second-quality military match rifle, with Davidson telescopic sight, serial number B547 (ca. 1861–62, imported 1863)

The Whitworth rifles purchased by the Confederate government were of a particular configuration known as second-quality military match (or target) rifles. These arms were built with a thirty-three-inch barrel secured to a checkered stock with two bands and, as expected for a sharpshooter rifle, no provision for a bayonet. The term "second quality" had nothing to do with the internal quality of the rifling, sights, or lock but referred only to the external finish and features. These "economy models" lacked the usual deep polish or engraving and dispensed with nonessential features such as the safety mechanism forward of the hammer and an implement compartment. Hence, the hand-engraved "2nd Quality" (sometimes with the cursive Q resembling a "2") on the trigger-guard tang is an indicator of Confederate purchase in much the same way as the "JS"-and-anchor view mark on English rifle-muskets.

The most distinctive feature of these rifles was the Davidson telescopic sight mounted to the left side of the stock. Unlike American telescopic sights of the day, which were mounted on top of the barrel and extended its full length, Davidson's sights were only about fifteen inches long and could be attached to the side of the arm, thus allowing the option of using the open sights on the top of the barrel (adjustable up to twelve hundred yards) for closer-range work. The rear mounting ring of the telescopic sight served as a pivot point, while the front mount could

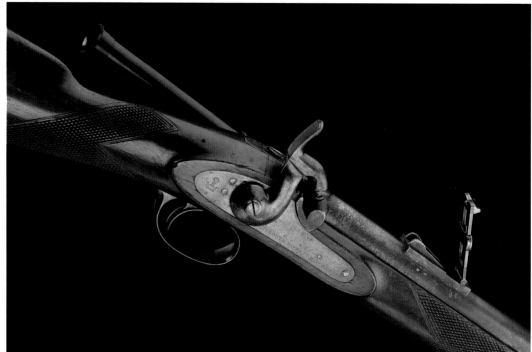

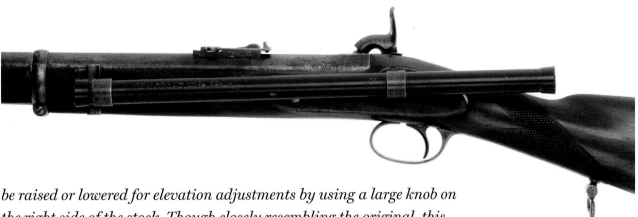

be raised or lowered for elevation adjustments by using a large knob on the right side of the stock. Though closely resembling the original, this particular Davidson sight is a restoration with twentieth-century optics.

The breech of this rifle is stamped with the obligatory Birmingham commercial proof marks, a bore gauge of 52 (.451 caliber), and serial number B547. Whitworth rifles were consecutively numbered regardless of configuration; after the first one thousand were produced, a letter prefix was added for each additional batch of one thousand arms. In theory, B547 should be the 1,547th rifle manufactured, but without a date stamp, the precise date of origin is unknown. Serial numbers for the few surviving Confederate-purchased Whitworth rifles range from B509 to C619. Although it is impossible to determine when or where this particular rifle was used, as one of the Confederacy's most valuable weapons, it certainly did see use. Just as certainly, it killed and wounded many Union soldiers.

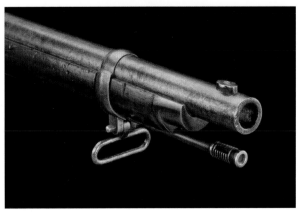

Whitworth bullets

Whitworth's hexagonal-bore rifle was designed for a lead bullet of the same hexagonal shape as the bore, with a wax lubricating plug at its base (right). It was found that elongated cylindrical bullets, which were much simpler to make, worked just as well, their hollow bases expanding to take the rifling. This one (left) is still wrapped in a paper patch. Each Confederate-purchased rifle was supposed to come with one thousand rounds of ammunition, but it is likely that sharpshooters also cast their own when supplies ran low, using molds such as the one below.

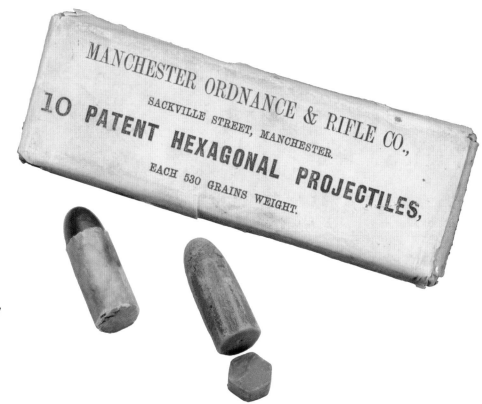

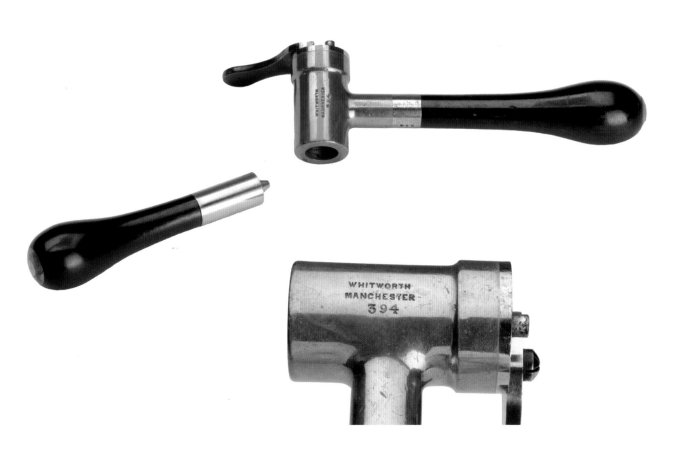

Whitworth cartridges

Left: *In 1859, Joseph Whitworth patented a special cartridge incorporating a cardboard tube around the bullet and powder charge. The tube was intended as a sort of false muzzle to hold the cylindrical bullet in place just before it was rammed down the barrel, thus seating it evenly. After loading, the tube was discarded.*

Right: *Some of the cartridges provided with Whitworth rifles were made in the "American" style, that is, with the cylindrical bullet wrapped in plain white paper. This bundle of ten cartridges was made by Eley Brothers of London, one of England's largest ammunition manufacturers.*

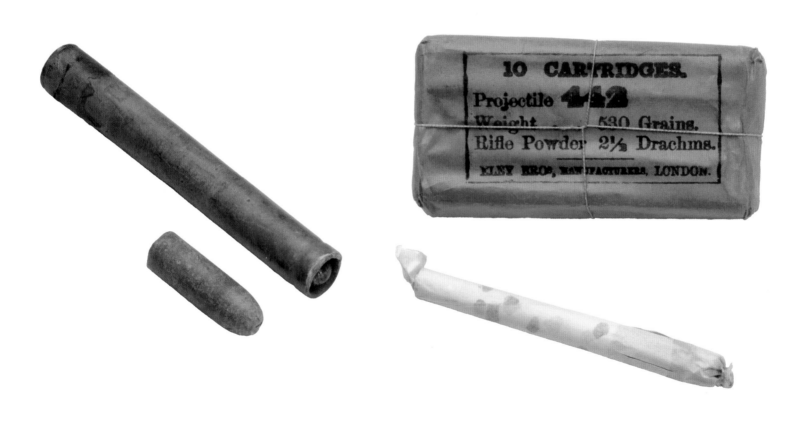

Whitworth second-quality military match rifle, serial number B933 (ca. 1861–62, imported 1863)

Bearing serial number B933, this is one of the only known second-quality military match rifles that was never meant to be mounted with a Davidson telescopic sight. One other, serial number B922, is virtually identical except for the front sight, suggesting that the two arms were built at approximately the same time and as part of the same order. Both clearly saw heavy use, but as seen here, the hexagonal bore had to be kept in pristine condition, as any powder residue or rust could not only throw off a bullet's trajectory but make loading impossible.

This example lacks the usual side-walled sliding ladder-type rear sight found on earlier second-quality military match rifles. Instead, it has the folding rack-and-pinion-type rear sight with no sidewalls, as found on many Whitworth civilian target rifles. The block front sight is consistent with other known military-style Whitworths, but the laterally adjustable peaked blade could be a factory variant, a field modification made by or for an individual sharpshooter, or a postwar replacement. In any event, this rifle certainly saw action in the hands of Confederate sharpshooters and perhaps continued in use after the war. There is no evidence of Whitworth rifles being surrendered in 1865, nor is there any mention of them in postwar sales by the U.S. War Department.

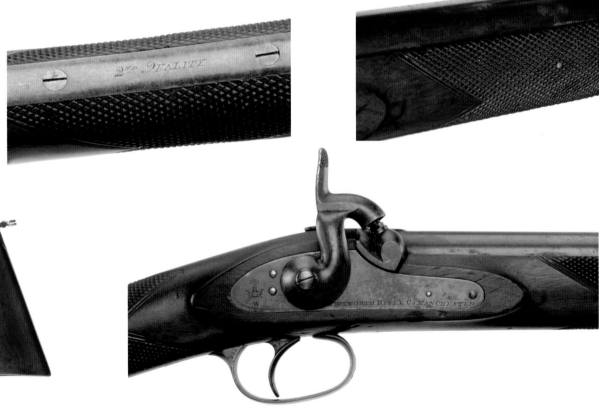

**Whitworth bullets recovered from an Army of Tennessee
shooting competition near Dalton, Georgia (1864)**

In his classic memoir, Company Aytch *(1882), the First Tennessee veteran Sam
Watkins recalled a shooting competition near the Army of Tennessee's winter
camp around Dalton, Georgia, in the early months of 1864. The winner was to
be assigned a Whitworth rifle and a place in one of the army's elite sharpshooter
squads. "All the generals and officers came out to see us shoot," Watkins
remembered. "The mark was put up about five hundred yards on a hill, and each
of us had three shots."*[7]

*In the 1980s, a local relic hunter located the target site for this famous
competition on a small hilltop northwest of Dalton, where he found six hexagonal
and thirty cylindrical Whitworth bullets, including the ones seen here. The fired
bullets were supposed to have been recovered and returned to the arsenals to be
melted down and recast, but these were left behind.*

Whitworth military match rifle, serial number B347 (ca. 1861)

Typical of most surviving Whitworth rifles of the 1860s, this one does not bear the characteristics of Confederate-purchased military match rifles. It has three bands instead of two, an implement compartment, no mounts for a Davidson telescopic sight, and a safety mechanism forward of the hammer. Most important, it lacks the telltale "2nd Quality" mark on the trigger-guard tang.

Yet unlike most Whitworth rifles, this one comes with a story. It was purchased in the 1970s from the descendants of a soldier believed to have served in Brigadier General George P. Doles's Georgia Brigade. Unfortunately, the name of this soldier is lost to time, and therefore the attribution can never be verified. But one of the five sharpshooters who claimed to have shot Major General Sedgwick on May 9, 1864, was Private Charles D. Grace of the Fourth Georgia Infantry, which was part of Doles's Brigade. "Grace was a fine shot and was armed with one of the few Whitworth rifles in our army," commented the brigade history, "which made the deed not only practicable but simple." [8]

A week later Grace was seriously wounded but survived to surrender at Appomattox, unlike General Doles, who was killed by a Union sharpshooter on June 2, 1864. No one will ever know who fired the shot that killed Sedgwick, but it was probably not Grace. Likewise, there is no firm evidence that he or anyone else in his brigade used this rifle. But it is still remotely possible, given that at least a few Whitworth rifles reached the South that were not purchased by the C.S. Ordnance Bureau. Interestingly, this one has had a hooded cover placed over the front sight to shield it from glare.

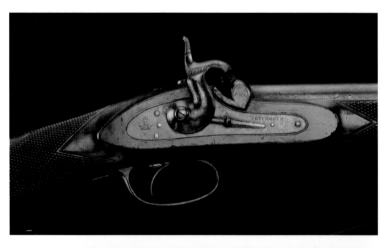

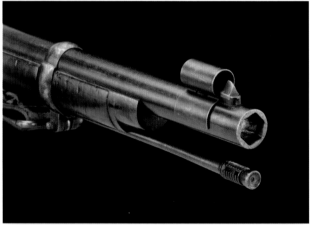

Whitworth military match rifle, with case and accessories, serial number B95 (ca. 1861)

This exquisite cased set was typical of those made for wealthy British officers or awarded as prizes in military target-shooting matches. It bears nearly all the same features as rifle B347, including the lack of the "2nd Quality" mark on the trigger-guard tang, but its folding rack-and-pinion-type rear sight is nearly identical to that of rifle B933. The front sight is a hooded globe type, with a center pin that can be adjusted laterally with a knob to compensate for windage. Whitworth produced an almost endless variety of made-to-order sights, especially front sights.

Remarkably, the oak case contains nearly all its original accessories, including a bullet mold, powder flask, tins for the lubricating bullet plugs, brass percussion-cap dispenser, an oil bottle, cleaning brush, spring vise, nipple wrench, and other tools. Probably manufactured in 1861, this rifle could have been among those imported into the South and sold by private speculators. If so, it would have been well beyond the means of an ordinary soldier, though not of a wealthy officer or a state purchasing agent. Nevertheless, there are no records indicating state purchases of such cased sets. It is also possible that it was sold privately in the North; it is more likely, however, that it never left England.

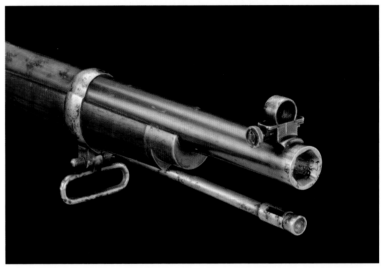

Sharpshooter's orthoptic spectacles

Though certainly originating in the mid-nineteenth century, these spectacles are not the ordinary "sunglasses" of the period, which were often made of blue or green glass. Instead, each amber-colored glass disc has a frosted finish with a round, clear center. It is believed that these spectacles, intended for target shooters, were designed to reduce glare and blurring by blocking out peripheral light, focusing the eye more clearly on the front sight.

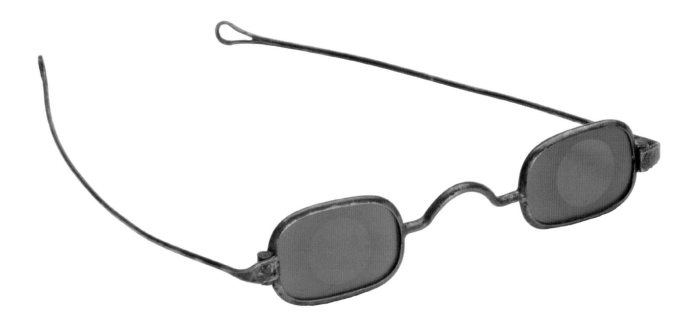

Kerr military target rifle, second type, made by the London Armoury Company, serial number 183 (1862)

In the early 1860s, Joseph Whitworth's rifles had many imitators. At least a dozen English gun makers produced cheaper versions of his rifles that had .451-caliber bores with a rapid spiral and deep grooves intended for specially shaped bullets. Designed and patented by the London Armoury Company superintendent James Kerr, this six-groove rifle became one of the most popular of these imitation arms, in large measure because all parts except the barrel and ramrod interchanged with the London Armoury Company's Pattern 1853 rifle-muskets.

At merely twice the cost of an ordinary rifle-musket, a Kerr rifle presented an attractive alternative for Confederate purchasing agents, especially since it could be used with the same cylindrical bullets as the more expensive Whitworth. In November 1863, twenty Kerr rifles were issued to the Army of Tennessee, ten of which went to General Patrick Cleburne's division. An unnamed Confederate sympathizer from England presented eleven more as a gift to General John C. Breckinridge, who had them issued in the spring of 1864 to the best shots in the famous Kentucky "Orphan Brigade" of the Army of Tennessee.

At least eight hundred of these special-purpose rifles were produced in a variety of configurations; probably no more than fifty ever reached the Confederacy. Bearing London commercial proof marks, serial number 186, and the "Kerr's Patent" mark on the top of the barrel, this well-worn example was probably not a Confederate purchase, though it is certainly representative of the type. The lockplate on this example has been stamped with a British government broad-arrow view mark, suggesting that it was left over from the London Armoury Company's rifle-musket contract.

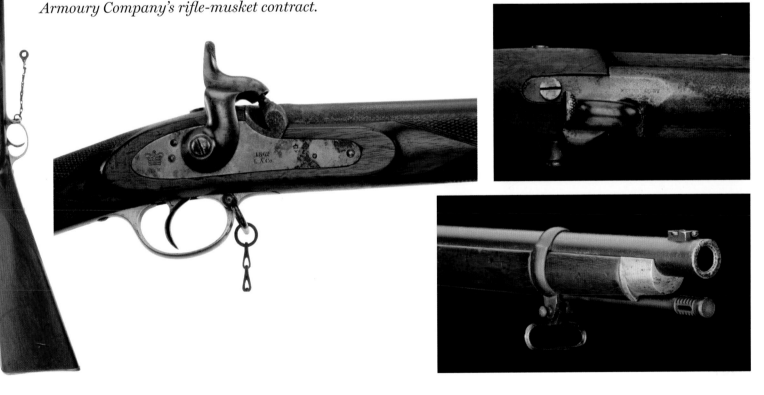

Whitworth muzzle-loading naval deck gun, 1.92-inch caliber (1864), with reproduction carriage (2003)

Although the British army was losing interest in mass-producing Whitworth's hexagonal-bore rifles, it was still interested in using his system for artillery pieces. So, too, was the Confederacy, which badly needed long-range artillery. Confederate army and navy agents purchased cannons from the Manchester Ordnance and Rifle Company in at least eight calibers, from the smallest "one-pounder" (1.25-inch) shipboard swivel guns to the largest "120-pounder" (6.4-inch) seacoast guns.

Extensive research by George Wray strongly suggests that this fifty-four-inch-long "three-pounder" naval deck gun was one of a pair made for a Confederate raiding ship or a blockade-runner, though the name of the ship remains unknown. The C.S. Navy agent George T. Sinclair purchased a pair of even smaller Whitworth "one-pounder" naval swivel guns in November 1864; it is possible that this pair of slightly larger deck guns was purchased at the same time. If so, it is unlikely they left British shores before the war ended.

This gun is marked identically on each trunnion: "MANCHESTER ORDNANCE & RIFLE COMPANY / CWT 2 / QRS 2 / WHITWORTH / PATENT / No. 316. / 1864." The mark "CWT 2 / QRS 2" gives the weight of the tube using British imperial measures of two centum weight (224 pounds) and two quarters (56 pounds), or 280 pounds in total. The mate to this gun, numbered 315, survives in the collection of the Royal Armouries in Great Britain, along with two others bearing 1863 dates. These four guns are the only known examples in the world. George Wray acquired this one in 1968, but unfortunately no further provenance is known.

Built by Historical Ordnance Works of Woodstock, Georgia, the naval slide carriage is an exact reproduction of the original on which gun number 315 is mounted. The original carriage does not conform to Royal Navy specifications but rather appears to have been specially ordered by George Sinclair with brass U.S. Navy–style mountings.

**Whitworth muzzle-loading field gun,
2.19-inch caliber (ca. 1861), with
reproduction carriage (2003)**

This muzzle-loading 2.19-inch-caliber "six-pounder" Whitworth rifle is the only known surviving example of its type. Its only marking is a barely discernible "WHITWORTH" stamped across the barrel just in front of the vent, though George Wray left notes indicating that it was once marked in the same area with "1861," "11" (or possibly "17"), and "4 CWT 1 QRS," indicating a weight of 476 pounds. Otherwise, there are no physical clues to the gun's origin or service history.

Records indicate that there were five Whitworth rifles of this size and configuration imported into the Confederacy. One of these was used in the Army of Northern Virginia. The other four were based in or near Fort Fisher, North Carolina, guardian of the South's most important blockade-running port at Wilmington. They were part of the famous quick-response force, or "flying battery," dispatched from Fort Fisher and moved from point to point along the beach to protect inbound blockade-runners and harass pursuing U.S. Navy ships. Although slight in caliber, these guns were accurate to three thousand yards or more, often beyond the range of blockaders' guns. A single shot could disable a steam boiler and prevent further pursuit.

After the war, this gun was taken north as a war trophy and displayed at the Grand Army of the Republic post in the town of Lititz, Pennsylvania, until the 1930s. It was then displayed outside a general store near Highland Falls, New York, until 1978, when Wray bought it from a local antiques dealer. It is mounted on a reproduction British-pattern field carriage built by Historical Ordnance Works.

Shells for Whitworth 2.19-inch muzzle-loading field gun (ca. 1863)

The perfectly angled spiraling planes of these three projectiles well illustrate the principle of Whitworth's "preguided" rifling. The shell on the left is an early type made with a straight base; later versions had a tapered base, which improved stability in flight and increased accuracy.

Most of the Confederacy's Whitworth projectiles were imported from Britain, where there was machinery to make these precisely measured and angled cuts. Some noticeably cruder but entirely functional projectiles were made in the Confederacy, probably by a very skilled machinist in Richmond. The only battlefield recoveries of projectiles for a 2.19-inch gun have come from around Fort Fisher, and all were made in Britain.

8. Blood and Honor

In large measure, the American Civil War was fought according to a nineteenth-century code of honor that expected unflinching personal courage and unquestioning commitment to the cause; battle was nothing less than a personal test of moral fiber. Early in the war, the means of conducting battle—long lines of men fighting within plain sight of one another without the benefit of cover—left little room for the fainthearted. The purpose of uniforms was not concealment but personal identification, pride, and even intimidation of an enemy. The tailored and padded chest of an officer's grandly embellished frock coat announced not only military rank and social status, but also masculine prowess. Battle flags, originally intended as means of identifying a particular regiment amid the smoke and confusion of battle, became the very embodiment of that regiment's esprit de corps; the loss of a battle flag to the enemy meant the loss of honor for the regiment. So it was that otherwise ordinary pieces of cloth became imbued with symbolic meanings far beyond those accruing to guns, accoutrements, or any other military tools; they were the patriotic emblems of honor for which men gave their lives.

For that reason most Confederate uniforms and flags in the Wray Collection have an often-tangible personal provenance: an old paper label, a name written into a collar, even newspaper accounts and veterans' reminiscences. Such provenance, combined with George Wray's penchant for genealogical research, make these the best-documented and most storied artifacts in the collection. Three of the soldiers who wore clothing illustrated in this chapter were killed in battle; one of them, Private Benjamin Schumpert, was wearing the coat pictured here at the moment of his death. We do not know how many men died under the flags illustrated here. In one battle alone, at least four men were hit while bearing the flag of the First Georgia Infantry. A flag flown over Battery Gregg in Charleston Harbor bears the punctures of exploding shrapnel that killed and wounded at least one hundred men in the fort in 1863. Undoubtedly, many more personal tragedies unfolded beneath these flags; we will never know their full extent.

Adding to the honorific value of these artifacts is the traditional perception that most of them were homemade, the handiwork of devoted mothers, wives, and

I may run, but if I do I wish that some of our own men would shoot me down.
—Confederate private G. L. Robertson to his mother, January 19, 1862

I at once forwarded my resignation to the Government I had served from early boyhood, and espoused the cause of my State, deeming it my sacred and honorable duty to take this step. I did not question my heart as to the pain involved. I knew it would be the severance of many pleasant ties and manly friendships. From this time my life seemed divided into two parts, and so I will divide this history of my life.
—John McIntosh Kell, *Recollections of a Naval Life* (1900)

daughters sending their men off to war. In 1861, that was largely true. Newspapers dutifully recorded the solemn speeches and prayers of hundreds of flag presentations across the South as volunteers vowed to defend their new flags to the death, thereby upholding the honor of those who had made them. Likewise, southern papers made a point of describing the homespun shirts and uniforms lovingly hand-sewn by local women for their menfolk, or else the wildly colorful coats, shakos, and white cross belts of the volunteer militias, virtually no two of which were uniformed alike. Based on such accounts alone, it would appear that Johnny Reb was supplied entirely from home, or at least from his local community, thus accounting for his supposedly ragged appearance as the war dragged on and home-front supplies ran short. Here was the perfect image for Lost Cause apologists: the more Johnny lacked in clothing and equipment, the more ennobling was his suffering, the more glorious his victories, and the more understandable his defeat.

The reality was much more mundane—and remarkable. Beginning in 1862, the Confederate central government abandoned the time-honored commutation system whereby each soldier purchased his own clothing and was reimbursed by the government. Understanding that a prolonged war would require a more efficient system of direct issues, the C.S. Quartermaster Bureau established the Clothing Bureau to oversee the mass production, storage, and issue of everything from jackets and trousers to socks, underwear, and shoes. The Clothing Bureau was responsible for battle flags too—as well as signal, marker, garrison, hospital, and headquarters flags. By 1862, Confederate uniforms and battle flags had become standard-issue equipment, the same as guns, knapsacks, and canteens. Throughout the war, most Confederate enlisted men were uniformed, shod, and equipped by their central government; even officers, who were responsible for providing their own uniforms, frequently relied on cloth made or imported by the government.

In accordance with the Confederacy's overall strategy of decentralization, the Clothing Bureau established at least a dozen major manufactories, or "depots," in six states, each supplying the Confederate army operating closest to it. As the Confederacy shrank, the bureau concentrated its operations in Richmond and in the network of textile manufacturing centers in Georgia: Atlanta, Athens, Augusta, and Columbus. Like the C.S. Ordnance Bureau, the Quartermaster Bureau operated with a heavy hand, using conscription exemptions as leverage, fixing prices below market value, or confiscating the production of privately owned textile mills, tanneries, and shoe factories. But unlike their comrades in the Ordnance Bureau, Confederate quartermasters preferred to dictate production rather than purchase it outright, thus avoiding the trouble and expense of running factories directly.

Not all uniforms were supplied by the Quartermaster Bureau. Individual soldiers often preferred clothing made by their homefolk (if or when they could get it), and the armies gave wide berth to personal preference. In the fall of 1862, as the commutation system broke down, some states established their own clothing bureaus. "Georgia troops in Confederate service are almost destitute of clothes and shoes and must suffer terribly this winter," reported Governor Joseph E. Brown in November 1862 as he requested (and got) authority to "seize all the factories and tanneries in this State and appropriate their whole products to this use, till a good pair of shoes and a good suit of clothes are furnished to every Georgia soldier in service."[1] In addition to Georgia, the states of Virginia, North Carolina, and Alabama, and even the C.S. Navy Department, competed directly with the Quartermaster Bureau to control the output of particular textile mills. For most of the war, North Carolina's governor Zebulon Vance refused to share his state's surplus production with the rest of the Confederacy. Meanwhile, government-made clothing and other stores were valuable commodities in a resource-starved civilian black market, especially when government wages lagged far behind inflation.

Nevertheless, by the last two years of the war, the C.S. Quartermaster Bureau had managed to mobilize nearly all the South's textile production, supplementing it with massive quantities of cloth, shoes, and even complete uniforms run through the blockade on the bureau's own ships. In 1864, its most successful year of operation, the bureau issued a staggering 458,000 jackets, 745,000 pairs of trousers, 745,000 pairs of shoes, and 316,000 blankets. At least two-thirds of the jackets and trousers were produced from domestically made cloth and assembled in government-operated depots; the rest of the cloth, as well as two-thirds of the shoes and nearly all the blankets, was imported through the blockade. During the course of the war, the Richmond Depot alone turned out one million knapsacks, haversacks, canteen slings, and saddle blankets; its total production of flags, of all descriptions, reached at least 2,000.[2]

In the end, the Confederacy fought a nineteenth-century affair of honor with a twentieth-century supply system. Seen in this wider context, the personal symbols of Confederate pride illustrated in this chapter were in fact symbols of a different kind of national achievement: near self-sufficiency in the manufacturing of almost everything Johnny Reb wore during battle.

Wearing of the Gray

For many years after the war, white southern writers celebrated an otherwise-ordinary color that became so synonymous with the Lost Cause that even today it is known as "Confederate Gray." The selection of gray as the uniform color for the Confederate army was rich with symbolic meaning. Dark blue had been the traditional uniform color for the U.S. Army since it was introduced by George Washington in 1779 as a means of distinguishing his own men from the scarlet red of the British. Dark blue thus became the symbolic color of liberty, and was later adopted by French revolutionaries in the 1790s. In the United States of the early 1800s, gray emerged as the traditional color for state or volunteer militias and cadets at military academies. In the minds of many Americans in the 1850s, blue and gray symbolized the tension between the potential authoritarian excesses of a national standing army and the noble citizen-soldier of the militia. Thus, gray was a natural choice for image-conscious Confederate leaders seeking to create their own revolutionary heritage. On June 6, 1861, the newly formed C.S. War Department issued its first and only set of uniform regulations, including the provision that officers and enlisted men alike were to wear cloth of a specific shade of blue gray known as cadet gray.

The department never established a standard shade of cadet or any other gray. Confederate uniforms in the Wray Collection range from light brown and grayish brown to blue gray and a gray so dark as to almost appear black. The exact shade depended largely on the quality of the dye. Cheaper gray vegetable dyes made from sumac or logwood quickly faded in the sunshine to the grayish brown or even olive green often termed "butternut." Just as Lost Cause writers celebrated home-spun clothing as evidence of southerners' devotion to their cause, so they claimed "butternut" dye—made from the husks of the butternut tree (a variety of walnut)—as a clever ersatz solution to shortages of gray dye. In fact, gray dyes were inexpensive, and there was never a significant shortage; the use of the term "butternut" to describe Confederate soldiers probably had more to do with the term's derogatory connotation of "country bumpkin" than with the color of their uniforms.

Besides the dye itself, a particular shade of gray depended on the kind of cloth being dyed. Wool was considered the only fabric sturdy enough to withstand the rigors of military use. Additionally, the oils in woolen fibers made the cloth naturally water resistant and even fire retardant, thus protecting the wearer to some degree from powder burns. With only limited supplies of wool available, the Clothing Bureau made extensive use of jean cloth, an equally sturdy but less expensive fabric woven with a cotton warp and a woolen weft. Depending on when the gray

When in the ranks of war we stood, and faced the deadly hail,
Our simple suits of gray composed our only coats of mail;
And of those awful hours that marked the bloody battle day,
In memory we'll still be seen a wearing of the gray.
—Anonymous, in W. L. Fagan, ed., *Southern War Songs* (1892)

We have employed in this depot about 60 cutters and trimmers and 2000 women to make the clothing, mostly wives and daughters of absent soldiers in the field and the poor of our city. . . . We average 2500 garments daily.
—Richmond Depot quartermaster William G. Ferguson to the *Richmond Whig*, November 18, 1862

A few days ago a large amount of clothing . . . were received from the Georgia Soldiers' Clothing Bureau, at Augusta, and distributed to the troops from that State. The arrival was quite opportune, as many of our brave boys were nearly nude from head to foot. The clothing, shoes and blankets were all home made, comfortable and well gotten up—much better in that regard than we usually receive.
—Anonymous Georgia soldier in General James Longstreet's command, Army of Northern Virginia, 1864

dye was applied — whether to the woolen yarn alone or to the already woven cloth — the color varied. Indeed, like the cotton warp, much of the woolen yarn was never dyed at all, leaving the cloth a natural light brownish-gray color — again, frequently mistaken for "butternut" but intended as "regulation" gray. More expensive woolen broadcloth, a heavy, smooth, finely woven cloth with little nap, was usually held in reserve for purchase by officers or even wealthy enlisted men who needed or wanted to provide their own uniforms. Some of the best fabric in the Confederacy was blockade-run English "army cloth," gray wool so dark that it was occasionally confused with blue on the battlefield — and with deadly results.

In the 1860s, the frock coat was considered the pinnacle of military fashion: a knee-length coat cut to emphasize the chest, a traditional symbol of masculinity. Padding in the chest (but not the shoulders) presented an overall appearance of rounded shoulders with the wearer's arms tucked back and the chest thrust out, symbolically daring the enemy to strike at his heart. Although the Confederate uniform regulations specified "tunics" or frock coats for men of all ranks, the Clothing Bureau's standard issue for enlisted men was the eminently more practical waist-length shell jacket. This jacket was a frock coat with the "skirt" removed, making for greater ease of motion and saving up to two yards of cloth on each garment. Though lacking extra padding, shell jackets were still cut to emphasize the chest. Meanwhile, the frock coat remained the garment of choice for officers, who were expected to purchase their own uniforms from a tailor. Because officers' uniforms were never issued by the Clothing Bureau, no two are alike; each is distinguished by its own grade of cloth, trim, braid, and buttons, often applied according to the financial means of the officer or the whim of the tailor. Only officers' rank insignia and the branch-of-service colors (blue for infantry, yellow for cavalry, red for artillery) remained more or less standard and in accordance with the 1861 regulations.

Unlike the guns produced at C.S. armories, the products of the Clothing Bureau were truly mass-produced, using the textile equivalent of interchangeable parts. In the 1840s and 1850s, the U.S. Office of Army Clothing and Equipage at the Schuykill Arsenal near Philadelphia pioneered a system of standard-sized clothing based on predicted ratios of sizes of the average human body. Before then, all garments were custom-made for each person. Using the newly invented tape measure, tailors soon realized that men with a certain chest measurement were also likely to have a corresponding shoulder width, waist size, and torso, arm, and leg lengths. Successfully predicting an average range of common sizes meant that a single shop might produce in advance reasonably well-fitting uniforms at a fraction of the cost of traditional tailoring. Thus was born the ready-made clothing industry.

Unlike the Union army, however, the C.S. Quartermaster Bureau never issued standard patterns for all enlisted uniforms; quite sensibly, it was more concerned that its soldiers be clothed than uniformed. Hence the cut, trim, quality and color of cloth, and number of buttons varied according to the depot and the materials available to it at the time. Nevertheless, the "Schuykill System" of mass production was adopted at all Confederate depots: part factory work and part cottage industry. At the Atlanta Depot, for example, twenty-two men were employed in laying out patterns and cutting through multiple layers of cloth with heavy shears. The component pieces of cloth were separated, sorted, and placed in bundles along with sewing thread and buttons (many of which were northern-made or even U.S. Army issue). These bundles—essentially "kits"—were then distributed to a workforce of three thousand local seamstresses, many of them young women age twelve to twenty, some of them war refugees. They worked up to fifteen hours a day stitching all parts by hand. The seamstresses then returned the completed garments to the depot, where they were paid only for those that passed inspection. Unlike Union army uniforms, virtually no enlisted men's Confederate jackets or trousers were made on sewing machines or marked with size or inspection stamps except those made in Ireland and imported through the blockade. Using this system, the Atlanta Depot's projected production for 1863 was 130,000 jackets, 130,000 trousers, 175,000 cotton shirts, and 175,000 pairs of drawers—enough to provide two uniforms a year to every soldier in the nearby Army of Tennessee. Under this system, Johnny Reb was seldom ragged.

So massive was the Clothing Bureau's output of enlisted men's uniforms that most Confederate veterans considered them too common to be worthy of note—and hence, unworthy of saving by their descendants. After the war, many uniforms were used as work clothes and then thrown away when they wore out, not unlike blue jeans or T-shirts today. Many woolen garments fell victim to moths while stored in attics. Today the once-common Confederate enlisted man's jacket is among the rarest of Civil War artifacts. Of at least one million produced under Confederate government authority, perhaps only 150 survive today. State-produced garments are even rarer, as are genuine southern-made forage caps.

Of the six enlisted men's uniform garments in the Wray Collection, none was made by the C.S. Clothing Bureau, but four were products of particular states. Most surviving Confederate enlisted men's uniforms—perhaps another three hundred examples, including two in the Wray Collection—are homemade, valued and preserved because of who made them and what they represented, not unlike a present-day wedding dress. The higher rate of survival for homemade garments greatly skews the sample of surviving uniforms for enlisted men, thus lending improper credence to the old myth that Confederate soldiers were usually supplied from home. For similar reasons—and with similar consequences—Confederate officers' uniforms survive in far greater numbers than enlisted men's uniforms. Today perhaps as many as one thousand Confederate officers' uniforms are extant, many of which were reserved for dress occasions and never worn in combat. As with most items of everyday use from the past, that which was most common is today least common.

Frock coat, trousers, and cap of Second Lieutenant Thomas J. Nuckolls,
Company A, Fifteenth Alabama Infantry (ca. 1861–62)

Like most sons of the planter class, thirty-two-year-old Thomas J. Nuckolls enthusiastically supported secession and eagerly volunteered to defend the Confederacy. The Harvard-educated attorney and resident of Columbus, Georgia, enlisted in the state militia in December 1860 and joined the elite Columbus Guards in July 1861. His education and social status earned him a commission as a second lieutenant just across the state line in Company A of the Fifteenth Alabama Infantry, in which he served as regimental adjutant in 1862.

But status in civilian life did not guarantee success in military life. Suffering from "internal piles [hemorrhoids] and stricture of the urethra," Nuckolls was absent during the Seven Days battles and the Second Battle of Manassas. When his first sergeant was promoted to captain over him in August 1862, Nuckolls angrily submitted his resignation. But it was not until December that his resignation was finally accepted "as the shortest mode of ridding the service of an unworthy officer."[3] Unfit though he may have been for the army, Nuckolls went on to become a well-respected civic leader in Columbus after the war.

Regardless of his abilities as an officer, Nuckolls knew how to dress the part. His royal blue kepi (complete with rubberized rain cover) made for a natty appearance when paired with his gray wool double-breasted frock coat, tailor-made precisely in accordance with the 1861 regulations. The buttons, made by Steele and Johnson of Waterbury, Connecticut, were produced especially for the Alabama Volunteer Corps, which was formed in February 1860, to organize the state's independent militia companies. Although the buttons alone make this coat rare, the simple fact that it bears the insignia of a second lieutenant makes it even rarer, since the survival rate of second lieutenants in combat was quite low. Apparently, Nuckolls did not see much combat.

The trousers are made from a sturdy wool-cotton jean material, with machine-stitched seams and hand-finished details. It is likely that the red-brown cotton warp threads were originally black, giving the trousers a darker brown or gray appearance. Likewise, the black satinette stripe down the outside seams was probably dark blue.

Colonel Robert C. Wood, ca. 1875

Frock coat of Colonel Robert C. Wood, First Mississippi Cavalry (ca. 1863)

Born at Fort Snelling in the Iowa Territory (present-day Minnesota), Robert Crooke Wood was raised in a family of famous American soldiers. His mother was the daughter of general and president Zachary Taylor, his father was assistant surgeon general of the U.S. Army, and his uncle was the future Confederate general Richard Taylor. In July 1850, eighteen-year-old Robert Wood was admitted to the U.S. Military Academy, but two years later, after proving to be a poor and unruly student, was given a medical leave of absence by Superintendent Robert E. Lee. Probably through the influence of Secretary of War Jefferson Davis, who had also wed one of Taylor's daughters, Wood went on to serve briefly as a second lieutenant in the elite Second U.S. Cavalry Regiment, experience sufficient to gain him a Confederate lieutenant colonel's commission in 1861.

While his brother served in the C.S. Navy, Wood fought with Colonel Wirt Adams's First Mississippi Cavalry Regiment in innumerable skirmishes across Tennessee and Mississippi. His battlefield conduct was the stuff of legend. On May 6, 1862, Wood and sixty-five men of the rear guard were trapped in the Oddfellows Hall in Lebanon, Tennessee, where they held off Union troopers for several hours before finally being forced to surrender by a threat to burn the building. After almost a year of imprisonment, Wood was exchanged, succeeded to command of his regiment, and in November 1863 was promoted to full colonel. Wood's badly depleted regiment fought to the last, joining Nathan Bedford Forrest in his futile attempt in April 1865 to halt James Wilson's raiders as they cut a swath through Alabama and Georgia. Wood and his regiment finally surrendered on May 4, 1865.

Modestly adorned with yellow piping (instead of the solid yellow cuff and collar as specified in the 1861 regulations), Wood's nearly pristine silk-lined frock coat evidently saw use only on special occasions. Unusually, the collar insignia of a Confederate colonel is made up of three separate and removable copper stars instead the usual cloth or embroidered stars sewn to the collar. At the same time, the back seam of each sleeve is adorned with a row of tiny brass beads, a nonregulation feature typical of officers' frock coats originating in the Western Theater. The coat bears the buttons of Wood's home state of Louisiana, where he remained active in veterans' affairs until his death in 1900.

Frock coat of Captain Augustin L. Taveau, staff officer (ca. 1863)

Augustin Louis Taveau was never much of a businessman or a soldier. Son of a French émigré who had done quite well as a rice planter, Taveau showed little interest in following in his father's footsteps or in practicing law, the usual pursuits for young men of his class in antebellum South Carolina. According to his father, at least, the young man's passions focused mainly on spending money and writing poetry. Indeed, Taveau contributed his work to the prestigious Southern Literary Messenger *and in 1855 published a book of poems under the pseudonym "Alton."*

In March 1861, the thirty-three-year-old Taveau received a state commission as first lieutenant of cavalry; he raised his own company at Adams Run, South Carolina, just west of Charleston. A year later, he was promoted to captain, serving as a volunteer aide-de-camp for Colonel John Black of the First South Carolina Cavalry until late 1862, when the regiment was sent to fight in Virginia. Taveau then volunteered in the same capacity for Brigadier General Nathan George "Shanks" Evans until his brigade was ordered west to help defend Vicksburg, Mississippi. Finally, Taveau was assigned to the C.S. Treasury Department office in Charleston, where he served through 1865.

Typical of the richly apportioned frock coats of the wealthy, this one was made of fine woolen broadcloth and adorned with the best trimmings money could buy, including the beige, or "buff," colored piping of a staff officer and gold braid at the cuffs and collar, both signifying the rank of captain. The fine English-made South Carolina–seal buttons, traditionally associated with the elite Palmetto Guard of Charleston, are especially unusual: the design features a snake coiled around the palmetto tree, on either side of which are the letters "CS" for "Confederate States" rather than the usual "SC." Taveau is seen wearing this frock coat in a hand-tinted photographic portrait, but the artist has incorrectly tinted beige the entire lower portion of the

Captain Augustin L. Taveau, ca. 1863

cuffs. Note that Taveau's right hand rests on a stack of books, symbolizing his literary interests.

Although Augustin Taveau almost certainly never saw combat—and indeed may have intentionally avoided it—he was nevertheless devoted to the Confederate cause. He served without pay throughout the war and invested all his money in Confederate bonds. After the fall of Charleston, the penniless Taveau and his wife took refuge with her family in Massachusetts before later taking up residence in Baltimore. There he became a noted poet, publishing two more books of poetry in the 1880s, including the epic Montezuma: An Historical Poem of the Ancient Aztecs of Mexico. *He never returned to Charleston.*

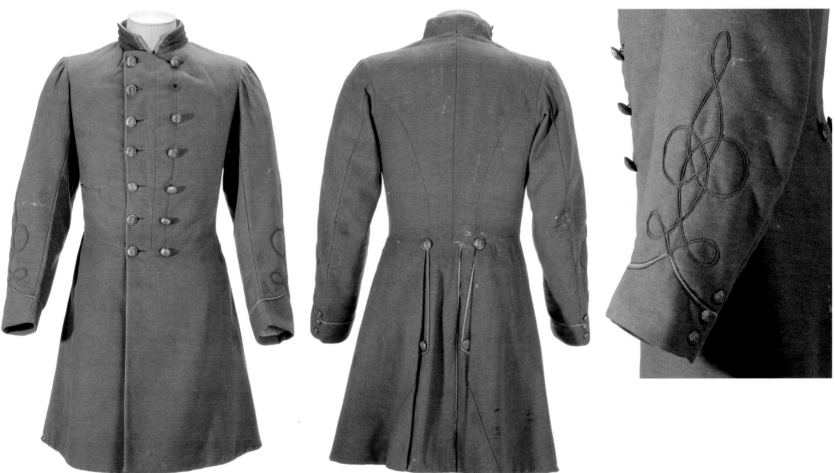

Frock coat of an unidentified North Carolina captain (ca. 1863)

Some Confederate officers' coats survive without personal attribution or provenance; whatever stories they might once have told were long ago lost. The only clues to the owner of this coat are its prewar northern-made North Carolina state seal buttons and the braid collar trim indicating the rank of captain.

The coat typifies the plight of Confederate captains and lieutenants who were expected to purchase their own uniforms but lacked the financial means to do so. As a result, many field-grade officer uniforms were as simple as this one: single-breasted, no branch-of-service color on the collar or cuff, and simple strips of braid stitched directly to the collar as an insignia of rank. The greatest expense was usually the cloth itself, which could often be purchased at below-market rates from Confederate or state clothing bureaus. Sometimes, for the sake of both economy and practicality, junior officers purchased enlisted jackets from the C.S. Quartermaster Bureau and attached rank insignia to the collar.

Frock coat and trousers of Major John A. A. West, chief of artillery, Department of Alabama, Mississippi, and East Louisiana (ca. 1864)

Major John Augustus Asbury West spared no expense when he had this dress uniform made in the fall of 1864, perhaps in Mobile, soon after his appointment as chief of artillery. With its red trim, gold braid on the sleeves, and red stripes on the trouser legs, his uniform is unusual in that it follows most of the 1861 regulations, with the notable exception of the beaded cuffs, a peculiarity of coats from the Western Theater. As befitted West's new position, the coat bears two rows of fine English-made Confederate staff officers' buttons.

Born in 1839 to a modestly wealthy slaveholding family in Madison, Georgia, West was an extremely bright young man, eager for a technical education. By far the best engineering school in the nation was the U.S. Military Academy, where he was admitted as a cadet in 1858. Soon after Georgia seceded, West resigned from the academy and immediately began seeking a Confederate commission. After attending the constitutional convention in Montgomery, Alabama, West was rewarded with a regular army commission as a second lieutenant in the First Battery, Confederate Light Artillery. It was a job that suited him well. Operating with fast-moving cavalry along the banks of the Mississippi River, West and his guns preyed on Union transports and harassed the garrisons of small towns and forts along the river. By late 1863, West was acting captain of the battery; in September 1864, he was promoted to departmental chief of artillery, a position he held under Lieutenant General Richard Taylor's command until its formal surrender on May 8, 1865.

After the war, West taught at Louisiana State University, received a degree from the medical college in Augusta, Georgia, ran his own coal-supply business, and served as treasurer for a railroad and banking company. In 1890, he was shot dead by his brother during an argument over the management of their father's estate in Hinds County, Mississippi.

Frock coat believed to have been worn by Master John Low, CSS *Alabama* (ca. 1862–63)

Confederate naval officers' uniforms in any condition are extremely rare, with fewer than fifteen examples known. The coarse gray wool broadcloth of this frock coat suggests that it was meant for everyday use, which might explain its well-worn appearance and its lack of original C.S. Navy buttons. Though dating to the Civil War era, the U.S. Navy buttons are replacements.

*Believed to have originated in a Georgia estate, this coat was once attributed to the Georgia native John McIntosh Kell, lieutenant and executive officer of the commerce raider CSS *Alabama*, which became famous for capturing or destroying sixty-five northern merchant ships between August 1862 and June 1864. At the outbreak of war, Kell was commissioned a first lieutenant, a rank he held before being promoted to commander in 1864. While the cuff braid of this coat indicates the rank of lieutenant, the plain blue shoulder straps (without a star insignia) indicate the rank of master,*

making it unlikely that Kell ever wore it. George Wray believed this coat belonged to another officer of the css *Alabama, John Low, who held the rank of master but served on board as fourth lieutenant.*

Low, a native of Aberdeen, Scotland, was an experienced merchant sailor and businessman, having established a naval supply company in Savannah, Georgia, with the aid of his wealthy uncle Andrew Low before the war. In 1861, John Low was commissioned a master in the C.S. Navy. He reported to Commander James Dunwoody Bulloch in London, where he assisted the navy's purchasing efforts. Low's first assignment was on board the blockade-runner Fingal, *which steamed into Savannah in November 1861, bearing a massive cargo of British-made armaments.*

As a lieutenant on the Alabama, *Low regularly commanded boarding parties responsible for seizing and burning merchant ships. In June 1863, Low was given command of the captured* Conrad, *which was armed with two small cannon and recommissioned as the* css Tuscaloosa. *After taking only one prize, the* Tuscaloosa *was seized by British authorities near Cape Town, South Africa, the following December. Low returned to England in February 1864, where he was promoted to lieutenant and oversaw the construction of gunboats meant for the C.S. Navy. After the war, Low went into business in England and never returned to Savannah.*

Another coat belonging to Low, bearing the rank of lieutenant, has survived among his descendants in England. In 1991, George Wray purchased the coat from a collector in Maryland, but he was never able to positively identify the original owner. If it did indeed belong to Low, he probably wore it aboard the Alabama *and the* Tuscaloosa.

Enlisted man's forage cap, believed to have been made by the C.S. Clothing Bureau at Richmond (ca. 1863)

Believed to have been made and inspected under C.S. government authority, this cap is constructed with a sturdy cotton and wool jean fabric that was also used for trousers and jackets. It may, indeed, have been made from worn-out clothing turned in to a government depot. When first made, it was probably much grayer in color than its current brownish green.

Instead of leather, the visor is made of heavy cardboard covered with painted and varnished cloth and edged with a strip of the same material; the top surface has been coated with black enamel for further waterproofing. The chinstrap (in this case probably never intended for actual use) is made of a single layer of painted cloth secured by two U.S. prewar buttons. Lined with flower-print cotton calico, the cap has a painted cloth sweatband stamped with a size mark "7/8." Other caps bearing these same features are known to have a Richmond provenance; furthermore, the size mark strongly suggests mass production in a governmental facility. Although clearly not of the same quality as its U.S. counterparts, this cap was certainly sturdy enough to do the job. Given that so few of these once-common uniform items survive, this is one of the rarest items in the Wray collection.

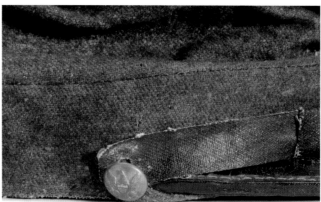

Military or political cap, maker unknown, date unknown

Unfortunately for present-day historians, forage caps and kepis were ubiquitous the world over among military formations, police forces, and even political clubs from the 1850s through the 1890s, making the identification of specific examples extremely difficult.

This cap is a good case in point. The painted red band around the base suggests that this cap was made for Confederate artillerymen, while the visor, made of leather coated with black enamel, is probably a restoration. The leather chinstrap, taken from a U.S.-issue cap, is anchored by two Georgia buttons made just before the war by the Steele and Johnson Manufacturing Company in Connecticut. Yet the body of the cap does not appear to be durable enough for extended wear; it is made of lightweight cotton canvas with a wicker ring support around the top of the crown.

Most important, this cap bears a close resemblance to ones made for members of the "Wide Awakes" political clubs, famous for their rallies in support of Abraham Lincoln's candidacy in 1860. If the Georgia buttons are original to the cap, it may have been used by a southern secessionist club such as The Minutemen. At the same time, the buttons could have been added by a modern collector or dealer to make the cap appear to be Confederate in origin, thus making it immensely more valuable (though perhaps less interesting) than a political cap.

Shell jacket of Sergeant James T. Lewis, Company I,
Sixty-First Virginia Militia, and Company F,
Fifth Virginia Cavalry, privately made (ca. 1862)

At the outbreak of war, a thirty-three-year-old house carpenter named James T. Lewis lived in Mathews County, Virginia, on Chesapeake Bay, with his wife, two children, and Lucy Cook, a fourteen-year-old enslaved house servant. His younger brothers, Thomas Lewis and James M. Lewis, lived nearby and worked as oystermen. In July 1861, all three brothers enlisted in the Mathews County Battalion of the Sixty-First Virginia Militia Regiment. James T. Lewis was immediately elected second sergeant. By March 1862, he had been promoted to first sergeant and was overseeing the distribution of rations to the men of Company I.

After passage of the Conscription Act (April 1862) and the reorganization of the Confederate army, James T. and Thomas Lewis joined Company F of the newly formed Fifth Virginia Cavalry, and James M. Lewis enrolled in the Nineteenth Regiment, Virginia Heavy Artillery. James T. retained his rank of first sergeant as the Fifth Cavalry fought in all the subsequent campaigns of the Army of Northern Virginia, including the Seven Days, the Maryland campaign, Fredericksburg, Brandy Station, and Gettysburg.

Just before noon on May 11, 1864, James T. and Thomas Lewis were in the line of battle near Yellow Tavern, about six miles from Richmond, as part of General J. E. B. Stuart's force of three thousand cavalrymen trying desperately to hold off ten thousand Union troopers headed toward the capital under General Phillip Sheridan. Stuart asked Colonel Henry Clay Pate, who commanded the line, how long he thought he could hold the position. "Until I die, General," came the response. A few minutes later, as his position was overrun, Pate fell dead, shot in the right temple. The Fifth Virginia lost at least half its men. Of the forty-nine troopers in Company F, twenty-three were captured and nineteen were killed or wounded, including First Sergeant James T. Lewis, who was shot and killed instantly, and Thomas Lewis, who was wounded and died two months later in a Richmond hospital. General Stuart himself was mortally wounded later that afternoon. James M. Lewis was the only one of the three Mathews County brothers to survive the war.

In 1999, George Wray purchased this gray jacket from a Boston-area collector who had discovered it in a New Hampshire attic along with a Union enlisted man's frock coat. The jacket was missing its buttons and

lacked any known provenance. Its gray color did not automatically mean the jacket was Confederate: many northern militias also wore gray. Additionally, its padded chest, slit breast pockets, and careful tailoring hardly resembled most mass-produced Confederate enlisted men's jackets. At the same time, its general construction, belt loops, and shoulder straps strongly suggested that it had been modeled on a Confederate jacket pattern, especially that of the C.S. Clothing Depot at Richmond. George Wray discovered the most essential clue in the partly legible letters inked onto the brown velvet lining of the collar: "1st / 1 Sgt / JT / James L_w_s." Additionally, the outer edges of the first sergeant's chevrons are sewn into the sleeve seams, indicating that they were applied before the jacket was completed. After combing dozens of Union and Confederate service records, Wray identified First Sergeant James T. Lewis as the only possible match. He then purchased a set of pre–Civil War Virginia state seal buttons and had them sewn to the jacket.

This privately made dress jacket may have been made as early as March 1862, when Lewis attained his rank as first sergeant; indeed, the piped black trim on the belt loops and shoulder straps resembles that of the first Richmond Depot jackets being made at the time. Yet there are enough differences between this jacket and the early Richmond Depot jackets (including plain cuffs and a solid-color collar) that it could easily have been made later. Lewis was not killed while wearing the jacket; instead, it may have been in his baggage when it was discovered by a Union soldier, who kept it as a souvenir.

Overshirt of Third Lieutenant Lucius W. Gash, Company K, Eleventh North Carolina Infantry, issued by the State of North Carolina (ca. 1863)

Led by the reluctant secessionist and soon-to-be-governor Captain Zebulon B. Vance, the "Rough and Ready Guards" of Buncombe County, North Carolina, marched off to fight against the Union in May 1861. Among them was an eager seventeen-year-old farm boy named Lucius W. Gash.

Just four months later, on September 17, Gash was abruptly discharged from the company, by then designated Company F of the Fourteenth North Carolina Infantry, when it was discovered that he was under the legal age of enlistment. Undeterred, Gash reenlisted on April 20, 1862, in another Buncombe County organization, Company K of the Eleventh North Carolina (famously known as the "Bethel Regiment" for its role in the Battle of Big Bethel, Virginia, June 10, 1861). On the first day at Gettysburg, Gash suffered a wound in the foot and was subsequently sent to a hospital in Lynchburg, Virginia, to recover. The wound may have saved his life; half the Bethel Regiment was killed or wounded during the famous Pickett-Pettigrew charge two days later.

In August or September 1863, Gash, now a corporal, returned to duty. He rose quickly in the rapidly diminishing ranks and was commissioned as third lieutenant in January 1864. On May 12, 1864, during intense hand-to-hand fighting near Spotsylvania Court House, Virginia, Gash was bayoneted through the back. He died two days later in a field hospital. Gash was not wearing this garment when he was killed, but a family story tells of a younger relative named Thomas (probably a cousin) who traveled to Virginia to retrieve his personal effects, including, possibly, this overshirt.

With a front opening all the way to the waist (rather than the usual placket), this overshirt resembles the bodice of a woman's dress. Yet its pockets, lining, collar, and cuffs are consistent with men's military-style overshirts (or "battle" shirts) of the period. Many of these shirts were made for local volunteer companies or regiments early in the war as substitutes for uniform jackets, which required more time, labor, and material to manufacture. This one was almost certainly issued by the State of North Carolina in 1863 or 1864, which was well known for supplying its own troops even after the Confederate government assumed authority for clothing its soldiers. Its soft, tightly woven cotton-and-wool twill cloth is very similar to that used for jackets issued by the State of North Carolina; its civilian buttons are English made, perhaps imported by the state through the blockade. A nearly identical overshirt has been positively identified as having belonged to Theophilus Frank, a forty-year-old conscript in the Forty-Eighth North Carolina Regiment, who served from October 1863 until about August 1864, when he was sent home on sick furlough. His service record indicates that he was issued clothing (though the source and type are not recorded) in April, June, and August.

It is possible that the state never intended these overshirts to be worn in place of jackets, which were being produced in large quantities by 1863. Instead, these roomy, comfortable, and eminently practical shirts may have been meant for fatigue duty or recovery in a hospital or convalescent camp, an experience both Gash and Frank shared. The oddly shaped patches inserted into the left sleeve are probably postwar attempts at restoration.

Fatigue jacket of Cadet Private John M. Hazelhurst, Georgia Military Institute, issued by the State of Georgia (ca. 1862)

In mid-1861, fourteen-year-old John McNish Hazelhurst, the only son of a wealthy Lowcountry Georgia rice-planting family, enrolled as a cadet at the Georgia Military Institute in Marietta, where his uncle served as an instructor. Opened in 1851 and acquired by the State of Georgia in 1858, the school combined military training with a rigorous academic curriculum based on that of the U.S. Military Academy. Young "Mac" Hazelhurst began his studies in science, mathematics, languages, literature, and engineering with about 150 fellow cadets, many of them also sons of the planter elite, including one of his cousins.

The cadets drilled daily in their West Point–inspired black shakos and full-dress gray tailcoats, each adorned with three rows of buttons bearing the Georgia state seal and the initials "GMI." But for work details and classroom "recitations," the boys wore these blue fatigue jackets, fitted with plain flat brass buttons more suitable for everyday wear. Bearing Hazelhurst's handwritten name in the lining, this jacket is believed to be the only surviving example of its type.

Almost immediately, the war interrupted the normally clockwork routine at the institute. The more experienced cadets were called upon to serve as drill instructors at nearby Camp McDonald; others served as provost guards, on funeral details, or as prison guards. Many joined the army. Governor Joseph E. Brown managed to keep the school open and the older cadets exempted from conscription by officially designating them the state's Engineer Corps.

Shell jacket, trousers, vest, and cap of Cadet Private John M. Hazelhurst, Georgia Military Institute, issued by the State of Georgia (1864)

*As Sherman's armies advanced into northern Georgia in May 1864, Governor Brown called out the state militia and, with it, the cadets of the Georgia Military Institute. Always prepared to provide for its own, the state issued the boys with brown jean uniforms and caps, perhaps made at the state factory in Augusta, where five hundred women sewed uniforms exclusively for Georgia troops. The left pocket of these well-worn trousers is stamped "*GEORGIA SOLDIERS CLOTHING BUREAU / AUGUSTA GA.*" It is believed that the entire uniform, including the badly deteriorated cap, was issued by the state, although it is possible that the vest (not usually an issue item) and jacket may have been made privately. Typical of many Confederate enlisted men's uniforms, both are fitted with prewar U.S. buttons: the jacket with seven U.S. general staff buttons, and the vest with six slightly smaller general service buttons and one civilian button with a flower pattern.*

With their knapsacks, accoutrements, and Austrian rifles, the cadets joined the Georgia Militia in the defenses around Atlanta in July 1864 before being

Cadet Private John M. Hazelhurst, 1864, wearing the uniform at right

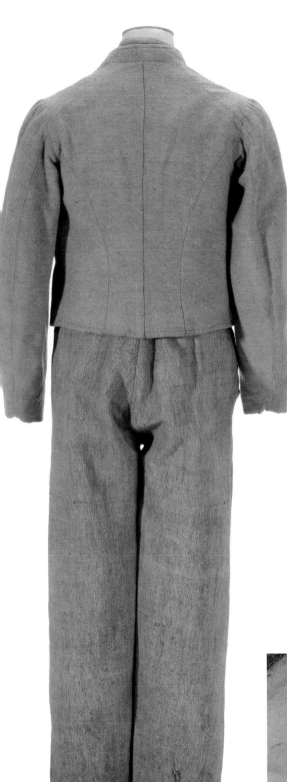

withdrawn the next month to protect the capital at Milledgeville from possible Union cavalry raids. There Hazelhurst and his fellow cadets drilled, paraded, and even resumed their studies until mid-November, when Sherman's armies began their march to Savannah. Before evacuating Marietta, Sherman's men burned the campus of the Georgia Military Institute, just as they would the public buildings in Milledgeville. Virtually powerless in the face of the Union onslaught, the cadets fought two skirmishes while defending railroad bridges before they were withdrawn to the defenses of Savannah. The end of the war found "Mac" Hazelhurst and the corps of cadets in Augusta, assigned to maintain order and protect public property. There, they were officially disbanded in May 1865.

Hazelhurst went back to his home in Glynn County, accompanied by two horses and an enslaved (soon freed) black servant. After the war, he worked in railroad construction with his uncle, but developed cancer and died at the age of thirty-seven in 1884. The uniform, which was passed down through the family, was acquired by George Wray in the 1980s.

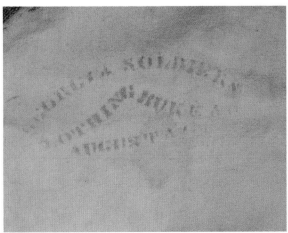

Enlisted man's shell jacket and trousers, believed to have been made by the Virginia quartermaster depot at Wytheville, Virginia (ca. 1863)

In May 1864, Union brigadier general George Crook (later famous as an Indian fighter) led a division of six thousand men from Fayetteville, West Virginia, toward the town of Dublin in the southern part of the Shenandoah Valley, there to break up the last remaining railroad connecting Virginia to Tennessee. Future U.S. president Rutherford B. Hayes commanded one of Crook's brigades in the ensuing Battle of Cloyd's Mountain, fought on May 9. After a short but costly fight, Crook's forces drove off about twenty-four hundred Confederate defenders and reached their objective. In addition to destroying railroad and telegraph lines around Dublin, they burned the vital Confederate supply depot there, with its stockpiles of tobacco, rations, uniforms, and accoutrements.

Among Crook's victorious soldiers was twenty-five-year-old Reuben B. Taylor, first sergeant of Company E, Fourteenth West Virginia Infantry. While preparing to torch the depot warehouses, he decided to make a souvenir of a Rebel uniform. It had evidently been worn before (and probably turned in for new clothing), but there was no evidence of the previous owner's identification except for an 1862-dated New Testament, *which Taylor found in the breast pocket of the jacket. He inscribed the frontispiece: "Lt. R.B. Taylor / Book Captured at Dublin Depot May 9th, 1864." Evidently, Taylor carried his pocket testament with him for some time, since he was not commissioned a lieutenant until October.*

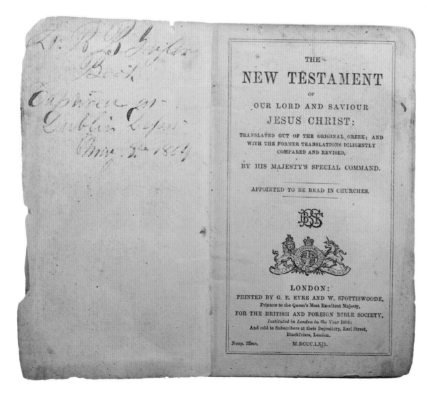

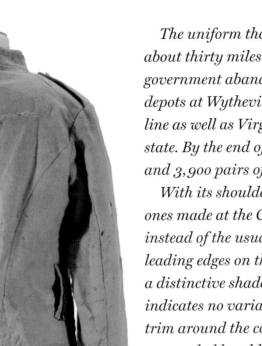

The uniform that Taylor took as a souvenir probably originated at Wytheville, about thirty miles southwest of Dublin. In the fall of 1862, as the Confederate government abandoned the commutation system, Virginia established clothing depots at Wytheville and Lynchburg to supply the reserve regiments of the state line as well as Virginia regiments in Confederate service in the western part of the state. By the end of December, these depots had turned out more than 3,300 jackets and 3,900 pairs of trousers.[4]

With its shoulder straps and belt loops, the shell jacket closely resembles the ones made at the C.S. Clothing Depot at Richmond, but with a six-button front instead of the usual nine, a slash pocket on the left breast, and squared-off leading edges on the collar. Wytheville clothing is thought to have been made of a distinctive shade of gray, but an examination of the seams of both garments indicates no variation from the present tan color. The origin of the decorative tape trim around the collar and on the belt loops of the jacket is unknown, though it was probably added by the soldier who wore it. The 1830s-era Virginia buttons on the jacket were added during a modern restoration, as were the silk crepoline patches over areas of moth damage.

Frock coat and trousers of Private Benjamin H. G. Schumpert,
Third South Carolina Infantry, privately made (1863)

In May 1862, sixteen-year-old Benjamin Howell Gray Schumpert lied about his age and enlisted at Newberry, South Carolina, for service in Company E of the Third South Carolina Volunteers, part of Joseph Kershaw's brigade. At his side was his first cousin, Osborn L. Schumpert, as well as many of their fellow students from Newberry College. Aside from patriotic fervor and a sense of youthful adventure, Ben (as his widowed forty-seven-year-old father, Amos, called him) had a very personal reason for enlisting: his older brother, Reuben, a member of the Eleventh Georgia Artillery Battalion, had died of typhoid fever the previous September while encamped near Manassas, Virginia—making Ben his father's only child.

At first, Benjamin Schumpert was lucky. He fought in every battle from the Seven Days through Gettysburg without suffering so much as a scratch and tasting victory at almost every turn. Probably in the summer of 1863, Ben received a new homemade uniform—perhaps the handiwork of twenty-one-year-old Sarah Pickett Schumpert, whom his father had recently married. It was an odd sort of uniform: the lightweight, unlined frock coat and trousers were made from beige cotton ticking, distinctively striped with brown, yellow, and blue, perhaps woven by one of Amos Schumpert's slaves. Although Ben may have been so proud of his homemade uniform that he insisted on wearing it into battle, surely he was aware of how much it made him stand out among his comrades. In September 1863, most of James Longstreet's Corps—including Kershaw's Brigade—was issued dark gray jackets and royal-blue trousers made from woolen cloth imported from England.

At the Battle of Chickamauga, the Third South Carolina suffered its greatest number of casualties, including seventeen-year-old Ben Schumpert. At about 1:15 on the afternoon of September 20, 1863, Schumpert and his regiment charged up the slope of what became known as Snodgrass Hill. There his luck finally ran out as a single Union minié ball found its mark. Schumpert's wound was catastrophic. His head virtually exploded, sending a shower of blood, bone, and brains out the back of his skull. Osborn Schumpert almost certainly witnessed his cousin's violent death and perhaps was close enough to have been splattered with his blood. It was the type of wound that unnerved even the most hardened veteran.

According to family lore, Osborn retrieved his cousin's body later that night. So that his father and stepmother might have some physical evidence of their son's death, Osborn carefully removed Ben's bloodstained coat before wrapping the body in a blanket and burying it at the foot of Horseshoe Ridge. Osborn received a

furlough from the army to take the coat and a pair of matching trrousers to Ben's bereaved father, then living in Americus, Georgia.

George Wray bought the uniform in the 1970s from an Americus man who had acquired it from the family and added the heavy Confederate cast-brass I ("Infantry") buttons. Although it is not known what kind of buttons originally adorned this coat, it is likely they were made of much lighter bone or hard rubber.

Although Amos Schumpert lost both his sons to the war, he at least knew what had happened to them, unlike thousands of others on both sides. Yet Amos Schumpert's ordeal was not over. Conscripted into Georgia service in 1864, he served as a prison guard at Camp Sumter, infamously known as Andersonville. Here was a father who literally gave all he had to his country. If any single object in the Wray Collection epitomizes the personal tragedy of the Confederate odyssey, then this is it.

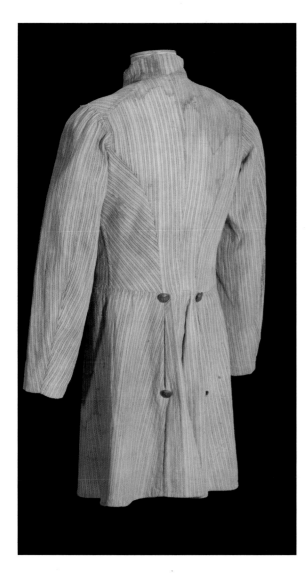

The Tools of the Trade

In addition to manufacturing firearms, the C.S. Ordnance Bureau was responsible for making ammunition, percussion caps, and the leather accoutrements needed to carry them. The accoutrements included a waist belt to which was attached a bayonet, scabbard, and a pouch for percussion caps. At the soldier's right hip (usually suspended by a sling over the left shoulder) was a cartridge box in which were carried forty rounds of paper-cartridge ammunition. These were the most essential tools of a soldier's trade. But for personal survival, the most important pieces of equipment were those issued by the C.S. Quartermaster Bureau: a canteen for water, a haversack for food rations, and, above all else, a good pair of shoes.

From the beginning, the South suffered from a critical material disadvantage that affected both army bureaus: nearly 70 percent of all leather tanned in the United States came from the North, mainly Massachusetts, New York, and Pennsylvania. It could take six to twelve months to tan a hide and much longer to put a tannery into operation—assuming that water, lime, acid, and bark were available. As a result, leather was always in short supply in the Confederacy. It quickly became a top priority for purchasing agents in Britain, who shipped tons of dried and salted hides as well as finished leather through the blockade. Meanwhile, southern manufacturers often improvised with canvas cloth painted black and varnished with linseed oil to make it water repellent.

In the fifty years before the war, the U.S. Army developed standard patterns for all its accoutrements, constantly working to improve them as the result of field testing, and paying attention to the smallest details. Throughout the war, the U.S. Army's Ordnance and Quartermaster Departments provided standard patterns to its arsenals and private contractors, thus ensuring that all accoutrements were made alike; a rigid system of inspection guaranteed consistent quality. By contrast, the Confederate army never issued standard patterns. Accoutrement makers at government workshops and in private businesses simply copied existing U.S. patterns, but often with practical shortcuts: pewter finials in place of scarce brass, a single belt loop rather than the U.S. Army standard of two, thicker thread, and less uniform stitching. The quality of Confederate accoutrements often improved over time as workers became more skilled at their ersatz craft.

Although all such accoutrements were subject to inspection, the standards were by no means as rigorous as those of the U.S. Army. Confederate inspectors were less concerned with perfect uniformity than with basic functionality, durability, and, above all else, quantity. Thus, like the products of the Clothing Bureau, the pattern and finish of Confederate accoutrements reflected where and when they were made, and by whom. Because very few were stamped with the place of manufacture or even a date, slight variations allow collectors and historians to identify items that likely came from the same source, even if that source remains unknown because of the lack of any marked examples.

Northern manufacturers also enjoyed the advantages provided by the latest industrial technology, such as sewing machines for making everything from haversacks to tents, or machine presses for stamping out hundreds of identical parts for canteens or other gear. Southern accoutrement makers often worked without machinery, relying on traditional craft technology and handwork. But they were extremely well organized: task specialization in the workshops resulted in a rudimentary but successful form of mass production. The Richmond Arsenal alone produced more than 375,000 sets of infantry and cavalry accoutrements during the war, and manufacturers in Georgia probably made even more. This domestic production, supplemented by imports through the blockade and scavenging on the battlefields, meant that Confederate soldiers never lacked the basic tools of the trade. In this barely industrialized war industry, the Confederacy nearly achieved logistical self-sufficiency.

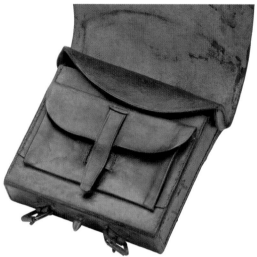

Confederate infantry cartridge boxes and cap pouch, makers unknown (ca. 1863)

Top: *With its neat stitching, brass closure finial, and embossed edging around the outer flap, this .69-caliber cartridge box is unusually well made, though it lacks the reinforcing rivets required for U.S.-made boxes.*

Middle: *The coarse thread and black color of this .54-caliber cartridge box is more typical of Confederate production. Note that the bottom of the right belt loop has started to tear, a problem the U.S. Army had solved by using rivets in addition to sewing.*

Bottom: *This cap pouch is a faithful copy of a prewar U.S. pattern made at the Allegheny Arsenal near Pittsburgh. As with the cartridge box pictured previously, the belt loops have started to stretch, and its closure finial has already broken off.*

Cavalry cartridge box and infantry cap pouch made
by the **C.S. Arsenal at Richmond** (1862–63)

Top: *With leather in short supply, Confederate accoutrement makers frequently had to reuse old or damaged items. To make this cavalry cartridge box, workers cut off two inches from all four sides of an infantry cartridge box and then attached a new bottom panel, sewing over the exposed belt loops in the process. The interior tin liner (not pictured) was also cut down. This 1863-dated box has a brass finial and is marked on the inner flap with the same type of lettering used on the cap pouch. A soldier carved his initials, "CRW," on the back of the box.*

Bottom: *This well-made cap pouch is a simplified version of a standard U.S. Pattern 1850 pouch. It substitutes a single sewn belt loop for two sewn and riveted loops. Unusually, its closure finial is made of brass instead of lead or pewter, which were often used by other Confederate manufacturers. The stamping die used for the small, 0.1-inch-high "RICH. VA." on the inner flap was made by a local printing shop; it is in the same font and only slightly larger than the stamping die used to mark the lockplates of rifle-muskets.*

Rifle cartridge box, believed to have been made by the C.S. Depot at Montgomery, Alabama, used by Powers's Cavalry Regiment (1862–63)

Though completely unmarked and adorned with a single brass C on its outer flap, this cartridge box is identical to an example in a private collection stamped "Montgomery Arsenal, 1862," with the brass letters "PC" on the flap. That cartridge box came with a note indicating its capture from Powers's Regiment of Mississippi Cavalry.

Formed from several independent cavalry companies in May 1863, Colonel Frank Powers's cavalry participated in the defense of Vicksburg and Port Hudson before keeping up more or less continual skirmishing with Union troops in Mississippi and Alabama through the end of the war. It is believed that this cartridge box was taken as a souvenir by a Union soldier when troopers of Captain A. J. Lewis's company were captured in a skirmish near Port Hudson in February 1864.

Intended for .54-caliber rifle ammunition, this cartridge box features single vertical loops on the back, indicating it was meant to be carried on a waist belt and not a shoulder strap, in typical rifleman's fashion. It is constructed with a minimum of sewing: the flap, belt loops, and closure tab are attached only with rivets, a production shortcut that would have been unacceptable in the Union army, and perhaps even at other Confederate depots. The spherical brass finial for the closure tab appears to be of prewar Union manufacture.

U.S. Pattern 1861 haversack (ca. 1863)

Wherever victories left Confederate soldiers in control of a battlefield, northern-made haversacks, canteens, blankets, and shoes invariably became part of their kit. Meanwhile, leather accoutrements, ammunition, and firearms were collected by Ordnance Bureau teams that combed every inch of a battlefield looking for anything that could be salvaged or reissued.

The standard-issue U.S. Army haversack was ubiquitous among Confederate soldiers, especially in Virginia, where they were equipped as often by their enemies as by their own government, especially early in the war. Made of burlap painted to make it water repellent, this example is missing its buckle for the closure strap. Because they were once so common as not to be deemed worthy of saving, even northern-made haversacks are today among the rarest of Civil War artifacts.

U.S. Pattern 1857 canteens and Confederate canteens (ca. 1863)

Top left: *The U.S. Pattern 1857 canteen was the standard-issue canteen for all Union soldiers during the Civil War. Designed especially for the purpose by the U.S. Quartermaster Department, it was easily mass-produced by using stamping dies to press out its two halves, leaving only one seam to join. As issued, these canteens were covered in wool cloth, which reduced noise on the march and, when dipped in water, kept the contents cool. These were by far the most sought-after canteens among Confederate soldiers, who took them whenever they could be found, with or without covers.*

Top right: *In 1862, the U.S. Quartermaster Department improved its canteen design by adding concentric rings to make it sturdier and less prone to dents.*

Middle left: *While there was no single standard-issue canteen for the Confederate army, the most common type at the beginning of the war was made of two round tin faces with a single tin strip forming the side. Unlike the U.S. Pattern 1857, these "tin drum" canteens were more difficult to construct, requiring twice the amount of soldering to join the faces.*

Bottom left: *Facing shortages of tin and lacking the stamping dies to make copies of the U.S. Pattern 1857, the C.S. Quartermaster Bureau in late 1862 decided to revert to making wooden canteens. Using barrel- and wheel-making technology little changed since the 1700s, wooden canteens such as this one were commonly made by local suppliers, especially in the Western Theater. The U.S. Army had not issued wooden canteens since 1839.*

Bottom right: *As designed by Francis Gardner of the Richmond Arsenal, the C.S. Quartermaster Bureau's canteens had slightly curved faces to make them sturdier, and the curved ends of the wooden staves were secured by iron bands. By 1863, perhaps a quarter of the Army of Northern Virginia was equipped with cherrywood or cedarwood Gardner-pattern canteens, an antiquated design revived by wartime necessity.*

Nuckolls patent canteen (1862)

Based on the French military pattern, this double-spouted canteen was discovered among Second Lieutenant Thomas J. Nuckolls's personal effects. It is believed to be the "Army Canteen" for which his father Nathaniel received Confederate patent number 129 on December 11, 1862. Because all the records and drawings of the C.S. Patent Office burned in 1865, identified examples of Confederate-patented products are extraordinarily rare. It is unlikely that canteens of this pattern were ever produced in any quantity; this may be the sole surviving example.

Work shoes, believed to be of Confederate manufacture (ca. 1863)

Throughout the war, the C.S. Quartermaster Bureau's top priority — and its greatest challenge — was to provide enough shoes for the army. Soldiers in the field could easily wear out a pair of shoes in three or four months, and with as many as 900,000 men mobilized over four years, demand often outstripped supply, especially early in the war. Yet by 1864, the bureau was producing 200,000 pairs a year, in addition to another 545,000 pairs imported through the blockade. Despite popular images of a barefoot Johnny Reb, the reality was far less dramatic.

These pegged-sole work shoes are representative of the type mass-produced for Confederate soldiers. Contrary to myth, nearly all shoes of the 1860s were made with separate lasts for left and right feet. This pair is unusual in that the uppers are made of two pieces of leather machine-stitched together.

Banners of Honor

From its inception, the Confederate States of America struggled to establish national symbols worthy of its conservative yet revolutionary cause. In 1861, southern volunteers rallied beneath hundreds of homemade secession banners, state flags, and company colors, each blessed in an elaborate presentation ceremony symbolically binding the volunteers to the communities they defended. Over the next four years, Confederate soldiers marched and fought under three national flag designs, ten battle flag designs, and innumerable variations of each. Most were mass-produced under Confederate government contract; regiments received them from the back of a wagon after signing a receipt, as with uniforms or tents. But even mass-produced battle flags were imbued with symbolic significance. Each was blessed in its own way by the men who held it aloft, both literally and figuratively.

In February 1861, the Provisional Confederate Congress in Montgomery, Alabama, formed a committee to design a new national flag. The hundreds of proposed designs were of two basic types: those that bore some resemblance to the national flag of the United States (using the same colors but different patterns of stars and stripes), and those that departed from it completely (using different colors as well as heraldic shields, sunburst patterns, and other difficult-to-produce designs). In the end, the conservatives won out over the revolutionaries. Designed by the flag committee and appropriately nicknamed the Stars and Bars, the new national flag intentionally mimicked the Stars and Stripes of the United States, thus reflecting the belief of many white southerners that their new republic was simply a reformed version of their old one. At first, the newly adopted national flag doubled as a battle flag; regiments placed their names or patriotic slogans amid the stars in the canton or on the single white bar.

Just as its detractors feared, at the First Battle of Manassas in July 1861, the Confederate Stars and Bars was easily confused, amid the smoke and dust, with the U.S. Stars and Stripes. For Generals P. G. T. Beauregard and Joseph E. Johnston, then commanding the Confederate forces in Virginia, the function of a battle flag, like the color of a uniform, was to differentiate friend from foe and regiment from regiment, nothing else. Instead of each regiment carrying the national colors and a distinctive regimental banner — a British tradition continued by the Union army — Beauregard and Johnston sought a single, standard battle flag for all Confederate regiments, differing only in the specific regimental designation to be painted onto each. Fortunately for Beauregard, his aide-de-camp, South Carolina representative William Porcher Miles, was the former chairman of the congressional flag committee. Miles had a helpful suggestion: one of the most attractive of the rejected

A new banner is entrusted to-day, as a battle-flag. . . . Soldiers: Your mother, your wives, and your sisters have made it. Consecrated by their hands, it must lead you to substantial victory, and the complete triumph of our cause. It can never be surrendered, save to your unspeakable dishonor. . . . Under its untarnished folds beat back the invader, and find nationality, everlasting immunity from an atrocious despotism, and honor and renown for yourselves — or death.
—General P. G. T. Beauregard, presenting new battle flags to Confederate regiments in Virginia, November 28, 1861

national flag designs was a red flag with a blue and white cross intersecting the flag from corner to corner. This "southern cross" design not only would make a distinctive and even spectacular battle flag, but also just happened to be the one that Miles himself had submitted for consideration in February 1861. Beauregard and Johnston loved the idea and the design. In November and December 1861, what would become known as the Army of Northern Virginia received the first batch of southern-cross battle flags. Each featured an even arrangement of twelve stars, including one for Missouri; in May 1862, a thirteenth star in the center of the cross was added for Kentucky, the last state formally recognized by the Confederacy. Meanwhile, the use of state and other flags in the field was banned, though many remained in unofficial use through 1865.

Beauregard and Johnston took "their" battle flag design with them wherever they were posted, which, as it turned out, was all over the South. Transferred west in February 1862, Beauregard found that corps commanders in Mississippi and Arkansas had created their own distinctive battle flags, including William J. Hardee's pattern (dark blue with a white disk or "moon" in the center) and Earl Van Dorn's pattern (red with a yellow crescent and a scattering of thirteen yellow stars). Beauregard wasted no time in ordering new flags of his preferred southern-cross design made for Braxton Bragg's and Leonidas Polk's corps. When Beauregard was transferred to the Department of South Carolina, Georgia, and Florida later that year, he had all the old state flags in his department replaced with the battle flags. Likewise, Johnston ordered variations of the southern-cross battle flag issued to the Department of Alabama, Mississippi, and East Louisiana in the fall of 1863, as well as to most of the Army of Tennessee when he took command of that army in the winter of 1863–64. The battle flag became so popular that it was incorporated into a new national flag in May 1863. Known as the "stainless banner," the official new flag of the Confederate nation featured William Porcher Miles's battle flag in the upper left corner on a field of white. Although other battle flag designs never completely disappeared, by the end of the war more Confederate soldiers had fought under the southern cross than any other flag pattern.

Given the unreliable nature of home supply and the sheer number of flags of all descriptions required by a modern military force, the Confederate government had to assume responsibility for flag production just as it had uniform production. The task fell naturally to the C.S. Clothing Bureau, which, in turn, supervised the mass production of flags from four centralized depots: Mobile, Augusta, Charleston, and Richmond. West of the Mississippi River, where the C.S. Clothing Bureau never established a regular system of supplying battle flags, individual Confederate units were usually responsible for providing their own flags. Only in Richmond were flags made under the direct supervision of a government depot; all others were made by private contractors, typically sign painters, sailmakers, or tent makers. Either way, manufacturing methods were similar to those used in making ready-made clothing: male tailors laid out the pattern and cut the cloth; female seamstresses, working either in their homes or on the premises, stitched the pieces together.

The general battle flag pattern remained consistent, but all else, including size, materials, and border or trim colors varied from depot to depot and from theater to theater. Infantry battle flags produced in Richmond and Charleston were about forty-eight inches square, while those made in Augusta and Mobile were rectangular, generally about fifty-four inches long. Occasionally, flags of the same pattern in smaller dimensions were produced for cavalry and artillery units. In the Trans-Mississippi Department, most battle flags were at least inspired by the William Porcher Miles design, but virtually none were exact copies; some were variations to be found nowhere else in the Confederacy.

Like many of the flags carried to war in 1861, the first battle flags issued in Virginia were made by ladies' sewing circles from locally procured silk originally intended for women's dresses. But silk was neither easy to obtain in bulk nor very durable or colorfast. By mid-1862, battle flags were being constructed of bunting, a lightweight, worsted wool fabric woven expressly for flags. Virtually all the bunting used for Confederate flags was made in England and run through the blockade; only the stars and tape trim were made from southern cotton.

Without doubt the Confederate flags of the Wray Collection are its most historically significant and emotionally powerful artifacts. They are also its rarest. Despite their deep honorific value, perhaps half of all Confederate flags did not survive the war. Some worn-out flags were cannibalized for cloth or destroyed by the C.S. Clothing Bureau when replaced by new issues. Many flags were torn up or burned to prevent their capture. Others were simply lost after the war. In 1865 there were 538 Confederate flags in the hands of the U.S. War Department, which had offered a wartime incentive for their capture: any Union soldier who turned in a Confederate battle flag was awarded the Medal of Honor, regardless of how he had obtained it. In 1905, in a show of national reconciliation, the War Department gave 231 flags that could be identified as having belonged to a particular state regiment to that state's authorities, where most survive today in public collections. The following year, the War Department gave another 252 unidentified flags to the Confederate

Memorial Literary Society in Richmond; these survive at the Museum of the Confederacy, along with an additional 283 flags donated by Confederate veterans and southern states in the early 1900s.

Many captured flags were never turned in through official War Department channels and thus remained in the hands of the soldiers or states that had captured them; some of these were subsequently returned to Confederate veterans organizations in the same spirit of reconciliation in the early 1900s. Other Confederate flags were never captured at all, but were simply retired from service and then awarded as souvenirs to a recipient deemed worthy of the honor, usually an officer or a color bearer. These flags predominate in private collections today, including all six examples from the Wray Collection. These six flags represent an excellent cross-section of national and battle flags, made by at least five different depots or makers from South Carolina to Texas.

**First national-pattern flag, maker unknown (1861), believed to have
flown over Battery Gregg during the siege of Charleston (1863)**

*Bearing eleven shrapnel holes, this flag is believed to have flown over Confederate
fortifications at Battery Gregg on Morris Island in the summer of 1863 during
one of the worst Union bombardments of the war. Today it measures just over five
feet wide by seven-and-a-half feet long, though when first made, the fly end (right
edge) was probably about eighteen inches longer. According to standard wartime
practice, cloth from the fly end was used to patch holes in the rest of the flag, thus
preventing any further tearing. In the 1980s, a conservator stitched strips of white
cotton to secure the ragged fly end as well as the damaged left hoist edge, leaving
only the embroidered "E. MARTIN 1861" visible.*

*Private Edward H. Martin was twenty years old in November 1862 when he
was detached as a signal operator in a special seventy-six-man unit of the C.S.
Signal Corps at Charleston Harbor. Martin used flags in the daytime and torches
at night to send encrypted messages between the forts and batteries protecting
the harbor or to communicate with entering or exiting blockade-runners. In the
summer of 1863, Martin's post was especially crucial: located at Cummings Point
on Morris Island, just three-fourths of a mile north of Fort Wagner, Battery Gregg
was the only communication link between Charleston and the besieged fort, which
was the key to defending the harbor and its symbolic prize of Fort Sumter.*

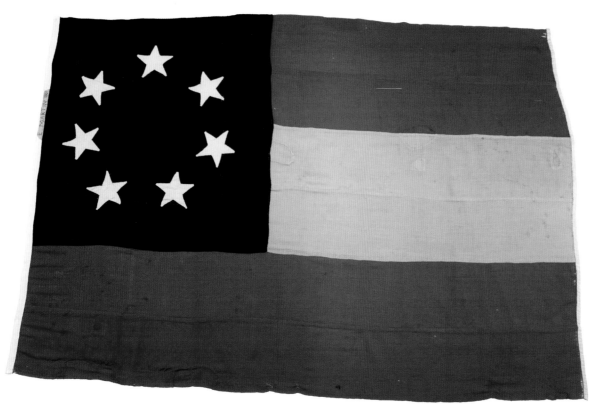

Martin was no ordinary private soldier. Described by one of his officers as "a gentleman of education and position," he had started the war as a member of the Charleston Light Dragoons, an elite volunteer company formed from the well-born sons of Charleston. In addition, he worked as an assistant clerk for the South Carolina State Senate, a job for which he was allowed temporary furloughs from the army. Evidently, he was also a highly skilled and fearless signalman.[5] Standing atop Battery Gregg's earthworks amid exploding enemy shells, Martin and five comrades sent more than five hundred messages during the month of July while also intercepting Union messages. "Their labors have been very heavy," reported their lieutenant, and although none were killed, "their station has suffered from the enemy's fire and is full of holes."[6] For their actions at Battery Gregg, Martin and his signal detachment were later listed in the Confederacy's official Roll of Honor.

It is not known how or when Martin acquired this shot-torn banner, but it is possible he was awarded it as a souvenir when it was replaced by a new, second national-pattern flag, perhaps at the end of July, when he was temporarily rotated out of Battery Gregg for a rest. Given the date "1861" on the hoist edge and the presence of only seven stars, this flag was probably made early that year, and may also have had some connection to Martin's service in the Charleston Light Dragoons on nearby Sullivan's Island in 1861. By coincidence, ten men from that company served as couriers between Battery Gregg and Fort Wagner during the siege. Thus, it is also possible that the flag was presented to Martin after the war via some of his many personal and political connections in Charleston.

First national-pattern lancer pennant, believed to have been made in Richmond, Virginia (ca. 1861)

Early in the war, several southern states raised units of mounted soldiers armed with long spears, or lances, instead of sabers and carbines. This small, seventeen-inch-long pennant was designed to be attached just below the point of the lance. As it became obvious that lancer units were impractical in combat, some pennants were repurposed as guidons to mark the flanks of a troop of cavalry. Made entirely of cotton and featuring eleven four-pointed stars, this one was probably made by a local seamstress, perhaps under contract for the Richmond firm of Burger and Brother, which also made lances.

Evidently, far more of these pennants were made than were ever issued or used. A large number of them, including this one, were taken as souvenirs from a Richmond warehouse by Union soldiers after the city was captured in April 1865. As indicated by a label written in the 1890s by the Philadelphia collector Reginald L. Hart, this pennant was captured along with a lance, which has since disappeared. The deep brown and black stains are the result of contact with rusty iron and water, perhaps while it was still in the warehouse.

Battle flag of an unknown regiment of General James Longstreet's command, first bunting issue, made by the C.S. Depot at Richmond (1862)

Many Confederate battle flags remain unidentified, their stories lost to time and failing memories. Sometimes the families, descendants' organizations, or museums to which such flags were entrusted confused one story with another, especially when there were so many unlabeled or unmarked flags that looked so much alike. When George Wray acquired this flag in the early 1980s, it was accompanied by an 1895 affidavit from a South Carolina veteran named S. B. Thomas, who had served with an artillery battery on the coast of South Carolina in 1864 and 1865. But the flag he described was a first national-pattern flag presented in 1861, not this battle flag made at the Richmond Depot in May 1862.

This flag was one of about fifty orange-bordered bunting flags issued to the infantry regiments and battalions of General James Longstreet's command in June 1862. After the Battles of Williamsburg (May 5, 1862) and Seven Pines (May 31–June 1, 1862), the depot produced strips of white cotton stenciled with battle honors to be sewn to the flags of an estimated thirty units eligible to receive them. Of the original fifty flags, fewer than twenty survive today, of which nearly half, including this one, may never be identified.

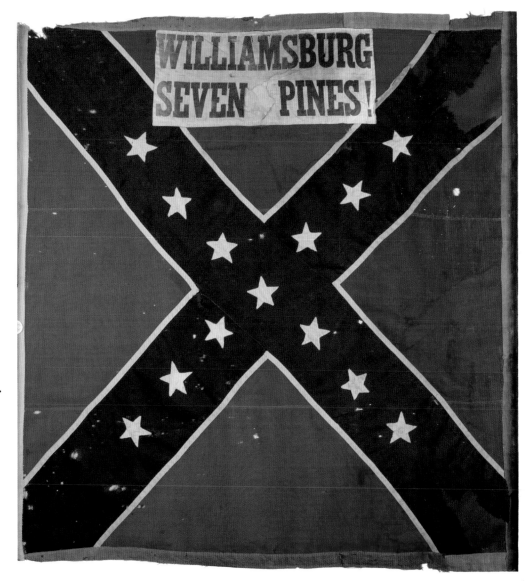

During the war, the Richmond Depot supplied six more issues of bunting battle flags, each slightly different from the one before. No other Confederate flag pattern was designed so efficiently for mass production. Its field comprised three horizontal strips of red bunting over which was sewn a cross of blue bunting (narrowed by three inches in 1862 to save cloth). The red field behind the cross was then cut away, and white polished cotton tape was stitched along the seams, serving both as decoration and reinforcement. Flags manufactured elsewhere were usually made by using traditional and much slower quilting techniques, sewing together four precisely cut triangular pieces to form the red field. Using the faster method, the Richmond Clothing Bureau turned out at least 491 flags from May through November 1862.

Battle flag of the First Georgia Infantry (Olmstead's), made by Charles W. Stiles and issued through the C.S. Depot at Charleston (1863)

Assigned to command the Department of South Carolina, Georgia, and Florida in August 1862, General P. G. T. Beauregard made sure that the C.S. Clothing Depot in Charleston adopted "his" flag design. In 1863 and 1864, the depot contracted with Charles W. Stiles, a forty-one-year-old Canadian-born painter, to produce nearly two hundred flags of all sizes, shapes, and uses. Aside from hospital and signal flags, all of them were of the William Porcher Miles pattern.

This forty-eight-inch-square example is one of at least twenty-eight infantry regimental battle flags made by Stiles, all of which are easily distinguished by a half-inch blue sleeve (symbolizing infantry) on the hoist edge for attaching the flag to a staff. Unlike the battle flags produced at the Richmond Depot, Charleston flags were pieced together using four triangular pieces of red cloth stitched directly to the white and blue stripes. Additionally, the white stars are larger and more evenly spaced than those of Richmond-made flags.

In May 1863, this flag was issued to Colonel Charles Olmstead's First Georgia Infantry Regiment. Composed of the most prominent volunteer militia companies in Savannah, the regiment was stationed on the Isle of Hope, where it manned heavy artillery batteries defending the approaches to the city. In early July 1863, four companies of the First Georgia were ordered north to reinforce the defenses around Charleston Harbor. It is believed that this battle flag went with them. Those four companies fought in the defense of Fort Wagner during the first Union assault on July 11, though they were stationed at Fort Johnston during the second assault on July 18 (made famous by the 1989 film Glory).

In May 1864, Olmstead's regiment was ordered to northern Georgia, where it was incorporated into the Army of Tennessee as part of Brigadier General Hugh W. Mercer's brigade. The First Georgia fought under this flag during the ensuing Atlanta Campaign, including the Battle of Kennesaw Mountain and the Battle of Peachtree Creek. On July 22, 1864, in what became known as the Battle of Bald Hill or the Battle of Atlanta, Mercer's brigade was part of the flanking attack on the Union Army's Sixteenth Corps just east of Atlanta along present-day Interstate 20. Here four men fell while carrying this flag: Privates Joseph J. Singer and Robert K. Dimond were killed; Private Henry Leaptrot and Corporal William H. Rose were wounded. Every man in the color guard was hit.

Although replaced by a Hardee-pattern battle flag soon after the July 22 battle, this flag was the one that the veterans of the First Georgia remembered most vividly after the war. In March 1904, fifty-nine-year-old William Rose carried this flag at the head of a memorial procession to mark the unveiling of a Confederate memorial stone at Cathedral Cemetery (today known as Catholic Cemetery) in Savannah. George Wray acquired this flag from family descendants in the 1970s.

Second national-pattern flag, used as a battle flag by the
Thirty-Third Texas Cavalry, maker unknown (ca. 1863)

In the spring of 1863, several independent companies of Texas cavalry were consolidated with Colonel James Duff's Fourteenth Texas Cavalry Battalion (better known as Duff's Partisan Rangers) to form the Thirty-Third Texas Cavalry Regiment. In 1862, Duff, a Scottish émigré, former U.S. Army sergeant, and San Antonio merchant, became famous (and later infamous) for rounding up German-born Union loyalists in the Central Texas Hill Country. The ten companies of his new regiment, made up largely of Tejanos, patrolled hundreds of miles of the Lower Rio Grande Valley, from San Antonio to Corpus Christi, and Brownsville to Eagle Pass, where they fought Mexican bandits and Union raiders while guarding Confederate cotton being traded across the border.

The Thirty-Third Texas Cavalry acquired this hand-stitched bunting national flag upon its formation and used it as a battle flag through the end of the war. Although the law adopting the "stainless banner" specified that it was to be twice as long as it was wide, at forty-nine by seventy-one inches, the flag of the Thirty-Third follows the much more common (nonregulation) length-to-width ratio of about three to two. This example has two features peculiar to Texas flags: an enlarged center star in the canton as well as thirteen eyelets along the canvas hoist edge through which a cord attached the flag to its staff. An additional strip of white bunting has been stitched onto the fly end to protect against fraying. The maker has yet to be identified.

The most famous men to fight under this flag were three hard-fighting and politically powerful brothers from the border town of Laredo. A merchant, rancher, and secessionist leader named Santos Benavides was second in command of the regiment, and his brothers Refugio and Cristóbal were company commanders. Promoted to colonel in command of his own cavalry regiment in November 1863, Santos Benavides became the highest-ranking Mexican American in Confederate service; his cavalry helped win a Confederate victory in the last battle of the Civil War at Palmito Ranch, Texas, May 12–13, 1865. The most infamous man to fight under the flag was a Marylander named Isaac D. Surratt, a sergeant in Company A and veteran of Duff's campaign against the Hill Country Unionists. Surratt was the first son of Mary E. J. Surratt, who was executed in 1865 for her involvement in the plot to assassinate Abraham Lincoln.

In April 1864, in reaction to the Union's Red River Campaign, the Thirty-Third Texas Cavalry was transferred to northeastern Texas, from where it operated against Union supply lines in Arkansas and the Indian Territories (present-day Oklahoma). Thirteen months later, beset by wholesale desertions and the news of surrenders in the East, Colonel Duff disbanded what was left of his regiment and fled to Mexico. His veterans presented their well-worn but never-surrendered battle flag to the widow of Captain Joseph B. Weyman, who had commanded Company G. The thirty-two-year-old New York–born captain had raised cattle in Columbus, Texas, before the war. While posted on the Arkansas border, Captain Weyman contracted typhoid fever and died in a private home in Titus County, Texas, on December 24, 1864. The battle flag was passed down through Weyman's descendants; George Wray purchased it from the family in 1981.

Captain Joseph B. Weyman, ca. 1864

Second national-pattern naval ensign from the blockade-runner *Pocahontas*, maker unknown (1864)

Shortly before midnight on July 8, 1864, the USS *Azalea and the* USS *Sweetbriar, two of the navy's newest steam-powered screw tugs, sighted an unknown sailing ship attempting to leave the Port of Charleston. Quickly overtaking the slow, sixty-five-foot-long schooner, the navy tugs discovered it was the* Pocahontas, *outbound for Nassau and loaded with 53 bales of cotton and 299 boxes of tobacco. Its captain-owner was thirty-five-year-old Joseph G. Hester, who, along with his wife and six crewmen, promptly surrendered. Concealed in his cabin was "the uniform of a lieutenant in the Confederate States Navy, which he states he purchased in England a few months since" as well as "a large Confederate flag."* [7]

This is the six-foot-by-nine-foot flag found in Hester's cabin. The rope loops on the hoist edge—intended for attachment to a halyard—distinguish it as a naval ensign. Like most Confederate flags, it is entirely hand sewn, assembled from English-made wool bunting and cotton stars. The red field of the canton was made from four triangular pieces, a construction feature typical of flags produced for the Confederate government by Charleston flag makers.

Despite the evidence found aboard the Pocahontas, *Joseph G. Hester was not a navy lieutenant — or at least there is no record of his having achieved that rank — and the* Pocahontas *was a private venture. When his native state of North Carolina seceded in 1861, the experienced seaman and packet-boat captain enlisted in the C.S. Navy, and his three brothers joined the army. From late 1861 through 1862, Hester served as acting master's mate aboard the commerce raider* css Sumter, *famous as the first command of the future* css Alabama *captain Raphael Semmes. But on October 15, 1862, as the decommissioned* Sumter *awaited sale in Gibraltar, Hester's seemingly promising Confederate navy career took a bizarre turn. That night he crept into the cabin of Midshipman William Andrews, pulled out a revolver, and shot him three times at point-blank range. Hester later claimed that Andrews, then commanding a skeleton crew of ten, was a traitor planning to turn over the ship to federal authorities. Hester's shipmates claimed that Andrews had caught him pilfering supplies. The embarrassing case reached all the way to the Confederate secretary of state, who arranged for Hester to be transported aboard a British warship first to London and then to the Confederacy, where he would be tried for murder. But during a stop in Bermuda, word reached the warship that the British government had ruled that it lacked jurisdiction in the case, and Hester was released. He never went to trial.*

In May 1864, Hester appeared in South Carolina, where he got married and purchased the Pocahontas, *registering the ship under his own name. Three weeks before Hester's capture, Confederate government authorities (who by law controlled half the ship's cargo) had denied him permission to run the blockade, stating that the risks for a slow vessel with a small cargo outweighed the potential gain to be earned by a large, fast steamer. Hester finally received approval for his venture, but Union spies were listening. On the night of July 2, the blockading fleet off Charleston received "positive information" that the* Pocahontas *would make a run through Breach Inlet; three tugs were ordered to "close in well and be particularly vigilant." The warning paid off. Hester later told his captors that "being desirous of leaving the Confederate States, he invested a sum of Confederate money" in the schooner and cargo, which he intended to sail either to Nassau, for which he was officially cleared, or to Bermuda.[8] The* Pocahontas *incident ended Hester's seafaring career and probably his Confederate allegiance as well. While imprisoned in Philadelphia, he proclaimed his willingness to take the oath of allegiance to the United States, yet it appears that he never did, and may have been exchanged in late 1864. Though his whereabouts in 1865 are unknown, there is some suggestion that he began working secretly for U.S. military intelligence at or before the end of the war.*

For ten years beginning in 1866, Hester worked as an undercover agent for the U.S. government, investigating and infiltrating the Ku Klux Klan in North Carolina, South Carolina, and Alabama. He later accepted several political plums from President Ulysses S. Grant, including a consulship in Chile and a special mission to Austria. At his death in 1901, he was engaged in real estate work in Washington, D.C. Newspaper obituaries made no mention of his Confederate past.

The strange story of Joseph Hester's flag does not end with his death. On the canvas heading of the hoist edge, the ink marking "A.H.S. / STRONG MM" refers to Frederick W. Strong, master's mate on the USS Azalea, who kept the flag as a souvenir, and to the Amherst Historical Society in Massachusetts, where his descendants placed the flag on loan beginning in 1907 and continuing through the 1950s. After passing through the hands of several private owners, the flag was purchased by George Wray in 1975. Seven years later, Wray sent the flag to West Virginia for appraisal, but under extremely mysterious circumstances, it was stolen from the mail while being returned. In 1994, a friend reported to Wray that he had seen the flag for sale in Knoxville, Tennessee. Armed with Wray's detailed drawings, correspondence with the U.S. Postal Service, and other proof of ownership, local law enforcement authorities were able to recover the flag, preserving a tangible reminder of one the most unusual stories of the Civil War.

Epilogue Confederate Defeat

In 1861, the eleven states that formed the Confederacy went to war with about 15 percent of their former nation's manufacturing capacity, 20 percent of its military-age manpower, and 30 percent of its railroads. Over the course of the war, the Confederacy mobilized an estimated 900,000 men, or about 75 percent of all white males of military age in its territory. They were pitted against about 2.1 million men fighting for the Union, which was only about 40 percent of its available manpower. As the historian and novelist Shelby Foote famously remarked, it would seem that "the North fought that war with one hand behind its back," making Union victory virtually inevitable.[1] Thus Confederate defeat has often been described in the simple eloquence of its greatest champion, penned at the surrender of its greatest army: "compelled to yield to overwhelming numbers and resources." That famous phrase tells us much about Confederate defeat and its imagined causes. The many stories behind the objects in the George Wray Collection reveal a much more complex reality.

Most of the Wray Collection consists of firearms. This body of evidence goes a long way toward justifying the "overwhelming numbers and resources" explanation of Confederate defeat. The total output of all governmental and private arms makers in the Confederacy from 1861 through 1865 only amounted to an estimated 78,000 new long arms, less than 10 percent of what Confederate armies required. In producing even that amount, the Confederacy was lucky: had the machinery at the Harpers Ferry Armory been destroyed on the night of April 18, 1861, the Confederate government would have been denied the capacity for making about 48,000 of those 78,000 arms. The rest of the Confederacy's long arms came from three outside sources: an estimated 260,000 arms (all but about 60,000 originally made under U.S. authority) were seized at U.S. arsenals in 1861 or issued from state arsenals; perhaps 250,000 U.S.- or foreign-made arms were scavenged from the battlefields by the C.S. Ordnance Bureau; and, most important, around 500,000 long arms were imported from Britain and another 100,000 from Austria. At the same time, the U.S. Armory at Springfield and twenty-two private contractors turned out 1,477,000 rifle-muskets, and other northern factories turned out at least 470,000

I have succeeded beyond my utmost expectations. . . . Where three years ago we were not making a gun, a pistol nor a sabre — a pound of powder — no shot nor shell (except at the Tredegar Works) we now make all these in quantities to meet the demands of our large armies. In looking over all this I feel that my three years of labor have not been passed in vain.
—Confederate chief of ordnance Josiah Gorgas, April 8, 1864

After four years of arduous service, marked by unsurpassed courage and fortitude, the Army of Northern Virginia has been compelled to yield to overwhelming numbers and resources.
—Confederate general Robert E. Lee, General Order Number Nine, April 10, 1865

409

breech-loading and repeating arms, not to mention 1,367,000 long arms purchased by Union agents in Europe. All told, the Union held a three-to-one numerical advantage in firearms, exceeding even its overall manpower advantage of just over two-to-one.

The North's advantage in firearms was not just quantitative. Virtually all arms manufactured under U.S. authority during and just before the war were assembled from interchangeable parts, and all rifle-muskets were made to standard caliber. Even using the U.S. machinery captured from Harpers Ferry, the C.S. Armories at Richmond and Fayetteville never fully achieved interchangeability; the only Confederate arms that were truly and consistently interchangeable were those purchased abroad from the London Armoury Company. Instead, Confederate-made arms are known for their many variations, to the point that virtually no two are alike. Most famously, the Richmond Armory was known for improvisation: damaged rifle-musket barrels were cut down into carbines, while barrels, bands, buttplates, and entire locks from U.S.-made arms were cleaned, repaired, and re-used to fill out production. Of fifteen Richmond Armory weapons in the Wray Collection, only two are composed entirely of Confederate-made parts. At the same time, ersatz "artillery muskets" believed to have been made in Mobile, the first-type rifle made at the Asheville Armory, the Texas contract rifles, and other products of small manufactories were so poorly made that it seems almost impossible to imagine soldiers actually using them. Yet clearly they were used — and like nearly all surviving Confederate arms, heavily used. Indeed, it is possible that many of these arms survive today only because they were taken as Union trophies to demonstrate how inferior were Rebel guns, and hence how corrupt was the Confederate cause.

Probably the most lethal of the North's technological advantages was its overwhelming superiority in breech-loading arms, in numbers alone outstripping Confederate production by a staggering sixty-five to one. By 1865, northern breechloaders — especially repeaters — were being produced in sufficient quantities to have a profound impact both on the battlefield and on Confederate morale, even at the highest levels. "Sheridan is to-day reported to be about 15 miles from the city [Richmond] with his whole force," lamented Josiah Gorgas in March 1865, "8000 men each armed with a 16 Shooter & four revolvers, a moving Armory truly!"[2] Despite his mild exaggeration of the enemy's weaponry, Gorgas obviously understood its impact, all the while recognizing that his Ordnance Bureau simply could not provide a creditable defense against it. Herein lies the most convincing evidence that the Confederacy was indeed "compelled to yield to overwhelming numbers and resources."

Even so, northern victory was by no means inevitable. To deny Confederate independence, the North had to raise and equip armies to invade the South, occupy strategic positions throughout its 750,000 square miles (including 3,500 miles of coastline), and destroy not only its material capacity to make war but also its popular will to do so. All that the Confederacy had to do was to exhaust the Union's will to continue the war; it could win by simply not losing. Hence, Confederate leaders and soldiers alike had reasonable grounds for expecting victory (or at least independence) through the summer of 1864. Former U.S. secretary of war Jefferson Davis and the many former U.S. Army officers in his armies understood full well the extent of northern material superiority, but hardly considered their cause lost as a result. They understood that victory or defeat lay primarily with the success or failure of their armies. In the end, armies were the currency of Confederate nationalism, not cities, territories, or morale, all of which could be regained or rebuilt. But armies could not. As long as Confederate armies survived, the cause survived; the outcome would ultimately come down to which side could put the heaviest battalions in the field and keep them fed, armed, equipped, and motivated.

Ultimately—and largely to Josiah Gorgas's credit—the Confederacy ran out of men long before it ran out of guns. Only a year before Lee yielded to "overwhelming numbers and resources," the Union cause had yet to capture Richmond, Atlanta, or the next presidential election, leaving the outcome still very much in doubt. At the time, Gorgas had good reason to count his many successes. Most notably, Confederate armies had never lost a battle because of a lack of military materiel. And incredibly, the South had achieved near self-sufficiency in the production of edged weapons, gunpowder, ammunition, accoutrements, uniforms, and other equipment—essentially in all areas except the technologically sophisticated field of arms manufacture. All this was achieved in a region only recently touched by the Industrial Revolution, one sorely lacking in financial, industrial, and transportation infrastructure. Along the way, there were unexpected and sometimes spectacular success stories: the Confederate Powder Works, the Tredegar Iron Works, the Griswold and Gunnison revolver factory (demonstrating that slave labor could be used in an industrial environment), and the C.S. Clothing Bureau (demonstrating that home production could be fused with mass production).

There were also hard realities. From the beginning, the Confederate national government pumped millions of dollars into the private sector to encourage the manufacturing of war materiel, especially firearms. The private sector responded with enthusiasm, patriotism, and more than its share of mechanical creativity. But few private entrepreneurs—and even fewer governmental officials—understood the complexity of manufacturing modern firearms. Southern newspapers were filled with glowing predictions of a coming Confederate industrial boom, apparently to be conjured from sheer willpower alone. "These arms, we are advised, can be made here with comparative rapidity," observed the Atlanta *Daily Intelligencer* of George Morse's breech-loading carbine. "If so, we see no good reason why the large work shop of the enterprising firm referred to above should not be engaged by the Government to turn them out by the thousands."[3] The "large work shop" was that of Hammond Marshall and Company, a small facility barely equipped to make swords, let alone the most advanced breech-loading design in the Confederacy. Furthermore, many of the would-be entrepreneurs lacked managerial proficiency, and their unskilled laborers lacked industrial work habits. The Confederacy's fragile infrastructure could not supply iron, steel, or even walnut in quantities sufficient for all who needed it. In the end, no amount of mechanical improvisation could transform the small cotton-gin manufactory of Henry J. Davis and David W. Bozeman in rural Coosa County, Alabama, into an armory capable of supplying tens of thousands of arms. Not even the famed gun makers of Guilford County, North Carolina, with all their collective skill and experience, could build another Harpers Ferry Armory.

Yet as perhaps these small gun makers came to understand after months of trial and error, they could supply a few hundred or even a few thousand rifles to their states, and even those few were better (but rarely more profitable) than none at all. Furthermore, despite all obstacles, the quality of many southern-made arms improved over the course of production as managers and workers alike gained experience. Even at the state level, arms were subjected to inspection, and as seen by records in Alabama and North Carolina, inferior-quality arms were regularly (and sometimes frequently) rejected. At the national armories, the quality of work was considerably higher. After all, they were run by former U.S. Army ordnance officers; the core of their workforce was composed largely of former Harpers Ferry mechanics, skilled men who knew how to improvise without sacrificing functionality. Although they could not afford to be as picky as their northern counterparts, Confederate armorers watched over the details of production, inspected finished arms, and consistently tried to obtain the best materials.

But success in any southern war industry came at a price. As the enormous size of the task became apparent, the Confederate national government resorted to industrialization by force, leveraging its control of labor, railroads, and raw materials in order to monopolize military-industrial production. By the end of the war, nearly all state and private arms factories were under the direct control of the C.S. Ordnance Bureau, and with good reason: the southern economy was simply not built to withstand what was being asked of it. With a finite and ever-shrinking supply of manpower and raw materials, the Confederate government, acting as a central-economic planner, rationed out resources to those government manu-factories that needed them most. By 1864, Gorgas and other Confederate leaders viewed private and state production as wasteful and occasionally dangerous be-cause of the diversion of precious resources away from governmental works.

The Confederacy's greatest success was not in domestic production but in foreign procurement. Here, Louis T. Wigfall was almost proved correct: an independent southern republic rich with slave-grown cotton could easily afford to buy guns, equipment, or anything else it needed from Europe, thus, at least theoretically, eliminating the need for domestic industry. In the end, it was not the valuable machinery taken at Harpers Ferry that proved decisive for Confederate survival; rather, it was 500,000 imported English-made rifle-muskets, along with saltpeter, tin, lead, leather, and other raw materials procured abroad, that allowed the young nation to approach self-sufficiency in the production of almost all other war mate-riel. These resources kept Confederate armies in the field and allowed the Confed-erate cause to survive its last three years. Yet without the industrial capacity to build a navy to defend its ports—even the fourth-wealthiest nation in the world had neither time nor money to buy one—the transatlantic lifeline was ultimately only a temporary expedient. In "numbers and resources," the 671 U.S. Navy warships and gunboats in service at the end of the war must count heavily in any reckoning of Confederate defeat, as must the capture of the vital port of Wilmington, North Carolina, in early 1865.

The Confederacy's survival owed much to its superintendent of armories, James H. Burton, perhaps the most experienced and knowledgeable expert in arms production on either side. In 1862, understanding the temporary nature of foreign procurement, he began planning for the long term, advocating the development of a Confederate government arms industry modeled on that of its northern neighbor: a centralized armory for manufacturing rifle-muskets (to be built in Macon) with ancillary (and personally remunerative) public-private partnerships for produc-ing revolvers (the "Spiller and Burr" model) and carbines (perhaps the Alexander model). It was a logical plan, already proven to work in the United States and Great Britain and well known to Burton. But for the Confederacy, such a plan depended on successfully defending its own territory, at least to the extent of maintaining a few open ports and some portion of its hinterland free from Union incursion, where manufacturing and supply facilities could operate unmolested. While the survival of the Confederacy depended on its armies, the survival of the armies depended on a steady supply of military materiel. Therein lay the fatal flaw, for as Burton soon discovered, no place in the Confederacy was truly safe.

Within the first year of the war, the large Confederate arsenals at Nashville and

Memphis were forced to relocate to safer confines in Georgia and Mississippi. In Richmond, the C.S. armory stocking machinery, the pistol factory, and later the carbine works were moved to prevent their possible capture. Even in one of the remotest places in the South, the C.S. Armory at Asheville fell victim to Union pressure in the fall of 1863 — just at the moment when full-scale production was finally getting under way. The decision to relocate its machinery to Columbia assumed that the Confederacy still had time to reestablish the armory in a safer place. In 1863, perhaps it did. But by the fall of 1864, Burton's efforts to move vital machinery out of harm's way had degenerated into a giant shell game, shifting men and materiel between Richmond, Columbia, Savannah, Macon, and Tallassee, all the while trying to guess where Union armies would go next. Linked by an increasingly fragile and unreliable railroad system, the armories at Richmond and Fayetteville were starved for parts and materials, and production slowed to a crawl. Thus, there are virtually no 1865-dated Richmond or Fayetteville Armory weapons in the Wray Collection and, for that matter, only a few dated 1864. Gorgas had succeeded beyond his utmost expectations, but it was not enough.

It was worse for the private manufacturers. In quests to find safe havens for their operations, the Cook and Brother Armory moved twice; Dickson, Nelson, and Company moved four times; Louis Froelich's sword and bayonet manufactory burned down, moved, was burned again in a Union raid, and was rebuilt a third time. Some entrepreneurs were less fortunate. In the fall of 1864, deciding they had nowhere else to run, Ferdinand and Francis Cook closed the most successful private armory in the Confederacy and led its entire workforce into battle. Weeks later, Major Ferdinand Cook — the moving force behind the armory and one of the South's best mechanical engineers — was killed in combat. Here was the Confederacy's ultimate vulnerability revealed in personal terms: its home front was also its battlefront. And Cook was only the most famous of many skilled mechanics lost in battle.

In November 1864, with much of the South occupied or destroyed and further prosecution of the war confirmed by the reelection of Abraham Lincoln, Confederate armies began to disintegrate. Like the war industries that had supplied them, southern soldiers had no place of refuge. Many were forced to choose between staying in the Confederate army to somehow carry on the fight or going home to protect their loved ones from the depredations of Union armies. By February 1865, over a hundred thousand men had decided that question in favor of home and family. As exemplified by Sherman's march through Georgia and the Carolinas and, even more spectacularly, by James H. Wilson's raid through Alabama and Georgia in the spring of 1865, the Union army put the heaviest battalions in the field and kept them there, armed with the best weapons, led by the best generals, and backed by the most efficient logistical infrastructure. In the end, it was not "numbers and resources" alone that brought about Confederate defeat; rather, it was also the Union's will to employ those resources, to use what Sherman called "the hard hand of war" to destroy the Confederacy's burgeoning military-industrial complex, defeat its armies in the field, break its morale, liberate its slaves, and leave it nothing to fight for.

Confederate soldiers were neither ignorant of their cause nor deceived into fighting for it. In their time, in their place, in their worldview, it was a cause worth dying for. And die they did: by 1865, nearly one-third of all Confederate soldiers had been killed on the battlefield or had died of disease; at least another third were wounded. It was by far the highest toll ever suffered by an American army, and it was suffered in defeat. The material story of that defeat is spelled out in intimate detail in the Wray Collection, written into the weapons, uniforms, and flags of the men who fought and lost the bloodiest war in American history.

Notes

1. Guns of the Industrial Revolution

Epigraphs were drawn from the following works: Hall quotation from Merritt Roe Smith, *Harpers Ferry Armory and the New Technology* (Ithaca, N.Y.: Cornell University Press, 1977), 199; rule number 15 quoted from Brooke Hindle and Steven Lubar, *Engines of Change: The American Industrial Revolution* (Washington, D.C.: Smithsonian Institution Press, 1986), 233; Ripley quotation from U.S. Chief of Ordnance James W. Ripley to Secretary of War Simon Cameron, June 11, 1861, in *The Executive Documents of the House of Representatives of the United States, 37th Cong., 2d sess., 1861–1862,* vol. 5, no. 67, 30–31; Whitney quotation from Lewis F. Southard, "The Origin of the Palmetto Pistols," *American Society of Arms Collectors Bulletin* 81:37; Sykes quotation from Madaus, "The Percussion Martial Firearms of Eli Whitney, Jr.," *Armax* 2, no. 1: 40–41; Manigault quotation from Report of Edward Manigault, South Carolina Chief of Ordnance, to the State Ordnance Board, November 21, 1861, quoted in Report of William H. Gist, chief of the Department of Construction and Manufacture, to Governor Francis Pickens, August 29, 1862, in *Journal of the Convention of the People of South Carolina Held in 1860, 1861 and 1862 together with the Ordinances, Reports, Resolutions, Etc.* (Columbia: R. W. Gibbes, 1862), 715; Petigru quotation from Walter B. Edgar, *South Carolina: A History* (Columbia: University of South Carolina Press, 1998), 355.

1. Quoted in Madaus, "Percussion Firearms of Eli Whitney," 21.

2. Southard, "Palmetto Pistols," 30.

3. Quoted in Jack A. Meyer, *William Glaze and the Palmetto Armory,* 2nd ed. (Columbia: South Carolina State Museum, 1994), 54.

2. Plowshares into Swords

Epigraphs were drawn from the following works: Benjamin quotation from *The War of the Rebellion: A Compilation of the Official Records of the Union and Confederate Armies,* ser. 1 (Washington, D.C.: Government Printing Office, 1902), 4:474; *Columbus (Ga.) Sun* quotation from Chad Morgan, *Planters' Progress: Modernizing Confederate Georgia* (Gainesville: University Press of Florida, 2005), 37; appeal to Walker from John M. Murphy and Howard M. Madaus, *Confederate Rifles and Muskets: Infantry Small Arms Manufactured in the Southern Confederacy, 1861–1865* (Newport Beach, Calif.: Graphic, 1996), 664; Walker to Harris from Murphy and Madaus, *Confederate Rifles and Muskets,* 663; *Richmond Daily Dispatch* quotations from "The War in the Southwest," May 15, 1862, and "The True Spirit" (speech of Rufus Barringer, Concord, N.C.), May 10, 1861; Armistead quotation from Mark Grimsley and Mark D. Simpson, *Gettysburg: A Battlefield Guide* (Lincoln: University of Nebraska Press, 1999), 150.

1. Quoted in Murphy and Madaus, *Confederate Rifles and Muskets,* 391.

2. Quoted in ibid., 651.

3. I am grateful to John Phillips of Christiansburg, Virginia, for this information.

4. Quoted in William A. Albaugh, *Confederate Edged Weapons* (1960; Wilmington, N.C.: Broadfoot, 1993), 95.

5. *Wilmington Daily Journal,* May 16, 1861, quoted in John W. McAden Jr. and Chris E. Fonvielle Jr., *Louis Froelich: Arms-Maker to the Confederacy* (Carolina Beach, N.C.: Slapdash, 2008), 3.

3. The Confederate National Armories

Epigraphs and pull quotes for this chapter were drawn from the following sources: Gorgas quotation from Benjamin LaBree, ed., *The Confederate Soldier in the Civil War* (Louisville, Ky.: Courier-Journal Job Printing Company, 1895), 324, originally published in *Southern Historical Society Papers,* vol. 12: *Jan.–Dec. 1884,* exact date of composition unknown; Kingsbury quotation from *Reports of the Committees of the Senate of the United States,* 37th Cong., 2nd sess., 1861–1862 (Washington, D.C.: Government Printing Office, 1862), 246; *Kansas State Journal* quotation from Erich Langsdorf, "Jim Lane and the Frontier Guard," *Kansas Historical Quarterly* 9, no. 1 (February 1940): 16, digitized on the Kansas Historical Society web page, http://www.kshs.org; Benjamin quotation from *The War of the Rebellion: A Compilation of the Official Records of the Union and Confederate Armies,* ser. 4 (Washington, D.C.: Government Printing Office, 1900), 1:988; Burton and Adams quotations from Paul J. Davies, *C.S. Armory, Richmond: A History of the Confederate States Armory, Richmond, Virginia, and the Stock Shop at the C.S. Armory, Macon, Georgia* (Gettysburg, Pa.: Thomas, 2003), 226, 199; stipulations for the location of a new U.S. arsenal in the South Atlantic region from Tom Belton, "A History of the Fayetteville Arsenal and Armory" (MA thesis, North Carolina State University, 1979), 8; Childs and Burkhart quotations from John M. Murphy and Howard M. Madaus, *Confederate Rifles and Muskets: Infantry Small Arms Manufactured in the Southern Confederacy, 1861–1865* (Newport Beach, Calif.: Graphic, 1996), 212; Downer quotation from Murphy and Madaus, *Confederate Rifles and Muskets,* 45.

1. Quoted in Davies, *C.S. Armory, Richmond,* 347.

2. Henry K. Craig to John B. Floyd, quoted in Belton, "A History of the Fayetteville Arsenal," 20.

3. Warren Winslow to Leroy P. Walker, July 11, 1861, quoted in Murphy and Madaus, *Confederate Rifles and Muskets,* 188.

4. Amasa King to James H. Burton, quoted in ibid., 47.

5. Benjamin Sloan to Josiah Gorgas, September 14, 1863, quoted in Gordon B. McKinney, "Premature Industrialization in Appalachia: The Asheville Armory, 1862–1863," in Kenneth W. Noe and Shannon H. Wilson, eds., *The Civil War in Appalachia: Collected Essays* (Knoxville: University of Tennessee Press, 1997), 233.

6. Master armorer Amasa W. King to acting superintendent of armories William S. Downer, August 26, 1863, in "Confederate Papers Relating to Citizens or Business Firms, 1861–1865," A.W. King file, Fold3.com, 23.

4. A War between the States

Epigraphs and pull quotes were drawn from the following sources: first Brown quotation from Chad Morgan, *Planters Progress: Modernizing Confederate Georgia* (Gainesville: University Press of Florida, 2005), 67; Benjamin quotation from *The War of the Rebellion: A Compilation of the Official Records of the Union and Confederate Armies*, ser. 4 (Washington, D.C.: Government Printing Office, 1900), 1:988; Hogg quotation from John M. Murphy and Howard M. Madaus, *Confederate Rifles and Muskets: Infantry Small Arms Manufactured in the Southern Confederacy, 1861–1865* (Newport Beach, Calif.: Graphic, 1996), 426; Burton quotation from National Archives and Records Administration, Washington, D.C., Record Group 109, chap. 4, vol. 31, quoted in Confederate States Armory at Macon, Georgia, "Military Operations Affecting the C.S. Armory at Macon," csarmory.org/military.htm♯repair; second Brown quotation from *War of the Rebellion*, ser. 1, vol. 52, pt. 2 (Washington, D.C.: Government Printing Office, 1898), 789; Bennett quotation from "Confederate Papers Relating to Citizens or Business Firms, 1861–1865," Alabama Arms Manufacturing Company file, Fold3.com, 9; C.S. Nitre and Mining Bureau quotation from Joseph H. Woodward II, "Alabama Iron Manufacturing, 1860–1865," *Alabama Review* (July 1954): 202; DuBose quotation from *War of the Rebellion*, ser. 1, vol. 34, pt. 2 (Washington, D.C.: Government Printing Office, 1891), 998; Short, Biscoe, and Company quotation from William A. Albaugh III, *Tyler, Texas, C.S.A.: The Story of the Confederate States Ordnance Works at Tyler, Texas, 1861–1865* (Falls Church, Va., 1958; repr., Wilmington, N.C.: Broadfoot, 1993), 26.

1. Quoted in Michael J. Black, "Clapp, Gates & Company: An Example of the Confederate Arms Production Effort," *Military Collector and Historian* 41, no. 4 (Winter 1989): 190.

2. Joseph E. Brown to "the Mechanics of Georgia," February 20, 1862, in Allen D. Candler, ed., *The Confederate Records of the State of Georgia, Compiled and Published under the Authority of the Legislature* (Atlanta: Charles P. Byrd, state printer, 1909), 2:199–200.

3. Walter C. Hodgkins to Richard E. Cuyler, July 16, 1862, quoted in William A. Albaugh III, Hugh Benet Jr., and Edward N. Simmons, *Confederate Handguns: Concerning the Guns, the Men Who Made Them, and the Times of Their Use* (New York: Bonanza, 1963), 26.

4. "New Orleans Rifle Factory," *New Orleans Bee*, August 5, 1861, 1.

5. Quoted in Murphy and Madaus, *Confederate Rifles and Muskets*, 158.

6. "Statement of Albert Nanney," St. Louis, Missouri, May 23, 1863, and undated endorsement of Captain Marcellus V. G. Strong, in "Compiled Service Records of Confederate Soldiers Who Served in Organizations Raised Directly by the Confederate Government," Seventh Kentucky Mounted Infantry, Albert Nanny file, Fold3.com, 21, 23, 12.

7. Acts of the Second Called Session, 1861, and of the First Regular Annual Session of the General Assembly of Alabama (Montgomery, Alabama: Montgomery Advertiser Book and Job Office, 1862), 75.

8. F. M. Gilmer Jr., Red Mountain Iron and Coal Company, to Josiah Gorgas, March 8, 1864, in "Compiled Service Records of Confederate General and Staff Officers and Non regimental Enlisted Men," James H. Burton file, Fold3.com, 626.

9. James H. Burton to Josiah Gorgas, April 1, 1864, in "Compiled Service Records of Confederate General and Staff Officers," Burton file, Fold3.com, 616, 618.

10. John T. Truss to Shorter, July 17, 1862, quoted in Murphy and Madaus, *Confederate Rifles and Muskets*, 655.

11. Acting Brigadier General Smith P. Bankhead to Captain Edmund P. Turner, August 23, 1863, quoted in ibid., 679.

12. Short to Governor Lubbock, September 6, 1862, quoted in Albaugh, *Tyler, Texas*, 17.

13. Texas Military Board to unknown recipient, October 12, 1863, quoted in ibid., 28.

14. Service record card in "Compiled Service Records of Confederate Soldiers Who Served in Organizations Raised Directly by the Confederate Government," Twenty-Ninth Texas Cavalry, William Malloy file, Fold3.com, 3.

15. James R. Nichols to the Texas Military Board, December 7, 1863, quoted in Howard Michael Madaus, "Contract Rifles of the Texas State Military Board, 1862–1864," *Journal of the American Society of Arms Collectors* 77 (Fall 1997), 27.

16. Contract between Short, Biscoe, and Company and the State of Texas, November 5, 1862, quoted in Albaugh, *Tyler, Texas*, 18.

5. Guns for Cotton

Epigraphs were drawn from the following sources: Wigfall quotation from James M. Perry, *A Bohemian Brigade: Civil War Correspondents — Mostly Rough, Sometimes Ready* (New York: Wiley, 2000), 15; Walker quotation from *The War of the Rebellion: A Compilation of the Official Records of the Union and Confederate Armies*, ser. 4 (Washington, D.C.: Government Printing Office, 1900), 1:494; Goodman quotation from John D. Goodman, "The Birmingham Gun Trade," in Samuel Timmins, ed., *The Resources, Products, and Industrial History of Birmingham and the Midland Hardware District: A Series of Reports, Collected by the Local Industries Committee of the British Association at Birmingham, in 1865* (London: Hardwicke, 1866), 393; Anderson quotation from W. Stanley Hoole, ed., *Confederate Foreign Agent: The European Diary of Edward C. Anderson* (University, Ala.: Confederate Publishing, 1976), 39; Huse quotation from *War of the Rebellion*, ser. 4, 1:344, 345; Brown quotation from "Governor's Message" in the *Journal of the Senate of the State of Georgia at the Annual Session of the General Assembly, Begun and Held in Milledgeville, the Seat of Government, in 1862* (Milledgeville, Ga.: Boughton, Nisbet and Barnes, State Printers, 1862), 13.

1. Goodman, "Birmingham Gun Trade," 392.

2. *Illustrated Catalogue of United States Cartridge Company's Collection of Firearms* (Lowell, Mass.: United States Cartridge Company, 1903), 68, item 263.

3. Report of Commander G. H. Scott, USS *Keystone State*, to U.S. secretary of the navy Gideon Welles, October 25, 1861, in *Official Records of the Union and Confederate Navies in the*

War of the Rebellion, ser. 1 (Washington, D.C.: Government Printing Office, 1894), 1:111.

4. Confederate secretary of war George W. Randolph to Georgia governor Joseph E. Brown, April 2, 1862, in *War of the Rebellion*, ser. 1 (Washington, D.C.: Government Printing Office, 1898), 53:229.

6. Southern Ingenuity

Epigraphs in this chapter were drawn from the following sources: Floyd quotation from John B. Floyd, "Report of the Secretary of War, December 3, 1860," in *Message from the President of the United States to the Two Houses of Congress at the Commencement of the Second Session of the Thirty-Sixth Congress* (Washington, D.C.: Bowman, 1860), 161; report of the U.S. Army Ordnance Board quoted in Benjamin Perley Poore, *The Life and Public Services of Ambrose E. Burnside: Soldier, Citizen, Statesman* (Providence, R.I.: Reid, 1882), 86; Mennigerode quotation from "Confederate Papers Relating to Citizens or Business Firms, 1861–1865," Samuel C. Robinson file, Fold3.com, 32; Report of Committee on Patents quotation from "Report of Committee on the Memorial of George W. Morse," in *Reports of Committees of the House of Representatives for the Third Session of the Forty-fifth Congress, 1878–79* (Washington, D.C.: Government Printing Office, 1879), 1:23; Morse quotation from South Carolina Ordnance Department Records, box 1, South Carolina Department of Archives and History, Columbia; Downer quotation from H. L. Sutherland, "Arms Manufactory in Greenville County," in Albert N. Sanders, ed., *Proceedings and Papers of the Greenville County Historical Society, 1968–1971* (Greenville, S.C.: Greenville County Historical Society, 1971), 4:52–53, courtesy of Bob Seigler.

1. Contract between Duff Green and C.S. Ordnance Bureau, represented by Josiah Gorgas, April 2, 1862, in "Confederate Papers Relating to Citizens or Business Firms," Duff C. Green file, Fold3.com, 49.

2. Josiah Gorgas to James H. Burton, March 13, 1862, in James Henry Burton Papers, MSS 117, box 2, folder 28, Yale University Library, New Haven, Connecticut (hereafter cited as Burton Papers).

3. Robert E. Lee to Josiah Gorgas, June 8, 1863, quoted in *The War of the Rebellion: A Compilation of the Official Records of the Union and Confederate Armies*, ser. 1, vol. 27, pt. 3

(Washington, D.C.: Government Printing Office, 1889), 872.

4. Draft affidavit of James H. Burton for submission to Confederate commissioner of patents Rufus R. Rhodes, January 29, 1863, in Burton Papers. The final version, dated February 4, 1863, is quoted in Claud E. Fuller and Richard D. Steuart, *Firearms of the Confederacy* (Lawrence, Mass.: Quarterman, 1944), 202.

5. Burton also stated: "At this time Mr. Alexander seemed to be ignorant of the construction of the Lawrence gas check until it was explained by the deponent" (ibid.).

6. "Gun Locks," *Hampden Whig* (Springfield, Mass.), October 19, 1831; courtesy of Bob Seigler, Greenville, South Carolina.

7. George W. Morse, "Improvement in Cartridges," U.S. Patent 15,996, issued October 28, 1856; available at www.google.com/patents.

8. William H. Bell, "Memoranda for the Honorable Henry Wilson, member of Military Committee of the Senate, concerning the Application of Morse's Breech-Loading Principle to the Muzzle-Loading Arms of the United States," in *The Congressional Globe: Containing the Debates and Proceedings of the First Session of the Thirty-Fifth Congress* (Washington, D.C.: Rives, 1858), 2441.

9. Erskine S. Allin to George W. Morse, November 8, 1860, reprinted in *Memorial of George W. Morse, to the 44th Congress of the United States in Regard to His Claim as the Inventor of the Modern Metallic Cartridge System of Fire-arms* (Washington, D.C.: Moran, 1878), 48.

10. George W. Morse to Confederate secretary of war Leroy P. Walker, March 1861, quoted in *Cases Decided in the Court of Claims at the term of 1891–92, with Abstracts of the Decisions of the Supreme Court in Appealed Cases, October 1891 to May 1899* (Washington, D.C.: Government Printing Office, 1893), 27:367.

11. Quoted in John M. Murphy, *Confederate Carbines and Musketoons: Cavalry Small Arms Manufactured in and for the Southern Confederacy, 1861–1865* (Santa Ana, Calif.: Graphic, 2002), 177–78.

12. William S. Downer to Josiah Gorgas, February 2 or 3, 1863, quoted in ibid., 177–78.

13. William S. Downer to Josiah Gorgas, October 5, 1863, quoted in Sutherland, "Arms Manufactory in Greenville County," 4:52–53; courtesy of Bob Seigler.

14. Petition of George W. Morse, exhibit A in *Memorial of George W. Morse*, 11.

15. Ibid.; "A Bill to Compensate George W. Morse for His Labor and Expenses in Adapting His System of Breech-Loading Fire-Arms and Ammunition to the Arms of the United States," in ibid., 3, 24.

16. Senate Committee on Patents, Report 866 [to accompany S. 1434], March 1, 1879, in *Reports of Committees of the Senate of the United States, Third Session of the Forty-Fifth Congress, 1878–79*, vol. 2 (Washington, D.C.: Government Printing Office, 1879).

17. George W. Morse to the South Carolina General Assembly, December 1, 1863, in *Records of the General Assembly: Petitions, 1863*, number 6, s165015, South Carolina Department of Archives and History, Columbia; courtesy of Bob Seigler.

7. The Specialists

Epigraphs were drawn from the following sources: Confederate veteran quoted in C. A. Stevens, *Berdan's United States Sharpshooters in the Army of the Potomac, 1861–1865* (St. Paul, Minn.: Price-McGill, 1892), 462–63; Berdan sharpshooter poster from Earl J. Coates and John D. McAulay, *Civil War Sharps Carbines and Rifles* (Gettysburg, Pa.: Thomas, 1996), 18; Berdan quotation from Wiley Sword, *Sharpshooter: Hiram Berdan, His Famous Sharpshooters, and Their Sharps Rifles* (Lincoln, R.I.: Mowbray, 1988), 64; Hill quotation from F. S. Harris, "Sharpshooting in Lee's Army," *Confederate Veteran* 3, no. 4 (April 1895): 98; Sedgwick quotation from Martin T. McMahon, "The Death of General John Sedgwick," in *Battles and Leaders of the Civil War* (New York: Century, 1888), 4:175; Strong quotation from Robert Hale Strong, *A Yankee Private's Civil War*, ed. Ashley Halsey (Chicago: Regnery, 1961), 20.

1. Stevens, *Berdan's Sharpshooters*, 205.

2. Josiah Gorgas to Richard Cuyler, May 5, 1862, quoted in John M. Murphy and Howard M. Madaus, *Confederate Rifles and Muskets* (Newport Beach, Calif.: Graphic, 1996), 439.

3. Undated story in "Fred Baker's Scrapbook," unpublished manuscript, Lancaster, New Hampshire Historical Society. See also Faith M. Kent, Lancaster, New Hampshire Historical Society, to George W. Wray Jr., Atlanta, Georgia, May 15, 2000, in Wray Collection object files, Atlanta History Center.

4. Quoted in "Davidson's Telescopes for Fire-Arms," *Engineer*, August 7, 1863, 87; see also Stephen Roberts, "Davidson's Telescopic Rifle Sights" (2010), available at http://springfield arsenal.files.wordpress.com/2010/10/davidson -telescope.pdf.

5. Edward C. Anderson, August 2, 1861, quoted in W. Stanley Hoole, ed., *Confederate Foreign Agent: The European Diary of Edward C. Anderson* (University, Ala.: Confederate Publishing, 1976), 26.

6. Josiah Gorgas to Braxton Bragg, May 29, 1863, quoted in Russ A. Pritchard Jr. and C. A. Huey, "The English Connection: Arms, Material, and Support Furnished to the Confederate States of America by Great Britain," unpublished manuscript in author's possession, draft of November 2011, 171.

7. Sam R. Watkins, *Company Aytch, or, A Side Show of the Big Show* (Nashville: Cumberland Presbyterian Publishing House, 1882), 139–40, quoted in John Anderson Morrow, *The Confederate Whitworth Sharpshooters*, 2nd ed. (published by the author, 2002), 35.

8. Henry W. Thomas, *History of the Doles-Cook Brigade, Army of Northern Virginia, C.S.A.* (Atlanta: Franklin, 1903), 76.

8. Blood and Honor

Epigraphs in this chapter were drawn from the following sources: Robertson quotation from Bell I. Wiley, *The Life of Johnny Reb: The Common Soldier of the Confederacy* (New York: Bobbs-Merrill, 1943), 29; Kell quotation from John McIntosh Kell, *Recollections of a Naval Life, including the Cruises of the Confederate States Steamers "Sumter" and "Alabama"* (Washington, D.C.: Neal, 1900), 134; lines from "Wearing of the Gray" in W. L. Fagan, ed., *Southern War Songs: Campfire, Patriotic, and Sentimental* (New York: Richardson, 1890), 366–67; anonymous Georgia soldier from "Soldiers' Clothing Received," *Richmond Whig*, April 13, 1864; Davis quotation from Jefferson Davis, *A Short History of the Confederate States of America* (Seneca, N.Y.: Belford, 1890), 117–18; Beauregard quotation from Alfred Roman, *The Military Operations of General Beauregard*, 2 vols. (New York: Harper, 1884) 1:148, quoted in John M. Coski, *The Confederate Battle Flag: America's Most Embattled Emblem* (Cambridge, Mass.: Belknap Press, 2005), 10.

1. Joseph E. Brown to the General Assembly of Georgia, November 6, 1862, in Allen D. Candler, *The Confederate Records of the State of Georgia, Compiled and Published under the Authority of the Legislature* (Atlanta: Charles P. Byrd, state printer, 1909), 2:266.

2. Harold S. Wilson, *Confederate Industry: Manufacturers and Quartermasters in the Civil War* (Jackson: University Press of Mississippi, 2002), 176–79.

3. Report of the physician Thomas M. Grimes, October 28, 1862, and Major A. A. Lowther to headquarters of the Army of Northern Virginia, December 2, 1862, in "Compiled Service Records of Confederate Soldiers Who Served in Organizations Raised Directly by the Confederate Government," Fifteenth Alabama Infantry, Thomas J. Nuckolls file, Fold3.com, 15, 18.

4. I am grateful to Bryan Beard of Virginia for this information.

5. Captain J. H. Brooks to General Samuel Cooper, November 14, 1864, in "Compiled Service Records," Edward H. Martin file, Fold3 .com, 53.

6. Report of Captain Frank Markoe in Edward H. Cummins, "Signal Corps of the Confederate States Army," in Benjamin LaBree, ed., *The Confederate Soldier in the Civil War, 1861–1865* (Louisville, Ky.: Courier-Journal Job Printing Company, 1895), 198.

7. Report of F. W. Strong, commanding the USS *Azalea*, July 9, 1864, in *Official Records of the Union and Confederate Navies in the War of the Rebellion*, ser. 1 (Washington, D.C.: Government Printing Office, 1902), 15:564.

8. Captain J. F. Green to Commander J. C. Williamson, commanding the USS *John Adams*, July 2, 1864, in ibid., 15:558; Report of F. W. Strong, July 9, 1864, in ibid., 15:564.

Epilogue

Gorgas epigraph from Sarah Woolfolk Wiggins, ed., *The Journals of Josiah Gorgas, 1857–1878* (Tuscaloosa: University of Alabama Press, 1995), 98.

1. Quoted in James M. McPherson, "American Victory, American Defeat," in Gabor S. Boritt, ed., *Why the Confederacy Lost* (New York: Oxford University Press, 1992), 20.

2. Wiggins, *Journals of Josiah Gorgas*, 157.

3. *Atlanta Daily Intelligencer*, December 19, 1862, quoted in John M. Murphy, *Confederate Carbines and Musketoons: Cavalry Small Arms Manufactured in and for the Southern Confederacy, 1861–1865* (Santa Ana, Calif.: Graphic, 2002), 178.

Researching the Wray Collection An Essay on Sources

What was true for Fuller and Steuart in 1944 is still true today, even after seventy years. We know much more about Confederate military production today than at any point in the past, yet that knowledge inevitably leads to the humbling realization that there is so much more yet to be uncovered. Those of us fortunate enough to be able to work with collections such as George Wray's stand on the shoulders of giants: in addition to Fuller and Steuart are William A. Albaugh, William B. Edwards, Howard M. Madaus, and many others whose lifetimes were devoted to collecting, studying, and researching Confederate artifacts. This book could be written only because of their work, but with the understanding that its information will be challenged and superseded as future generations continue building upon previously published (and in many cases, unpublished) work.

Given the large number of primary and secondary historical sources consulted in the writing of this book, it was decided to create endnotes only for direct quotations, virtually all of which were taken originally from primary sources. Otherwise, there was a real possibility of flooding the text with superscript numbers, thereby distracting readers from the central purpose of the book. As a result, general context and technical information, including data on markings, production numbers, methods of manufacturing, and so forth, are not specifically noted. Instead, such information was derived chiefly (but not solely) from secondary sources. These are discussed here in the hopes that they will serve as an aid for future works on the same or related topics.

General Reference and Battlefield Tactics

There are several general reference works that no arms researcher should be without. Chief among them is Norm Flayderman, *Flayderman's Guide to Antique American Firearms and Their Values*, 9th ed. (Iola, Wisc.: Gun Digest Books, 2007). Since its first edition in 1973, *Flayderman's Guide* has been the best-organized and most authoritative quick reference guide to the vast array of nineteenth-century arms. Another classic is Arcadi Gluckman and L. D. Satterlee, *American Gun Makers* (Harrisburg, Pa.: Stackpole, 1953), an alphabetical listing of all known gun makers, with a brief entry on each. Similarly, Bruce S. Bazelon and William F. McGuinn, *A Directory of American Military Goods, Dealers, and Makers, 1785–1915* (Manassas, Va., 1990), lists makers of accoutrements, uniforms, edged weapons, and other military materiel. A useful primer in identifying metals and the techniques of their finish for firearms and edged weapons is Art Gogan, *Fighting Iron: A Metals Handbook for Arms Collectors* (Lincoln, R.I.: Mowbray, 1999).

The most popular among many fine picture reference books covering Civil War artifacts are two classic volumes from Time-Life Books, *Echoes of Glory: Arms and Equipment of the Confederacy* and *Echoes of Glory: Arms and Equipment of the Union* (Alexandria, Va., 1991). Another excellent visual reference is Shannon Pritchard, *Collecting the Confederacy: Artifacts and Antiques from the War between the States* (New York: Savas Beatie, 2005). Featuring detailed line drawings by the illustrator George Woodbridge, the three-volume set *American Military Equipage, 1851–1872*, by Frederick P. Todd and Michael J. McAfee (Providence, R.I.: Company of Military Historians, 1977), remains a useful, even if somewhat outdated, resource. A wonderful reference covering the history of Civil War collecting and its more famous collections is Stephen W. Sylvia and Michael J. O'Donnell, *The Illustrated History of American Civil War Relics* (Orange, Va.: Moss, 1978).

This book is presented in as much detail as the present limited data permits but THERE IS SO MUCH WE DO NOT KNOW that it will devolve upon some future writer, with more complete information, to give the final story.
—From the introduction to Claud E. Fuller and Richard D. Steuart, *Firearms of the Confederacy* (1944)

The best single summary of how Civil War combat worked—and hence how the artifacts in the Wray Collection were used—is Paddy Griffith, *Battle in the Civil War: Generalship and Tactics in America, 1861–1865* (Mansfield, UK: Fieldbooks, 1986; also published in the United Kingdom by the Crowood Press as *Rally Once Again* and in the United States by Yale University Press as *Battle Tactics of the Civil War*). This book is an excellent companion to Earl J. Hess, *The Rifle Musket in Civil War Combat: Reality and Myth* (Lawrence: University Press of Kansas, 2008). Hess demonstrates conclusively that the new technology of the minié ball and the rifle-musket was less decisive than previously asserted, especially in Grady McWhiney and Perry D. Jamieson, *Attack and Die: Civil War Military Tactics and the Southern Heritage* (Tuscaloosa: University of Alabama Press, 1984). Additionally, two well-written works by Joseph G. Bilby provide enlightening summaries of the tactical uses of muskets, rifle-muskets, carbines, and revolvers from the standpoint of a modern shooter: *Civil War Firearms: Their Historical Background, Tactical Use, and Modern Collecting and Shooting* (Cambridge, Mass.: Da Capo, 1997) and *Small Arms at Gettysburg: Infantry and Cavalry Weapons in America's Greatest Battle* (Yardley, Pa.: Westholme, 2008).

The American System and Mass Production

A central theme in *Confederate Odyssey* is the evolution of the American System of manufacturing, for which there is an extensive body of literature extending well beyond firearms. Two outstanding overviews are David A. Hounshell, *From the American System to Mass Production: The Development of Manufacturing Technology in the United States* (Baltimore: Johns Hopkins University Press, 1984), and Brooke Hindle and Steven Lubar, *Engines of Change: The American Industrial Revolution, 1790–1860* (Washington, D.C.: Smithsonian Institution Press, 1986). A fascinating study of the extent to which interchangeability of parts was achieved in firearms production before the Civil War is Robert B. Gordon, "Who Turned the Mechanical Ideal into Mechanical Reality?," *Technology and Culture* 29, no. 4 (October 1998): 744–78. Gordon's compelling case that interchangeability relied on skilled laborers using hand tools to bring machined parts to their final dimensions helps explain why a shortage of skilled labor was so crippling to the Confederacy.

By far the best case study of the practical challenges involved in the adoption of the American System in firearms manufacture is Merritt Roe Smith, *Harpers Ferry Armory and the New Technology: The Challenge of Change* (Ithaca, N.Y.: Cornell University Press, 1977). Smith's work is ably supported by Richard Colton, ed., *Forge of Innovation: An Industrial History of the Springfield Armory, 1794–1968* (Fort Washington, Pa.: Eastern National, 2008), which was originally a report, "Conservative Innovators and Military Small Arms: An Industrial History of the Springfield Armory, 1794–1968," prepared for the National Park Service in 1989. Though less insightful, two works by Daniel D. Hartzler and James B. Whisker, *The Northern Armory: The United States Armory at Springfield, Massachusetts, 1795–1859* and *The Southern Arsenal: A Study of the United States Arsenal at Harper's Ferry* (Bedford, Pennsylvania: Old Bedford Village, 1980, 1996), provide much useful data, including a list of known employees at Harpers Ferry, with brief biographical information on each.

The adoption (and adaptation) of the American System by the man most often associated with it is addressed by Karyl Lee Kibler Hall and Carolyn Cooper in *Windows on the Works: Industry on the Eli Whitney Site, 1798–1979* (Hamden, Conn.: Eli Whitney Museum, 1985). The definitive work on Whitney firearms of the 1840s and 1850s is Howard M. Madaus, "The Percussion Martial Firearms of Eli Whitney, Jr.," *Armax* [Journal of the Winchester Arms Museum] 2, no. 1 (1988): 7–76, which attempts to classify extant arms into specific types, an attempt since shown to be practically impossible because of the many variants now known in the Wray and other collections. Whitney's work for the State of Connecticut is thoroughly examined in David James Naumec, "The Connecticut Contracted '61 Springfield: The Special Model to the 'Good and Serviceable' Arm," *American Society of Arms Collectors Bulletin* 90 (Spring 2004): 1–16. A good summary of South Carolina's attempt to buy into the American System is Jack A. Meyer, *William Glaze and the Palmetto Armory*, 2nd ed. (Columbia: South Carolina State Museum, 1994). Since the publication of Meyer's work, there has been additional research documenting the northern origins of these arms; see especially Lewis F. Southard, "The Origin of the Palmetto Pistols," *American Society of Arms Collectors Bulletin* 81 (Fall 1999): 29–42. In the same bulletin, see also John R. Ewing, "Asa Holman Waters and the 1842 Musket," 43–52.

U.S. Arms

The best among many reference books on U.S.-made arms before and during the Civil War is George D. Moller, *American Military Shoulder Arms*, vol. 2, *From the 1790s to the End of the Flintlock Period*, and vol.3, *Flintlock Alterations and Muzzleloading Percussion Shoulder Arms, 1840–1865* (Albuquerque: University of New Mexico Press, 2011). These works, along with a previous volume covering the Revolutionary War, provide detailed technical descriptions of every model of U.S. long arm, along with alterations, contract variants, and state production. Besides the works by Moller, the classic reference is Robert M. Reilly, *United States Military Firearms: The Federal Firearms of the Civil War* (Highland Park, N.J.: Gun Room, 1970). Although some of its information is now outdated, the clarity of its line drawings is unsurpassed. Another classic that belongs on every collector's bookshelf is Claud E. Fuller, *The Rifled Musket* (New York: Bonanza, 1958), which covers U.S. muzzle-loading and breech-loading arms. For information on the field use of U.S. arms during and after the war, the best sources are a pair of works by John D. McAulay: *Rifles of the U.S. Army, 1861–1906* and *U.S. Military Carbines from the Civil War and Indian Campaigns to the Spanish-American War and the Philippine Insurrection* (Lincoln, R.I.: Mowbray, 2003, 2006). For additional photographic detail, see James B. Whisker, Larry W. Yantz, and Daniel D. Hartzler, *United States Rifle-Musket Model 1861* and *U.S. Civil War Carbines* (Rochester, N.Y.: Rowe, 2000, 2001). John W. Jordan, *The Eagle on U.S. Firearms* (Union City, Tenn.: Pioneer, 1991), is a highly specialized yet fascinating study of the marks of authority applied to U.S. arms in the nineteenth century.

The U.S. bayonets that served as the models for so many Confederate copies are described in two articles in the *American Society of Arms Collectors Bulletin*: Richard L. Bergland, "Harpers Ferry Sword Bayonets Model 1841 and Model 1855," vol. 90 (Spring 2004): 53–59; and Bergland and Peter A. Albee, "Beautiful Rifles with Pointy Things," vol. 97 (Spring 2008): 23–29. The definitive work on U.S. bayonets is a forthcoming book by Paul D. Johnson, *Civil War Bayonets and Scabbards of the Union Infantryman* (Woonsocket, R.I.: Mowbray). Johnson's work on the subject is covered also in a series of four articles published in *North South Trader's Civil War* in 2013 and 2014. The classic reference on bayonets—and one that heavily influenced George Wray—is Albert N. Hardin Jr., *The American Bayonet, 1776–1964* (Philadelphia: Riling and Lentz, 1964).

C.S. Arms

The starting point for any research on Confederate firearms is still Claud E. Fuller and Richard D. Steuart's classic *Firearms of the Confederacy* (Lawrence, Mass.: Quarterman, 1944). This work is well known as the first comprehensive reference book on the topic, the guidebook for a generation of collectors and historians. Its texts and charts drawn from primary sources are as relevant and useful today as they were in 1944, even if some of the authors' conclusions have been overturned. The other great classics from the mid-twentieth century are William A. Albaugh and Edward Simmons, *Confederate Arms* (New York: Stackpole, 1957), a work whose conclusions have held up remarkably well over the years, and William B. Edwards, *Civil War Guns: The Complete Story of Federal and Confederate Small Arms* (Harrisburg, Pa.: Stackpole, 1962).

Today the standard references on Confederate firearms are two books by John M. Murphy and Howard M. Madaus: *Confederate Carbines and Musketoons: Cavalry Small Arms Manufactured in and for the Southern Confederacy, 1861–1865* (1986; revised and expanded ed., Santa Ana, Calif.: Graphic, 2002), and *Confederate Rifles and Muskets: Infantry Small Arms Manufactured in the Southern Confederacy, 1861–1865* (Newport Beach, Calif.: Graphic, 1996). These works, especially *Confederate Rifles and Muskets*, are by far the most definitive to date and form the basis for the majority of the information presented in *Confederate Odyssey*. As with any reference sources, Madaus and Murphy's books are not without the occasional error or outdated conclusion. Close examination of some of the fourteen Wray Collection arms featured in *Confederate Rifles and Muskets* (Asheville Armory rifles, for example) reveals new evidence not sufficiently accounted for by the authors' conclusions.

The best general overview of Confederate Ordnance Bureau operations is still Frank E. Vandiver's classic *Ploughshares into Swords: Josiah Gorgas and Confederate Ordnance* (Austin: University of Texas Press, 1952). There has been only one biography of James H. Burton, and despite its rather uneven writing, Thomas K. Tate, *From under Iron Eyelids: The Biography of James Henry Burton, Armorer to Three Nations* (Bloomington, Ind.: AuthorHouse, 2006), is an extraordinarily useful work. Although slightly outdated, another critical examination of Burton's contribution to Confederate manufacturing is Eugene K. Wilson III, "James H. Burton and the Development of the Confederate Small Arms Industry" (MA thesis, Old Dominion University, 1976).

Unquestionably the finest study on any of the Confederate national armories is Paul J. Davies's meticulously researched *C.S. Armory, Richmond: A History of the Confederate States Armory, Richmond, Virginia, and the Stock Shop at the C.S. Armory, Macon, Georgia* (Gettysburg, Pa.: Thomas, 2003). This exhaustive work touches also on operations at Harpers Ferry, Fayetteville, Asheville, and elsewhere. There is currently no similar work on the Fayetteville Armory except for Thomas W. Belton's solid but brief "A History of the Fayetteville Arsenal and Armory" (MA thesis, North Carolina State University, 1979). Among the first to attempt histories of the Asheville and Tallassee Armories was William B. Floyd in "The Asheville Armory and Rifle" (*American Society of Arms Collectors Bulletin* 44 [Spring 1981]) and "The Tallassee Armory" (*American Society of Arms Collectors Bulletin* 74 [Spring 1996]), both reprinted in volume two of *Longarms in America* (Easton, Pa.: Mack, 1997; 55–59, 73–87), compiled by George E. Weatherly for the American Society of Arms Collectors. The best scholarly study of the Asheville Armory is Gordon B. McKinney, "Premature Industrialization in Appalachia: The Asheville Armory, 1862–1863," in Kenneth W. Noe and Shannon H. Wilson, eds., *The Civil War in Appalachia: Collected Essays* (Knoxville: University of Tennessee Press, 1997), though the author's focus is on the development of the armory as an industrial enterprise and not on the technical details of the rifles produced there. An outstanding book-length work with a similar focus is Charles B. Dew, *Iron Maker to the Confederacy: Joseph R. Anderson and the Tredegar Iron Works* (Richmond: Library of Virginia, 1999), perhaps the finest case study of a Confederate war industry, including its use of slave labor.

The most comprehensive treatment of state and private arms manufacturing in the Confederacy are Murphy and Madaus's two books, but a number of other sources provide valuable additional information. Chief among them is William A. Albaugh III, *Tyler, Texas, C.S.A.: The Story of the Confederate States Ordnance Works at Tyler, Texas, 1861–1865* (Falls Church, Va., 1958; repr., Wilmington, N.C.: Broadfoot, 1993). This work is so comprehensive in its treatment (including an annotated transcription of the armory's record, or "day," book) that Murphy and Madaus did not attempt additional research on the topic. Madaus updated the information on Texas contractors in *Confederate Rifles and Muskets* with "Contract Rifles of the Texas State Military Board, 1862–1864," *American Society of Arms Collectors Bulletin* 77 (Fall 1997): 17–31. In it, the Wray Collection's rifle attributed in *Confederate Rifles and Muskets* to the Arkadelphia Arsenal in Arkansas is (probably correctly) identified as a product of N. B. Tanner and Company. The best general source on Texas arms of the nineteenth century is Chris Hirsch, *The Texas Gun Trade: A Guide to the Guns Made or Sold in the Lone Star State, 1790–1899* (Woonsocket, R.I.: Mowbray, 2008). In his lavishly illustrated work *North Carolina Schools of Longrifles, 1765–1865* (Thomasville, N.C.: Stone Commercial Printing and Graphics, 2010), William Ivey addresses the Guilford County rifles produced during the Civil War. Michael J. Black adds additional information regarding the field use of these arms in "Clapp, Gates & Company: An Example of the Confederate Arms Production Effort," *Military Collector and Historian* [Journal of the Company of Military Historians] 41, no. 4 (Winter, 1989): 188–93. Another fine article supplementing information given in Murphy and Madaus is Douglas E. Jones, "The Dickson, Nelson Company: Alabama Civil War Gunmakers," *American Society of Arms Collectors Bulletin* 60 (Spring 1989): 29–37. On the only state to maintain its own armory before the war, the standard reference is Giles Cromwell, *The Virginia Manufactory of Arms* (Charlottesville: University of Virginia Press, 1975), which has been supplemented by Craig D. Bell, "Virginia Manufactory of Arms: The Original Operating Years from 1802 through 1821," *American Society of Arms Collectors Bulletin* 104 (Fall 2011): 2–20.

Unsurprisingly, given its central role in Confederate manufacturing, Georgia has its own body of scholarly literature devoted to the subject, beginning with T. Conn Bryan, *Confederate Georgia* (Athens: University of Georgia Press, 1953). Two groundbreaking works are Chad Morgan, *Planters' Progress: Modernizing Confederate Georgia* (Gainesville: University Press of Florida, 2005), and Mary A. DeCredico, *Patriotism for Profit: Georgia's Urban Entrepreneurs and the Confederate War Effort* (Chapel Hill: University of North Carolina Press, 1990). Though focused on Georgia, both studies have broader implications for Confederate manufacturing; Morgan's book is also an excellent microstudy of the internal conflicts that contributed to Confederate defeat. An especially useful work documenting slave labor in Confederate manufacturing is Clarence L. Mohr, *On the Threshold of Freedom: Masters and Slaves in Civil War Georgia* (Athens: University of Georgia Press, 1986). There has been no book-length study of the Cook and Brother Armory, though there are a number of good summary articles, such as Penn Templeman, "Cook and Brother, Confederate Armory, Athens, Georgia," *Man at Arms for the Gun and Sword Collector* 34, no. 3 (June 2012): 27–30.

Edged Weapons and Revolvers

Though not strongly emphasized in the Wray Collection, Confederate edged weapons have their own body of reference works, beginning with two excellent books by William A. Albaugh. Even after fifty years, *Confederate Edged Weapons* and *A Photographic Supplement of Confederate Swords* (Falls Church, Va., 1960, 1963; both repr., Wilmington, N.C.: Broadfoot, 1993) are standard references for collectors. Albaugh's fine work has been supplemented recently by more-detailed studies such as John W. McAden Jr. and Chris E. Fonvielle Jr., *Louis Froelich: Arms-Maker to the Confederacy* (Carolina Beach, N.C.: Slapdash, 2008), and Jack Melton, Josh Phillips, and John Sexton, *Confederate Bowie Knives* (Woonsocket, R.I.: Mowbray, 2012). Richard H. Bezdek, *American Swords and Sword Makers*, 2 vols. (Boulder, Colo.: Paladin, 1994, 1999), provides valuable data on the locations and working dates of Confederate weapons makers. By far the best technical references on the U.S. edged weapons that served as models for so many Confederate copies are John H. Thillmann's *Civil War Cavalry and Artillery Sabers: A Study of United States Cavalry and Artillery Sabers, 1833–1865* (Lincoln, R.I.: Mowbray, 2001) and *Civil War Army Swords: A Study of United States Army Swords from 1832 through 1865* (Mowbray, 2008). For additional articles on all aspects of American edged weapons, see George E. Weatherly and Robert A. Sadler, eds., *Book of Edged Weapons* (Ephrata, Pa.: Cadmus, 2004), a compilation of articles from the *American Society of Arms Collectors Bulletin* from the previous fifty years.

On Confederate revolvers, the classic reference books are William A. Albaugh III, Hugh Benet Jr., and Edward N. Simmons, *Confederate Handguns: Concerning the Guns, the Men Who Made Them, and the Times of Their Use* (New York: Bonanza, 1963), and Albaugh's *The Confederate Brass-Framed Colt and Whitney* (Falls Church, Va., 1955; repr., Wilmington, N.C.: Broadfoot, 1993). These classics are supplemented by William A. Gary, *Confederate Revolvers* (Dallas: Taylor, 1987). One of the most comprehensive case studies of any Confederate manufacturing facility is Matthew W. Norman, *Colonel Burton's Spiller and Burr Revolver: An Untimely Venture in Confederate Small-Arms Manufacturing* (Macon, Georgia: Mercer University Press, 1996). See also George E. Weatherly and Robert A. Sadler, eds., *Book of Historic Handguns* (Lancaster, Pa.: Cadmus, 2011), another compilation of articles from the *American Society of Arms Collectors Bulletin*.

Imported Weapons and Blockade-Running

Given the large number of foreign arms imported by both the Union and the Confederacy, the subject has received surprisingly little attention until recently. The only work approaching a comprehensive reference is David Noe, Larry W. Yantz, and James B. Whisker, *Firearms from Europe* (Rochester, N.Y.: Rowe, 1999), which provides a useful and reliable classification of British, French, Belgian, Austrian, German, and other European arms of the Civil War era. The authors rely in part on Daniel M. Roche, "The Acquisition and Use of Foreign Shoulder Arms by the Union Army, 1861–1865" (PhD diss., University of Colorado, 1949), which attempts to quantify the number of foreign arms in use during the war and provides the figure of 250,000 arms captured on the battlefield by Confederate forces. The best work to date on imported bayonets is David Noe and Joseph Serbaroli Jr., *European Bayonets of the American Civil War* (Woonsocket, R.I.: Mowbray, 2013).

For French-made arms, the best single reference source is Jean Boudriot, *Armes à Feu Françaises Modèles Réglementaires, 1833–1918* [French Regulation Model Firearms] (La Tour-du-Pin, France: Editions du Portail, 1997), which is well illustrated with detailed line drawings. Jack Puaud and Christian Mery, *Les Armes à Feu de la Défense Nationale et Leurs Baïonnettes, 1870–1871* [Firearms for National Defense and Their Bayonets] (Chaumont, France: Éditions Crépin-Leblond, 2007), provides excellent summaries of the numbers of French, British, and U.S. Civil War–era arms used in the Franco-Prussian War, with useful descriptions and photographs of each type of arm.

The starting point for any study of British firearms is a series of detailed studies published in the United Kingdom, the most important of which is C. H. Roads, *The British Soldier's Firearm: From Smoothbore to Smallbore, 1850–1864* (London: Jenkins, 1964; repr., Livonia, N.Y.: R and R Books, 1994), followed closely by a brief but definitive guidebook: Dewitt W. Bailey, *British Military Longarms, 1815–1865* (Harrisburg, Pa.: Stackpole, 1972). To this list should be added Howard L. Blackmore, *British Military Firearms, 1650–1850* (London: Jenkins, 1961), as well as a deft summary by Peter Smithurst, *The Pattern 1853 Enfield Rifle* (Botley, UK: Osprey, 2011). A fine technical reference book spelling out the many and often-confusing British government markings found on nineteenth- and twentieth-century arms is Ian D. Skennerton, *The Broad Arrow: British and Empire Factory Production, Proof, Inspection, Armourers, Unit, and Issue Markings* (Labrador, Australia, 2001; distributed in North America by Arms and Militaria Press, Grants Pass, Oregon). A useful summary of proof marks is a booklet issued by the Worshipful Company of Gunmakers of the City of London and the Guardians of the Birmingham Proof House, *Notes on the Proof of Shotguns and Other Small Arms* (Birmingham: Kynoch, 1960). On bayonets, the best general guidebook is R. J. Wilkinson Latham, *British Military Bayonets from 1700 to 1945* (New York: Arco, 1969). An excellent summary of the methods of noninterchangeable arms production in the United Kingdom is Craig L. Barry, "The Birmingham System of Gun Manufacture," *Military Collector and Historian* 64, no. 4 (Winter 2012): 226–30, as well as David Williams's book-length study covering the entire nineteenth century, *The Birmingham Gun Trade* (Stroud, UK: History Press, 2004).

The first comprehensive reference work on British-made arms and military equipment imported into the Confederacy is the forthcoming volume by Russ A. Pritchard Jr. and C. A. Huey, *The English Connection: Arms, Material, and Support Furnished to the Confederate States of America by Great Britain* (Gettysburg, Pa.: Thomas). This work, which was used extensively in the writing of chapter 5 of *Confederate Odyssey*, addresses the configurations and markings of British-made weapons, whose proliferation and seemingly enigmatic variations had previously discouraged researchers from attempting such a work. Another recent book that unravels many of the same mysteries is a small but well-illustrated volume by Steven W. Knott, *The Confederate Enfield* (published by the author, 2013). A solid overview originally provided for the benefit of historical reenactors is Craig L. Barry, *The Civil War Musket: A Handbook for Historical Accuracy*, bound with *Lock, Stock, and Barrel: Modifications for Reproduction Civil War Era Enfield and U.S. Pattern Muskets and Rifle-Muskets*, 2nd ed. (Warren, Mich.: Watchdog Quarterly, 2011). Barry and David C. Burt provide a great deal of valuable information on English gun and accoutrement makers, in *Suppliers to the Confederacy: British Imported Arms and Accoutrements* (Atglen, Pa.: Schiffer, 2012). See also a small paperback book by the same authors, *Supplier to the Confederacy: S. Isaac Campbell & Co., London* (Sandy, UK: Authors OnLine, 2010), which is a revised and expanded edition of David Burt's *Major Caleb Huse C.S.A. and S. Isaac Campbell & Co.* Before these works, the only reliable similar reference was Wiley Sword, *Firepower from Abroad: The Confederate Enfield and LeMat Revolver* (Lincoln, R.I.: Mowbray, 1986).

On the famous LeMat revolvers, the most definitive work to date is Doug Adams, *The Confederate LeMat Revolver* (Lincoln, R.I.: Mowbray, 2005). This book updates previous research by Valmore J. Forgett, Alain F. Serpette, and Marie-Antoinette Serpette, *LeMat: The Man, the Gun* (Ridgefield, N.J., 1996; also available through Arms and Militaria Press, Grants Pass, Oregon). Further useful and practical observations on the field use of LeMats are contained in Frederick R. Edmunds, "Some Thoughts on the Confederate LeMat Revolver," *American Society of Arms Collectors Bulletin* 100 (Fall 2009): 25–28. For information on Kerr revolvers and the London Armoury beyond what is covered in Pritchard and Huey's work, see Valmore J. Forgett, "Why Kerrs?," *American Society of Arms Collectors Bulletin* 97 (Fall 2007): 5–19.

By far the best work to date on Confederate blockade-running is Stephen R. Wise, *Lifeline of the Confederacy: Blockade Running during the Civil War* (Columbia: University of South Carolina Press, 1988), with appendices listing all known ships engaged in the trade, along with their physical characteristics, lists of ships entering and clearing southern ports, and other technical data. This work is an excellent source for understanding the intricacies of the trade and the complicated logistics of running steamers past the blockade. Wise's work is ably supported by C. L. Webster III, *Entrepot: Government Imports into the Confederate States* (Roseville, Minn.: Edinborough, 2010), which gives detailed information on the contents of specific cargoes, organized by port of entry. Thomas Boaz, *Guns for Cotton: England Arms the Confederacy* (Shippensburg, Pa.: Burd Street, 1996), is a useful thumbnail sketch of blockade-running operations, as is Catherine L. Deichman, *Rogues and Runners: Bermuda and the American Civil War* (Hamilton, Bermuda: Bermuda National Trust, 2003). Two works outlining the financial underpinnings of the Confederacy's transatlantic arms trade are Richard I. Lester, *Confederate Finance and Purchasing in Great Britain* (Charlottesville: University Press of Virginia, 1975), and Ethel Trenholm Seabrook Nepveux, *George A. Trenholm: Financial Genius of the Confederacy* (Anderson, S.C.: Electric City, 1999). A fascinating study on the extent to which the C.S. Ordnance Bureau shifted distribution priorities according to the types of arms that it was able to obtain through the blockade is Howard M. Madaus, "Small Arms Deliveries through Wilmington, N.C. in 1863: The Impact on Confederate Ordnance Policy," *American Society of Arms Collectors Bulletin* 85 (Spring 2002): 51–58.

Breech-Loading Arms and Sharpshooter Rifles

There is surprisingly little reference material on Confederate breechloaders other than that contained in the classic sources such as Fuller and Steuart's *Firearms of the Confederacy* and Murphy and Madaus's *Confederate Carbines and Musketoons*. The use of Maynard carbines by southern states is given detailed treatment in John D. McAulay, "Dr. Maynard's Secessionist Gun (1st Model Maynard)," *Man at Arms*, May–June, 1990, 29–38, and Howard M. Madaus, "The Maynard Rifle and Carbine in Confederate Service," *American Society of Arms Collectors Bulletin* 52 (Spring 1985), collected in *Longarms in America* 2:95–108. A similar contribution is William B. Floyd, "The Confederate Sharps," *American Society of Arms Collectors Bulletin* 35 (Fall 1976), also in *Longarms in America*, 2:89–94. Northern-made Sharps rifles are described through the use of reprinted primary sources in Martin Rywell, *Sharps Rifle: The Gun That Shaped American Destiny* (Harriman, Tenn., 1957; repr., Union City, Tenn.: Pioneer Press, 1979). Their battlefield use is documented in Earl J. Coates and John D. McAulay, *Civil War Sharps Carbines and Rifles* (Gettysburg, Pa.: Thomas, 1996). Although his focus is ammunition, Dean S. Thomas presents a great deal of well-documented information on Union and Confederate breechloaders in *Roundball to Rimfire: A History of Small Arms Ammunition*: part 2, *Federal Breechloading Carbines and Rifles*, and part 4, *A Contribution to the History of the Confederate Ordnance Bureau* (Gettysburg, Pa.: Thomas, 2002, 2010). H. Jackson Knight, *Confederate Invention: The Story of the Confederate States Patent Office and Its Inventors* (Baton Rouge: Louisiana State University Press, 2011), is an incredible resource, with biographical profiles of all Confederate patentees and extended notes on the most significant patents, including that of Charles W. Alexander.

There are no significant articles or books on George W. Morse, though his prewar alterations for the U.S. Army are covered in volume two of George D. Moller's *American Military Shoulder Arms*. Robert Seigler of Greenville, South Carolina, is preparing a book tentatively titled *George W. Morse: His Breech Loading Carbine and the South Carolina State Military Works*. Some of Seigler's research is incorporated into chapter 6, in addition to primary-source material compiled by George Wray. William Ray Cresswell provides additional data on the Linder alterations of the same period in "Combat Elegance: Edward Linder, His Carbines, and the Amoskeag Manufacturing Company," *American Society of Arms Collectors Bulletin* 98 (Spring 2008): 70–78.

Perhaps the best place to begin a study of Civil War sharpshooting is Earl J. Hess's previously mentioned *The Rifle Musket in Civil War Combat*, which devotes three chapters to the topic, exploring the practical differences between skirmishing and sniping on the battlefield. Hess's conclusions on the evolution of Confederate sharpshooting units are supported by Gary Yee, "Confederate Sharpshooter Selection: From Falstaff's Army to Fighting Elite," *Military Collector and Historian* 61, no. 2 (Summer 2009): 136–40. The best work on Berdan's Sharpshooters is Wiley Sword, *Sharpshooter: Hiram Berdan, His Famous Sharpshooters, and Their Sharps Rifles* (Lincoln, R.I.: Mowbray, 1988). For the full story on the gun-making career of Thomas Morse, see Michael Carroll and Gordon L. Jones, "Thomas Morse: A Yankee Confederate Yankee Gunsmith," *American Society of Arms Collectors Bulletin* 105 (Fall 2012): 47–57.

The fabled Whitworth rifle is a collecting specialty in itself, with a body of literature too extensive to mention in its entirety here. Two seminal articles describing the guns and their production were written by the noted British arms historian Dewitt W. Bailey, "Whitworth's Percussion Rifles," *Guns Review*, March 1969, 96–102, and "The Whitworth Rifle: A Great Milestone in Rifle History," in John T. Amber, ed., *Gun Digest 1971: Silver Anniversary Deluxe Edition* (Northfield, Ill.: Gun Digest Company, 1971),

94–105. The best work detailing the battlefield use of Whitworth rifles is John A. Morrow, *The Confederate Whitworth Sharpshooters*, 2nd ed. (published by the author, 2002). Also indispensable is Steven Roberts, "Davidson's Telescopic Rifle Sight" (2010), available at www.springfieldarsenal.files.wordpress.com/2010/10/davidson-telescope.pdf. Another useful article describing the "second-quality" rifles is R. E. Neville, "The Confederate Whitworth Rifle," *North South Trader's Civil War* 29, no. 2 (2002): 38–44. Jack W. Melton Jr. describes one of the Confederate-used Whitworth rifles from the Wray Collection in "Confederate Imported Whitworth Rifle B933," *Man at Arms for the Gun and Sword Collector* 35, no. 1 (February 2013): 27–30. A useful article especially focused on Whitworth artillery pieces is William E. Brundage, "Joseph Whitworth and His Guns," *American Society of Arms Collectors Bulletin* 64 (Spring 1991): 45–51. Reliable insights on the Kerr rifle are provided by Bill Adams in "Thoughts on the Confederate Kerr Rifle: The 'Poor Man's Whitworth,'" *Black Powder* [Quarterly Magazine of the Muzzle Loaders Association of Great Britain], Spring 2013, 28–32, found under the larger heading "The Kerr Rifle Project."

Uniforms, Flags, and Accoutrements

Any research on Confederate enlisted uniforms should begin with Leslie D. Jensen's landmark "A Survey of Confederate Central Government Quartermaster Issue Jackets," part 1, *Military Collector and Historian* 41, no. 3 (Fall 1989): 109–22, and part 2, *Military Collector and Historian* 41, no. 4 (Winter 1989): 162–71. The result of many years of research and observation, this article provided the first classification of extant Confederate uniform jackets based on their probable points of origin at depots of the Confederate Clothing Bureau. Jensen provides further information and detailed analyses of clothing as seen in period photographs in *Johnny Reb: The Uniform of the Confederate Army, 1861–1865* (Mechanicsburg, Pa.: Stackpole, 1996). For additional descriptive material taken from Confederate letters, newspapers, and other accounts, see Thomas M. Arliskas, *Cadet Gray and Butternut Brown: Notes on Confederate Uniforms* (Gettysburg, Pa.: Thomas, 2006). A useful visual reference for Union and Confederate clothing, headgear, and accoutrements is Earl J. Coates, Michael J. McAfee, and Don Troiani, *Don Troiani's Regiments and Uniforms of the Civil War* (Mechanicsburg, Pa.: Stackpole, 2002).

There is a considerable body of literature addressing nineteenth-century men's fashions and the evolution of the ready-made clothing industry. These include Lois W. Banner, *American Beauty* (New York: Knopf, 1983), Anne Hollander, *Sex and Suits* (New York: Knopf, 1995), and Claudia B. Kidwell and Margaret C. Christman, *Suiting Everyone: The Democratization of Clothing in America* (Washington, D.C.: Smithsonian Institution Press, 1974). Patrick Brown, *"For Fatigue Purposes": The Army Sack Coat of 1857–1872* (Warren, Mich.: Watchdog Quarterly, 2003), addresses the mass production of Union army clothing, as does John P. Langellier, *Army Blue: The Uniform of Uncle Sam's Regulars, 1848–1873* (Atglen, Pa.: Schiffer, 1998). Of the number of works addressing the impact of the sewing machine, perhaps the best is Grace Rogers Cooper, *The Sewing Machine: Its Invention and Development* (Washington, D.C.: Smithsonian Institution Press, 1976).

Also essential for the identification of enlisted men's and officers' uniforms are several reference books on buttons, another field of specialized collecting. These works include Warren K. Tice, *Uniform Buttons of the United States, 1776–1865* (Gettysburg, Pa.: Thomas, 1997), which updates Alphaeus S. Albert's classic *Record of American Uniform and Historical Buttons, Bicentennial Edition* (Boyertown Pa.: Boyertown, 1976). Another valuable source is William F. McGuinn and Bruce S. Bazelon, *American Military Button Makers and Dealers: Their Backmarks and Dates*, expanded ed. (Chelsea, Mich.: BookCrafters, 1988).

The most impressive scholarly work to date on Confederate flags is John M. Coski, *The Confederate Battle Flag: America's Most Embattled Emblem* (Cambridge, Mass.: Belknap Press, 2005), a superb study of the origins, uses, meanings, and mythologies surrounding the southern-cross design. An essential illustrated primer on Confederate flags is Devereaux D. Cannon Jr., *The Flags of the Confederacy: An Illustrated History* (Memphis, Tenn.: St. Luke's, 1988), as well as *Flags of the Confederacy*, an extensive website maintained by Gregg Biggs, Tom Belton, Robert B. Bradley, Bruce Graetz, and other contributors at Confederate-Flags.org. Essential published sources include Howard M. Madaus and Robert D. Needham, *Battle Flags of the Confederate Army of Tennessee* (Milwaukee: Milwaukee Public Museum, 1976), and Madaus and Needham, "Unit Colors of the Trans-Mississippi Confederacy," published in three parts in *Military Collector and Historian*: part 1 in vol. 41, no. 3 (Fall 1989): 123–41; part 2 in vol. 41, no.

4 (Winter 1989): 172–82; and part 3 in vol. 42, no. 1 (Spring 1990): 16–21. See also Howard M. Madaus, "Rebel Flags Afloat: A Survey of the Surviving Flags of the Confederate States Navy, Revenue Service, and Merchant Marine," *Flag Bulletin* 115, nos. 1–2 (January–April 1986). An important article on the origin of many of the Confederate flags now in state collections and the Museum of the Confederacy in Richmond is Charles M. Nusbaum, "The Return of the War Department Captured Flags to the States, 1905–1906," *Military Collector and Historian* 60, no. 4 (Winter 2008): 261–73. Glenn Dedmondt has produced a fine series of illustrated paperbacks on the Civil War flags of South Carolina, Alabama, North Carolina, Missouri, and Arkansas (Gretna, La.: Pelican, 2000–2009).

The best work to date on the operations of the Confederate Quartermaster Bureau is Harold S. Wilson, *Confederate Industry: Manufacturers and Quartermasters in the Civil War* (Jackson: University Press of Mississippi, 2002), followed closely by Richard D. Goff's classic volume, *Confederate Supply* (Durham, N.C.: Duke University Press, 1969). Reference books and articles on Civil War accoutrements are numerous, but a good starting point is Paul D. Johnson, *Civil War Cartridge Boxes of the Union Infantryman* (Lincoln, R.I.: Mowbray, 1998), which provides a solid foundation for understanding the essential forms and construction techniques copied and adapted by Confederate accoutrement makers. Two articles by David Jarnagin and Ken R. Knopp in *Military Collector and Historian* further define the differences between northern and southern production: "Military Leather in the Nineteenth Century: Its Methods and Secrets," vol. 61, no. 1 (Spring 2009): 56–61, and "Confederate Leather: Black or Brown? How and Where?," vol. 61, no. 2 (Summer 2009): 111–18. By far the most exhaustive research on canteens is Michael J. O'Donnell, *U.S. Army and Militia Canteens, 1775–1910* (Alexandria, Va.: O'Donnell, 2008), which is supplemented by an excellent article by David Burt, "Canteens of the Army of Northern Virginia: The Emergence of the Gardner," available on the web page of the American Civil War Society (UK), www.acws .co.uk/archives/military/anvgardner.htm. Essential studies of Confederate belt plates include the Sydney C. Kerksis classic, *Plates and Buckles of the American Military, 1795–1874* (Kennesaw, Ga.: Gilgal, 1974), as well as the authoritative work on the subject by Steve Mullinax, *Confederate Belt Buckles and Plates* (Alexandria, Va.: O'Donnell, 1991), and additional work by Michael J. O'Donnell and J. Duncan Campbell, *American Military Belt Plates* (Alexandria, Va.: O'Donnell, 1996).

Primary Resources

The vast majority of information presented in *Confederate Odyssey* relating to the provenance of its objects and the personal stories surrounding them was derived from primary sources, especially the sixteen file boxes of research material assembled by George Wray over his fifty years of collecting. Research that took George Wray months to accomplish can now be done in a matter of minutes by accessing some of the records of the National Archives and Records Administration through an online subscription to Fold 3 (Fold3.com). Especially valuable are materials from Record Group 109 (the U.S. War Department Collection of Confederate Records), particularly the Confederate Citizens Files, which document transactions between the Confederate government and private contractors for war materiel and other supplies. Also important are the personnel files of Confederate Ordnance Bureau officers such as James H. Burton, Richard M. Cuyler, and Amasa W. King. A subscription to Ancestry.com, another essential research tool, enables the identification, through census and other records, of many (though not all) individual gun makers and soldiers. Ancestry.com is linked to Find a Grave (Findagrave.com), a searchable database containing more than 100,000,000 grave records.

Google Books, another indispensable resource, contains thousands of nineteenth-century congressional reports, technical manuals, and other relevant volumes, especially *The War of the Rebellion: A Compilation of the Official Records of the Union and Confederate Armies*. Containing mainly after-action reports and communications from commanders of both sides, the *Official Records* (usually known simply as the "ORs") is the most extensive collection of primary sources on the Civil War. The Internet Archive (Archive.org), which is maintained by a consortium of libraries around the world, contains thousands of period military manuals and books in easily downloadable formats, including PDFs. All the specifications and drawings for nineteenth-century U.S. patents are available by searching Google Patents (www.google .com/patents). Another wonderful resource is *Confederate Veteran* magazine (1893–1932), a complete run of which is available online through the University of Pennsylvania (onlinebooks.library.upenn.edu).

The Library of Virginia has a searchable index to *Confederate Veteran* on its website (www.lva.virginia.gov). The Library of Congress maintains digital copies of newspapers from all over the United States at its *Chronicling America: Historic American Newspapers* site (chroniclingamerica.loc.gov), which is searchable by keyword. A collection of digitized and searchable Georgia newspapers covering the Confederate manufacturing centers of Columbus, Macon, Atlanta, and Athens is available through the Digital Library of Georgia (dlg.galileo.usg.edu).

The most essential primary sources for the study of Confederate artifacts are the artifacts themselves. The Atlanta History Center collection includes approximately 12,000 Civil War–related objects, most of which were originally assembled in private collections by Sydney C. Kerksis, Thomas S. Dickey, the DuBose Family, and George W. Wray. Similarly, the private collections assembled by the pioneer arms researchers Claud E. Fuller and Richard Steuart (*Firearms of the Confederacy*) are housed in museums. Fuller's collection of nearly 350 long arms from the Revolutionary War through World War I is exhibited at the Chickamauga and Chattanooga National Military Park, and more than 860 pieces from Steuart's collection of Confederate arms are housed at the Virginia Historical Society in Richmond. The collections of William A. Albaugh (*Confederate Arms* and *Confederate Edged Weapons*, among others) and William B. Edwards (*Civil War Guns*) were dispersed into private collections after their deaths, and a few pieces from those collections are now part of the Wray Collection. John M. Murphy and Howard M. Madaus's *Confederate Carbines and Musketoons* and *Confederate Rifles and Muskets* are based on the Murphy Collection of some 150 arms, now exhibited at the Greensboro Historical Museum in North Carolina. The Murphy Collection is the most comprehensive and specialized collection of its type, differing from the Wray collection in that it includes only Confederate-made or Confederate-altered arms, and does not include U.S.-made arms in their original state or British-made arms.

Most famously, the Museum of the Confederacy in Richmond maintains 15,000 objects related to the Confederacy, including the nation's largest collection of identified Confederate flags and uniforms as well as objects relating to the southern civilian experience. The National Museum of American History (Smithsonian Institution) includes an impressive Civil War collection, including all the Civil War uniform and clothing samples saved by the U.S. Quartermaster Department. In addition to the Fuller Collection, the National Park Service houses a number of fine collections in visitors' centers at the national battlefields, military parks, and historic sites maintained by the service, including the Sweeney Collection at Wilson's Creek National Battlefield, the Rosensteel Collection (among others) at Gettysburg National Military Park, and the massive collection of some 9,000 arms at the Springfield Armory National Historic Site. This collection is the American equivalent of the much larger collections of arms (including many used in the Civil War) at the Royal Armouries museums in England, the Musée de l'Armée in Paris, and the Musée Royal de l'Armée et d'Histoire Militaire in Brussels.

Significant state collections—many of which were first assembled by the United Daughters of the Confederacy in the early twentieth century—include the North Carolina State Museum (Raleigh), the South Carolina Confederate Relic Room and Military Museum (Columbia), the Confederate Museum (Market Hall, Charleston), the Tennessee State Museum (Nashville), Louisiana's Civil War Museum at Confederate Memorial Hall (New Orleans), and the Texas Civil War Museum (Fort Worth). In addition, there are dozens of superb private collections throughout the United States and in other parts of the world, essential resources informing the many reference books and articles mentioned in this essay, nearly all of which were researched and written by private collectors.

Index

Craig, Henry, 35
Cranberry Iron Works (N.C.), 133, 139, 147, 148
Crenshaw, Robert, 298
Crenshaw and Collie and Company, 211
Crescent Regiment (La.), 82
Crimean War, 45, 215, 222, 252
Cromwell, Giles, 424
Crook, George, 382
Cross, Nathaniel D., 198
Crystal Palace exhibition (1851), 236
C.S. Armory, Asheville, N.C., 111, 145–49, 414, 424; guns made at, 150–54, 423; markings of, 123, 149–53; production figures for, 111, 147–48; slave labor at, 147
C.S. Armory, Athens, Ga., 182
C.S. Armory, Columbia, S.C., 111, 148–49
C.S. Armory, Fayetteville, N.C., 138–39, 221, 414; ammunition made at, 285; bayonets made at, 143, 145; capture of, 112, 139; guns made at, 26, 63, 140–45; machinery at, 109–10; markings of, 23, 141, 143; production figures for, 112, 139, 145; shortages at, 111
C.S. Armory, Holly Springs, Miss., 74–75, 278
C.S. Armory, Macon, Ga., 122, 210, 237, 424; machinery at, 110–12, 148; revolvers of, 176–77; sharpshooter rifles of, 3–4, 332–33; slave labor at, 7
C.S. Armory, Richmond, Va., 6–7, 119–22, 414, 424; accoutrements made at, 387; bayonets made at, 88, 135; breech-loading arms made at, 276, 281; guns made at, 26, 121–34, 136, 285; and interchangeable parts, 120–21; machinery at, 109–10, 113; production figures for, 112, 122, 130; shortages at, 111
C.S. Armory, Tallassee, Ala., 120, 182, 273, 277, 290
C.S. Armory, Tyler, Tex., 201–2, 205–8, 424
C.S. Arsenal, Atlanta, Ga., 74, 169
C.S. Arsenal, Augusta, Ga., 169
C.S. Arsenal, Charleston, S.C., 107
C.S. Arsenal, Columbia, Tenn., 68
C.S. Arsenal, Columbus, Ga., 169, 196
C.S. Arsenal, Columbus, Miss., 76–78
C.S. Arsenal, Danville, Va., 287
C.S. Arsenal, Macon, Ga., 169
C.S. Arsenal, Memphis, Tenn., 68, 69, 76–78, 414
C.S. Arsenal, Nashville, Tenn., 68, 69, 74, 169, 414; Morse, George Woodward, at, 308; saber made at, 95
C.S. Arsenal, Selma, Ala., 76, 190
C.S. Ordnance Bureau, 88, 111, 157, 412–13; and Alabama Arms Manufacturing Company,

190–91; ammunition made by, 386; and Atlanta Arsenal, 169; blockade-running ships of, 211–12, 234; and breech-loading carbines, 272–73, 309; and Cook and Brother Armory, 181; European imports of, 249–50; inspectors of, 284, 308, 310; state purchases competing with, 249–50, 256
C.S. Powder Works, Augusta, Ga., 110, 411
C.S. Quartermaster Bureau, 386–93, 429; blockade-running ships of, 211–12, 357; canteens of, 392; Clothing Bureau of, 268, 356–61, 372, 395–96, 411; European imports of, 211–12, 250–51; and Georgia textiles, 171, 356–57; literature on, 429; railroad control by, 156
Cuba, blockade-runners from, 211
Curtis, Isaac, 221
cutlasses, 96, 98, 180, 189. *See also* swords
Cuyler, Richard M., 332–33

Danville, Va., 287
Davidson, David, 340, 342–43, 428
Davies, Paul J., 424
Davis, Henry J., 193, 412
Davis, Jefferson, 155, 212, 250, 272, 308; family of, 364; in Mexican War, 18, 42; as U.S. secretary of war, 26, 35, 274, 275, 411; as U.S. senator, 42, 294
Davis and Bozeman Company (Coosa County, Ala.), 191, 193–96
DeCredico, Mary A., 424
Dedmondt, Glenn, 429
Deichman, Catherine L., 427
Deringer, Henry, 78
Dew, Charles B., 424
Dickey, Thomas S., 5, 136, 430
Dickson, Nelson, and Company, 158, 169, 190, 414; carbines made by, 199; production figures for, 191; rifles made by, 198; sharpshooter rifle made by, 338
Dickson, William, 198
Dimond, Robert K., 403
Doles, George P., 348
Downer, William S., 146, 147, 148; on Morse, George Woodward, carbines, 309, 314; on South Carolina State Military Works, 308, 310
DuBose, Beverly M., Jr., 4
DuBose, Beverly M., III, 4
DuBose, Julius J., 200
DuBose Collection at Atlanta History Museum, 4–6, 152, 220, 260, 430
Duff, James, 404, 405

Edward Brooks and Son (Birmingham, England), 230
Edwards, William B., 261, 421, 423, 430
E. J. Johnston and Company (Macon, Ga.), 94
Eley Brothers (London, England), 345
Ellis, John W., 110, 138
Elwell, Henry, 76
Enfield (British Pattern 1853) rifle-muskets, 30, 45, 155, 172, 190, 201; bayonets for, 226, 230; of Belgian toy maker, 235; Confederate purchases of, 209–10, 249–50, 255, 256, 258; gunstocks of, 217; interchangeable parts of, 30, 215, 236; literature on, 426; locks of, 206, 216; markings on, 215–20, 223, 224; as model for Confederate arms, 172, 190, 201, 222–23; Union purchasing of, 249, 250; and Whitworth rifles, 339
E. Remington and Sons (Ilion, N.Y.), 329
Erhard, Adolf A., 204
Erlanger and Company, 210, 237
Estvan, Bela, 98
Evans, Nathan George "Shanks," 366

Fall and Cunningham Company, 70
Farragut, David, 92, 180
Fayetteville, N.C., 138, 159. *See also* C.S. Armory, Fayetteville, N.C.
Fingal (ship), 230, 257, 265, 269, 371
Fire Arm Manufacturing Company (Baltimore, Md.), 306
Flagg, Benjamin, 47, 53
flags, 5, 80, 183, 355–56, 394–408; literature on, 428–29
Flayderman, Norm, 421
flintlocks, 15–17; alterations to, 53, 56, 57, 60; breech-loading, 274, 278, 287, 288
Florence, N.C., state armory at, 159, 160
Floyd, John B., 56, 64, 271, 274, 294, 304
Fonvielle, Chris E., Jr., 425
Foote, Shelby, 409
Forgett, Valmore J., 426
Forrest, Nathan Bedford, 188, 364
Forsyth, John, 18
Fort Fisher, N.C., 139, 212, 353
Fort Johnston (Charleston, S.C.), 403
Fort Leavenworth, Kans., 21
Fort Sumter (Charleston, S.C.), 1, 47, 79, 81
Fort Wagner (Charleston, S.C.), 398, 399, 403
Frank, Theophilus, 378
Frankford, Pa., U.S. Arsenal at, 294, 296, 310, 312, 319
Fraser, Trenholm and Company (London, England), 250, 256